THE SECRET APPARATUS

THE MUSLIM BROTHERHOOD'S INDUSTRY OF DEATH

CYNTHIA FARAHAT

FOREWORD BY DANIEL PIPES

BOMBARDIER
BOOKS

Published by Bombardier Books
An Imprint of Post Hill Press
ISBN: 978-1-64293-865-4
ISBN (eBook): 978-1-64293-866-1

The Secret Apparatus:
The Muslim Brotherhood's Industry of Death

Cover Design by Tiffani Shea

BOMBARDIER
BOOKS
Post Hill
PRESS

Post Hill Press
New York • Nashville
posthillpress.com

Published in the United States of America
1 2 3 4 5 6 7 8 9 10

For Jeffrey James Higgins, my husband, my hero,
and the man who embodies every benevolent
value I respect, cherish, and strive to protect

Note on Transliteration

In *The Secret Apparatus,* I have followed the guidelines of the *International Journal of Middle East Studies,* with some deviation. For familiar Arabic names of individuals and organizations, common English spellings were substituted for transliteration.

CONTENTS

ACKNOWLEDGMENTS

I WROTE THIS BOOK IN loving memory of Michael Mos'aad, a classic liberal human rights activist and my friend. Michael was murdered by Muslim Brotherhood soldiers during the Maspero Massacre. Michael suffered and died under a repressive regime, and this book is for him and the millions of others who have been tormented and oppressed by the Muslim Brotherhood, their affiliated regimes, and their terrorist offshoots.

My husband Jeffrey James Higgins is my kindred spirit, my inspiration, my hero, and the love of my life; I would not have written this book without his help, love, and support.

My mother, Sanaa Amin, has endured countless sleepless nights and endless sacrifice because of the path I sought. She supported my values, even though they came with a hefty price. She always encouraged me to follow an uncompromising trail for liberty, integrity, and justice.

My brother, Amir Abdelmalek, was apolitical, but he became a victim when Brotherhood-affiliated government agents kidnapped and tortured him to try to coerce me into working with them. My brother's support, kindness, and intelligence helped me win many battles.

My late grandmother Elaine Iskandar was my role model and my best friend, whom I miss every day.

Thanks to Gamal Helal, whose belief and relentless support helped me finish this manuscript. I will always be grateful for his kindness.

Dr. Daniel Pipes has been both a friend and colleague. I want to thank him for giving me a fellowship at The Middle East Forum. Dr. Pipes has believed in me since we first communicated in 2009, when I was risking my life in Cairo by fostering ideas of classic liberalism. Dr. Pipes provided support when my brother was kidnapped, and through the Middle East Forum, he has helped spread my ideas around the world.

Thanks to my editor Adam Bellow at Bombardier Books and everyone at Post Hill Press for publishing this book. They have given me a platform to voice my research and analysis, which has been shunned in the insular and corrupt foreign policy community.

This book is also for the heroic Muslims who face constant threats to their lives and their families—the uncompromising heroes Amira Abdel Fattah, Sahar Elgaara, Fatima Naout, Ibrahim Eissa, Islam al-Behery, Tharwat al-Kherbawy, Khaled Montaser, Hassan Ismail, Ahmad Subhy Mansour, Ahmed Abdu Maher, Sayyid Al-Qemany, and Muslim and non-Muslim soldiers and law enforcement everywhere who sacrificed their lives to protect the innocent in the face of this unbridle evil. This book is also for you.

FOREWORD TO *THE SECRET APPARATUS: THE MUSLIM BROTHERHOOD'S INDUSTRY OF DEATH* BY DANIEL PIPES

IN THIS AMBITIOUS AND POWERFUL book, Cynthia Farahat argues that the Muslim Brotherhood (MB), founded nearly a century ago, presents a far greater threat than is usually perceived, being nothing less than "the world's incubator of modern Islamic terrorism" and "the world's most dangerous militant cult." She traces leading Egyptian groups such as al-Takfir wa'l-Hijra, al-Jama'a al-Islamiya, and Egyptian Islamic Jihad back to the MB, as well as non-Egyptian ones like Ansar al-Shari'a in Libya, Jama'at al-Tawhid wa'l-Jihad in Jordan, Talai' al-Fateh in several countries, Hamas, the Taliban, al-Qaeda, and ISIS. With such an array of accomplishments, she concludes that the MB presents an "existential threat" to the United States. Those not alarmed by the MB, in brief, Farahat wants urgently to alarm.

The author is an Egyptian who immigrated a decade ago to the United States, where she has written on jihad for American publications, penned a column for an Egyptian newspaper, testified before Congress, and advised US law enforcement about Islamism and jihad. Before that, in Egypt, she co-founded the Liberal Egyptian party, whose platform endorsed capitalism, separation of mosque and state, and peace with Israel. She studied Islamic jurisprudence and history and co-authored a book (in Arabic) titled *Desecration of a Heavenly*

Religion in 2008. For her efforts, al-Azhar University banned the book while she herself was banned from Lebanon and landed on the hit list of an Qaeda-affiliated group.

This book, *The Secret Apparatus*, contains a wealth of names, dates, events, and other granular facts, all needed to establish the author's case; accordingly, it is not a book to be speed read but studied and returned to. Much of the evidence is original, Farahat having taken advantage of archives opened after the 2013 revolution in Egypt or relying on new sources, such as memories of the hyperthymestic Tharwat al-Kherbawy. To help the reader approach and appreciate the pages that follow, therefore, I propose to sketch out their main lines in this foreword, adding some reflections of my own.

The book has five main parts: background influences, the MB founder, deceptions, impact, and US policy.

BACKGROUND INFLUENCES

Farahat argues that the Muslim Brotherhood, established on March 22, 1928, began modern Islamism; and that the Secret Apparatus was "the first covert Islamic terrorist organization in modern history." She traces the MB's origins to two main sources:

(1) Iran and the Shi'i branch of Islam: the medieval Assassins served as "the biggest influence on the Brotherhood's formation," something made possible by *taqrib*, the effort to narrow theological differences between Shi'i and Sunni Islam, with the ultimate goal of re-establishing the caliphate and jointly waging jihad against their common enemies. The Iranian Jamal ad-Din al-Afghani, founder of the modern jihad project, may have been "the most important figure in the revival of Islamism" because he combined Western secret societies with Islamic clandestine proselytism. MB founder Hasan al-Banna drew heavily on this legacy to create a "twentieth-century equivalent of the order of the Assassins."

Farahat reports the surprising news that Ayatollah Khomeini visited Banna in Cairo in 1938. She speculates that "Banna swayed Khomeini, as Banna's influence on Khomeini would become apparent years later." In the mid-1960s, Ali Khamenei took advantage of his time in an Iranian prison to translate two of the MB's key books, by Sayyid Qutb, into Persian. The Iranian revolution of 1978–79 saw an MB branch formally established in Iran. Also at that time, Khomeini apparently suggested the wording of the MB's key slogan, "Islam is the solution." During the Iraq-Iran war, the MB used its influence to help Tehran; in turn, Tehran generously funded Hamas. When Khamenei became Iran's supreme leader in 1989, he included those two Qutb books in the curriculum of the Islamic Revolutionary Guard Corps' schools; in return, MB leaders included Khomeini among its most important teachers along with Banna, Qutb, and Abul A'la Maududi. The two sides forged new bonds following the overthrow of Hosni Mubarak in 2011, when the MB fervently supported Iran's nuclear program.

From this long record, Farahat concludes that "The Muslim Brotherhood and Iranian cooperation is one of the most dangerous and complicated relationships in the world of international politics, jihadism, and transnational terrorism."

(2) Modern Western ideas and institutions: These many and eclectic influences included: the Freemasons (especially the idea of a clandestine organization) and a range of twentieth-century dictators: Kaiser "Hajji" Wilhelm II and his World War I propaganda (especially the subversive work of Max von Oppenheim), the Nazis (especially the brutality of the Sturmabteilung or S.A.), and the Soviets (especially Lenin's ideas, the Comintern's dual model of public party and secret apparatus, and Stalin's NKVD). Although Banna admired Hitler and the MB personnel "continue to adhere to Hitler's values until today," Stalin had the most influence on the MB's structure, which copied his domestic and international institutions of power as well as the Comintern model. Indeed, "Banna modeled his organization after

Stalin's governing apparatuses, a structure still used by the Muslim Brotherhood today." A more brutal model one cannot imagine.

HASAN AL-BANNA

In addition to these influences lies the character of the MB's founder, Hasan al-Banna, which remains dominant long after his death: his "paranoid, obsessive, and criminal vision endures through the chameleon-like entity he created." For example, the organization's by-laws demanded that members "prioritize the interest of the group over the interest of the individual" and the group viewed members' children as fodder for its ambitions. Ultimately, every member must vow total obedience to the leader, known as the General Guide. Lesser officers of the organization, known as emirs, then involve themselves in every aspect of a member's life, including marriages, illnesses, and hardships, with an eye to pressure, blackmail, or bribe the member. For example; MB operatives must marry within the organization and to someone from a family with a status similar to their own.

Beyond these internal matters, Banna stressed two themes especially: the caliphate and death. "The Muslim Brotherhood's raison d'être is to establish an Islamic caliphate" that will apply Islamic law, the Shari'a. That is because for it, as for many other Islamists, "the answer to every problem—from trouble with their in-laws, to health issues, to public policy concerns—is the return of the Caliphate." Toward this end, the MB uses all methods, lawful or criminal.

Banna's renowned definition of the MB's principles hints at his peculiar preoccupation with death: "God is our goal, the Prophet is our model, the Qur'an is our law, jihad is our path, and martyrdom is our aspiration." The mention of an "Industry of Death" (*sina'at al-mawt*) in the title of this book refers to a memorably perverse article by Banna in which he discusses the glory of dying for Islam:

> Death is an art, sometimes a beautiful art despite its bitterness, it might even be the most beautiful of arts if it is created by the hands of a masterful artist. The Qur'an honorably presented it to its believers and compelled them to cherish and love it more than others love life ... Muslims will not be saved from their reality unless they adopt the Qur'an's philosophy of death and embrace it as an art, a truly beautiful art.

Banna exalted death over all else. He "believed that loving life was a deadly sin which prevented Muslims from entering paradise. He held that Muslims could only go to heaven if they 'shed their blood as tax for [loving] life.'" His leading disciple, Qutb, then "continued Banna's doctrinal principle that all Muslim who aren't members in jihadists groups are infidels and deserved to get killed." It gets worse:

> While it is widely known that the Muslim Brotherhood believes in the extermination of all non-Muslims, it is not common knowledge that they also consider all Islamic nations houses of war, and the vast majority of Muslims as infidels whom they believe should be killed.

In short, the MB is a perfected killing machine.

Mixed together, influences of the Assassins, Stalin, and Banna created an organization summed up by Banna's statement that "the laws and teachings of Islam are a total system complete unto itself as the final arbiter of life in this world and the hereafter."

THREE DECEPTIONS

Farahat offers three key insights about MB methods to explain the institution's success, all based on deception.

The first concerns a deception based on a duality, namely the existence of a somewhat benign public face, the General Apparatus, and a demonic covert militia, the Secret Apparatus. The organization has engaged in doublespeak about its two halves since 1951, with the one opportunistically spouting liberal democratic values and the other expressing "extremist and pro-terrorism rhetoric." At the same time, it has been clear that the leader of the Secret Apparatus, known as the Secret Guide has, since 1971, been the MB's ultimate leader; during this half-century, the General Guide merely "acts as a public relations figure." Those public relations duties have included persuasively to perpetuate "the myth that the Secret Apparatus is no longer operational" when in fact it very much is. Both the public and clandestine divisions operate on the basis of Banna's permanent jihad, thereby permitting all sorts of criminal and other illegal undertakings.

Part of this deception includes the pretense of having abandoned force in favor of legitimate politics: "every time the Muslim Brotherhood publicly renounced violence, it engaged in clandestine jihadist activities under a different banner." Indeed, the MB cannot give up force under any circumstances: "If the Brotherhood were to give up violent jihad, it would mean the leaders had dismantled the organization, because the Muslim Brotherhood would lose its legitimacy and its sole reason for its existence."

The second deception concerns the MB practice of directing members formally to sever ties with it and to found seemingly unrelated offshoots. The Free Officers "perpetrated the 1952 coup d'état" that ended Egypt's monarchy. Egypt's various Salafi organizations make the MB look moderate. Hamas so successfully infused the Palestinian-Israeli conflict with violence that it became "a model" for other MB franchises. Al-Jama'a al-Islamiya and the Muslim Brotherhood,

President Anwar al-Sadat once noted, "are one and the same." Rif'at Qumsan, an Egyptian general, includes more groups, stating that

> We should not be fooled with names such as Daesh [ISIS], Nusrat al-Haq, Nusrat al-Islam, Hamas, etc. They are all one. We can say the Brotherhood is the frame for all these organizations, whether so-called peaceful ones, like Jama'at al-Tabligh wa'l-Da'wa, or the most violent ones, such as Al-Qaeda, Tanzim al-Jihad, and Daesh.

This pattern of "franchising the Brotherhood terrorism model" makes the MB a far greater menace than if it acted as a solitary organization, especially as each branch operates its own Secret Apparatus.

The third deception involves infiltration. The Secret Apparatus unit dealing with intelligence systematically "infiltrates and internally subverts political parties, militaries, intelligence agencies, media, educational systems, governmental and nongovernmental organizations, and other influential groups." The Egyptian government has been the primary target of this campaign; other institutions include charitable organizations, Egypt's Communist party and al-Azhar University.

Indeed, al-Azhar University has a unique role in spreading the MB message, starting with "the theological legitimacy of inflicting pain upon infidels"; for example, the "Muslim is allowed to murder an apostate and eat him, [as well as] kill [an infidel] warrior, even if they are a child or female. It is permissible to eat them because they are not [granted] protection." With such an education, it hardly shocks one to learn that jihadis sometimes "conceal their terrorism manifestos as masters and PhD theses" at al-Azhar. As a result, "Some of the world's most brutal jihadists received their formal religious training" at one of al-Azhar's many affiliated mosques, schools, learning centers, and universities around the world. Burhanuddin Rabbani, who had a major role in forwarding Islamism in Afghanistan, offers one such example.

Farahat considers in detail the case of Omar Abdel-Rahman, known as the Blind Sheikh. Remembered in the West for spending decades in prison following his inciting jihad against New York City monuments, she argues he had a much larger role, calling him "the most influential theologian for Sunni militant groups over the past fifty years" and "the Godfather of Islamic jihad." Specifically, he was "the ideological founder" of al-Jama'a al-Islamiya and al-Qaeda, both of which he mentioned in his doctoral thesis. She also reports that he received "direct institutional support and theological legitimization" from al-Azhar University for these activities and that he "couldn't have created this massive wave of transnational terrorism without al-Azhar." Finally, she speculates that al-Azhar was "directly involved" in the founding of al-Qaeda.

Infiltration has paid great dividends. "Decades of infiltration have allowed active Muslim Brotherhood members to control Qatar, Turkey, Sudan, and formerly Egypt. Western nations deeply affected by the Brotherhood's destabilizing tactics include the United States, United Kingdom, and Germany." In brief, funded by Egyptian taxpayers, al-Azhar "militarizes its students and turns them into jihadists." Farahat concludes that not only infidels must fear al-Azhar's teachings but "all Muslims are also in danger" from them.

IMPACT

Noteworthy MB acts of jihadi violence have included the assassination of Egypt's Prime Minister Ahmad Maher Pasha in 1945, former Prime Minister Mahmoud Fahmi al-Nuqrashi in 1948, and Sadat in 1981. In addition, it nearly assassinated Gamal Abdel Nasser in 1954. Also, MB members actively participated in the burning of much of central Cairo in 1952.

But the MB's Civilizational Jihad Operation using lawful means to extend its influence, Farahat argues, is even "more damaging" than violence. Egypt, home of the MB, is the model for Civilizational Jihad. In Egypt, the MB since the late 1950s "has almost full control over al-Azhar University," the Cairo-based institution that enjoys worldwide prestige among Sunni Muslims. Within Egypt itself, al-Azhar's personnel effectively controlled the legislative branch of government by virtue of their ability to draft or vet laws prior to their being taken to parliament.

Both the first and second presidents of Egypt, Mohamed Naguib and Gamal Abdel Nasser, were clandestine MB members (Nasser had joined in 1942). Nasser may have been "a totalitarian dilettante who adopted far-left-wing ideologies" but he released all MB jihadis from prison and employed German Nazis to "dismantle the Egyptian education system and ideologically subvert the country." Nasser visited Banna's grave in 1954 along with his successor Sadat; there, they both pledged allegiance to the MB founder. Nasser swore, "As God is my witness, I will uphold [Banna's] values and wage a jihad on their behalf."

Sadat had long been an MB member, as was his successor Mubarak (who joined in 1944). Farahat describes the latter as someone "armed with the audacity of profound ignorance, the rigidity of the peasantry, and a lust for power." So complete was the MB infiltration of the military under Mubarak that Abbas Mukheimar, the army major general he appointed to oversee the purge of officers with MB or other Islamist affiliations, himself was an MB member. Also, during Mubarak's rule, MB "terrorism recruitment was state sponsored and broadcast around the clock on the Egyptian government's Radio and Television Union's communications satellite, Nilesat."

Muhammad Hussein Tantawi, who carried out a coup d'état in 2011 on the MB's behalf, probably was a member and the military council he headed was openly Islamist, to the point of funding the MB and its affiliated Salafi political parties. Of course, Mohamed Morsi, who ruled Egypt in 2012–13 was publicly a member and, indeed, had been overtly chosen by the MB to run for president. In a key appointment, Morsi made Abdel Fattah al-Sisi his minister of defense, relying on the fact that Sisi came from MB royalty, being a descendant of MB co-founder Abbas al-Sisi.

Under Morsi, things changed radically, with the MB becoming "openly jihadist. The group installed torture and murder tents or camps across Egypt, where they abducted, tortured, and murdered protesters and sometimes random civilians." Worse, it had drawn up plans for mass extermination of Egyptians, both Christian and Muslim, in keeping with Banna's eschatological doctrine of annihilating the Muslim population as a blood sacrifice, what he called a blood tax (*daribat ad-damm*).

With this, however, the MB finally went too far: "Widespread, indiscriminate torture and murder carried out by the Brotherhood resulted in wide opposition to it," spurring the largest political rally in all history on June 30, 2013, followed immediately by a revolution headed by Sisi, who came to power riding a massive wave of popularity. Then, against nearly all expectations, Sisi turned on the MB and became Egypt's first anti-MB president. When the MB refused to accept this reality, instituting a wave of violence against the new regime, Sisi responded in December 2013 by designating it a terrorist organization.

In all, "From 1952 to 2012, each of Egypt's transitions of power resulted from a coup d'état by [military] officers belonging to the Muslim Brotherhood." More than that, for much of this era, they "were the power behind decision making" and, indeed, "dominated the country." During this time, MB influence in Egypt meant that most government institutions were but "decorative structures [intended] to give the country a superficially modern guise," even as the MB actually ruled. Also, the MB only pretended to fight the government during that sixty-year period while in fact serving as the "government-sponsored fake opposition" which the government went so far as to subsidize via its business enterprises.

The MB also wields extensive power outside of Egypt. Amin al-Husseini, the mufti of Jerusalem, helped the MB establish itself in Mandatory Palestine and Transjordan. In Afghanistan, the MB "played a pivotal role" in the Soviet-Afghan war" by helping jihadis from the Middle East to reach Afghanistan. In the middle of that war, in 1985, three MB leaders (Abdullah Azzam, Osama Bin Laden, Ayman al-Zawahiri) founded an organization that later morphed into al-Qaeda. Other MB figures had a key role in founding the Taliban. In Sudan, Omar Al-Bashir seized power in 1989, making him "the first member of the Muslim Brotherhood publicly and officially to rule a country." In Tunisia, a MB coup d'état deposed Tunisia's President Zine El Abidine Ben Ali in 2011, initiating the "Arab Spring." Most remarkably, Farahat finds numerous indicators to suggest that the Turkish strongman, Recep Tayyip Erdoğan is both the General and the Secret Guide of the MB as well as head of its International Apparatus. Under his leadership, "Turkey became the command-and-control center for Islamic terrorism," while Istanbul has become "a haven for recruiting terrorists, smuggling jihadists in and out of Turkey, and plotting international terrorist attacks."

As Muslim immigration to the West has increased, so too have MB activities there, relying as usual on the dual structure of an overt organization, which operates benign-appearing schools, mosques, and the like, and a covert one that establishes, funds, and partially or fully operates violent jihadi groups. The Blind Sheikh, Omar Abdel-Rahman, is perhaps the most notorious MB exemplar of the latter strain.

US POLICY

Turning to US policy, Farahat is dismayed to find that MB deceptions have succeeded: "veiled terminology was a contributing factor to the infiltration of the US government, and led to policies that supported the Muslim Brotherhood." To help fix this problem, she offers a guide to MB use of language. *Truth* means the implementation of the Shari'a. *Freedom* means the freedom from transgressions against the Shari'a. *Tyranny* means opposing the Shari'a. *Justice* means Shari'a over every aspect of life. *Peace* means accepting the rule of Muslims. *Islamic revival* means the subjugation of all people on earth to Allah. This coded Islamist terminology, entwined with infiltration, she concludes, "has allowed the world's most violent jihadist group to gain power in America."

She also finds that Washington has abandoned its old approach of peace through strength with a "nineteenth-century, German-Ottoman strategy of employing jihadist mercenaries to carry out broken policies." This has had devastating consequences: misguided Western policy vis-à-vis the MB

> has contributed to hundreds of thousands of deaths and the displacement of 2.7 million people by the Muslim Brotherhood's regime in Sudan alone. Furthermore, the riots and protests that erupted across the Middle East in 2011 were a direct result of a lenient US policy toward the Muslim Brotherhood.

During just the past decade, Farahat argues, mistaken US policies "resulted in the loss of hundreds of thousands of lives and the displacement of millions of people in the Middle East."

To sustain its "security and for freedom to thrive internationally," she argues, Washington "must criminalize the Muslim Brotherhood" by designating it a terrorist organization. Doing so not only will clarify the identity of the enemy but also it will help with the crucial distinction between Muslims and Islamists: Muslim Brothers "have desecrated their own religion by weaponizing theological terminology and poisoning it with violent and terroristic definitions that are alien to the vast majority of Muslims." *The Secret Apparatus* ends with these sobering words: "Either you are with the overwhelming majority of

Muslims, and every peaceful individual on earth, or you are with the Muslim Brotherhood."

Over two decades of research on the Muslim Brotherhood led Cynthia Farahat to a horrified appreciation of its achievement as "one of the world's most complex criminal enterprises." The book in your hands makes a compelling case to see the MB not as one of many contending Islamist organizations but as a historic trailblazer and the source of untold misery.

Mr. Pipes (DanielPipes.org, @DanielPipes) is president of the Middle East Forum.

INTRODUCTION

THIS BOOK IS AN INTELLECTUAL salvo in one of the most important wars of our time. It is about a battle of ideas within Islam and a struggle between good and evil. *The Secret Apparatus* reveals new information, never before seen in the West. The research, analysis, and conclusions presented herein do not come from third-party opinions or translations but mainly from original texts and the words of Muslim Brotherhood leaders themselves. It is the culmination of more than two decades of research.

I wrote it because nothing else like it exists about the Muslim Brotherhood's "Secret Apparatus," which has transformed the group into the world's incubator of modern Islamic terrorism.

There is a strict and clear distinction between Muslims and Islamists. Islamists are intent on subjugating all Muslims and the entire world under an oppressive militant theocracy. While Islamists often claim their main challenges stem from Western governments and Western colonialism, the real threat to their violent caliphate—and the majority of their victims—are other Muslims. A millennia-long battle within Islam has been waged between Sunni Islamists and the Mu'tazila, one of the most moderate Islamic sects. Currently, the ideological war for the soul of Islam is at its height in the Middle East, and the peaceful neo-Mu'tazila sect and other moderate Islamic interpretations have gained unprecedented popularity.

During the twentieth century, the US government departed from its Jeffersonian foreign policy of peace through strength. It was replaced by the nineteenth-century German-Ottoman strategy of employing jihadist mercenaries to carry out broken policies. The government of the United States supported the growing influence of the Muslim Brotherhood in the US, Egypt, Qatar, Turkey, Sudan, Syria, Yemen, Saudi Arabia, and Iran. Today, they are employing the same destructive strategies in Afghanistan.

My journey to understanding the true scope and nature of the Muslim Brotherhood began when I was a teenager, then living in Egypt, monitoring Islamists online, leading to more than twenty years of daily study. I read the same material Omar Abdel Rahman, the Blind Sheikh, studied to become the most prominent ideological figure in the history of modern militant Islamic organizations. My path led to unexpected discoveries about the Brotherhood, the clandestine incubator of Islamic terrorism that is currently waging war against America and the West. I argue that the US must criminalize the Muslim Brotherhood for her own security and for freedom to thrive internationally.

The Muslim Brotherhood is a militaristic clandestine organization founded in 1928 by Hassan al-Banna (1906–1949). Banna was reared in a devout Muslim household, where he was inculcated in the Hanbali school of Islamic jurisprudence, popular among Wahhabi and Salafi jihadists. Fascinated by secret societies, cults, and clandestine orders, Banna founded the Muslim Brotherhood as a fraternity cult.

He modeled the Brotherhood after the eleventh-century *Hashashin* (the order of the Assassins) and launched a century of terror. The Brotherhood became the command and control center for all Sunni jihadists, establishing most modern Islamic terrorist groups, including Hamas, al-Qaeda, al-Gama'a al-Islamiyya (Islamic Group), and Egyptian Islamic Jihad. Even the caliph of that Islamic State was a former Brotherhood operative.

The Brotherhood has its own secret militia, *al-jihaz al-khass* or *al-jihaz as-sirri* (the Special Apparatus or the Secret Apparatus), which is deliberately modeled on the internal power structure of the Soviet Union. This secret directorate is responsible for strategy, funding, military training, and transnational terrorism. Many Western policy experts believe the Secret Apparatus was disbanded, but it is active and has become the wellspring of jihad.

For a century, the Brotherhood has operated under different banners and spread terror around the world. Stopping them begins with uncloaking their Secret Apparatus.

CHAPTER ONE

THE INCUBATOR OF TERROR

"We are war…"

—Hassan al-Banna[1]

THE MOST DANGEROUS TERRORIST GROUP in the world is not hiding in the caves of the Hindu Kush or dwelling in the wilderness of the Sahara. It is an order with an international political, military, and clandestine apparatus that is the fountain of the world's Islamic terrorist groups. It is a fraternal cult inspired by *al-Hashashin* (the Assassins) with an internal structure modeled after Joseph Stalin's Secret Apparatus and a pledge for eternal jihad. It is an *imperium in imperio* with a one-hundred-year plan to destroy America and the West, and its operatives have infiltrated and influenced the United States government, think tanks, universities, and mainstream media.[2]

The failure to recognize the fact that the Muslim Brotherhood is the command and control for almost all Sunni Islamic jihadist groups contributed to the catastrophic American withdrawal from Afghanistan in August 2021. President Joe Biden's administration negotiated with the Taliban, as Presidents Donald Trump and Barack had before him, claiming the Taliban wanted to be accepted into the community of nations. Islamic State, Hamas, and al-Qaeda were

1 Al-Nazir (Cairo), May 30, 1938; The Official Muslim Brotherhood Website, https://ikhwanonline.com, accessed April 9, 2011.

2 FrontPage Magazine (California), https://www.frontpagemag.com/, accessed May 11, 2006.

characterized as terrorist enemies, while the Taliban was portrayed as a reasonable alternative that could be trusted to govern Afghanistan without running it as a terrorist training base, even as they violated the negotiated agreement numerous times and publicly flaunted their defiance. The Taliban directly supported al-Qaeda's attack on the US on September 11, 2001, and they have been killing Americans ever since.

In the aftermath of the attacks, President George W. Bush demanded that the Taliban surrender al-Qaeda terrorists to the United States. When they refused, the US and Britain invaded Afghanistan to destroy and dismantle the Taliban, a regime that had protected terrorists and turned Afghanistan into a jihadist training camp. The initial effort succeeded, until the Bush administration succumbed to decades of infiltration and corruption in Washington.

This failed US policy in Afghanistan laid bare America's misunderstanding of the enemy in what is known as the War on Terror. There is almost no ideological difference among Sunni and Shi'ite terrorist groups and the Taliban when it comes to their common enemies in the West and the rest of humanity, including the overwhelming majority of Muslims. All subscribe to radical Islam and seek a global Islamic state. Often the same members of Islamic terrorist groups fight for different organizations at different times, based on tribal loyalties, allegiances to warlords, sources of funding, or other familial or geo-political squabbles. Differences and conflict among these groups are driven by internecine warfare, but their ultimate goals are identical. The failed US policy in Afghanistan has proven that any hope of victory against jihadists must acknowledge the ideological enemy and seek to destroy the leadership behind it—namely, the Muslim Brotherhood.

The Western mind often struggles to comprehend the altruistic suicidal patience of an Islamist whose most prized goal is to die as a martyr. Martyrdom is motivated not just by an Islamist's lust for reward in the afterlife and to terrorize their enemies; it is also a political, social, and religious duty to help recruit others and inspire allegiance to their vision of a global Islamic state. Every major political action taken by an Islamist is designed to serve long-term goals. Thus, a profound epistemological gap exists between Western politicians who focus on an upcoming election cycle and an ideological soldier who conscripts every cell in his body to achieve goals that surpass his and his children's lifetimes.

The short-term nature of American foreign policy comes with an equally short-term memory. It is also sometimes combined with cynicism regarding human life and lust for power. In the US Department of State and foreign policy circles, antisocial behaviors and ideas are normalized and even encouraged. President Biden's horrific policy disaster in Afghanistan is the culmination of decades of corruption, subversion, negligence, and betrayal of American values.

The world has witnessed and will witness the regurgitated jihadist terror of the Taliban, just as it witnessed the terror of Islamic State (IS), also known as the Islamic State of Iraq and the Levant (ISIL) and the Islamic State of Iraq and Syria (ISIS). Before Islamic State, Manhattan watched al-Qaeda operatives fly airplanes into her tallest buildings in 2001. In 1993, *al-Jama'a al-Islamiyya* or *al-Gama'a al-Islamiyya* (The Islamic Group) planted bombs in the World Trade Center, while Hamas routinely massacred Israelis and Americans. Prior to those incidents, *at-Takfir wa'l-Hijrah* (Excommunication and Emigration) committed mass murder and, before that, *Tanzim 1965* (The Group of 1965) attempted assassinations in Egypt. Preceding all of them, at the beginning of modern terrorism, was *al-Jihaz as-Serri* (the Secret Apparatus), also known as *al-Jihaz al-Khas* (the Special Apparatus), *al-Nizam al-Khas* (the Special Order), and *at-Tanzim as-Serri* (the Secret Order or Secret Group)—all names for the clandestine military wing of the Muslim Brotherhood.

Despite overwhelming evidence that the Brotherhood founded numerous Islamic terrorist groups—and many of its current leaders have admitted the existence of the Secret Apparatus—many Western academics, policymakers, and terrorism experts believe the clandestine jihadist apparatus has been dissolved. This is not true. Not only is the Secret Apparatus still operational, but also it remains the main governing body of the Muslim Brotherhood. It is responsible for establishing the world's most dangerous terror groups and ideologically and militarily guiding them with the help of state sponsors such as Iran, Turkey, and Qatar.

After the world witnessed the brutality of al-Qaeda, it was hard to imagine that another group could surpass its savagery until the Islamic State emerged. They in turn will be followed by a new terrorist group, and another will follow them. The vicious circle will end only when the Muslim Brotherhood, the founder of all these groups, is itself designated as a terrorist organization.

Brotherhood founder Hassan al-Banna (1906–1949) officially constructed the Secret Apparatus in the mid-1930s with the assistance of Nazi collaborator and Mufti of Jerusalem, Amin al-Husseini (1897–1974). The Secret Apparatus became the first covert Islamic terrorist organization in modern history.[3]

To understand the Secret Apparatus, it is crucial to reexamine obscure and mysterious elements in Islamism and the Muslim Brotherhood's history, which have never been presented to a Western audience—until now. For example, the Brotherhood's leadership was fascinated with secret fraternal orders, such as the Freemasons and Shi'ite secret cults. Shi'ite elements in the Brotherhood's ideology have created widespread confusion in the West about the true nature of the Sunni-Shi'ite conflict. Academics and policy experts have focused on sectarian division, but ignored military cooperation between Islamists from both sects.

Early Muslim Brotherhood leaders were intrigued by Shi'ite secret theology, known as *batiniyya* or batin (inner esoteric or hid-

3 Al-Jazeera (Doha), December 28, 2003; "Farid Abdul Khaliq ma'Ahmed Mansour: An-Nizam as-Sirri" September 13, 2020.

den doctrine). Shi'ite Assassins adopted this theology in the late eleventh century. According to Brotherhood Secret Apparatus operative Ali Ashmawi, the Assassins were the biggest influence on the Brotherhood's formation.[4] The Muslim Brotherhood was a project designed to revive the Assassins, and the group remains a modern version of them, employing *ad-da'wa as-sirriyya* (clandestine proselytism) to infiltrate and subvert the social, political, and intelligence communities of targeted nations.[5]

Today, the Secret Apparatus is the governing body of the Muslim Brotherhood. Interestingly, scholars in the West have not noticed that the reason the Muslim Brotherhood still calls its public governing frame the "General Apparatus" is that they also have a Special Apparatus. Brotherhood leaders and members have publicly articulated this distinction. Hassan al-Banna chose this compelling language when he structured the organization, because the group's ideology and methodology were heavily influenced by Joseph Stalin, and they modeled its internal structure after Stalin's Secret Apparatus.

Many leaders of the Brotherhood's Secret Apparatus were both officers in the Egyptian military and members of the Egyptian Communist Party, which explains their knowledge of the Soviet model. Among the most notable early members were Egyptian President Gamal Abdel Nasser (1918–1970) and the "Red General," Khalid Mohieddin (1922–2018). There is evidence to suggest the Muslim Brotherhood's militia cell may still be operating inside the Egyptian military.

Muslim Brotherhood members deny the existence of the Secret Apparatus when they communicate with their Western targets, but this strategy of denial is not new and dates back to Hassan al-Hudaybi (1891–1973), who succeeded al-Banna as the Brotherhood's *al-mur-*

---

4 Ali Ashmawi, *At-Tarikh as-Sirri li-Jama'at al-Ikhwan al-Muslimin* (Cairo: Ibn Khaldun Center, 2006), 8.

5 Hussein bin Muhammad bin Ali Jaber, *Al-Tariq ila Jama'at al-Muslimin* (Cairo: Dar al-Wafa, 1990), 190-9.

shid al-am, or General Guide (also known as the Supreme Guide). Hudaybi falsely claimed to have dissolved the Secret Apparatus in an effort to ease the Egyptian government's suspicion of the group. He was arrested in 1965, alongside other Brotherhood leaders, and charged with forming a new militia and engaging in military training with the goal of assassinating then-President Nasser. This resulted in the execution of the Brotherhood's foremost ideologue, Sayyid Qutb (1906–1966), and two other Brotherhood leaders in 1966.[6]

Hudaybi's false denial of the Brotherhood's military wing became a standard tactic of the group, as did their strategy of operating their militia under independent banners—a policy that birthed terrorist organizations as we know them today. The first terrorist groups founded by the Brotherhood under different names were *Tanzim 1965* (The Group of 1965); *Gama'at al-Muslimin* (the Muslim's Group) commonly known as *at-Takfir wa'l-Hijrah* (Excommunication and Emigration); and *al-Gama'a al-Islamiyya.* [7] Decades later, the Brotherhood founded Hamas, al-Qaeda, and Islamic State.[8] Overwhelming evidence suggests that most active Sunni terrorist groups in the twenty-first century are operating as the Muslim Brotherhood's military divisions.

The Brotherhood's second most important operation is its International Apparatus, a body that few Western academics have explored. The dearth of information on the International Apparatus has made it easy for the Brotherhood to spread disinformation about the group's relationship with its international chapters. For example, the International Apparatus' bylaws state that every international Muslim Brotherhood affiliate is required to fulfill its mandatory commitment to "jihad and martyrdom."[9] Yet, some experts in the West

6 Salah Shadi, *Safahat min at-Tarikh* (Cairo: Islamic Publishing House, 1987), 79.

7 Tharwat al-Kherbawy, *Sirr al-Ma'bad* (Cairo: Nahdat Misr Publishing, 2012), 220; "Al-Sadat Yatahadath an al-Gama›a al-Islamiya wa'l-Ikhwan," YouTube.com, May 9, 2012.

8 Al-Arabiya (Dubai), October 14, 2014.

9 Hassan al-Banna, "Al-La'iha al-Alamiyya li Gama'at al-Ikhwan al-Muslimin," Philipps-Universität Marburg, www.Uni-Marburg.de, accessed May 4, 2018.

claim that these chapters have "complete operational independence."[10] This book will explore the various reasons many experts don't convey the full truth about the Muslim Brotherhood.

The Secret Apparatus operates an International Apparatus. Its leadership has targeted the West with a propaganda campaign and has successfully penetrated Western governments and intelligence agencies. Their clandestine, subversive activities work in parallel with their strategy of cowing nations through terrorism. This tactic was spelled out in a Muslim Brotherhood document published in 2018.[11] The document was written by Mahmoud Fathi Badr, an Egyptian national residing in Turkey. He is a Brotherhood leader in the organization's youth wing and a cofounder of its terrorist militia, *Harakat Sawa'd Misr* (HASM) (the Forearms of Egypt Movement).[12] In January 2018, the United States designated HASM as Specially Designated Global Terrorists (SDGTs).[13] In the document titled "*Rasa'il al-Istiqlal*" (Epistles of Independence), Badr urged Brotherhood operatives to set fires across Egypt to "follow a procedural policy of shock and awe to exhaust the government by making it constantly occupied with the next [jihadist] operation."[14]

Badr's comments reflect a recurring Brotherhood tactic against targeted nations. It is common for its current leaders and public figures to incite violence and boast about their involvement in terrorism, torture, and kidnapping in Arabic, while denying their participation in these crimes in other languages. The truth about the Brotherhood's activities is often conveniently lost in translation.

---

10 Interview with Lorenzo Vidino, "Is it Time to Designate the Muslim Brotherhood as a Terrorist Group?" European Eye on Radicalization, June 27, 2019, https://eeradicalization.com/is-it-time-to-designate-the-muslim-brotherhood-as-a-terrorist-group/.

11 Mahmoud Fathi Badr, "*Rasa'il al-Istiqlal: Tayyar al-Umma Misr,*" Tayyar al-Umma Official Facebook Page, www.Facebook.com/NationStream, May 25, 2018.

12 Under Secretary for Public Diplomacy and Public Affairs, Bureau of Public Affairs Press Release, "State Department Terrorist Designations of Ismail Haniyeh, Harakat al-Sabireen, Liwa al-Thawra, and Harakat Sawa'd Misr (HASM)," January 31, 2018, https://il.usembassy.gov/state-department-terrorist-designations-ismail-haniyeh-harakat-al-sabireen-liwa-al-thawra-harakat-sawad-misr-hasm/.

13 13. Mubtada' News (Cairo), January 25, 2017.

14 Mahmoud Fathi Badr, "Rasa'il al-Istiqlal."

Sudanese Muslim Brotherhood leader Hassan al-Turabi (1932–2016) revealed important information about the Secret Apparatus and provided another example of how its leaders frequently tell the truth in Arabic. Turabi is important because Sudan is a vital and unique model. Until now, no expert in the West has acknowledged that Sudan was the first country to be directly and officially ruled by the Muslim Brotherhood. The Sudanese model became more relevant after it was emulated during Arab upheavals, euphemized as the "Arab Spring." Perpetrators of the coup d'état against Egyptian President Hosni Mubarak said that Sudan was their model.

Examining the ideological, theological, and structural foundation of the world's most dangerous militant cult is necessary to understand why the Muslim Brotherhood has targeted the United States. This background is needed to understand diverse elements of their war against America and the world and the only way to predict the future behavior of the worldwide Islamic insurgency.

The modus operandi of the Muslim Brotherhood's internal structure has allowed its operatives to gain unprecedented political power in the US. Concealing the existence of the Secret Apparatus has allowed the group to penetrate critical intelligence and political positions. America's friendly relationship with the Brotherhood has had destructive consequences. It has allowed the Brotherhood to hijack the representation of overwhelmingly peaceful Muslim Americans whom the Brotherhood systemically terrorizes. It has also empowered Brotherhood leaders to advise several US administrations on policy.

One annual event in Washington, DC, embodies the US government's failure in dealing with the Brotherhood and demonstrates a fraction of the magnitude of the national security crisis caused by Islamist infiltration. Once a year, the halls of Congress swarm with Brotherhood operatives—individuals directly connected to Islamic

State and al-Qaeda.[15] Islamists with ties to terrorism have met with members of Congress every spring since 2015 when the US Council of Muslim Organizations (USCMO), a coalition of national and local Islamist organizations, hosts its "Muslim Advocacy Day," an annual lobbying event held in the auditorium of the Capitol Visitor Center.

MORE DANGEROUS AS FRIENDS THAN AS ENEMIES

While the Muslim Brotherhood's project in America began in the 1960s, operating under both Republican and Democratic administrations, it was commonplace for Westerners to portray the Muslim Brotherhood as a moderate option to "more radical" Muslim groups. For example, James Clapper, former US Director of National Intelligence, described the Brotherhood as "largely secular."[16] Georgetown University Professor John Esposito claimed that "Muslim Brotherhood-affiliated movements and parties have been a force for democratization and stability in the Middle East."[17] While Esposito was speaking to a Western audience, his university's branch in Qatar was mediating between Iran, the world's largest state sponsor of terror, and the Muslim Brotherhood-affiliated regime in Qatar.[18]

On the other hand, in 2014, the United Arab Emirates formally designated the Muslim Brotherhood and its local and international affiliates, including the US-based Council on American-Islamic Relations (CAIR), as an international terrorist group.[19] A British gov-

15 Cynthia Farahat, "Islamists with Direct Ties to Terrorists Lobby Congress," The Middle East Forum, Philadelphia, www.meforum.org, accessed May 17, 2018.

16 "James Clapper: Muslim Brotherhood 'Largely Secular'," ABC News, February 10, 2011, https://abcnews.go.com/Politics/video/james-clapper-muslim-brotherhood-largely-secular-12886575.

17 John Esposito, *"The Muslim Brotherhood, Terrorism and U.S. Policy," Huffington Post,* March 22, 2016 (New York).

18 Iran Daily, December 6, 2015; Muhammad al-Honi, *Saif al-Gaddafi* (United Arab Emirates: Madarik Publishing House, 2015), 171.

19 Reuters, November 15, 2014; *The Washington Post*, November 17, 2014.

ernment review, commissioned the same year, also found that parts of the Muslim Brotherhood have a highly ambiguous relationship with violent extremism. The Muslim Brotherhood has been a gateway for some individuals and groups who have gone on to engage in violence and terrorism.

In the United States, Senator Ted Cruz (R-TX) and Congressman Mario Diaz-Balart (R-FL) have introduced legislation to designate the Muslim Brotherhood as a terrorist organization. In February 2016, the US House Judiciary Committee approved a bill that called on the State Department to designate the Muslim Brotherhood as a foreign terrorist organization. In July 2016, then-Congressman Dave Brat (R-VA) introduced the "Naming the Enemy within Homeland Security Act," a bill that would have prohibited the Department of Homeland Security from funding or collaborating with organizations or individuals associated with the Muslim Brotherhood.[20]

While these are remarkable efforts, the US government's procrastination in designating the Muslim Brotherhood as a terrorist group has had devastating consequences. Internationally, Western policy toward the group has contributed to hundreds of thousands of deaths and the displacement of 2.7 million people by the Muslim Brotherhood's regime in Sudan alone. Furthermore, the riots and protests that erupted across the Middle East in 2011 were a direct result of a lenient US policy toward the Muslim Brotherhood.[21]

Ignorance, arrogance, infiltration, or a combination of these factors have led many regimes and governments around the world to imagine they can ally with the Muslim Brotherhood. This has almost always resulted in the Muslim Brotherhood either overthrowing these regimes or infiltrating and subverting government policies.

Decades of infiltration have allowed active Brotherhood members to control Qatar, Turkey, Sudan, and formerly Egypt. Western nations

20 Rep. Dave Brat, press release, http://www.brat.house.gov, July 19, 2016.

21 Marlise Simons, Lydia Polgreen, and Jeffrey Gettleman, "Arrest Is Sought of Sudan Leader in Genocide Case," *New York Times*, July 15, 2008,

deeply affected by the Brotherhood's destabilizing tactics include the United States, United Kingdom, and Germany.

The most serious danger posed by the International and Secret Apparatuses is not their founding of terrorist groups; it is the clandestine Civilization Jihad Operation and the Brotherhood's employment of both Sunni and Shi'ite clandestine proselytism. Civilization Jihad has had more damaging implications for Western nations than Islamic terrorism, according to statements made by Hassan al-Turabi and in the policies adopted by recent US administrations.

It is impossible to counter the Brotherhood's attacks without first understanding the ideological, operational, and covert elements of the Secret Apparatus.

CHAPTER TWO

HISTORY IS NOT HISTORY

Ideological Origins of the Muslim Brotherhood's Secret Warfare

"The effects of the secret doctrine had, indeed, manifested themselves in the bloody traces of the dagger..."

—Joseph Von Hammer[1]

THE MUSLIM BROTHERHOOD'S RAISON D'ÊTRE is to establish an Islamic caliphate through jihad. The study of the Muslim Brotherhood's history is imperative to understand its current stratagem and to predict its future behavior. The Brotherhood's contemporary goals, strategies, and tactics are almost identical to its past operations and objectives. Their ritualistic repetition of history is not merely meant to preserve tradition, it is a religious obligation and a devout demonstration of submission and blind allegiance to this occultist society. The Brotherhood's obsession with history is deeply rooted in Islamist mystical epistemology.

Islamists possess an absolute belief in predestination. They believe that the only means to overcome modern challenges is to revive a romanticized and sometimes fictional version of the early Islamic caliphate. For Islamists, the answer to every problem—from trouble

1 Joseph Von Hammer, *The History of the Assassins*, trans. Oswald Charles Wood (London, 1835), 105.

with their in-laws, to health issues, to public policy concerns—is the return of the caliphate.

While Westerners generally examine history critically, Islamists consider a critical view of history to be a condemnation of religion, Islamic jurisprudence, and the validity of Islamic theocracy. While Westerners may believe that "those who cannot learn from history are doomed to repeat it," Islamists believe, "those who cannot learn from history cannot accurately repeat it."

Islamic political history is consecrated, and its critical examination is punishable under blasphemy laws in many Muslim-majority countries. The Sunni and Shi'a theocratic practice of Islam sanctifies historic figures and repeats their modus operandi in governance as a religious duty. The attempt to deter critical examination of Islamic history compelled a lawmaker, Amr Hamrush—a member of Parliament and the general secretary of the Religious Committee in the Egyptian Parliament—to introduce a bill proposing a maximum five-year imprisonment and a fine of up to 500,000 Egyptian pounds on critics of "historic figures."[2]

Theocratic organizations like the Brotherhood attempt to revive Islamic history by using the broad electoral slogan, "Islam is the solution." The term was originally inspired by former Supreme Leader of Iran Sayyid Ruhollah Khomeini (1902–1989), known in the West as Ayatollah Khomeini. The Brotherhood believes all problems can be cured by Islam. As Saudi scholar Saleh bin Fawzan, a member of The Council of Senior Scholars in Saudi Arabia, said, "Islam is the solution to all people's problems." Bin Fawzan stated that whether the problems were related to aging, poverty, marriage, or women's issues, the solution was "Islam."[3]

The Brotherhood's understanding of Islam is a combination of Wahhabism, a fundamentalist Sunni Islamic subsect, and *ad-da'wa*

2 Ramadan Al Sherbini, "Egypt Could Make It a Crime to Insult Historic Figures," *Gulf News* (Dubai), November 9, 2017.

3 Salih bin Fawzan, "Al-Islam Hua al-Hal li Gami 'Mushakilat an-Nas," https://alfawzan.af.org.sa/ar, accessed October 14, 2017.

as-sirriya (clandestine proselytism or the clandestine call). Islamist scholar Hussein bin Ali Jaber explains clandestine proselytism as "secrecy during the founding of a group, where any information regarding its operational plan is only restricted to those assigned to implement it. At the same time, the individuals implementing a secret plan should stay anonymous to one another, and any information they acquire should be limited to their role and they shall remain ignorant of the any tasks assigned to other members."[4]

Three main contributing factors played a significant role in the creation of the Muslim Brotherhood. First was the theological basis for cooperation between Sunni and Shi'ites militants. Second was the Muslim Brotherhood founders' fascination with cults and secret orders. Third was the ideological war between classical liberal renaissance and the Islamic Awakening. The modern Islamist theological term for the Islamic Awakening Project is *Mashrou' as-Sahwah al-Islamiyya.* It is sometimes translated as the "the Resurgence of Islam Project." That battle of ideas is still being fought in most Muslim-majority countries, and it is a struggle over their national identities, languages, philosophies, and government. There is an ongoing ideological war surrounding the soul of Islam, between non-theocratic reformists and Islamist who are still working to unify militants from the Sunni and Shi'a sects against the vast majority of Muslims and the West.

SUNNI AND SHI'ITE COOPERATION

For the first time, this chapter presents to Western readers a comprehensive view of the historic theological and operational cooperation between militants from both Sunni and Shi'ite sects. This information challenges the current foreign policy and academic orthodoxy regarding jihadist groups from these sects, their allegiances, and their

4 Hussein bin Muhammad bin Ali Jaber, *Al-Tariq ila Jama'at al-Muslimin* (Cairo: Dar al-Wafa, 1990) pp. 190-9.

relationship with each other. To understand the current relationship between the Brotherhood and Iran, one has to understand how Hassan al-Banna delivered an almost millennium-old Shi'ite political project.

This chapter also provides the ideological basis for covert jihadism in both sects. It presents a new question: Was the Islamic Awakening Project a revival of the *al-Hashashin* (the Assassins)?

The Brotherhood's ideological underpinnings are tied to the theological cooperation between Sunnis and Shi'as. The alliance between Sunni and Shi'ite militants is seldom discussed in reference to the creation of the Muslim Brotherhood. Competition between them has caused most experts, academics, and policymakers to focus more on their sectarian conflict rather than on their jihadist cooperation. This common misunderstanding has led to numerous policy mistakes and underestimation of the Shi'ite influence on the Muslim Brotherhood.

It is hard to decipher the relationship between them using Western epistemological tools. The mind of an Islamist operates in a different mystical realm that resides on three inseparable pillars. An Islamist combines monastic patience (transcending the span of his lifetime), the vision of a military strategist, and the bloodlust of a predator. These elements allow a jihadist to think in terms of centuries, not in years or decades. The eternal vigilance of an Islamist is dangerously underestimated in the West. His altruistic philosophical approach manifests itself in martyrdom, and more dangerously, in the militant dedication of his every resource to satisfy his hunger for power and absolute dominance.

To prove the long tradition of partnership between Sunnis and Shi'ite jihadists, it is necessary to explain the theological basis for their division and cooperation. Two major Shi'ite projects have deeply influenced the Muslim Brotherhood's ideology and operations.

The first project is what the Brotherhood and Shi'a militants call the *taqrib* (also spelled *taghrib*), or (proximity) project. It is the pinnacle of a millennium of patience, conspiracy, and military strategy, and it has created a relationship between the Brotherhood and Iran.

The Sunni-Shi'a proximity project is more than one thousand years old. The theological movement toward alliance was driven by four Shi'ite forefathers. They established a foundation upon which the Brotherhood and Iran have built their proximity project—a modern operation that began in the twentieth century and is still active today.

While a peaceful relationship between Sunnis and Shi'ites can bring significant benefits to the Middle East and the entire world, the proximity project aims to do the opposite. It aspires to unify militants from both sects to wage joint jihad against their common enemies, both inside and outside their faith. According to a statement on the Iranian government's proximity website, Taghrib New Agency (TNA), the agency aims to "explicate resistance groups and movements which counter occupation and Zionism," declaring the Republic of Iran "as the leader of revolution in the Islamic world." The proximity project leaders in Tehran are playing a significant role in networking terrorists worldwide.[5]

The second project, which resulted from proximity, was the revival of clandestine proselytism, which incorporates *al-jihad as-sirri* (clandestine jihad). This element is perhaps the most important ideological tenet of the Muslim Brotherhood's critical operation of the Secret Apparatus. The theological elements of clandestine proselytism allowed the Brotherhood to model its organization after the Shi'ite order of the Assassins, perhaps the deadliest cult in history. Fourteen centuries of conflict between Sunnis and Shi'ites are often superficially analyzed within the confines of their sectarian rivalry. This oversimplification dismisses the historical fact that the Sunni-Shi'a relationship is a history not merely of conflict but also of competition and, sometimes, cooperation.

---

5 Iranian government's Taghrib News Agency website, http://taghribnews.com/, accessed October 18, 2020.

THE THEOLOGY OF PERPETUAL JIHAD AND THE ROOTS OF THE SUNNI-SHI'ITE DIVISION

From a Western perspective, war is war, but from an Islamist perspective, war is a way of life—it is perpetual. It is an everyday tactical necessity employed in different ways, in various degrees, and toward different parties, to serve a multitude of strategic goals. In the Islamist's mind, war is not a temporary condition, nor is it a necessary evil. To Islamists, war is an all-encompassing system that can incorporate other aspects of daily existence and is a stable constant. The continuous state of jihad is known in Sunni theology as *dawam al-jihad* (the permanence of jihad). In Sunni eschatology, perpetual jihad ends only when Islamists kill *al-masih ad-dajjal* (the false messiah).[6] In the Shi'a eschatology, jihad is practiced until the appearance of the Mahdi—the redeemer of Islam, after the earth is "cleansed" from non-Muslims and the sun rises from the West.[7]

In 2018, Egyptian president Abdel Fattah al-Sisi protested the theology of perpetual war, asking, "Is war an exception or is it a constant? War is the exception. When the thought of a nation is exclusively centered on war—at least for the past one hundred to two hundred years, their understanding of their religion is that war is a constant and peace is an exemption. How is this a religious interpretation?" The Egyptian president was the first Muslim leader to comment on this specific aspect of the fundamentalist interpretation of Islam. Al-Sisi made this remark during one of his many calls for religious reform. During his speech, he also called for peace between Sunnis and Shi'ites.[8]

---

6 Abu Dawud Sulayman as-Sijistani, *Sunnan abi Dawud* (Beirut: Dar Ibn Hazm, 1997), 3: p. 10,

7 Sulaiman Al-Alwan, *Al-Niza'at fil-Mahdi*, Central Intelligence Agency Library, www.CIA.Gov/Library, accessed November 1, 2018; Muhammad ibn Ya'qub al-Kulayni, *Al-Kafi* (Tehran: Dar al-Kitab al-Islamiyya, 1948), 5: 9–10.

8 Al-Masry Al-Youm, "Egypt's People Are the Real Hero of the Reform Process, Sisi Says During Youth Conference," *Egypt Independent* (Cairo), July 28, 2018.

The division between the two sects started after the death of the Prophet of Islam in 632 and began before his burial.[9] The conflict between them centered around the Prophet's successor, the caliph, the shadow of God on earth and the sole rightful ruler of Muslims. The dispute split the Prophet's followers into two camps. The first argued that succession should be awarded to Abu Bakr as-Siddiq, the Prophet's father-in-law. Others insisted that the only legitimate ruler must come through his bloodline and should be awarded to his cousin and son-in-law, Ali ibn abi Talib. After Abu Bakr claimed his position as caliph, Ali and his wife, Fatimah bint Muhammad, only temporarily accepted him after Bakr's allies threated to burn down their house if they opposed him.[10]

Even when the conflict between Bakr and Ali over the caliphate was at its height, they still allied militarily in 632 to fight the Wars of Apostasy against Arabs who had abandoned Islam. This alliance set the precedent for military cooperation between jihadists from the two camps, and since that time they have joined forces against their common enemies.[11]

There is a general consensus among Sunni and Shi'a militants regarding their foreign policy strategies, theology of treaties, war, and international affairs. The common agenda regarding the West, which militants from both sects agree upon, has resulted in one of the most dangerous alliances in modern history—the cooperation between the Muslim Brotherhood and Shi'a militants. They both employ similar theological tools to achieve their goals.

9 Ibn Hisham, *As-Sirah an-Nabawiyya* (Beirut: Dar Al-Kitab Al-Arabi, 1991), 4: 308.
10 Ali ibn Abdul Malik al-Hindi, *Kanz al-Ummal* (Beirut: Mu'asat al-Resala, 1985), 5: 651.
11 Muhammad Abduh, *Nahj al-Balagha* (Beirut: Dar al-Marefa, 1963), 3: 119.

DISSIMULATION AND CONCEALMENT IN CLANDESTINE PROSELYTISM

During a time of war, Sunnis and Shi'a militants are theologically permitted to ally against their shared enemies. Sunni groups, such as the Muslim Brotherhood, adhere to the Islamic jurisprudence concept known as *fiqh al-awlawiyat* (the jurisprudence of priorities) and *fiqh al-muwazanat* (the jurisprudence of balances).[12] Both concepts prioritize short-term, pragmatic, tactical alliances if they improve conditions to allow jihadists to dominate non-Muslim nations.

In 2006, Brotherhood jurist Yusuf al-Qaradawi issued a *fatwa* (religious edict) titled *Mabade' at-Taqrib bain as-Sunna wa'l-Shi'a* (The Principles of Dialogue and Proximity Between Sunnis and Shi'ites), in which he discussed the importance of unifying the Islamic front against the United States and Israel. The fatwa, which was posted for years on the leading Sunni theology website, IslamOnline.net, was recently removed. In the fatwa, Qaradawi said that Iran urged Sunnis to focus on the jurisprudence of priorities in order to foster common grounds—something Qaradawi also asked of Sunnis. He discussed his philosophy in his book about the proximity project, *Mabade' fi al-Hiwar w'at-Taqrib bain al-Maddahib al-Islamiyya* (The Principles of Dialogue and Proximity between Islamic Sects).[13]

The Shi'a Imamate or Twelver rulers of Iran adopted proximity strategy under the umbrella of *taqiyya* (dissimulation) and *batiniyya or batin* (inner esoteric or hidden theology). In both Sunni and Shi'ite theologies, *taqiyya* is a pragmatic Islamic juridical term that allows Muslims to lie and to forge alliances with their rivals, if doing so serves the long-term agenda of Muslim rulers or nations.

---

12 Yusuf al-Qaradawi, *Fiqh al-Awlawiyat* (Cairo: Al-Risala Institute, 1994); Abdul Mijid Muhammad as-Susoua, *Fiqh al-Muazanat* (Dubai: Dar al-Qalam, 2004).

13 Yusuf al-Qaradawi, *Mabade' fi al-Hiwar w'at-Taqrib bain al-Maddahib al-Islamiyya* (Cairo: Maktabat Wahba, 2006).

The Shi'ite Twelvers believe that every Qur'anic verse has both a *zahir* (outer exoteric) and *batin* interpretation.[14] Many Sunni Islamists use "*batiniyya*" as a derogatory term when they refer to Shi'ism, as a propaganda tactic to instill suspicion and fear of Shi'ites, but batiniyya also exists in Sunni theology. *Batinyya* is frequently used in Sunni theology under the term *kitman* (concealment), and it relates to concealing intentions and ideology of an Islamist individual or group during a weak stage of their operation.[15]

According to Sunni theologian and Shari'a law jurist Muhammad Khair Haikal, "Secrecy and *kitman* in Islamic *da'wa* incorporate even the secrecy of the act of *da'wa* in itself. It should be secretly practiced in its totality, including its rituals, and the secrecy of [its] order. The directive is, those who join the Islamic da'wa are a unified group that should be morally, ideologically, and doctrinally segregated from the society in which they exist, abiding by the laws of [their] leadership."[16]

Hidden theology or concealment has been a core aspect of clandestine orders in both sects. The Muslim Brotherhood is not among the group of Islamists that denounce batiniyya. Brotherhood cofounder and leader Farid Abdul Khaliq admitted the Brotherhood's adherence to *batiniyya* and stated, "The *batiniyya* aspect of *taqiyya* is to maintain the secrecy of values, to only be revealed to followers and a few selected people, and this is why it is a strategic necessity."[17]

These ideological tools have been critical since the inception of proximity between Sunnis and Shi'ites. Islamists from both sects who attempt to unify militants from the *ummah* (Muslim nation) against their common enemies have employed dissimulation and

14 Sayyid Hashim bin Sulaiman al-Bahrani, *Al-Burhan fi Tafsir al-Qur'an* (Beirut: Mu'asset al-Ilami, 2006), 2: 9.

15 Ibn Kaldun, *Shifa as-Sa'il* (Ankara: Ankara Universitesi Ilahiyat Fakultesi Yayinlari, 1957), 7-9.

16 .Muhammad Khair Haikal, *Al-Jihad wa'l-Qital fi as-Siasa ash-Shar'iyya* (Damascus: Dar ibn Hazm, 1996) 1: 378-385.

17 Farid Abdul Khaliq, *Al-Ikhwan al-Muslimun fi Mizan al-Haq* (Cairo: Dar as-Sahwah fil Nashr w'at-Tawze', 1987), 118.

concealment, both against each other and against their common enemies during their alliances. In this context, "common enemies" is an extremely loose term that encompasses most of humanity, including the vast majority of Muslims who don't adhere to violent Sunni or Shi'ite interpretations of Islam. Despite the current competitive and often hostile relationship between both sects in the Middle East, the Sunni revolutionary jihadist project of Muslim Brotherhood and the Shi'ite revolutionary goals of the Iranian mullahs have allowed them to find common theological and political grounds.

SUNNI-SHI'A PROXIMITY PROJECT

The modern cooperation between Sunni and Shi'ite Islamists developed through three major phases. The first dates to the early founding of the Muslim Brotherhood and to Hassan al-Banna, who had strong ideological and organizational ties to radical Shi'a imams in Iran. The second stage took place when a Muslim Brotherhood's International Apparatus delegation visited Iran in 1979, following the Islamic revolution. The third stage of the cooperation followed the uprisings and coup d'états in the Middle East in 2011.

It is essential to understand the ideological roadmap that led to the inception of the Muslim Brotherhood, as it is still at the heart of the group's current operations. This journey puts into context many unexplained questions regarding how a Sunni group came to revive the Sunni version of the secret order of Assassins.

The Shi'ite project to unify Islamists predates the Muslim Brotherhood. Analyzing the roots of the Shi'ite project is necessary to understand the depth of the current policy, because modern Islamists revere and emulate the past.

The *taqrib* or proximity project is more of a Shi'ite initiative than a Sunni one. While Sunnis often dominated Shi'ites militarily throughout history, as a minority, the Shi'ites were more politically savvy and relied heavily on their theological elements of dissimulation. This allowed the Shi'ites to be more advanced in their clandestine operations. It has been their strongest attribute since the era of Nizari Isma'ilism, which was originally formed as a clandestine sect.

The Sunni-Shi'ite military alliance is a complex, multilayered puzzle, impossible to decrypt outside the context of its historic building blocks. It is imprecise to refer to past events in Islamic thought as merely "historic," as the word holds different connotations in Islamist epistemology, and, in some cases, past events are more relevant in the Islamist mind than their current reality. History is used as a manual, and repeating some of the most violent and tyrannical elements of Islamic history is often a sanctified religious obligation.

For Islamists in both sects, their most important objective is reviving the caliphate. According to former Brotherhood operative and al-Gama'a al-Islamiyya terrorist group leader Yasser Sa'ad, "the Muslim Brotherhood views the caliphate as *fard ain* [individual religious obligation] on every Muslim."[18]

Continuing the Sunni-Shi'ite alliance to achieve a caliphate should be expected.

THE FIRST PIONEER OF PROXIMITY

The first of the Shi'ite figures to foment the basis for the alliance was the Persian theologian Abu Ja'far Muhammad ibn Hassan at-Tusi (995–1067), known as *Shaikh at-Taifah* also spelled Sheikh al-Taifah (sheikh of the sect). Ja'far at-Tusi is the author of major theological books upon which Shi'ites rely. He was the first theologian to officially attempt to bridge the gap between both sects. As a Shi'ite minority living under the brutal rule of the Sunni Abbasid dynasty (750–1258), Ja'far at-Tusi adjusted the Shi'ite theological discourse by elevating the status of the sixth Shi'ite imam, Ja'far ibn Muhammad

18 Dotmsr News (Cairo), September 2, 2014.

as-Sadiq (700 or 702–765), in his writing and sermons. This served two strategic objectives and changed the course of Shi'ism. The first objective was to unite the Shi'ite sect through elevating the status of the sixth imam, after Ali bin abi Talib, whom Shi'ites agreed upon before their internal division. The second and more important reason Ja'far at-Tusi focused on as-Sadiq may have been because Sadiq is also revered in Sunni thought.

The two major sects in Shi'ite Islam are the *Ithna Ashariyyah* (Twelvers), and *al-Isma'iliyya* (Isma'ilis), or Seveners. The Twelvers believe in the authority of twelve imams, who were appointed by God to lead the Muslim nation. The Isma'ilis believe in only seven imams. Both sects agree upon the first six imams, the last of whom was Ja'far as-Sadiq. The battle for succession between the two sects surrounds Sadiq's sons. The Isma'ilis argued that the custodian of the religion should be as-Sadiq's oldest son, Isma'il. The Twelvers believe his younger brother, Musa al-Kazim, was the legitimate imam and his lineage continued until the twelfth imam, who disappeared in 873.

The Isma'ilis' largest subsect is the Nizari. After the death of the Fatimid Caliph al-Mustansir Billah in Egypt in 1094, an issue over succession emerged between two of his sons, causing a divide in the Isma'ili sect. When al-Mustansir died, his minster appointed his son, Abul-Qasim al-Musta'li, as caliph. Al-Musta'li's older brother, Nizar, and his followers dissented against the appointment, claiming Nizar was the rightful successor. This led to the imprisonment and death of Nizar in prison, in 1097. After his death, his followers developed the Nizari Isma'ili sect.

In 1171, the Shi'ite Fatimid dynasty ended with the death of its last ruler and was replaced by a series of invasions by the Sunni Turks that brought dramatic economic and military restructuring to the old Fatimid order. This inspired the formation of the Nizari clandestine terror group under the leadership of jihadist Hassan as-Sabbah (1050–1124). As-Sabbah, like a significant number of jihadist leaders throughout history, received his religious training at al-Azhar University in Cairo. He would become an inspiration for the Brotherhood and its founder, Hassan al-Banna.

The Nizaris worked in secret for many years. They combine elements from both Sunnism and Shi"ism. Isma'ilis provided an early organized framework that elevated the value of self-sacrifice and absolute devotion to their imam, whom they viewed as the God's chosen prophet and sole leader.[19]

This theological tactic carried out by Ja'far at-Tusi led to another historic precedent in the cooperation between Sunnis and Shi'ites, when Ja'far at-Tusi became the first Shi'ite honored by a Sunni ruler. He was appointed by the Sunni caliph, al-Qa'im bi-A'mri Allah (1001–1075), to *Kursi al-Kalam* (the Council of Islamic Scholastic Theology), which would be an equivalent to today's Council of Senior Scholars in the Kingdom of Saudi Arabia.[20] This was highly unusual, and it is considered the first official act of ideological proximity between the two sects.[21]

Muhammad Abu Zahra (1898–1974), an Egyptian Muslim Brotherhood sympathizer and former head Faculty of Shari'a Law at al-Azhar University, praised Ja'far at-Tusi's reliance on Ja'far as-Sadiq in his work and said that he "filled a void" in the Shi'ite sect, which wouldn't have occurred without him.[22] Zahra is correct, because the decision to elevate the status of Ja'far as-Sadiq narrowed the gap between Twelvers and Seveners, and between Sunnis and Shi'ites. This move proved to be very influential in the future of the proximity movement.

Perhaps the other main reason the Sunni caliph honored Ja'far at-Tusi was because he avoided the small areas of sectarian conflict during his popular mosque sermons, which were usually attended

---

19 Bernard Lewis, *The Assassins* (New York: Basic Books, 2002), 27.

20 Islamic Republic of Iran Broadcasting (IRIB), February 20, 2010.

21 Muhammad Abu Zahra, *Al-Imam as-Sadiq* (Cairo: Dar al-Fikr al-Arabi, 1960), 458.

22 The Official Muslim Brotherhood Encyclopedia, "Mustafa as-Siba'i al-Muraqib al-A'am al-Awal li al-Ikhwan al-Muslimin fi Suria," https://ikhwanwiki.com/, accessed April 20, 2018.

by three hundred clerics from different Islamic sects.[23] The caliph probably hoped it would create internal stability, while he was busy fighting the external threat of the Seljuks. Ja'far at-Tusi's motives remain debated among some Islamic scholars who argue that Tusi's attempt to initiate proximity with Sunnis may have been a form of dissimulation.[24]

CONQUERING THE CONQUERORS

The second important political employment of dissimulation, which is still cited among Islamists as another unification precedent took place between Shi'ites and non-Muslims. It was the alliance forged between Nasir ad-Din at-Tusi (1201–1274) and the Mongols. The protagonist of this incident was born in the city of Tus in Khorasan (northeastern Iran). He was a philosopher, theologian, and astronomer. When Genghis Khan invaded his hometown from 1219 to 1221, Nasir sought refuge with the Isma'ili Assassins in Alamut, a region in Iran the Assassins had chosen as their headquarters. There, he authored some of their treaties, which the sect still considers authoritative.[25]

According to Bernard Lewis, Nasir later "claimed to be a Twelver Shi'ite, whose association with the Isma'ilis had been involuntary. Which of his allegiances, if either, was *taqiyya* remains uncertain." This is a recurring theme in the chameleon movements of Islamists through the present day.

The Mongol advancement against the Isma'ilis led to the capture of Nasir, who made himself indispensable to the Mongols and was appointed as an advisor to Mongol Prince Hulagu during his campaign against Iraq, which the Mongols captured in 1258. As British historian Michael Axworthy puts it, "the Persian class of schol-

23 IRIB, February 20, 2010.

24 Nasir al-Qaffari, *Mas'alatu at-Taqrib bain as-Sunna wa'l-Sh'ia* (Riyadh: Dar Tiba, 1992), 2: 148.

25 Bernard Lewis, *The Assassins*, 84.

ars and administrators had pulled off their trick of conquering the conquerors."[26]

Nasir's successful infiltration of Hulagu's regime was praised and used as an example of essential use of *taqiyya* by Ayatollah Khomeini. In his book *Hukumat-e Islami* (Islamic Government), Khomeini wrote, "*Taqiyya* is my religion and the religion of my forefathers."[27] Khomeini borrowed the quote from Ja'far as-Sadiq. Islamists miss the irony that the man who is called *as-Sadiq* (the truthful) claimed dissimulation as his religion and the religion of his forefathers.

THE COUNCIL OF NAJAF IN 1743

The third pioneer of the Sunni and Shi'a unity project was Nader Qoli (1688–1747). While Nader's attempts failed in his lifetime, his vision eventually would be actualized by the Muslim Brotherhood.

Nader was a successful Shi'ite lieutenant in the Persian army of Tahmasp II (1704–1740). When Afghanistan won the Battle of Gulnabad against the Persians in 1722, it encouraged Russia and Turkey to attack Persia. Russia had to withdraw following the death of Peter the Great in 1725, but the Ottomans remained. After almost a decade of war against the Ottomans, Tahmasp faced another humiliating defeat, which resulted in the Treaty of Ahmad Pasha, the Ottoman governor of Baghdad in 1732. In this treaty, Tahmasp gave five cities in the Caucasus to the Ottomans. The treaty led Nader to overthrow Tahmasp and install Tahmasp's infant son in power. Within three years, Nader defeated the Ottomans and the Russians in Persia. This victory paved the road for him to be known later as "the Napoleon of Iran."[28]

26 Michael Axworthy, *A History of Iran* (New York: Basic Books, 2016), 104.

27 Ruhollah Khomeini, *Hukumat-e Islami* (third edition, 1969), 142; Ruhollah Khomeini, *Islamic Government: Governance of the Jurist* (Tehran: The Institute for Compilation and Publication of Imam Khomeini's Works, International Affairs Division), 120.

28 Yahya Armajani, *Iran* (New Jersey: Prentice Hall, 1972), 101–2.

In 1736, after the death of Tahmasp's son, Nader took his position as Shah of Iran and assumed the title Nader Shah Afshar. He ruled as a brutal tyrant and ended up killing his own son.[29]

One of Nader's most prominent achievements was on the ideological front, although it is unclear whether Nader was a Sunni, a Shi'ite, or an atheist.[30] Before he officially seized power, he gathered Persian notables, provincial governors, officials, military leaders, and officers and gave them conditions for accepting his position as shah. The first condition was that they halt support for any member of the former shah's family. The second condition was that Persians refrain from cursing the early Sunni caliphs Omar ibn al-Khattab and Usman ibn Affan and abandon the Shi'ite tradition of self-flagellation to draw blood during *Ashura* celebrations, which commemorated the death of the Prophet's grandson. Shi'ites were asked to accept the Sunni religious practices and take Imam Ja'far as-Sadiq as the symbolic head of their sect. The third condition was that they should accept Nader's children as successors after his death. While Nader framed these conditions as requests, it's safe to assume that he knew the dignitaries would accept them, given that he was widely known for his brutality.[31]

Soon after Nader seized power, he introduced ideological alterations to the Shi'ite state religion. These alterations and Nader's vision would become the foundation for an alliance project revived more than two centuries later, between the Muslim Brotherhood and Iran.

Prior to officially becoming shah, Nader articulated his vision more precisely and communicated it to the Ottoman ambassador, Ganj Ali Pasha:[32]

> (1) Persians will refrain from cursing the first three caliphs, and from cutting themselves during the Ashura festi-

29 Ibid.
30 Michael Axworthy, *The Sword of Persia* (London: I.B.Tauris, 2006), 168.
31 Axworthy, *The Sword of Persia,* 161–2.
32 .Armajani, *Iran,* 79; Axworthy, *Sword of Persia*, 164..

val. Persians should accept Sunnis' religious practices, and take Imam Ja'far as the symbolic head of their sect. Sunnis should recognize the Ja'fari Shi'a sect as a fifth school of thought in Islam.

(2) Persians should be allowed to participate in Hajj with their Ja'fari sect.

(3) During Hajj, Persians should be accompanied by a representative.

(4) Ottomans and Persians should exchange prisoners of war.

(5) Ottomans and Persians should exchange ambassadors.

Nader banned elements of Shi'ism previously introduced by the Safavid dynasty (1501–1736). For example, he instructed Shi'a clerics to refrain from referring to Imam Ali as the deputy of God, because of enmity between Shi'as and Sunnis.[33] Nader killed the chief mullah to show his subjects and enemies that he was serious about his policies. Axworthy notes, "the killing of the leading cleric in Persia marked a break with the old order."[34]

The Ottomans agreed to only four of Nader's conditions. They rejected Nader's first condition to make the Ja'fari a fifth school of jurisprudence and insisted that it was heretical.[35]

Like his predecessors, Nader had a strategic objective behind elevating Imam Ja'far to symbolize the Shi'ite sect, a move that would pay off two centuries later. The fact that Ja'far is revered by both Sunnis and Shi'ites dramatically bridges the gap between the two sects. It became harder for Sunnis to excommunicate Shi'ites when they were referred to as *Ja'farites*. It will never be known whether Nader decided to bridge the gap for ideological reasons or as a political strategy to rule Sunnis.

---

33 Ibid.,166.

34 Ibid.

35 Abbas Iqbal, *Tarkikh Iran ba'd al-Islam* (Cairo: Dar al-Thaqafa al-Arabiyya, 1989), 717.

Nader understood the strategic importance of Iraq's geographic position. But after failing three times to capture various Iraqi cities militarily in 1733, 1734, and 1743, he finally resorted to ideology, a tactic that would later be followed by the militant regime in Iran.

In Najaf, Nader hosted an assembly of Shi'ite and Sunni scholars in the presence of a representative from the Ottoman governor Ahmad Pasha. Explaining the purpose of the assembly, and sending a message to the Pasha, Nader said:

> [In] my realm there are two areas, Afghanistan and Turkestan, in which they call the Iranians infidels. Infidelity is loathsome and it is not fitting that there should be in my domains a people that call another infidels. Now I make you my representative to go and remove all of the charges of infidelity and witness this in front of three groups with whatever is required. You will report everything that you see and hear to me and relay your account to Ahmad Khan.[36]

Nader hoped that the Najaf council would result in a treaty with the Ottomans through which his army would retreat from Iraqi cities and in return, the Ottomans would accept the *Ja'afri madhab* (sect) as the fifth school of Islam.[37]

The Najaf council was the first proximity conference ever held between the two sects. The convention proposed three major issues. First was the accusation of apostasy between Muslims. Second, insulting the early caliphs. Third, accepting the Shi'ite sect, and the school of Ja'far as-Sadiq as the fifth school of thought in Islam. The convention ended with a document that both parties signed, listing Nader's five earlier demands to the Ottomans. As soon as the convention was over, so was the relevance of the document. The convention failed, but his vision endured.

---

36 Michael Axworthy, *The Sword of Persia*, 256.
37 Ibid., 258.

PAN-ISLAMISM, PROXIMITY, AND THE REVIVAL OF THE ASSASSINS

The fourth major figure of the Islamic unification project and clandestine proselytism in the nineteenth century was Persian political agitator and pan-Islamism activist Jamal ad-Din al-Afghani (1838 or 1839–1897).[38] Afghani may be the most important figure in the revival of Islamism. He started a clandestine jihadist project, and his disciples influenced the founding of the Muslim Brotherhood.

There are several parallels between Afghani and his predecessor in the Islamic unification project. As with Nader, many wondered where Afghani stood ideologically. He has been called a Sunni, a Shi'ite, an atheist, and even a Russian agent.[39] Perhaps the question that should be asked is: Was Afghani an Isma'ili Assassin?

In his early years, Afghani received traditional Shi'ite Islamic education as well as education influenced by Persian Islamic philosophers—such as the famous proponent of *taqiyya*, Nasir ad-Din Tusi.[40] Similar to his Shi'a jihadist predecessors who influenced the militant unification project, Afghani also relied on dissimulation and clandestine proselytism.[41] While Afghani's teachings are often described as "liberal" in the West, the opposite is more accurate.[42] Afghani believed in the caliphate under a newer term: pan-Islamism. The enigmatic leader's modus operandi is more consistent with radical theologies within the Shi'ite faith. Afghani's path appears more concordant with the Nizari Isma'ili creed of the Assassins than with any other Islamic faction.

While the Nizari sect is peaceful today, they did create the deadliest cult in history. Austrian orientalist Joseph Von Hammer alerted

38 Nikkie R. Keddie, *Sayyid Jamal Ad-Din Al-Afghani: A Political Biography* (ACLS Humanities E-Book, 2008), 35.
39 Armajani, *Iran*, p. 117; Keddie, *Sayyid Jamal Ad-Din Al-Afghani*, 38, 51.
40 Ibid., 18.
41 Ibid.
42 Wilfrid Scawen Blunt, *Secret History of the English Occupation of Egypt* (New York: Alfred A. Knopf, 1922), 78.

the world to their history in his book *History of Assassins* in 1818. Von Hammer warned against "the pernicious influence of secret societies... and...the dreadful prostitution of religion to the horrors of unbridled ambition." When Hammer wrote these words, secret societies were common in the Middle East and Europe.[43]

Afghani was among the earliest modern Islamists to combine the Western model of secret societies with Islamic clandestine proselytism. Afghani had three common core elements with the Assassins. First, he used secret societies to further his conspiracies. Second, he believed in using secret emissaries to mobilize his pan-Islamism project, and who could resort to assassinations to further his missions.[44] One of his disciples, Mizra Riza Kirmani, was involved in the 1896 assassination of the ruler of Iran, Nasir ad-Din Shah.[45]

The third core element he shared with the Assassins was that his followers sanctified him. After Afghani's disciple killed the Shah, Kirmani said he believed Afghani was the Mahdi.[46] Fundamentalist Shi'ites believe the Mahdi will someday return to establish an Islamic state and kill all infidels, according to the current leader of Iran, Ayatollah Ali Khamenei.[47]

In Afghanistan from 1866 to 1868, Afghani clearly stated that his ideological mission was to unify the Muslim nation. According to Afghani's disciple and friend, Muhammad al-Makhzumi, Afghani said the Sunnis of Afghanistan "should collaborate with their Iranian brothers, there is no conflict in their general interests. They are all from one origin, unified by the honorable Islamic association."[48]

---

43 Bernard Lewis, *The Assassins*, 12.

44 Jacob M. Landau, *Pan-Islam History and Politics*, (Routledge Library Editions: Politics of the Middle East, 2015), 15: 30; Landau, *Middle Eastern Themes: Papers in History and Politics* (Routledge Library Editions: Politics of the Middle East, 2016), 14: 36.

45 Keddie, *Sayyid Jamal Ad-Din Al-Afghani*, 412.

46 Ibid., 211.

47 The Daily Caller, June 15, 2014, www.dailycaller.com.

48 Muhammad Pasha Makhzumi, *Khatirat al-Afghani* (Egypt: Maktabit ash-Shoruq ad-Dawliyya, 2002), 232.

Afghani's words were similar to those uttered by Nader Shah in Najaf, more than 120 years earlier. Afghani attributed all forms of backwardness and "total decay" of the ummah to Islamic sectarianism, and believed that unity would be the most effective means to combat their enemies.[49] Afghani stated, "Islamic unity is a priority for the Iranians. They aspire to be the pioneers of renewing Islamic unification."[50]

Afghani used the term "renewal" because the concept of Shi'a-Sunni unity already had a Persian tradition. Afghani was an intelligent man, and in an attempt to entice Sunnis to accept his call for unification, he reminded them that several of the most renowned scholars in Sunni Islam were Persian. For example, five of the authors of *al-kutub as-sittah*, the six Sunni books of Hadith, the collection of traditions of the Prophet of Islam, were Persian.[51]

THE LIBERAL RENAISSANCE VERSUS THE ISLAMIC AWAKENING

Afghani traveled to Egypt in 1871, where he stayed for eight years. The trip was fruitful for his two Islamist projects: the jihadist unification project—using clandestine proselytism—and his pan-Islamism project. Upon his arrival in Egypt, Afghani was given a government pension and he briefly taught at al-Azhar University, where he was able to recruit *ulama* (Muslim clerics) to his ideas. At the time, Egypt saw rapid modernization and the governmental and societal abandonment of Islamic fundamentalism, which began under the rule of Sa'id Pasha (1822–1863).

Soon after assuming power in Egypt in 1854, Sa'id introduced several reforms to move Egypt toward capitalism and property rights

49 Ibid., 231.
50 Ibid.
51 Ibid., 233.

and to abolish the *dhimmi* status. In Shari'a law, "*dhimmi*" status means that Christians and Jews are governed by different legal and societal laws and rules. Under *dhimmi* status, people have few or no individual or property rights, and have to pay a *jizyah* (religious ransom tax) to stay alive.[52]

This status was perpetrated against Coptic Christians and Jews for centuries under Islamic rule. When Sa'id abolished the *jizyah* tax, Coptic Christians and Jews significantly flourished and transformed Egypt's economy into a booming capitalist society. Sa'id also elevated the prominence of a Muslim classical liberal, Sheikh Rifa'a at-Tahtawi (1801–1873). Tahtawi was a proponent of Western civilization, and Sa'id gave him vast power to control the education system.

In 1835, Tahtawi founded Madrasat at-Tarjama (the school for linguistics) as a foundation for his renaissance project, which translated Western philosophy, literature, and the sciences into Arabic. Tahtawi's school still exists as Al-Alsun College, in the Ain Shams University in Cairo. He was also a strong advocate of women's rights, individual liberty, and the Western model of the rule of law.[53]

The movement toward Western civilization resumed under the rule of Sa'id's successor, Isma'il Pasha (1830–1895), also known as Isma'il the Magnificent, who governed Egypt from 1863 to 1879. Under Isma'il's rule, the calls for a renaissance became more mainstream and popular. The openness to Western civilization had opponents among Islamic fanatics.

While Tahtawi and Afghani are sometimes lumped together as members of the same "renaissance" project, they were on opposing ends.[54] Afghani's activism was a repudiation of Tahtawi's, Isma'il's, and Sa'id's classical liberal legacies. Afghani's project was a regressive

52 Al-Ahram (Cairo), https://gate.ahram.org.eg/daily/News/203257/3/745338/تاقيقحت/يفتتح-غدا-ويرسل-رسالة-سلام-إلى-العالم-عبد-«إيلاه».aspx, January 9, 2020.

53 Rifa'a at-Tahtawi, *Takhlis al-Ibriz fi Talkhis Paris* (California: Kitab Inc., 2005), 113.

54 Mark Juergensmeyer and Wade Clark Roof, *Encyclopedia of Global Religion* (London: SAGE Publications, 2011), 1: 587.

Islamic *sahwa* (awakening) in the face of the progressive renaissance civilization project.

Research by the Qatari government's al-Jazeera media network accurately describes the conflict between these figures as "the second greatest conflict in our history after the conflict between Ali and Mu'awiyya," in reference to the first and largest Islamic civil war in 657 AD.[55] The Islamic Awakening Project instigated by Afghani would later be organized by the Muslim Brotherhood, in what they currently call their *an-nahda* also spelled *al-nahda* (resurrection or renaissance) project.

Afghani's political agitation is as misunderstood as the Brotherhood's mission. Afghani is sometimes inaccurately described as a "modernist" by experts in the West for his call to use Western scientific innovation to advance his pan-Islamic cause.[56] He hoped Western sciences could be "adopted without the foreigners' cultural and linguistic baggage."[57] What he viewed as cultural and linguistic baggage was Western morality, values, rule of law, and rational epistemology. Afghani hoped for a fundamentalist, totalitarian, and scientifically advanced Islamic nation to be able to militarily defeat the West. The ideological war between Afghani's and Tahtawi's ideas remain an ongoing battle in terms of understanding of Islam and its role in society and politics.

Afghani's ideas were not mainstream in Egypt, or in his native Iran.[58] But his political activism gained momentum after he joined the Freemasonry for political reasons. According to historian A. Albert Kudsi-Zadeh, Afghani's earliest known contact with the Freemasons in Egypt was in 1875; this "proved to be useful because it offered a ready-made organization for those interested in subversive activities."[59] The Freemasons gave Afghani an outlet to propagate his ambi-

55 Wa'el Ali, "Bain at-Tahtawi wa'l-Afghani," Al-Jazeera (Qatar), September 9, 2016.
56 Keddie, *Sayyid Jamal Ad-Din Al-Afghani,* 165–6.
57 Ibid.
58 Yahya Armajani, *Iran,* 117.
59 A. Albert Kudsi-Zadeh, "Afghani and Freemasonry in Egypt," *Journal of the American Oriental Society* 92, no. 1 (January-March 1972), 27.

tions and practice his clandestine proselytism. His activism in the Freemasons allowed him to be involved with Isma'il Pasha's oldest son, Muhammad Tawfiq Pasha (1852–1892), in a conspiracy that successfully deposed Isma'il.

Shortly after Tawfiq attained power in 1879, Egyptian police notified Tawfiq that Afghani planned to assassinate him.[60] While Afghani denied the accusation, it's likely he did want to assassinate Tawfiq, just as he suggested Isma'il Pasha ought to be assassinated.[61] Afghani's conspiracy to kill Tawfiq led to his arrest and deportation to India the same year. Afghani's assassination aspirations failed with Isma'il and Tawfiq, but they were successful with their Persian counterpart Nasir ad-Din Shah.

A year before departing Egypt, Afghani founded a secret society in Alexandria called *Misr al-Fatat* (Young Egypt), and he acted as its president. The organization issued a weekly newspaper under the same name until Afghani was forced to leave Egypt in 1879 and settle in Hyderabad, India.[62] The organization eventually turned into an Islamic-socialist, fascist political party decades after Afghani's death.

In India, Afghani founded a clandestine anti-European pan-Islamic organization called *al-Urwah al-Wuthqa*, in 1882.[63] Two years later, Afghani travelled to Paris where he was joined by his protégé, al-Azhar scholar Muḥammad Abduh (1849–1905), who eventually would assume the powerful position of Grand Mufti of Egypt in 1899. Abduh and Afghani established the society's branch in Paris and under its auspices, they published an Arabic periodical using the same name as their secret society.[64]

---

60 Ibid., 34.

61 Ibid., 31.

62 Ami Ayalon, *The Press in the Arabic Middle East: A History* (Oxford: Oxford University Press, 1995), 44.

63 Nihayah Muhammad Salih al-Himdani, *Al-Haraqa al-Wataniyya at-Tunisiyya* (Dubai: Al-Minhal, 2016) , 146–7.

64 Albert Hourani, *Arabic Thought in the Liberal Age 1798—1939* (Cambridge: Cambridge University Press, 1988), 109; Fathi Hassan Mikawi, *Ash-Shaikh Muhammad Tahir ibn Ashur* (Virginia: International Institute of Islamic Thought, 2011), 64–5.

From December 1884 to January 1885, Abduh traveled to Tunisia to recruit important figures to their secret society. Abduh's choice of Tunisia was strategic, as its al-Zaytuna Mosque had become a hub for clandestine *da'wa* and Islamist secret societies. In Tunisia, Abduh met with many influential Islamist figures.[65] He returned to Tunisia in 1903 to resume his Islamist activities, and there he met the Tunisian Islamist Salih al-Sharif at-Tunsi (1869–1920), who later would become an instrumental figure in spreading global German-jihadist propaganda that would lead to the founding of the Muslim Brotherhood.

Despite Afghani's absence from Egypt, his two projects gained momentum with his followers from al-Azhar University and among military officers who were members of the Freemasons. According to a *Times of London* correspondent, Afghani "almost obtained the weight of a Median law among the lower and less educated classes," and he was also able to influence "fallah officers" (peasant officers).[66] These army officers, who were also members of Afghani's lodge, planted the seed that would later grow into an army revolt led by Freemason member and radical Colonel Ahmed Urabi (1841–1911).[67] The officers perpetrated a violent revolt from 1879 to 1882, which was later suppressed by Khedive Tawfiq with the help of British and French forces.

While many scholars and historians wonder whether Afghani was a Sunni, a Shi'ite, an atheist, a reformer, or a Russian agent, Afghani was most probably an Islma'ili Assassin.

His pan-Islamic awakening, proximity project, and clandestine work continued through three major actors. The first was Muhammad Abduh. The second was an influential Lebanese Islamist, Muhammad Rashid Rida (1865–1935), a pan-Islamism fundamentalist who was exiled to Egypt, in 1898, for supporting the Urabi revolt. The third

65 The Arab League Educational, Cultural and Scientific Organization, *Mawsu'at a'lam al-Ulamma wa'l-Udaba' al-Arab wa'l-Muslimin* (Beirut: Dar al-Jil, 2004), 430.

66 Kudsi-Zadeh, "Afghani and Freemasonry in Egypt," 31.

67 Ibid., 32.

and most successful manifestation of Afghani's vision was through the Muslim Brotherhood and the Islamic revolution in Iran.

The Sunni-Shi'a proximity project went smoothly during the early years of the Brotherhood's founding. The current divide between the two sects was almost culturally nonexistent at the time. The mainstream perception of relations between the two sects was not only peaceful but even positive. For example, in 1939, Sunni Princess Fawzia Fuad of Egypt (1921–2013) married the Shi'ite Shah of Iran, Muhammad Reza Pahlavi (1919–1980), in a historic ceremony with the blessing of the people from both nations. Fawzia became the Queen of Iran during their marriage until they divorced in 1948.

This indicates the peaceful atmosphere the Muslim Brotherhood and jihadist Iranian factions exploited to form a dangerous alliance with a violent revolutionary agenda. The forefather of the Muslim Brotherhood, Hassan al-Banna, was influenced by Muhammad Abduh's clandestine proselytism and was mentored by Rashid Rida's Manar's school of thought, which combined the teachings of Afghani and Abduh with Wahhabism.[68]

During the early years of its formation, Banna and other founding members of the Brotherhood studied Shi'a Islamic secret societies, such as al-Hashashin, and modeled the Muslim Brotherhood organization after them.[69] In the mid-1940s, prior to his involvement with the group, the Brotherhood's ideological leader, Sayyid Qutb, often referred to the Muslim Brotherhood as "al-Hashashin" and to Hassan al-Banna as "Hassan as-Sabbah"—the founder of the Assassins.[70]

The Brotherhood's infatuation with the most murderous Shi'a cult partially explains the group's ideological affinity to Iran, which goes beyond simple pragmatic causes for their alliance. The Brotherhood's

68 Muhammad as-Sayyid, "Muhammad Rashid Rida: Ra'id al-Aqlaniyya al-Islamiyya al-Mo'asira," The Official Muslim Brotherhood Encyclopedia, https://ikhwanwiki.com/, accessed February 12, 2018.

69 Ali Ashmawi, *At-Tarikh as-Sirri*, 8.

70 Tharwat al-Kherbawy, *A'imatu ash-Share* (Cairo: Dar Nahdat Misr Publishing: 2013), 17.

jurisprudence of priorities established a deep and continuing ideological relationship, not merely a tactical one. The proximity project was ingrained in the founding vision and structure of the organization. The Brotherhood's clandestine aspects capitalized on its wider acceptance of the Shi'ite sect. This explains why the Brotherhood attracted Shi'ite members during its early years and was even funded by Iran.[71]

Banna often repeated Rida's proximity aphorism about the cooperation between Sunnis and Shi'ites, saying, "We cooperate in what we agree upon between us, and excuse each other's differences."[72]

71 Azhari TV (Cairo), July 18, 2014; Al-Kherbawy, *A'imatu ash-Share*, 143–153.

72 Ibid., 119–120; Muhammad Rashid Rida, *Fatwatiyn min Fatawa al-Manar al-Islah'iyya* (Cairo: Dar al-Manar, 1921), 9.

CHAPTER THREE

WORLD DOMINATION

The Four Pillars of The Muslim Brotherhood Cult

"Our mission is world domination"
—Hassan al-Banna[1]

IT IS DIFFICULT TO UNDERSTAND any topic outside the context of its past. A psychiatrist or a physician does not examine an ailment in isolation. It has to be viewed within the context of a patient's medical history. The Muslim Brotherhood and its terrorist offshoots are the same. It is impossible to examine or predict their behavior without dissecting their history, especially since the Muslim Brotherhood aggravates old conflicts and grievances and repeats its early organization's modus operandi. The Brotherhood is stuck in a repetitive vortex, not out of ignorance but for ideological reasons that justify its existence.

Four major influences on the Brotherhood's founder led to the organization's creation. A deep examination of these factors reveals similar individual and organizational behavioral patterns among contemporary clandestine Islamist groups. Two covert Islamic groups that contributed to the founding of the Muslim Brotherhood have been reestablished and are operational today.

---

1 Hassan al-Banna, "*Risalat ila Aia Shai' Nad'ou an-Nas?*" The Official Muslim Brotherhood Encyclopedia, https://ikhwanwiki.com/, accessed November 13, 2020.

THE FOUR PILLARS

The first significant influence on Hassan al-Banna was his ideological upbringing, which was steeped in the fundamentalist orthodox Hanbali school of jurisprudence, adhered to by the vast majority of Sunni terrorist groups. The second factor was the growing movement of Islamic Awakening by the World War I-era Islamist cabal, originally developed in the Ottoman empire. The third influence on Banna was the growing wave of far-left-wing governments in Europe and the Soviet Union, which directly contributed to how Banna structured the Muslim Brotherhood. The fourth pillar was the trend of secret societies and clandestine fraternities in the region, which became breeding grounds for secret Islamist proselytism and models for Islamist secret societies.

THE CREATION OF THE SALAFI HASSAN AL-BANNA

In October 1906, Hassan al-Banna was born in Mahmudiyya, a rural Nile Delta town northwest of Cairo. Al-Banna was the son of an imam and mosque teacher, Ahmed Abdul Rahman al-Banna (1884–1958), also known as as-Sa'ati (also spelled al-Sa'ati), "the watch repairer." He operated a small watch repair shop, but his more influential endeavor was the ideological indoctrination of his children.

Sa'ati was an imam who received religious training at al-Azhar University when Muhammad Abduh was teaching there.[2] Sa'ati adhered to the fundamentalist Sunni Hanbali school of jurisprudence. His major work was his arrangement of religious works from legist Ahmad ibn Hanbal (703–855).[3] According to former advisor to Kuwaiti Ministry of Islamic Relations, Abdullah al-Aqeel, Banna's

---

2 Richard P. Mitchell, *The Society of the Muslim Brothers* (Oxford: Oxford University Press, 1993), 1.

3 Ahmed bin Abdul Rahman as-Sa'ati, *Al-Fattih al-rabbani fi Tartib Musnad al-Imam Ahmad ibn Hanbal ash-Shibanni* (Amman: Dar al-Afkar ad-Dawliyya, 2004).

father dedicated thirty-eight years compiling hadith and *fiqh* (interpretations of Islamic jurisprudence) from jurist ibn Hanbal, which he published in 1957.[4]

The Hanbali school of thought is the most radical of the four orthodox Sunni schools of jurisprudence. Ibn Hanbal influenced history's most radical theologians, such as thirteenth-to-fourteenth-century Ibn Taymiyah, and the eighteenth century founder of Wahhabism, Muhammad ibn Abdul-Wahhab.[5] Ibn Hanbal influenced Egypt's Salafi or Salafist movements. Salafism refers to *salaf*, which means ancestors, and is often used in reference to the first three generation of Muslims associated with the Prophet of Islam. Salafis believe in adhering to a fundamentalist and purist form of Sunni Islam, which should be propagated and practiced through a perpetual state of jihad. Salafism is not a sect, but rather a movement within Sunnism.

The Hanbali school is adhered to by most Sunni Salafi terrorist groups, including Islamic State and al-Qaeda.[6] The earliest and most prominent influence in Banna's life was his Salafi Hanbali upbringing.[7] The Salafi movement begun with Jamal ad-Din al-Afghani and Muhammad Abduh in 1883–1884.[8] The ideology was developed and propagated through their magazine *al-Urwah al-Wuthqa*, named after the clandestine group Afghani established in India.

In the eighteenth and nineteenth centuries, the Hanbali school of jurisprudence was generally shunned in Egyptian society. During that period, Egypt's mainstream culture associated it with backwardness, extremism, and rigidity.

The mass resentment of the Hanbali school gained momentum after an incident in 1884.[9] Two years into the British occupation of

---

4 Abdullah al-Aqeel, "Al-Imam al-Muhadith Shaikh Ahmad Abdul Rahman al-Banna as-Sa'ati," AlaqeelAbuMostafa.com, accessed August 30, 2019.

5 Sayyid Abdul Aziz as-Sayili, *Al-Aqida as-Salafiyya* (Cairo: al-Mannar, 1993), 26.

6 Al-Aqeel, Al-Imam al-Muhadith.

7 Asharq Al-Awsat (London), March 31, 2013.

8 J. Heyworth-Dunne, *Religious and Political Trends in Modern Egypt* (Washington, DC, 1950), 9.

9 Al-Ahram (Cairo), March 22, 2014.

Egypt, British forces issued a pamphlet urging Egyptians to use running water in mosques instead of washstands for *al-wudu'*, the Islamic purification ritual of rinsing parts of the body before prayer. The pamphlet created a controversy inside Egyptian mosques. Mosques led by Hanbali scholars issued a *fatwa* against using running water, stating that "prayers are blessed by [using] water which was previously used by the imam" who typically starts the *wudu'* ritual. The followers of the more moderate Hanafi school of jurisprudence accepted the invitation to use running water, and the Egyptian government ignored the Hanbali dissent and introduced running tap water into mosques. They tasked British toxicologist and irrigation engineer Sir William R. Wilcox to implement the project. The division over running water in mosques earned faucets its etymology: *hanafiyya*, the feminine noun of Hanafi, remains the Egyptian word for faucet. That incident also inspired the Egyptian aphorism "don't be a Hanbali"—a proverb still widely used in Egypt—to refer to someone who is rigid, unsympathetic, or stubborn.

The young Banna grew up in a society that told him not to be himself. When Banna was almost eight years old, his father enrolled him in the al-Rashad Islamic *madrassa* (Islamic religious school). There, local imam Muhammad Zahran instructed Banna in fundamentalist Islamic teaching.[10] Banna failed to memorize the Qur'an at al-Rashad and insisted upon joining middle school. His father agreed under the condition that he continue memorizing the Qur'an at home.[11]

In middle school, Banna first experienced organized activism when he joined the Society of Moral Behavior.[12] The society was founded by one of Banna's teachers and its purpose was to punish moral offenses, such as cursing one's parents or religion, by levying fines on offenders.

Banna and other students were not content with these activities, and when Banna was twelve years old, he said they wanted to

10 Hassan al-Banna, *Mudhakkirat ad-D'wa wa'l-Da'iyya* (Kuwait: Dar Afaq, 2012), 6.
11 Ibid., 8.
12 Ibid.

"work on rectifying society."[13] A representative of the Society of Moral Behavior met Banna's father and two other teachers at his school. Together, they established the "Society of Vice Prevention," a juvenile version of today's Saudi Committee for the Promotion of Virtue and the Prevention of Vice. Banna's teenage delinquencies became legitimized by society.

Banna admitted that the main activity of this Society was drafting anonymous threatening letters to Muslims whom they perceived as sinners, such as women who wore makeup and individuals who did not fast during the month of Ramadan.[14] In a 2014 television interview, Egyptian Muslim Brotherhood expert, author, and former Undersecretary of State Security Service General Fouad Allam said, "Banna's mob spread terror in his rural town by harassing and assaulting Christians, setting their property on fire, and sending secret and anonymous threats to Muslims."[15]

SUFI OR SALAFI?

When Banna turned thirteen years old, his Islamic activism led him to join a Sunni-Sufi group. Banna's affiliation with the group still creates a misunderstanding in the West about the nature of Banna's message. Sufism is Islamic mysticism, and it is often incorporated within religious rituals of Sunnism or Shi'itism. A Sufi Islamic sect exists, but it is shunned and condemned by fundamentalist Sunni and Shi'ite scholars and Islamists, including Banna himself, who strongly rejected it.[16] Banna said the Sufi sect "allowed every infidel, atheist, or corrupt [individual] the right to their opinion and faith." Thus, the Muslim Brotherhood makes a clear distinction between Sufi rituals incorporated within Sunnism, and the Sufi sect that was represented

13 Ibid., 11.
14 Ibid.
15 Misr al-Balad (Cairo), March 19, 2014.
16 Banna, *Mudhakkirat,* 21.

by mystics such as Mansur al-Hallaj (858–922) and Muhammad ibn al-Hasan al-Niffari (died 965). Islamists consider the Sufi sect a form of apostasy from Islam.

Most Islamists accept Sunni-Sufism, which manifests in *dhikr* circles. These circles take two forms: sitting or dancing *dhikr*.[17] The sitting *dhikr* can be either a silent meditation or an oral recitation of Islamic chants. The dancing *dhikr* involves Islamic chanting and spinning. The choice of the practice is often named after a local imam who leads the circle.

Hassan al-Banna joined the sitting *dhikr* of the Order of the Hasafiyya Brothers, which is named after a local imam, Hussein al-Hasafi (1848–1910). The circle was reestablished by Ahmad al-Sukari (1901–1993), and Banna's relationship with Sukari changed both their lives. The Hasafiyya Brothers became the first official seed in establishing the Muslim Brotherhood. Banna said what captivated him the most while reading the writings of Imam Hasafi was his "severity in enforcing virtue and prohibiting of vice."[18] This became the first objective of the Order of Hasafiyya Brothers. The second objective was to counter Christian evangelism.

In 1923, Banna joined Dar al-Ulum, a teacher-training school in Cairo, where Banna reconnected with the Hasafiyya Brothers. The young man surveyed the city with the "eyes of a religious villager" while the war of ideas reached its height in Cairo.[19]

Classic liberals, communists, and Islamists in Egyptian society debated individual freedom and the role of religion in society and governance. Mainstream classical liberal movements pushed for women's rights and the separation of mosque and state, some even advocated for the abolishment of classical Arabic. The Free Constitutionalists

17 Mahmoud Abdul Raouf al-Qassim, *Al-Kashf an al-Haqiqa as-Sufiyya* (Beirut: Dar al-Sahaba, 1987), 629.

18 Banna, *Mudhakkirat,* 15.

19 112. Ibid. ,55. Richard P. Mitchell, *The Society of the Muslim Brothers* (Oxford University Press, 1993) p. 4

Party and the old Wafd Party became the most powerful proponents for European renaissance values and classical liberalism.[20]

Following the 1919 revolution, Cairo underwent a mainstream reformist movement toward classical liberalism, which led to Egyptian women shedding the *hijab* (Islamic headscarf) and popularizing the values of freedom of speech. Cairo University's secular law school was established in 1908 and was inspired by the notion that it "could not be a law university unless it revolted against religion and fought the social tradition which derived from it."[21]

The libertarian movement inside Cairo University was part of the growing popularity of intellectual literary and social salons, societies, parties, books, and newspapers, that propagated ideas to "weaken the influence of religion."[22] Classical liberal politicians became mainstream figures in the government, and they drafted Egypt's most liberal constitution in 1924, a document that granted "absolute religious freedom," individual liberty, and free speech. This mainstream wave of liberation faced a vast network of secret Islamists movements that branched across the Middle East and Europe, and franchised jihadism under benign-sounding slogans. Several of these organizations still exist, and others are reemerging. Banna's early Islamic education in the Salafi Hanbali school, combined with his upbringing, made him a perfect target for recruitment by secret Islamist groups.

BANNA AND THE SECRET WORLD WAR I ISLAMIST CABAL

During the late 1800s, several jihad-propagating secret Islamic societies formed across the Middle East and in Constantinople, which

20 The Wafd Party was established in 1919 and operated until it was dissolved by the Free Officers' Islamic socialist coup d'etat in 1952. The New Wafd Party which was established in 1978, adheres to anti-Semitic, pan-Islamic and Pan-Arab ideas.

21 Banna, *Mudhakkirat*, 55; Mitchell, *The Society of the Muslim Brothers*, 4.

22 Ibid.

is modern-day Istanbul. Two efforts to revive the Ottoman Empire exist today, and they have succeeded in evading the attention of counterterrorism experts and the intelligence community. This repetition of historic secret warfare follows specific patterns. Islamic clandestine groups can be identified by (1) understanding their history from their own sources; (2) studying their ideology; (3) analyzing their discourse; and (4) monitoring their behavior and associations. While current Islamist literature and discourse is often loaded with codes and concealed terminology, it still reveals itself to those who are armed with these four indispensable tools.

When Islamists are in what they perceive as a state of *mihna* (crisis or adversity), they rebrand their mission under benign terms such as morality, principles, ethics, freedom, justice, etc. In Islamist discourse, words often mean more than their literal translation. For example, the term "mihna" does not just mean "crisis" but refers to a branch of jurisprudence in modern fundamental Sunni thought known as *fiqh al-mihna* (the Jurisprudence of Crisis). The general Islamic theological concept of *mihna* is classically referred to as *ibtila'* (hardship) and is defined as hardship or adversity, which tests the believer's faith and fortitude.

In 1954, Islamists weaponized the term "mihna" with elements of clandestine jihad after Brotherhood theologians coined their modern doctrinal terms, *lahzat al-mihna* (the moment of crisis) or *sa'at al-mihna* (the hour of crisis), in reference to the first public split within the group. The first *mihna* of 1954 resulted in Qutb's Muslim Brotherhood and Islamic terrorism manifesto, "Milestones," which he published in 1964.

According to current Brotherhood leader and Islamic scholar Hazem Sa'id, crises should be viewed as "Godly rewards which elevate its bearers and prepare them to uphold His message and defend His religion. God has preordained the people of the truth with the path of jihad, jihad is permanent till the end of days."[23]

The Brotherhood believes that to overcome a crisis, it is essential to revert to the eschatological concept of *permanence of jihad*. This theological tool becomes instrumental whenever Islamists encounter political or societal challenges.

During a speech to Brotherhood operatives, Yusuf al-Qaradawi said it was "evident from Islamic history that the nation is stronger and more solid in the hour of crisis."[24] What Qaradawi meant by a "stronger" Islamic nation is a fanatic, jihadist, expansionist, and theocratic one. His use of term *hour of crisis* is code for jihad. While his statement is not entirely correct, there is truth in it. Islamists operate better in covert settings, because their ideology requires criminal and illegal undertakings, which are prohibited by the laws of most countries.

The jurisprudence of mihna does not apply only to political challenges. If the majority population of a targeted nation considers Islamist ideas to be either criminal or morally reprehensible, the concept of mihna allows Islamists to revert to clandestine proselytism.[25]

THE MAKASSED FOUNDATION

According to the Iranian government's Taghrib News Agency, which aims to bridge the gap between jihadists from both sects, "charitable organizations and religious educational institutions" were "among the tools utilized by the proponents of the [Islamic] Awakening."[26] This is true. The tactic of employing charitable organizations as front groups for jihadist activities has been successful in funding terrorism

23 Hazem Sa'id, "Limaza Ibtalana Allah?" The Official Muslim Brotherhood Encyclopedia, https://ikhwanwiki.com/, accessed November 5, 2020.

24 "Nasr Allah ya'eti wa-Lawu Ishtadat al-Mihan," YouTube.com, April 11, 2020.

25 Yusuf al-Qaradawi, *Al-Mihna fi Waqi' al-Haraka al-Islamiyya al-Mu'asira* (Cairo: Maktabit Wahba, 2001), 35.

26 Taghrib News website, http://www.taghribnews.ir/, accessed November 17, 2020.

and hijacking the representation of Muslims and radicalizing them since the 1800s.

A prominent example of this tactic is *Jam'iyat al-Makassid al-Islamiyya* (The Foundation of Islamic Principle), also known as Makassid or Makassed Foundation. The Makassed Foundation was cofounded in 1878 by Lebanese pan-Islamism agitator, politician, and sheikh Abdul-Kadir Mustafa Kabbani (1848–1935). The Makassed Foundation still operates widely in Lebanon and has a branch in the United States, which was founded in 1999.

MAKASSED'S TWO-FAÇADES

This group was among the pioneers of the current Islamist charity organizations that function with two façades—overt and covert. When Kabbani founded his organization, it operated publicly as a charitable organization. Secretly, observers at the time labeled it a covert political organization working to overthrow the government and replace it.[27] Many controversial individuals helped found this group but the most important of them was Ahmed Sefik Midhat Pasha (1822–1883).[28] The study of Midhat Pasha's example provides identifying patterns of behavior of modern covert jihadists who are labeled as "liberal" or "moderate" in the West, while they are working to advance a violent Islamic caliphate. Jamal ad-Din al-Afghani's example is replicated with Midhat Pasha but on a smaller scale. The next chapters will demonstrate how these classic examples of two-faced agents are currently taking place in the West, where covert Brotherhood agents are celebrated as dissidents, human rights activists, academics, celebrities, politicians, and entrepreneurs.

27 Hassan Hallak, *Mudhakkirat Selim Ali Salam 1868–1938* (Beirut: Dar an-Nahda al-Arabiyya, 2015), 116.

28 Mustafa Dandishli, "Tarikh wa-Tatwur al-Makasad al-Khayriya" (Saida: Al-Markaz al-Thaqafi l'al-Behouth w'at-Tawthiq, 1986), accessed November 5, 2020.

A preliminary research into the history of Makassed would give the false impression that that its founders were "liberal." Makassed's leadership invokes propaganda to fake moderation.

Midhat Pasha was the real leader behind the Makassed Foundation.[29] He was an Islamist Ottoman politician and briefly a Grand Vizier (de facto prime minister of the Ottoman Empire). He was also an avid supporter of Jamal ad-Din al-Afghani when Afghani visited Turkey from 1869 to 1871.[30] Midhat Pasha also cofounded the secret Young Ottomans group and helped raise Sultan Abdulhamid II (1842–1918) to power in 1876. He also contributed to deposing the liberal Sultan Abdulaziz (1830–1876). Abdulhamid would become known in the Middle East as *Sultan ad-Dam* (the Bloody Sultan) for his role in the genocide of Armenians and the massacre of Assyrians.[31]

Just like another Afghani supporter, Midhat Pasha was an Islamist who would later become a murderer but, prior to engaging in jihad, was often described in West as a "liberal."[32] In 1877, American Ambassador to Turkey Horace Maynard wrote a letter to Ambassador Nicholas Fish II in which he stated Midhat Pasha was "a reformer and a true patriot" as well as "champion of a liberal policy."[33] The opposite was true. Midhat Pasha attempted to preserve Islamic law as the basis for governance but framed it as a Western-style constitution in a religious obscurantist fashion.

Midhat Pasha assigned Islamic scholars to write the constitution.[34] Constitutional theocracies have not performed well due to the inher-

29 Dandishli, "Tarikh wa-Tatwur."

30 Rafid Alaa al-Khaza'i, "As-Sayyid Jamal ad-Din al-Afghani: Guevara as-Sharq" (Baghdad: Thahifat al-Muthaqaf, August 20 2011, 1810.

31 François Georgeon, *Abdulhamid II: Le sultan calife* (Paris: Fayard, 2003), 33.

32 Editors, "The Liberal Midhat Pasha Forms Ministry in Constantinople," The Literary Encyclopedia, 2011, https://www.litencyc.com/php/stopics.php?rec=true&UID=18706, accessed November 6, 2020.

33 United States Department of State, Papers Relating to the Foreign Relations of the United States: Transmitted to Congress, with the Annual Message of the President, December 3, 1877; of Persons and Subjects (Classic Reprint, 2018), 558.

34 Geoffrey P. Nash, ed. *Marmaduke Pickthall: Islam and the Modern World* (Boston: Brill, 2017), 140.

ent contradiction between secular law and Islamic law. Shari'a law nullifies civil law and constitutional articles when contradictions exist. Despite this, Midhat Pasha's Young Ottomans succeeded in pushing for the Ottoman Empire's first constitution. The First Constitutional Era began in December 1876 and ended when the constitution was overthrown in February 1878. Its own theocratic articles preserved the status of the caliph and *Shaikh ul-Islam*, the chief mufti assigned by the caliph to oversee the hierarchy of the state-appointed Muslim scholars, imams, and sheikhs. Midhat Pasha and Sultan Abdulhamid eventually became adversaries due to a rift over power, not ideology.[35]

During Midhat Pasha's life, an alarming pattern begun. Just as Afghani's Persian protégé assassinated the Shah of Iran, Midhat Pasha was also convicted and charged with assassination of reformist Sultan Abdulaziz in 1881. Midhat Pasha was initially sentenced to death, but his sentence was later commuted to life imprisonment and he died in his cell in 1883.

A year before his death, the organization he founded in Lebanon came under scrutiny when the local government confiscated eighty-five barrels of gunpowder after they were shipped to Makassed's cofounder, Sa'id Turbah.[36] This incident led Ottoman statesman Ahmed Hamdi Pasha to open an investigation into the foundation. It also prompted him to make the common political mistake of assuming that he could engage these Islamists instead of dismantling their foundation and seizing its assets. Ahmed Pasha assigned an Islamist judge to contain the movement under the government's national group of Islamic associations, *Sho'bat al-Ma'araf al-Ahliyya*, under the leadership of Ottoman Shari'a law judge Abdullah Jamal ad-Din. Ad-Din strengthened the foundation and augmented it with more

35 *Mudhakkirat as-Sultan' Abdulhamid II*, trans. Muhammad Harb (Damascus: Dar al-Qalam, 1991), 76.
36 Al-Liwa' (Beirut), July 21, 2018.

radicals from Egypt, such as Abduh, who was exiled to Lebanon in 1882 for his role in the Urabi revolt.[37]

The other major founder of the Makassed Foundation, Kabbani, established several organizations, among them an Islamic madrassa he cofounded with Rashid Rida.[38]

During his time in Lebanon, Abduh also connected with Rida and Kabbani. According to the official website of the Kabbani clan in Lebanon, they originate from an Arabian tribe that was involved in early jihadist campaigns against several nations in the Middle East, including Egypt, Iraq, Morocco, and other nations in the Eastern Mediterranean region, such as modern Syria and Lebanon.[39] The Kabbani clan is still closely associated with the Makassed Foundation in Lebanon, and it can be described as a Muslim Brotherhood front group.

THE OTTOMAN-GERMAN JIHAD PROJECT AND ITS INFLUENCE ON THE MUSLIM BROTHERHOOD

The Makassed Foundation has an Egyptian equivalent that played a major role in the founding of the Muslim Brotherhood, and Banna became one of its most powerful recruits.

Banna retaliated against modernized cosmopolitan society by reverting to fundamentalism. During his second year in school, he joined the Salafi religious group *Jam'iyat Makarim al-Akhlaq al-Islamiyya*, which was sometimes translated in the West as the Islamic Society for Nobility of Character.[40] A more accurate translation is used by the society: Islamic Ethics Association. It is not exactly clear when the

37 Ibid.

38 The Official Website of the Kabbani Clan, "Tarikh Usrat Kabbani," http://kabbanifamily.org/, accessed November 4, 2020.

39 Ibid.

40 Azmi Bishara, *Fi al-Ijaba an Su'al: Ma as-Salafiyya* (Doha: Arab Center for Research & Policy Studies, 2018), 56.

group was established; it has the most obscure history of all Egyptian societies of the time.[41] Muhammad Rashid Rida said it was the only Islamic society in Egypt when he immigrated to Cairo in 1897.[42]

The Islamic Ethics Association's history is important not only for understanding the socio-political climate of Islamism in Egypt at the time but also because this dangerous organization is currently a Muslim Brotherhood front group and has reemerged across the Middle East. The group is attempting to revive underground practices of clandestine jihad, Islamist infiltration, and agitation. It is also attempting to restore the Ottoman Empire.

This mysterious organization was founded by a group of al-Azhar sheikhs, most of whom were Abduh's and Afghani's students. These sheikhs are the missing link between the original proponents of the Islamic Awakening Project and Banna. The organization predominantly relied on clandestine proselytism, and it had a strong connection to the Ottoman-German jihad project during World War I.

On July 30, 1914, soon after World War I began, Kaiser Wilhelm II stated: "Our consuls and agents in Turkey, India and Egypt are supposed to inflame the Muslim regions to wild revolts against the British."[43] The Kaiser was sometimes known in the Middle East as "Hajji Wilhelm" and the "protector of Islam."[44] He had a strong track record among Islamist activists. After Turkey perpetrated the massacres against Armenians from 1894 to 1896—known as "the Hamidian massacres" in reference to Abdulhamid II—the Kaiser proclaimed allegiance to the perpetrators. He did so in 1898 by giving a speech in Damascus at the tomb of An-Nasir Salah ad-Din ibn Ayyub, known in the West as Saladin, during which the Kaiser proclaimed himself a

---

41 Omar ash-Sharif, *A'alam Mansiyya: Derasa Tarikhiyya* (Cairo: Biblomania Publishing, 2017), 147-50.

42 Muhmmed Rashid Rida, *Al-Manar* (Cairo: Al-Manar, 1932), 32: 634.

43 Barry Rubin and Wolfgang G. Schwanitz, *Nazis, Islamists, and the Making of the Modern Middle East* (New Haven: Yale University Press, 2014), 32.

44 Henry Morgenthau, *Ambassador Morgenthau's Story* (New York: Doubleday, Page & Company, 1919), 101.

friend of Islam.[45] On his way to Damascus, the Kaiser and his wife, Augusta Victoria, stopped in Lebanon, where they received an organized celebration arranged by Kabbani, who personally entertained and hosted the Kaiser and his wife.[46]

The Kaiser relied on a major operative in the Islamic Awakening Project, Baron Max von Oppenheim (1860–1946). Oppenheim was a lawyer, diplomat, historian, and archaeologist. He successfully employed all these skills to awaken jihadism in the Middle East, and he ultimately became an instigator and architect of Islamic jihad against the Triple Entente association of Britain, France, and Russia.[47]

According to historian Lionel Gossman, in October 1914, Oppenheim issued a *Denkschrift betreffend die Revolutionierung der islamischen Gebiete unserer Feinde* (Memorandum Concerning the Fomenting of Revolutions in the Islamic Territories of our Enemies). Oppenheim's memorandum advocated that Turks "invade Egypt."[48] While it did not succeed militarily, after a failed raid on the Suez by a German-led Ottoman army in 1915, it eventually would succeed ideologically. When Thomas Paine said, "An army of principles can penetrate where an army of soldiers cannot," he could have been referring to Oppenheim and the Ottoman's conspiratorial project.

Oppenheim recruited Islamic agents for ideological subversion of British-occupied Muslim-majority countries. He had the assistance of three Ottoman pro-Germany leaders, known in the West as the Three Pashas: War Minister Isma'il Enver, Navy Minister Ahmed Djemal, and Interior Minister Mehmed Tal'at.[49] The Three Pashas were also members of the Islamist-controlled Ottoman Freemason branch, "Committee of Young Turkey at Constantinople," which was known

45 Lionel Gossman, *The Passion of Max von Oppenheim: Archaeology and Intrigue in the Middle East from Wilhelm II to Hitler* (Open Book Publishers, 2013), 98.

46 The Official Website of the Kabbani Clan, "Ash-sheikh Abdul-Kadir Mustafa Kabbani 1848–1935," http://kabbanifamily.org/, accessed November 4, 2020.

47 Gossman, *The Passion of Max von Oppenheim*, 18.

48 Ibid., 275.

49 Ibid.

by 1895 as the "Committee of Union and Progress" (CUP). It became a major ruling power in the Ottoman Empire until 1918.[50]

Oppenheim set up the *Nachrichtenstelle für den Orient* (Orient Intelligence Bureau) under the roof of the Federal Foreign Office in Berlin. Gossman states that its function "was to gather intelligence and to spread Pan-Islamist ideas among Muslims everywhere, including those serving in the armies of the Entente, encourage participation in the jihad against the British, French, and Russian enemies of Islam."[51] According to historians Barry Rubin and Wolfgang G. Schwantiz:

> Von Oppenheim, author of Germany's Islamic Strategy, returned to the Foreign Ministry on August 2 [1914], nominally as head of the news department but actually to run a covert warfare in the Middle East, implementing the program he had advocated for twenty years. As Von Oppenheim had put in in 1898, his mission was to unleash "Muslim fanaticism that borders on insanity."[52]

By the end of the war, Oppenheim had hired almost sixty emissaries, mostly Muslim non-Germans, to implement his project.[53] Among them were Abduh's acquaintance, Salih al-Sharif at-Tunsi; the Lebanese Druze pan-Islamist, Shakib Arslan (1869–1946), who was deeply influenced by al-Afghani; Abduh's student, the prominent Islamist Abul-Aziz Jawish (1876–1929); and the Tunisian-born Algerian imam and agitator, Muhammad al-Khidr Hussein (1873–1958), also known as Sheikh Khidr. These men would change history by fulfilling Von Oppenheim's promise of unleashing "Muslim

50 Gerhard Böwering, *The Princeton Encyclopedia of Islamic Political Thought* (Princeton and Oxford: Princeton University Press, 2013), 601.

51 Ibid., 92.

52 Rubin and Schwanitz, *Nazis, Islamists, and the Making of the Modern Middle East*, 32.

53 Ibid., 39.

fanaticism that borders on insanity" causing millions of deaths and also majorly influence the founding of the Muslim Brotherhood cult.

GERMANY'S AGENT WHO HEADED AL-AZHAR UNIVERSITY

Von Oppenheim's agent, Muhammad al-Khidr Hussein became an instrumental figure in the Islamic Awakening Project and eventually the head of the world's ideological base of jihadism, al-Azhar University in Cairo. Oppenheim's Orient Intelligence Bureau published a newspaper in Arabic and other languages titled *El Dschihad*, or *al-Jihad*. The three key authors and editors of *al-Jihad* were al-Sharif at-Tunsi, Khidr, and Oppenheim.[54]

Khidr became Oppenheim's most powerful recruit and the connection between Oppenheim's project and Banna. The author was able to identify the connection, which understandably eluded historians as there was seemingly a lack of direct connection between the two. This void could only be filled by exploring Khidr and the Islamic Ethics Association.

In Tunisia, Khidr studied Islam at al-Zaytuna Mosque until he graduated in 1898. He then worked as a Shari'a court judge and as an Islamic law teacher at Zaytuna where clandestine proselytism, pan-Arabism, and Islamist secret societies were prevalent under the leadership of Sheikh Muhammad Tahir bin Ashur, who was also an associate and friend of Khidr.[55]

In 1912 Khidr moved to Istanbul, where he worked for the Ottoman Ministry of War under the leadership of Enver Pasha. In 1916, Enver assigned him to travel to Germany with a group of

54 Mourir Fendri, *Le Maghreb et l'Islam dans la stratégie de l'Allemagne en 1914* (Rabat: Hespéris-Tamuda, 2018), LIII, no.1: 117; Muhammad as-Sayyid, "Al-Allama ash-Shaikh Muhammad al-Khidr Hussein al-Muslih al-Tha'ir," The Official Muslim Brotherhood Encyclopedia, https://ikhwanwiki.com/, accessed February 16, 2019.

55 Rachid al-Ghannouchi, *Min Taghrubit al-Haraqat al-Islamiyya fi Tunis* (London: Maghreb Center for Research and Development, 2001), 46–7.

sheikhs to train them to agitate Muslims in Tunisia and Algeria against Western colonialism.[56] This trend endures, as Western colonial grievances are still exploited by jihadists and communists to justify tyrannical and criminal political actions. Khidr stayed in Germany for nine months, and in 1917 he gave a speech at the opening ceremony of a mosque in Berlin for Muslim soldiers who had been captured while serving in the armies of the Entente.[57]

At the time, pan-Islamist agitation already had an audience in Egypt among al-Azhar sheikhs. The Islamic Ethics Association was at its heart and would become a significant factor in the creation of the Muslim Brotherhood. It was the first Islamist organization in the history of modern Egypt, and its secret activities explain why information about it is scarce.

The Islamic Ethics Association was founded by al-Azhar University imam Abdul-Wahhab al-Naggar (1862–1941). Naggar joined Dar al-Ulum briefly and became a colleague and friend of Jawish. They were both trained by Abduh.[58] Naggar graduated from Dar al-Ulum in 1897 and founded the Islamic Ethics Association with another al-Azhar Islamist, Muhammad Zaki ad-Din Sanad (1866–1903). While the organization was already active, according to Naggar, it was not officially established until 1899.[59] Naggar stated that among the members of the organization were "influential statesmen, judges, and ulama."[60] The association published a magazine and distributed pamphlets to propagate pan-Islamism.

The organization had a controversial reputation from its inception. After the Ottoman Empire's defeat in World War I, Khidr left Germany and settled in Damascus for almost three years until he fled to Egypt when the Franco-Syrian War erupted, in March 1920. After

56 Ibid.
57 Ibid.
58 Ahmad Zakaria ash-Shalaq, *Al-Ayamu al-Hamra'* (Cairo: Dar al-Wathaiq al-Qawmiyya, 2010), 5.
59 Abdul Wahhab al-Naggar, *Qissas al-Anbia'* (Beirut: Dar al-Kotob al-Alamiyah, 1971), 10.
60 Ash-Shalaq, *Al-Ayamu al-Hamra'*, 5.

the French army defeated the forces of the Hashemite monarch, King Faisal, they entered Damascus on July 24, 1920, and the newly pro-French government headed by Alaa ad-Din ad-Darubi cracked down on Islamist agitators and German agents. Among those was Khidr, who was sentenced to death in absentia for his jihadist activities.[61]

In the early 1920s the Islamic Ethics Association's official president was an obscure front man named Mahmud, but its actual leader was Khidr, and the organization became the headquarters for covert Islamist activity in Cairo.[62]

When Banna joined Dar al-Ulum, he became a student of Naggar, who worked there as an Islamic law teacher. Banna soon joined Naggar's organization, where he met weekly with prominent Islamists. Banna also frequented the Salafi bookstore run by Muhibb ad-Din al-Khatib. Banna said he received "guidance" from prominent Islamists there, and among them was Oppenheim's agent, Khidr. Banna also attended Rashid Rida's meetings. Rida carried the mantle of pan-Islamism handed down to him by Muhammad Abduh.[63] While Abduh contributed to the radicalization and recruitment of countless jihadists, many experts believe that he diverged from some of these ideas in his later years.

During the early 1920s, two major historic events contributed to the escalation of Islamist activities. The first was the defeat and dissolution of the Ottoman Empire, which ended in 1922 and was replaced by a nationalist secular system in Turkey. The second was the victory of Abdulaziz ibn Saud, known in the West as Ibn Saud (1880–1953). He consolidated his control over Najd in 1922 and conquered Hejaz in 1925 after he had seized control of Riyadh in 1902. Ibn Saud's military triumph would eventually lead to the creation of the Kingdom of Saudi Arabia. Ibn Saud's victory relied on a

61 Muhammad as-Sayyid, *Al-Allama ash-Sheikh*, accessed February 16, 2019.
62 Awni Faris, "*Al-Ikhwan al-Muslimoun fi Zakirat ash-Sheikh Al-Azhari Fatehallah as-Salwadi*" Al-Manhal e-Library, https://www.almanhal.com/ar.
63 Banna, *Mudhakkirat*, 56.

group of zealous jihadists called *Ikhwan* (Brotherhood or Brethren), which adhered to Wahhabism.

Two of Banna's revered religious figures, Rida and Khatib, both developed a relationship with Ibn Saud, and Rida became his advisor in 1924 after Ibn Saud declared himself the new Sunni caliph.[64]

The Islamic Awakening challenged Egyptian and Middle Eastern societies with a flurry of activity. One of the most important groups at the time was the Young Men's Muslim Association(YMMA), which was cofounded by Khidr in 1927. Another group formed was the Islamic Fraternity Association, led by Abdul-Wahhab Azzam, the grandfather of al-Qaeda's leader Ayman al-Zawahiri and great-uncle of the modern Egyptian-British Muslim Brotherhood agitator Maha Azzam.

In either 1938 or 1940, the Islamic Ethics Association established a mysterious branch in Lebanon.[65] The lack of information available on this division stems from its secretive nature, but it shares similarities with its Egyptian division. Just as German-Ottoman agent Khidr revamped the Islamic Ethics Association in Egypt, Enver's agent and Mufti of the Ottoman navy during World War I Ali Sheikh al-Arab founded the group's Lebanese chapter.[66] But the public face of the group was al-Azhar's envoy, Sheikh Salah ad-Din Abu Ali. Both the Islamic Ethics Association and the Makassed Foundation ultimately became precursors to the Muslim Brotherhood division in Lebanon.[67]

---

64 Sa'ad al-Hammid, "*Rihalat ash-Shaikh Muhammad Rashid Rida fi al-Jazirah al-Arabiyya,*" https://www.alukah.net/, April 5, 2011.

65 Youssef al-Mar'ashli, *Nathr al-Jawaher w'ad-Durar fil Ulama' al-Qarn al-Rabe' Ashr* (Beirut: Dar al-Marefeh, 2006) 1: 796; Jam'iat Makarim al-Akhlaq al-Islamiyya bi-Tarablus, "Al-Jam'iyya," http://almakarem.org/, August 18, 2018.

66 Yusuf al-Mar'ashli, *Nathr al-Jawaher w'ad-Durar fi-Ulama' al-Qarn al-rabe'ashr*, (Beirut: Dar al-Ma'arif, 200) 1: 919.

67 160. Amal Itani, Abdul-Qadir Ali, and Mu'in Manna', *Al-Jama'ah al-Islamiyya fi-Libnan* (Beirut: Markaz al-Zaitouna l'al-Derasat wa'l-wa'l-wa'l-Istesharat, 2009), 14, 16, 21.

BOLSHEVIKS AND THE MUSLIM BROTHERHOOD

The Classic Liberal era in Egypt faced challenges not only from pan-Arabism and pan-Islamism, but from the rise of communism, nationally and internationally. Afghani, Abduh, and Oppenheim's cabal had paved the way for a reversion to a totalitarian form of religion and society. The few but powerful radicals and extremists in the Middle East were prepared for the ideological, moral, and political totalitarianism of the 1917 Bolshevik Revolution in Russia. The Russian Empire was home to sixteen million Muslims, and among them, a few million radicals were ready to exploit new opportunities after the fall of tsarism.

During the same year, several Muslim congresses were held in Moscow and Kazan. On November 20, 1917, the Bolsheviks initiated their eastern policy with Vladimir Lenin's (1870–1924) decree "to the Toiling Muslims of Russia and the East," aiming to exploit Islamic fundamentalism and political grievances.[68] Lenin was keen on Islamist agitation in the Middle East. In 1919, he published an appeal to the Muslim of the world in which he declared:

> Muslims of the entire world, victims of the capitalists, wake up! Russia has abandoned the pernicious policy of the Czars with regard to you and offers you a helping hand in your efforts to overthrow British tyranny. Russia will give you full religious freedom and political autonomy. Pre-war frontiers will be respected, no Turkish territory will be given to Armenia, the Dardanelles will remain Turkish and Constantinople will remain the capital of the Muslim world.[69]

68 Ben Fowkes and Bülent Gökay, "Unholy Alliance: Muslims and Communists – An Introduction," *The Journal of Communist Studies and Transition Politics* 25, no.1 (2009): 2.

69 Rami Ginat, *The Soviet Union and Egypt* (London: Frank Cass & Co. Ltd, 1993), 4.

While the Ottoman Empire engaged in the Armenian Genocide (1915–1923), which took the lives of almost 1.5 million Armenians, Lenin decided to support Islamist perpetrators, like the Kaiser before him. Lenin's policies turned him into an ally of the Islamic Awakening Project, and his message was welcomed by many Islamists. The most prominent among them was Rida, who wrote an article in his *al-Manar* magazine defending Bolsheviks and stating that European politicians who criticized the revolution as "chaotic, blood thirsty, illegally and unlawfully seizing wealth" were engaged in "their usual criticism of the good, and glorification of ugliness, and turning truth on its head."[70]

Lenin's call was also heard by a group of Egyptian communists who would later become instrumental to the Muslim Brotherhood. In 1920, the Egyptian Socialist Party was established by five leaders: Muhammad Abdullah Anan, Salama Moussa, Joseph Rosenthal, Husni al-Urabi, and Antun Marun. In 1922, a delegation from the Egyptian Socialist Party went to Russia to request their party's membership in Communist International (Comintern).

According to Hassan al-Banna's younger brother, Gamal al-Banna (1920–2013), Husni Urabi was the only Egyptian socialist union leader to personally meet Lenin during their visit, and Lenin conditioned their Party's membership in the Comintern on their acceptance of twenty-one conditions of admission. Urabi agreed, and the party changed its name to the Egyptian Communist Party. Husni Urabi would later become an influential figure in deploying Soviet stratagems to jihadism.[71]

According to the *Programme of the Communist International*, "Communist Parties must be prepared for transition to illegal conditions...." The organizational requirements of the Comintern demanded the "existence of a secret apparatus even where a Party may operate openly."[72] The Egyptian Communist Party abided by these rules and established a secret apparatus.

70 Muhmmed Rashid Rida, *Al-Manar* (Cairo: Al-Manar, 1919) 12: 252.

71 Gamal al-Banna, "Man Huwa Gamal al-Banna", Secular Studies & Researches Centre in Arabic World, https://ssrcaw.org/, February 19, 2011.

72 Attorney General v. Communist Party, Reports on the Subversive Activities Control Board, 273.

The Comintern's model of having a public organization and a secret apparatus was replicated beyond the Communist Party in Egypt and adopted by several other Egyptian groups. The willingness to accept an underground machinery beyond the confines of communism can be attributed to the ideological and epistemological similarities between Soviet communists, left-wing nationalists, and Islamists. Among the most important of these epistemological tenets is employing conspiracy. In his book *The Special World*, Niels Erik Rosenfeldt explained this critical concept:

> The general belief in the value of secrecy was reflected in the fact that "conspiracy" and "conspiratorial" were positive terms in the Bolshevik's universe, at least so far as their *own* ideal behavior was concerned. Already by the 1920s regular reference was made to the need to ensure "maximum conspiracy at work."

Rosenfeldt further questioned:

> whether it is correct to translate the Russian word *konspirativnyi* as "conspiratorial," since the English term has clearly negative connotations. The alternative would simply be to use the term "secret." But this does not quite cover the meaning either. For one thing, it reduces the general semantic content of the Russian word, eliminating the specific associations attached to the term "conspiracy": i.e. the efforts of an organization, operating in secrecy, to conceal its activities from the outside world.[73]

Rosenfeldt's explanation of the Russian notion of conspiracy coincides to a large extent with both the Shi'a concept of *batinyya* and its

73 Niels Erik Rosenfeldt, *The" Special" World: Stalin's Power Apparatus and the Soviet System's Secret Structures of Communication* (Copenhagen: Museum Tusculanum Press, 2009), 1: 66.

Sunni concept of *kitman*, which are the theological tenets of clandestine proselytism and Islamist's chameleon-like behavioral adaptations toward their targeted societies and entities.

This factor prepared the grounds for Islamists to believe that it was theologically acceptable to adopt the methodological tactics of the Comintern into the structure and modus operandi of their emerging organizations. The next chapters will explain how Banna modeled his organization after Stalin's governing apparatuses, a structure still used by the Muslim Brotherhood today.

SECRET SOCIETIES AND CLANDESTINE FRATERNITIES IN EGYPT

The fourth element that played a significant role in the founding of the Brotherhood was Banna's and Islamists' infatuation with Western-style secret societies, cults, and fraternal orders. These secret groups were fashionable in aristocratic circles in Egypt and across the Middle East from the mid-1800s till the 1940s. These type of organizations, such as the Masonic High Council of Egypt, were banned in 1956.[74]

When Banna was in Cairo in the 1920s, aristocratic-led clandestine societies would not have been accessible to a young man from a rural town who attended an Islamic madrassa. In a television interview in 2014, Egyptian Major General Fouad Allam stated that "Banna remained obsessed with secret societies all of his life."[75]

It was a status symbol to become a member of a clandestine fraternity, and it gave Islamists connections to aristocratic circles they would not be able to interact with under normal circumstances. Secret societies played a critical role in the success of agitators such as Abduh, Afghani, Kabbani, and the pan-Islamic colonel Ahmed Urabi. During their last years in Egypt, the Freemasons recruited some of the world's most influential Islamists.

74 Masonic High Council of Egypt, www.rgle.org.UK, accessed August 30, 2016.
75 Misr al-Balad TV (Cairo), March 19, 2014.

While the Freemasons may or may not be a subversive entity, the inherent tribal, narcissistic nature of clandestine orders often attracted charismatic figures, social climbers, and individuals with antisocial personality traits and agendas. Banna emulated elements of the Freemasons' structure while building his organization.

Secret societies were also popular among Wahhabis in Arabia and not just in Egypt. Wide Sunni acceptance of covert Islamic proselytism increased Banna's ability to propagate for his organization.[76] Some early clandestine Islamist entities, such as the Makassed Foundation and the Islamic Ethics Association, remain operational and powerful, but many similar entities have reemerged today, especially in areas where the Muslim Brotherhood is faced with what the organization perceives as a crisis.

The Brotherhood's political machine is advanced. Many Islamist groups in the United States and across the world employ the tactic of creating organizations with two façades—a public one to cover the more important covert entity, which employs secret proselytism for subversive and sometimes illegal activities. These groups predominantly rely on a supply of activists, agitators, and jihadists, who are provided by Islamic madrassas, which recruit individuals such as Banna. These organizations are often involved with Islamic education to create a segment of society ready to operate on their behalf.

World War I ended, but Oppenheim, Hajji Wilhelm, and Enver's jihad lived on through their agent, Khidr, and subsequently Banna. Their goals and strategies are still pursued by the Muslim Brotherhood and their front organizations around the world. Today, the Muslim Brotherhood is continuing to revive the clandestine Islamist strategy of concealing their organizations under the seemingly benign banners of freedom, ethics, and morality.

---

76 Martin Kramer, *Islam Assembled* (New York: Columbia University Press, 1986), 15.

CHAPTER FOUR

TEMPTATION AND TERROR

The Creation of the General Apparatus and the Structure of its Public Divisions

"God is our goal, the Prophet is our model, the Qur'an is our law, jihad is our path, and martyrdom is our aspiration."

—The Muslim Brotherhood's Mission Statement[1]

THE MAIN PURPOSE OF LAYING out the forthcoming historical and contemporary events is to identify individual and organizational behavioral patterns that can be used to successfully counter terror threats. It is crucial to analyze behavior through a historical lens, as failure to do so blinds one to reality. Hassan al-Banna's paranoid, obsessive, and criminal vision endures through the chameleon-like entity he created. Banna's fanatical jihad, his fascination with clandestine orders, and his study of international criminal groups compelled him to combine these elements under an organization structurally similar to Stalin's power apparatuses and also to utilize some of the Comintern's twenty-one conditions. Coalescing these components allowed him to create a twentieth-century equivalent of the order of the Assassins.

While examining the Muslim Brotherhood's various departments, special attention must be given to the names of these divisions and the

1 Hassan al-Banna, "Risalat at-Ta'alim," The Official Muslim Brotherhood Encyclopedia, https://ikhwanwiki.com/, accessed January 11, 2021.

titles of their operatives. Islamists' relationship with the Arabic language is unique. While this doesn't apply to the overwhelming majority of Muslims, Islamists don't utilize language merely as a principal mean of communication, but also as a sacred tool in Islamic jurisprudence and often as a method of domination and supremacy. For example, until President Sisi's rule, it was prohibited in Egypt to teach the native Egyptian Coptic language, and it was mostly taught only inside the Coptic church or as part of Coptic religious studies. The government prohibited publishing books in the Coptic language, and its students had to rely on photocopied handwritten notebooks. This prohibition was an unwritten law enforced by Egypt's State Security Investigations Services from the late 1950s until President al-Sisi's administration, which not only allowed Egyptians to freely learn their spoken native ancient language, but he also commissioned an opera in the Coptic language honoring the Egyptian goddess Isis, whose name has been tarnished by Islamists. Is hard to ignore the similarities between Sisi and Isma'il the Magnificent, who also commissioned Giuseppe Verdi's opera Aida in 1871.

While most Muslims are tolerant and inclusive, the same cannot be said for Islamists. The means by which they utilize the Arabic language should not be taken at face value and must be given a thoughtful analysis. For Islamists, language is also sometimes used as a weapon for concealment and dissimulation, and it is fraught with code words and cryptic terminology.

When Banna decided to call the public governing body of the Muslim Brotherhood *at-tanzim al-am* (The General Department or the General Group, also known as the General Apparatus), he did so because his organization had established a Special Department or Special Order, commonly referred to as the Secret Apparatus in Brotherhood literature. The analysis of their public organ will reveal that this body's main function is to service the group's more important covert operation. It will also uncover that it is impossible to fully divide both wings of organization, as they entwine in most of the

General Apparatus' divisions. Each chapter in every single country where Muslim Brotherhood operatives exist must fully abide by the structure, rules, bylaws, and operation of the General Apparatus.

Some Muslim Brotherhood and jihad propagandists in the West falsely claim that each chapter of the Muslim Brotherhood is independent. The forthcoming information will demonstrate that according to the Muslim Brotherhood's own words and bylaws, almost every public and private act of its members worldwide is controlled by the Muslim Brotherhood's bylaws and rules.

TEMPTATION AND TERROR

In 1927, Banna graduated from Dar al-Ulum at the age of twenty-one. In his last school assignment, Banna wrote that his dream was "to become a guide and teacher" and to recruit the parents of his students "through lectures, conversations, writing, as well as through roaming [the streets]."[2] In the same essay, Banna showed his contempt for Egypt's modern aesthetics and its wide attraction to "earthy philosophies." Muslim Brotherhood supporter and historian Ishaq al-Husaini described this essay as the "first virus of the da'wa."[3]

Following his graduation, Banna became more active in religious circles, especially at the clandestine jihad base of the Islamic Ethics Association. In 1927, Banna was also active in Khidr's YMMA, but the association did not "heal Banna's vengeance," as al-Husaini described it.[4]

Banna was encouraged to become more openly fundamentalist like his mentors Rida and Khatib, who started to actively propagate on behalf of Ibn Saud, the new Wahhabi Caliph. This was one reason Banna and Sukari decided to expand and revamp the Hasafiyya

2 Banna, *Mudhakkirat*, 61–3.

3 Muhammad al-Khidr Hussein, *Mawsu'at al-A'mal al-Kamla l'al-Imam Muhammad al-Khidr Hussein* (Cairo: Dar al-Nour, 2010) 12: 137; Ishaq al-Husaini, *Al-Ikhwan al-Muslimun* (Dar Beirut, 1952), 17.

4 Ibid., 14.

Brothers and reestablish it as the *al-Ikhwan al-Muslimin* (The Muslim Brotherhood), on March 22, 1928. Banna officially founded his group in the Suez Canal city of Isma'iliyya, where he was employed as an elementary school Arabic language and handwriting teacher. The Wahhabi influence of Arabia's Ikhwan compelled Banna to emulate them. After all, it was the Ikhwan that had granted Ibn Saud control of Arabia. The Muslim Brotherhood intentionally concealed the influence of the Arabian Ikhwan on the Egyptian organization and portrayed the group as a religious association rather than a political one.[5] This became a continued pattern where jihadist groups create similar or affiliated groups while falsely claiming that they are ideologically and/or organizationally independent from each other to guarantee the continuation of the mission. If one groups fails or gets banned, another prêt à porter one can replace it.

While Banna strove to obscure his ideological influence from the Arabian Ikhwan, he still borrowed the sword from their flag when he designed his group's insignia, perhaps to signal the alliance to his base. In September 1930, Banna drafted a preliminary internal document for the organization's framework. In its second article, Banna practiced concealment and dissimulation when he said, "this association does not address any political affairs" and it "does not adhere to a specific sect and it is for all Muslims anywhere and at all times."

Banna's station in Isma'iliyya allowed him to continue his recruitment of uneducated segments of society under the guise of religious apolitical missionary work.[6] He focused his activism on three specific cafés frequented by working-class men, and gave two weekly lessons in each. Banna's supporters often fondly described his style of preaching as "reminding people of God and of the end of times through temptation and terror."[7] Banna's carrot–and–stick style of occultist teaching and recruitment appealed to fundamentalists.

---

5 Tharwat al-Kherbawy, *Sir al-Ma'bad* (Cairo: Nahdat Misr Publishing Group, 2012), 180.
6 Ibid., 175.
7 Ishaq al-Husaini, *Al-Ikhwan al-Muslimun*, 17.

Banna's jihadist intentions for his new association were present from the beginning and communicated through the Muslim Brotherhood's emblem, which depicts two crossed swords beneath a red Qur'an, both of which are contained within a green circle. Inscribed on the Qur'an is the phrase, "It is the generous Qur'an," and below the sword the word, "Prepare," from the Qur'anic verse (8:60): "And prepare against them whatever you are able of power and of steeds of war by which you may terrify the enemy of Allah and your enemy and others besides them whom you do not know [but] whom Allah knows. And whatever you spend in the cause of Allah will be fully repaid to you, and you will not be wronged." Some Islamic sects adhere to Qur'anic interpretations limiting religious warfare to the early years of da'wa of the Prophet of Islam, but according to Banna's Hanbali school of thought, holy war is a perpetual venture.

Banna's ideology legitimized his deep contempt for modern and cosmopolitan aspects of Isma'iliyya. At the time, Egypt had one of the world's strongest economies, and immigrants fled from across Europe to Egypt for employment and to escape persecution. European migrants were successfully assimilated into the country's culture and permanently influenced Egyptian Arabic. Islama'iliyya was an international city that embodied all aspects of civilization that offended Banna's rural religious outlook.

Banna particularly loathed the Suez Canal Company.[8] The Salafi Hanbali fundamentalist in him was enraged by Western influence on the industry of modernizing utilities and infrastructure. But his hatred did not stop him from requesting a grant from the Suez Canal Company for his new group, and he was awarded E£500, the equivalent of $2,450, which would be almost $37,000 today.

In 1930, Banna's activities disturbed many members of his community in Isma'iliyya, and the Prime Minister of Egypt, Isma'il Sidky Pasha, filed complaints against Banna with the Minister of Education.

8 Mitchell, *The Society of the Muslim Brothers*, 7.

The personal intervention of Sidky Pasha was highly unusual, as Egypt was a free country and the government did not impose limitations on speech or association. But according to Banna, Sidky Pasha alleged he was a communist agent, received communist funds, and engaged in subversive activities.[9] This was the first time the Muslim Brotherhood was accused of working with communists. Banna dismissed the complaints, and so did the Ministry of Education.

It wouldn't be until November 1948 that the Egyptian government discovered the Muslim Brotherhood had received monies and weaponry from the Soviet Union. According to a United States intelligence memorandum titled "Alleged Financial Support of Ikhwan al-Muslimin by Soviets," during a police raid on Muslim Brotherhood leader and jihadist sheikh Muhammad Farghali's house in Isma'iliyya, the police found correspondence between the Soviet legation and the Brotherhood, along with Farghali's arms cache.[10] While Banna's mission was predominantly political from its inception, he attempted to publicly tame this aspect only during his stay in Isma'iliyya. This changed when he relocated to Cairo in 1932, and Banna showed that he had acquired more from communists than just their money.[11]

THE STRUCTURE, FUNCTION, AND MISSION OF THE GENERAL APPARATUS

The structure of the General Apparatus evolved over the course of several decades until it ultimately morphed into its massive modern bureaucracy. One must learn the main governing elements of the Muslim Brotherhood's General Apparatus to understand the organization's deeper and more important covert mission.

---

9 Al-Banna, *Mudhakkirat*,101–2.

10 Central Intelligence Agency Library, CREST General Records, Document Number: CIA-RDP82-00457R002400240004-9, https://www.cia.gov/library/readingroom/document/cia-rdp82-00457r002400240004-9, accessed June 10, 2020.

11 Kamil ash-Sharif, *Al-Mukawama as-Sirriya fi Qanat as-Suez* (Cairo: Maktabat al-Mannar, 1987), 50.

In January 1932, Banna issued the group's first official bylaws. The cultist structure of the organization was prevalent throughout the document. The Brotherhood's earliest bylaws gave a glimpse into the ideological dynamics of his organization. For example, in its second article, Banna demanded "appreciation" and "obedience." He revealed his totalitarian, sacrificial nature by demanding his operatives "prioritize the interest of the group over the interest of the individual."[12]

The 1932 bylaws included an important indicator. In the document, Banna didn't simply describe himself as *murshid* (guide), but referred to himself as *al-murshid al-amm* (the General Guide). His choice to add the term "general" is far from incidental. Decades after his death, it would be revealed that there is also *al-murshid as-sirri* (the Secret Guide) with a secret identity.

The term *maktab al-irshad al-amm* (the General Guidance Bureau, or General Guidance Office) appeared for the first time in the 1932 document. The Guidance Office specialized in handling the organization's non-secret activities and committees. The General Guide is the head of *majlis al-Shura* (Consultative Assembly), also known as the Shura Council. The Shura Council was called *al-hay'a at-ta'sisiyya* (The Founding Assembly) until 1945. The General Guide is also head of the Guidance Bureau and Constative Assembly.

In January 1934, the Brotherhood's Shura Council had its second meeting, during which it restructured the Guidance Bureau and decided that the office would consist of sixteen members instead of ten. Currently, the Shura Council consists of over one hundred members. This bureaucracy was created to serve the more important ideological and recruitment endeavors of their propaganda, membership, and conscription divisions.

The General Apparatus has several *lijan* (committees) working under its leadership, including treasury, legal, political, *fatwa*, statistics, and services. These committees operate under Administrative

12 Hassan al-Banna, "La'hat 1932," The Official Muslim Brotherhood Encyclopedia, https://ikhwanwiki.com/, accessed March 1, 2020.

Office personnel appointed by the Guidance Office. Initially, the Guidance Office consisted of Banna and his secretary-general, but per the 1932 bylaws, it contained eleven operatives, including Banna's younger brother, Abdul Rahman as-Sa'ati, and Banna's cofounder, Ahmad Sukari. In later years, the Guidance Office would consist of fifteen to twenty members.

The ideological and propaganda departments handling political and jihadist membership divisions are called *aqsam* (sections). There are currently nine main sections tailored to propagandize, infiltrate, bribe, and recruit operatives from different segments of society.[13]

(1) The Propagation of the Message. This section is the main theological body of the Brotherhood, and it is mostly headed by al-Azhar trained scholars. It is the organ responsible for vetting the Islamic legitimacy of every action or public statement issued by any member Muslim Brotherhood worldwide.[14] It is as old as the group itself, but was officially founded in 1945 when Banna wrote its internal bylaws. This section's international branch currently operates under the title of the International Union of Muslim Scholars, which was founded by al-Qaradawi in 2004. This association is currently designated as a terrorist group by the United Arab Emirates.[15] The group is currently headed by Moroccan Brotherhood leader Ahmad al-Raysuni, and is based in Qatar. The United Arab Emirates designated Raysuni as a terrorist and considered his appointment to head this body as "Qatar's commitment to sponsoring terrorism and destructive activities against the United Arab Emirates, the Kingdom of Saudi Arabia, Egypt, and Bahrain."[16]

(2) Students. This is among the Muslim Brotherhood's most important enlistment departments, and provides recruits for the group's public organ and its militant divisions. Its leaders have access

13 Hassan al-Banna, "La'hat am 1948 l'al-Ikhwan al-Muslimin," The Official Muslim Brotherhood Encyclopedia https://ikhwanwiki.com/, accessed December 20, 2020.

14 Ibid.

15 Al-Jazeera (Doha), December 1, 2017.

16 Al-Bayan (Dubai), April 22, 2015.

to military-age males in the "crime-prone age group of 15- to 24-year-olds."[17] The body has established front groups that recruit Brotherhood operatives, militants, infiltrators, and sympathizers in the Middle East and in most countries in the West. Among these front groups are the Muslim Students' Association (MSA) and the Brotherhood Scouts in the United States.[18]

(3) Labor and Peasants. Banna targeted farmers and working men since founding the group, and he more concisely articulated this strategy in the 1948 bylaws. It is heavily influenced by Leninist and Marxists propaganda, but the Brotherhood offers Islamism as a solution instead of socialism.[19]

(4) Professionals and Unions. This section's purpose is to "propagate the message" and "Islamize the general atmosphere" in its operatives' milieu. The 1948 bylaws articulated the infiltration strategy to "insert Brotherhood [members] in every profession and employ their positions to serve the Brotherhood's message, individuals, and group" as well as "Islamize unions" and use them to advance the Brotherhood's mission. This division is tasked with penetrating every profession and union.[20]

(5) Physical Training. This innocent-sounding division has an intentionally vaguely worded definition in the 1948 bylaws, which state, "the physical training section implements Islamically required methodology and study [of means to] prepare Brotherhood [members] to fulfill their mission, and it oversees the implementation of the policy dictated by the Guidance Office."[21] In other words, it's physical training for carrying out jihadist attacks, as the Muslim Brotherhood will later admit in their own words. The earliest mention of this sec-

17 Jeffrey T. Ulmer, Darrell Steffensmeier, *The Age and Crime Relationship: Social Variation, Social Explanations* (California: Sage, 2014), 378.

18 Investigative Project on Terrorism, "Muslim Student Association Dossier," https://info.publicintelligence.net/VFCEducationalFacilitiesT hreatAssessment.pdf, January 2008.

19 "Al-Ikhwan al-Muslimin wa'l-wa'l-wa'l-Haraqa al-Umaliyya al-Masriyya," The Official Muslim Brotherhood Encyclopedia, https://ikhwanwiki.com/, accessed December 20, 2020.

20 Al-Banna, "La'hat am 1948."

21 Ibid.

tion was in 1934, when Banna wrote an essay titled *firaq al-rihalat* (Ranger Squads).[22]

(6) Press and Translation. This section is responsible for inspecting Brotherhood publications worldwide to guarantee their full compliance with the Guidance Office's policies. It also archives everything published about the Muslim Brotherhood, both nationally and internationally, and translates material that helps propagate the group's message in any language.[23]

(7) The Muslim Sisterhood. In 1933, Banna started targeting women by creating this section. He issued a document called *firqat al-akhawat al-muslimat* (Muslim Sisterhood Group) and urged this section to engage in Islamic gatherings, events, and lectures to recruit female members .[24] The Muslim Sisterhood leader directly reported to Banna. This body is currently active in most Western countries, including the United States. The activities and identities of some of its operatives in the United States will be revealed in forthcoming chapters.

(8) Liaison with the Islamic World. This section was first mentioned in Banna's address at the Muslim Brotherhood's fifth conference in 1938 when he articulated the section's official mission. Banna defined the division's operation stating, "The Brotherhood believes that the caliphate is a symbol of Islamic unity, a signal to the bond between Islamic nations, and an Islamic ritual which Muslims should contemplate and pay attention to, the caliph is entrusted to implement the Islamic law of God." Currently, this section is known as *at-tanzim ad-dawli* or *al-jihaz ad-dawli* (the International Group or International Apparatus).[25]

(9) The Family. The Brotherhood's membership department revolves around *al-usra* (the family) or *al-usar* (the families) section. The exact date this division was established is not known, and the first

22 Banna, *Mudhakkirat,* 125.
23 Al-Banna, "La'hat am 1948."
24 The Official Muslim Brotherhood Encyclopedia, "Awal La'hat l'al-Akhawat al-Muslimat," https://ikhwanwiki.com/, accessed March 1, 2020.
25 Hassan al-Banna, "Risalat al-Mu'tamar al-Khamis," The Official Muslim Brotherhood Encyclopedia, https://ikhwanwiki.com/, accessed December 23, 2020.

detailed documentation of this unit appeared when Banna wrote its memorandum in 1942. Muslim Brotherhood literature in the West rarely analyzes this section, yet it provides the most insight into the nature and dynamics of the organization's core, which has been emulated by various terrorist groups. The Family remains the nucleus of the Brotherhood.

The term used by the Brotherhood to describe its extensive initiation process is *tarbiyya*. *Tarbiyya* is the Arabic word for raising, rearing, or upbringing. The Brotherhood's leadership views its members as juveniles who need to be rewired in every aspect of life. The most authoritative Brotherhood manual on recruitment, initiation, and training is *Wasa'il at-Tarbiyya ind al-Ikhwan al-Muslimin*. Its literal translation is "The Muslim Brotherhood's Methodologies of Rearing." This manual was written by al-Azhar University imam and Brotherhood leader and member of the Propagation of the Message section, Ali Abdul Halim Mahmoud (1928–2014). It is not a coincidence that Brotherhood leaders chose not to use terms such as "education" or "training" to describe this process. They selected terminology that denotes raising children as they exercise complete and total restructuring of every aspect of their recruit's life in typical cultist fashion.

THE COSA NOSTRA BROTHERHOOD FAMILY

Cults and organized criminal syndicates often use the term "family" in reference to their organizations to enlist a sense of loyalty, hierarchy, and belonging. Secret Apparatus leader Ali Ashmawi said in his memoir, "the Brotherhood studied several mobs around the world when they established the Special Apparatus." While Ashmawi was discussing the clandestine wing, the same applied to the Guidance Office. The family section of the Brotherhood borrowed elements from the structure of the Cosa Nostra Sicilian mafia and merged them with the Muslim Brotherhood's cultish family dynamics in an Islamic framework.

In her book *Mafia Brotherhoods: Organized Crime, Italian Style*, Letizia Paoli writes about the Cosa Nostra:

> Heading each family is a *rappresentante* [representative] or *capofamiglia* [family head], who is elected by the members and constitutes the highest group authority. The family chief avails himself of one or more *consiglieri* [counselors], who are also elected by associates. They assist him in the most important decisions and, at the same time, check his management of the family.... The family is run by a *vice-rappresentante* [vice representative] chosen by the *capofamiglia* himself. In the larger families, he also selects one or more *capi decina*, who coordinate units of about ten people.[26]

Capi decina translates to "head of ten," and is the title of the individual assigned to oversee families consisting of ten criminals. In smaller families, each group is regulated by a chief, "who is called *capo rione* [district chief]."[27]

Paoli could have been describing the family structure of the Muslim Brotherhood rather than the Cosa Nostra. The Brotherhood family is also headed by *naquib al-usra* [the family chief]. The Brotherhood family also consists of ten operatives, and its chief has a deputy chief. Each operative has a potential replacement in case of his incarceration, death, or dismissal.

The Brotherhood family's main mission is (1) ideological, to reinforce its members with ideological consistency; (2) Islamic, and it unconditional acceptance of Islam as it is defined by the Brotherhood; (3) Islamic compassion, which the Brotherhood defines as "worshiping God as an absolute;" (4) justice and equality, described as speaking and acting justly toward one another; (5) demanding virtue and pro-

26 Letizia Paoli, *Mafia Brotherhoods: Organized Crime, Italian Style* (Oxford: Oxford University Press, 2003), 46.

27 Ibid.

hibiting vice, demanding all that is virtuous from everyone, and prohibiting anyone from engaging in vice; (6) jihad in the path of Allah, and "exerting every [resource] to destroy the enemy. Its three types are, jihad against the public enemy, jihad against Satan, and inner jihad."[28]

These slogans entail details on how to implement them in the lives of the family members. The instruction controls what members eat, drink, say, write, and think; whom they marry and when; and how and when they can kill others and themselves, and why.[29]

A Muslim Brotherhood family chief can only be nominated by another former family chief who also serves as a member of the Family Chiefs' Bureau, which directly reports to the Guidance Office. When a family chief is nominated, his nomination is kept secret, even from the candidate himself for a duration of six months. During this period, the subject undergoes vigorous surveillance to vet him ideologically, psychologically, and physically to make sure that he would be able to withstand the assignment of training his family members, and more importantly, to guarantee he is not a security threat.[30] After a chief is selected, he undergoes extensive training and monitoring to guarantee the success of the family's mission as well as to ensure the "ideological and operational propagation of Islam [both] intellectually and [through] jihad."[31]

The Family section operates within *ashira* (a clan) that consists of four families. Those forty clan members are headed by one family chief, and his deputies are selected from other family chiefs. Every five clans are organized under another body known as *raht* (group or tribe). The tribe—consisting of two hundred members—operates in a *katiba* (battalion), which comprises five tribes and one thousand operatives.[32]

28 Ali Abdul Halim Mahmud, *Wasa'il at-Tarbiyya ind al-Ikhwan al-Muslimin* (Mansoura: Dar al-Wafa', 1990), 18–9.
29 Ibid. ,112–218.
30 Ibid., 138–9.
31 Ibid., 211.
32 Ibid., 166.

Banna designed his military unit to "organize all members of the Brotherhood's General Apparatus in battalions."[33] The Muslim Brotherhood's definition of a battalion is, "Jihad within oneself, jihad against Satan and his temptations, and the military training of its operatives."[34]

Every Brotherhood family is a cell within a battalion, and every member of the Brotherhood's public organ operates in some capacity within a battalion. One of the main differences between the General Apparatus and the Secret Apparatus is the level of trust its members are given to secure the organization's secrets. The fact that every Brotherhood member is also a member in a battalion demonstrates that is not possible to divide the General Apparatus from the militant Secret Apparatus.

MEMBERSHIP IN THE MUSLIM BROTHERHOOD

The membership process in any terrorist or clandestine group follows specific criteria and vetting procedures to avoid infiltration and security breaches. It is the task of the Secret Apparatus to handle most membership affairs. Banna followed a classic terrorist recruitment route after he returned to Cairo. He targeted mosques to enlist members for his organization by distributing pamphlets and copies of his magazines, *Magalat al-Ikhwan al-Muslimin* (the *Muslim Brotherhood* magazine) and *al-Nazir* (*The Herald*). After approaching mosque attendees, Banna would invite them to join conferences, lectures, and seminars, before he vetted and initiated them in his group.

Subsequent to their recruitment, Banna organized his disciples in specific roles depending on their level of blind obedience and skills. At the Brotherhood's third conference, Banna officially adopted the

33 Ibid., 221.
34 Ibid., 220.

mujahid (jihadist) affiliation for his group, and it remains to this day. Since the conference, the Muslim Brotherhood leadership has introduced fifteen amendments to its internal bylaws.

Secret Apparatus leader Mahmoud as-Sabbagh stated that the membership process in both the General and Secret Apparatuses occurs over the course of three stages:

> The first stage is an orientation on [means] by which their message is propagated. The second, is training [conscripts] with the aim to select subjects who can endure the burdens of jihad, and during this phase [an operative] exercises a civilian spiritual role, and an actively militaristic one. The rule for those two stages is always obeying orders without questions or inquiries. The third phase is executing [orders].[35]

The current rules for membership and initiation into the group are mainly based on its 1994 bylaws, but in 2005, Lebanese Brotherhood operative Fadi Shamia published a document that revealed the updated seven levels of membership.[36]

(1) Novice or Fan (*mukarab, muhib*). This degree of association with the Brotherhood precedes formal organizational affiliation. In this stage, an individual is active within public events, such as public lectures, seminars, and prayer groups.

(2) General Affiliation (*indimam am or muntasib*). An individual is accepted to join this degree after a year of vetting and successfully undergoing its testing process. A new member has to endure many trials that scrutinize his level of loyalty, obedience, physical, and psychological endurance of hardships. If a member succeeds in every test

35 Mahmoud as-Sabbagh, *Hakikat at-Tanzim al-Khas*, The Official Muslim Brotherhood Encyclopedia, https://ikhwanwiki.com/, accessed January 15, 2021.

36 Fadi Shamia, "Sabil al-Qassid l'al-Hukm al-rashid," The Official Muslim Brotherhood Encyclopedia, https://ikhwanwiki.com/, August 28, 2005; "Al-Nizam al-Am l'al-Ikhwan al-Muslimin (1994)," The Official Muslim Brotherhood Encyclopedia, https://ikhwanwiki.com/, accessed January 5, 2021.

during this year, he signs the membership document where he pledges to pay the Brotherhood between three to seven percent of his monthly income depending on his level of wealth. Those accepted as a general affiliates must successfully remain in this stage for three years before they are initiated to the following phase. A successful fulfillment of this stage depends on the member's ability to prove his piety, obedience, and willingness to engage in jihad.

(3) Active Member (*udw amil*); handler (*munafiz*); and jihadist (mujahid). This degree provides the member the right to exercise leadership roles. Every single member who joins this level is obligated to recite this oath of allegiance to the General Guide:

> I contract with God Almighty to implement the laws of Islam and [wage] jihad in its cause, and to be a loyal soldier in the Muslim Brotherhood, to listen and absolutely obey [the leadership] in times of hardship and ease, in health and sickness, in everything except what transgresses against God, and to never argue with the leaders, and to sacrifice myself, my money, and my blood in God's cause, and everything it entails. I swear by God on this and make my oath of loyalty by Him. Of what I say, God is [my] Witness.

Contrary to what Muslim Brotherhood and jihad propagandists in the West claim, every single member of the Muslim Brotherhood worldwide, in any chapter and in any nation, has to vow obedience to the General Guide and uphold this oath. The third General Guide of the Muslim Brotherhood, Omar al-Tilmisani (1904–1986), famously said that a Brotherhood "member between the hands of his guide is like the cadaver between the hands of its undertaker."[37]

If members of the Brotherhood in the United States of America or any other Western nation did not pledge their allegiance to the

37 Ahmad Ban, "Qawa'id al-Fikr al-Ikhwani," Hafryat, February 13, 2018, https://hafryat.com/ar.

General Guide and commit to jihad, they wouldn't be members of the Muslim Brotherhood. While this might seem simplistic, Brotherhood propagandists audaciously claim otherwise.

(4) The Family Chief (*naquib al-usra*). Family chiefs assume the highest degree in the hierarchy of active members. Granting an operative this affiliation permits him to indoctrinate, train, and receive a pledge of allegiance from his subordinates. A chief is also allowed to participate in making major decisions and is entrusted with the secrets of the group.

(5) Commander (*emir or rukn*). A Brotherhood battalion commander is most commonly referred to as *emir*. The word literally means "prince," but in the context of terrorist organizations, it refers to the cell leader. In Syria and Lebanon, the emir is often also called *rukn*. While rukn's literal translation is "corner," in this context it means "pillar."

In a Brotherhood battalion, the emir is required to be the eldest in age with the longest duration as a member among the family chiefs. Shamia described the leader of a battalion as someone who illustrates "the characteristics of prophets."

(6) The Preacher (*da'iyya*). This position is assumed by individuals who successfully fulfilled all the previous degrees but who also have the advantage of having Islamic training at al-Azhar University in Cairo or at another fundamentalist equivalent, such the Shari'a College in Riyadh. A Brotherhood *da'iyya* is usually also a member of the Propagation of the Message section.

(7) Master (*ustadh*) or General Guide. While the word *ustadh* literally means teacher, it is most commonly used before a surname or full name to address or refer to a man without a higher honorific or professional title. In the context of Islamic militant groups, this honorific title is only given to highest ranking leader or leaders. While the term *ustadh* is generally used in reference to the General Guide, it can also be used to refer to members of the Guidance Office.

The Cosa Nostra Mafia, the Assassins, and clandestine groups throughout history are not the only influences on the Muslim Brotherhood. The Brotherhood was equally influenced by far-left-wing governments and their terrorism and secret warfare methodologies.

SOVIET INFLUENCE ON THE BROTHERHOOD'S INTERNAL STRUCTURE

While the Cold War between the United States and Union of Soviet Socialist Republics (USSR) has been relegated to history, the structure of the Soviet Union's most sensitive organs are still emulated by the Muslim Brotherhood and their tactics are used against unsuspecting and unprepared targets such as the United States.

The Brotherhood immortalized Banna's collectivist tendencies, which compelled him to promote growing totalitarian systems in Europe. The Brotherhood's early alliance with the Soviet Union was widely accepted within the organization.

Secret Apparatus leader Saleh al-Ashmawi said, "the Brotherhood does not find any real objections which would prevent it from establishing a common front with communists against our common enemies, the [Western] imperialists."[38]

Islamist acceptance of left-wing totalitarian governments was also due to the USSR's successful covert operation targeting al-Azhar University. The Soviet Union legation in Cairo was headed by Abdul Rahman Sultanov. His Muslim origins aided his advocacy for coexistence between Islam and communism during his several visits to al-Azhar University.[39] Prominent Egyptian Islamic-socialist and Soviet agent,[40] Husni al-Urabi, once claimed to "have close relations with

38 Ginat, *The Soviet Union and Egypt*, 39.

39 Ibid., 15.

40 British Intelligence file on Mahmud Husni El Arabi, United Kingdom National Achieves KV2/2668, Richmond England, September 15, 1924–September 28, 1950, Discovery.NationalArchives.gov.uk/details/r/C11377557.

Sultanov."[41] He was active in the Islamic agitation front, and he was a leader in the separatist Islamic group *Jam'iyat al-Usba al-Islamiyya ad-Dawliya* (the International Islamic League Association), which was described in a British Intelligence report as "spreading violent anti-British and pro-Nazi propaganda."[42] Urabi was one of the earliest examples of the effectiveness of communist propaganda on Islamists, which ultimately resulted in the elevation of Nazi and Soviet-affiliated Islamists to power.

In the early 1930s, Banna paid special attention to Stalin and Hitler's regimes and published articles and gave speeches praising them.[43] This gave Banna a reputation for replicating a combination of Stalin, Mussolini, and Hitler's regimes. This assertion was made by a prominent Egyptian intellectual of the time, Muhammad Husain Ahmad, in his book *Al-Ikhwan al-Muslimmin fil-Mizan* (The Muslim Brotherhood in the Balance).[44]

It could be argued that Banna's alliance with communists and Nazis went beyond mere cooperation against a common enemy. From the Revolution's earliest days, Islamists widely accepted the Bolsheviks' appeasement. Lenin's initial invitation of alliance compelled Islamists like Banna to study the structure of Stalin's power apparatuses and replicate them with great accuracy. Communist collaboration with Islamists became even more legitimized when Amin al-Husaini accepted communist funds for his jihad.[45]

While most experts in the West and Middle East are aware of the Soviet influence on the Muslim Brotherhood, they have missed Banna's borrowing of Soviet terminology and the structure of Stalin's power

41 Ibid.
42 Ibid.
43 Ishaq al-Husaini, *Al-Ikhwan al-Muslimun*, 6.
44 Muhammad Husain Ahmad, *Al-Ikhwan al-Muslimmin fil-Mizan* (Cairo: Al-Ikha' Printing Press, 1946), 102.
45 Central Intelligence Agency, Freedom of Information Act Electronic Reading Room, Nazi War Crimes Disclosure Act, Document Number: 51966ec8993294098d50a510," https://www.cia.gov/readingroom/docs/DADONE%2C%20UGO_0006.pdf, accessed April 2, 2020.

apparatuses when he formed his organization. Comparing Stalin's Special and Secret Apparatuses with the Muslim Brotherhood's, one can conclude that the Soviets were the main influence on the group's structure. The Brotherhood still operates almost the same way today, only on a much larger scale.

According to Rosenfeldt, in his study of Stalin's power apparatus:

> The titles "General Department" and "Secret Department" referred to two different departments that existed side by side until 1934. The General Department was set up in 1919 as a common chancellery for the central Party apparatus, but had the stage to itself only for one year. In 1920 a separate office was established for classified matters, which was called the "secret registry" (or the "secret subdepartment"). During the same period this had its counterpart in a "general registry" (or "general chancellery"), which was now confined to dealing with non-secret matters and certain joint office tasks.[46]

By the 1920s, Stalin had subdepartments such as the Bureau of Central Committee Secretariat, the Secretariat of the Organizational Bureau, the Code Bureau, the Secret Archive, and the Terror Apparatus.[47]

According to Rosenfeldt, "In 1923, the 'Bureau of the Central Committee Secretariat' was described in an official source as the most important part of the Communist Party's entire apparatus." Rosenfeldt adds that the "Bureau of the Central Committee Secretariat was simply another designation for the Secret Department, also known as the Secret Apparatus, as a whole."[48] He concluded that while they existed separately, they were closely associated institutions. It wasn't

46 Rosenfeldt, *The Special World*, 1: 113–4.
47 Ibid., 386–417.
48 Ibid., 114–6.

until 1934 that the Secret Department was replaced by the Special Department, while the General Department continued to exist.

The following Muslim Brotherhood departments were adopted from Stalin's power apparatuses.[49]

(1) The Soviet General Department or General Apparatus is called the General Department or General Apparatus in the Muslim Brotherhood.

(2) The Soviet Secret Department or Secret Apparatus is also called the Special Department, Secret Order, or the Secret Apparatus in the Muslim Brotherhood.

(3) The Soviet Bureau of the Central Committee Secretariat is called the Guidance Bureau or Guidance Office in the Muslim Brotherhood.

(4) The Bureau of International Information is the equivalent of the International Apparatus of the Brotherhood.

(5) The Soviet Union's Secret Apparatus operated a Terror Apparatus, and the next chapters will provide evidence that the Muslim Brotherhood's Secret Apparatus still operates as the group's terror apparatus.

The Muslim Brotherhood's most important defector is Tharwat al-Kherbawy. He was the group's general counsel for over a decade and represented them in historic terrorism cases. Kherbawy's extensive knowledge of the Brotherhood is enhanced by his hyperthymesia, a highly superior autobiographical memory. Kherbawy's condition allows him to remember nearly every detail of his life. Very few people in the world have been diagnosed with this condition.

During one interview with Kherbawy for this book about communist influence on the Muslim Brotherhood, Kherbawy relayed a 2002 conversation he had with the Muslim Brotherhood's official historian, Mahmoud Abdul Halim. According to Kherbawy, Halim said

49 Abdu Mustafa Desouki, "*Maktab al-Irshad wa-Marhlat at-Takwin w'at-Tarbiyya,*" The Official Muslim Brotherhood Encyclopedia, https://ikhwanwiki.com/, accessed May 1, 2020.

he had a conversation with Banna in the late 1930s, during which Banna claimed he had met Leon Trotsky (1879–1940). Kherbawy said that during Trotsky's exile in Turkey, he secretly visited Isma'ilia, "probably in 1932 when he stayed at the same pension hotel where Banna stayed when he first landed in Isma'ilia." It was run by a British woman they called "um Joseph," and Banna called it *pension um Joseph* (Joseph's mother hotel), "where he had a one-on-one meeting with Hassan al-Banna and no one knows what they discussed." Kherbawy said the meeting was arranged by an Islamist-socialist employee of the Suez Canal Company, labor union activist and Brotherhood cofounder Hafiz Abdul Hamid.

Kherbawy added that Trotsky was interested in "propagating for his concept of permanent revolution and the need for an armed paramilitary to protect it. He also met with Egyptian communists Husni al-Urabi and Joseph Rosenthal." Halim told Kherbawy that following this meeting, Banna established the Ranger Squads division. This author has not been able to corroborate the allegations that Banna met with Trotsky or that Trotsky was in Isma'ilia at the time.

MUSLIM BROTHERHOOD'S SUPPORT OF HAJJ HITLER

Adolf Hitler's rise to power in Germany in 1933 was not welcomed in Egypt except among Islamists. Banna showed genuine admiration toward Hitler and Mussolini when he said they "guided their peoples to unity, order, regeneration, power, and glory."[50] Banna was inspired by Hitler's use of propaganda and "its powers of inciting and enflaming enthusiasm," while he criticized Egyptian media, saying it was used "to spread love, passion, and debauchery."[51]

---

50 Robert St. John, *The Boss: The Story of Gamal Abdel Nasser* (New York: McGraw Hill, 1960), 41–2.

51 Ishaq al-Husaini *Al-Ikhwan al-Muslimun*, 6.

The National Socialist German Workers' Party, or *National sozialistische Deutsche Arbeiterpartei* (NSDAP), operated a foreign division commonly referred to as NSDAP/AO. AO is the abbreviation of the German compound word *Auslands-Organisation* (Foreign Organization). NSDAP/AO assigned Egyptian-born Alfred Hess (1897–1963) and a few hundred local German members of the Nazi Party to build the NSDAP/AO's *Landesgruppe Ägypten* (the Egyptian national committee) from 1926 to 1933. Alfred Hess was the younger brother of Hitler's future deputy, Rudolf Hess (1894–1987).[52]

According to historian Georges Bensoussan, "In 1933, Berlin set up an Arabic language press service and, in 1935, opened a radio bureau in Cairo. Several Egyptian movements made contact with the Bureau."[53] These groups included the Muslim Brotherhood and *Misr al-Fatat* (Young Egypt Society), originally founded by Afghani and in 1929, it was revived as a socialist and Arab nationalist left-wing fascist militia by Ahmad Husain, an Islamically educated lawyer.

Berlin's Arabic-language press service circulated Nazi propaganda, and Hitler found an avid fan base among Egypt's Islamists. The Muslim Brotherhood glorified Hitler's words. For example, during his speeches, Hitler would often use the common German expression "the hour will come," in different variations, such as "*Nun ist die Stunde der Abrechnung gekommen*, (now the hour of reckoning has come)," which he used in his speech before the Nazi Party on March 3, 1932.[54]

In his first speech as Chancellor at Berlin Sportpalast, on February 10, 1933, Hitler used the term "the hour will come."[55] This sparked rumors that Hitler had converted to Islam, as this expression vaguely resembles the Qur'anic verse (54:1): "The Hour of Resurrection drew

52 Mahmoud Kassim, *Die diplomatischen Beziehungen Deutschlands zu Ägypten 1919–1936* (Münster: LIT Verlag, 2000), 366.

53 Georges Bensoussan, *Jews in Arab Countries: The Great Uprooting* (Bloomington: Indiana University Press, 2019), 303.

54 Johannes Hohlfeld, *Deutsche Reichsgeschichte in Dokumenten 1931–1934* (Germany: Kraus Reprint, 1972), 454.

55 Volker Hentschel, *Hitler und seine Bezwinger: Churchill, Roosevelt, Stalin, de Gaulle. Band 1 (1870–1939) und Band 2 (1939–1970)* (Münster: Lit Verlag, 2013), 341.

near and the moon split asunder." The rumor that Hitler had converted to Islam earned him a title similar to Wilhelm's II, and Hitler was known in Egyptian and Middle Eastern Islamist circles as Hajji Hitler, Hajj Hitler, or Hajj Muhammad Hitler. [56]

Islamist provocateurs orchestrated several riots across the Middle East on behalf of Hitler between 1933 and the end of World War II. During these protests Islamists adopted the Muslim Brotherhood chant, *Allah hai, Allah hai, al-Hajj Muhammad Hitler jai* (God is alive, God is alive, Hajj Muhammad Hitler is coming).[57]

Contrary to Islamist attitudes, the mainstream sentiment in Egypt among both Muslims and Christians was generally one of sympathy and solidarity for the Jewish national homeland reemerging in British Mandate of Palestine.[58] The Egyptian reaction to the Nazi assumption of power instigated massive anti-Nazi protests led by seventy to eighty thousand members of the Jewish community, with strong support from almost all segments of society.[59] In March and April 1933, numerous anti-Nazi mass meetings took place, German goods and movies were boycotted, and the government banned the showing of German films.[60] Hess and his agents' mission was a failure in Egypt except among Islamists, who mobilized their militias to riot and protest. Among the groups that rioted in support of Nazis in 1933 were the Muslim Brotherhood and the YMMA.[61] A number of Brotherhood operatives even fought in Heinrich Himmler's Bosnian Handschar division of the Schutzstaffel (SS).[62]

On December 26, 1938, Banna wrote in an article in *al-Nazir*, "Some newspapers reported that Italy and Germany are considering

---

56 Kamal Abdullah, *Salsalat Kadat il-Harb: Adolf Hitler* (Beirut: Al-Maktaba al-Haditha, 1974), 38.

57 Amin al-Husaini, *Mudhakkirat Muhammad Amin al-Husaini* (Damascus: Al-Ahali Publishing, 1999), 73.

58 Matthias Küntzel, *Jihad and Jew-Hatred: Islamism, Nazism, and the roots of /11* (Telos Press Publishing, 2007), 16–7.

59 Küntzel, *Jihad and Jew-Hatred,* 18.

60 Ibid.

61 Küntzel, *Jihad and Jew-Hatred,* 20.

62 Georges Lepre, *Himmler's Bosnian Division: The Waffen SS Handschar Division 1943–45* (Schiffer Publishing, Ltd, 1997), 31–4.

converting to Islam, and Italy decided to teach Arabic in its schools in an official and compulsory capacity, and prior to this we heard that Japan is contemplating [converting to] Islam."[63]

The Nazi Party's Egypt office also funded the Muslim Brotherhood. On December 30, 2006, Egypt's *Ahram* newspaper published a document from the Nazi Party office in Egypt dating back to August 18, 1939. It read, "The mission sent Hassan al-Banna the same amount of money for a second time and through the same channels; but the Muslim Brotherhood requested more money, although I had already given them two thousand Egyptian Pounds."[64]

The Nazi Party and the Soviet Union were not the only ones who funded Egyptian Islamists and Arab nationalists. Italian Fascists also funded them. A declassified CIA document, "Cavalier Ugo Dadone," discussed the activities of the influential journalist, agitator, and fascist Ugo Dadone. Dadone cooperated with Mussolini in his newspaper *Il Popolo d'Italia*. According to the CIA document, the newspaper sent Dadone to Egypt as a special correspondent in 1934, where he "propagated sentiments favorable to Italy until his internment in 1941."[65]

Dadone funded a considerable number of Egyptian newspapers to run pro-fascist editorials. Among these periodicals were the influential newspaper *al-Ahram*, *Rose al-Yusuf* magazine, and the Young Egypt society's paper, *as-Sarkha*. Among the individuals funded by Dadon were Young Egypt society's leader Ahmad Husain and Muslim Brotherhood operative, Banna's friend, and personal attorney, Fathi Radawn.[66]

Brotherhood operatives and Islamists officially continue to adhere to Hitler's values until today. The support of Hitler is pervasive among Islamists, to the extent that some Islamists have named their children

63 Al-Nazir (Cairo), December 26, 1938.

64 Al-Ahram newspaper (Cairo), December 30, 2006.

65 Central Intelligence Agency, Freedom of Information Act Electronic Reading Room, Nazi War Crimes Disclosure Act, Document Number: 51966ec5993294098d509dd4, https://www.cia.gov/readingroom/docs/DADONE%2C%20UGO_0006.pdf, accessed April 2, 2021.

66 "Fathi Radwan wa-Ilaqatu bil-Ikhwan al-Muslimin," The Official Muslim Brotherhood Encyclopedia, https://ikhwanwiki.com/, accessed January 2, 2021.

Hitler. Among those was Hitler Tantawi (1941–2013), President Hosni Mubarak's Secretary General of the Egyptian Ministry of Defense and later the Director of the Administrative Control Authority until he retired in 2004.

The Secret Apparatus adheres to the fundamentalist Hanbali doctrine and is structured like Stalin's power apparatuses. These elements combine the methodology of Assassins with the Sicilian Mafia.

In 1818, Joseph Von Hammer wrote about the Assassins lodge in Cairo:

> The institution of their lodge at Cairo; the various grades of initiation; the appellation of master, companions, and novice; the public and the secret doctrine; the oath of unconditional obedience to unknown superiors, to serve the ends of the order; all agree completely with what we have heard and read, in our own days, concerning secret revolutionary societies; and they coincide not less in the form of their constitution, than in the common object of declaring all kings and priest superfluous.[67]

Von Hammer could have been describing the Muslim Brotherhood's *bai'a* (Islamic oath of allegiance) process and membership degrees. Criminologist Letizia Paoli's description of the Cosa Nostra Mafia family could have been describing the Muslim Brotherhood's family. Historian Niels Erick Rosenfeldt's study of Stalin's power apparatuses is strikingly similar to the Brotherhood's structure.

The next chapters will reveal how this matrix of crime, mysticism, covert warfare, and suicidal ideations has controlled, subverted, and influenced governments, militaries, and numerous institutions around the world.

---

67 Joseph Von Hammer, *The History of the Assassins,* 217.

CHAPTER FIVE

THE INDUSTRY OF DEATH

Creation of the Secret Apparatus, its Divisions, and the Secret Guide

"Yes, [it is] an industry of death, death is one of the industries. People who refine and know how to die an honorable death, and know how and when to choose a battlefield for their honorable death…are rewarded in life and the hereafter."

—Hassan al-Banna[1]

HASSAN AL-BANNA'S ORGANIZATION BECAME ONE of the world most complex criminal enterprises—what Banna described as his "industry of death." It is centered around the group's Secret Apparatus, the organ that currently controls the Muslim Brotherhood's headquarters in Egypt, Turkey, and Qatar, and dictates the policies of the Brotherhood's chapters worldwide.

Almost all Western Middle East policy experts and historians believe that the Secret Apparatus was dismantled and its existence confined to history books. This is a perilous falsehood. Not only is the

1 Hassan al-Banna, "Sina'at al-Mawt," Al-Nazir (Cairo), September 27, 1938; Hassan al-Banna, "Risalat al-Jihad," The Muslim Brotherhood official website, https://ikhwanonline.com/, accessed December 1, 2020; The Muslim Brotherhood official website, "Fikr wa-Athar al-Imam al-Banna," https://ikhwanonline.com/, accessed September 12, 2018.

Secret Apparatus still operational, but the organization is ruled by this militant division, and the main organization acts as its public façade.

The Brotherhood has become the blueprint for modern jihadism and the actualized vision of the father of the Islamic Awakening Project, Jamal ad-Din al-Afghani, to utilize Western technology to advance Islamist expansionism. Banna built one of the world's most complex criminal syndicates, and the group's real power lies in its operatives' patience and adaptability. They superficially integrate into their surroundings and study their adversaries enough to successfully camouflage themselves amongst them.

When Banna questioned his new members about their true allegiances, he demonstrated his psychological contamination from the empire he built on secrecy and concealment. Banna's paranoid edifice would not have succeeded without three critical subdivisions within the Secret Apparatus. The first of these organs is *jihaz al-mukhabarat* (the Intelligence Apparatus). The second is *jihaz dubat al-Ikhwan* (the Apparatus of the Brotherhood Officers), which ultimately ruled Egypt in 1952 and enabled the Muslim Brotherhood to franchise its brand of covert and overt terrorism across the world. The Secret Apparatus' third important division is the International Apparatus. The modern state of the International Apparatus and its role in founding the majority of modern terrorist groups will be explained in later chapters.

THE OFFICIAL CREATION OF THE SECRET APPARATUS

A clandestine terrorist order stays in the shadows, but proselytism combined with their operatives' tendencies to vaunt jihadist activities—whether out of narcissism or a desire to recruit terrorists—has revealed classified information about the Brotherhood. The Muslim Brotherhood is currently restructuring the Secret Apparatus, both within their jihadist wing and their terror offshoots, to revive its original form.

During its early founding, Secret Apparatus leader Ali Ashmawi, Banna, and other members of the Guidance Bureau studied covert movements around the world when they originally established the Secret Apparatus. According to Ashmawi, they were "very influenced with clandestine proselytism in Islamic history [and in] Shi'ite [thought] and its clandestine orders." Ashmawi also said the Brotherhood has been "significantly impacted by the Assassins...they were fascinated by their miraculous levels of attention and obedience [to their leader] even if they were asked to kill themselves."[2]

The exact date of the founding of the Secret Apparatus is not known, but Ashmawi stated that the Secret Apparatus "is as old as the group itself."[3] Public discussions about the existence of the Secret Apparatus within the Brotherhood date back to 1930 when some of its members directly accused Banna of "secret works."[4]

It is not commonly known that Banna and members of the Guidance Office officially founded the Secret Apparatus with Hajj Amin al-Husaini.[5] Husaini rose to prominence in 1931 in Jerusalem after he established the World Islamic Congress, which operated as a secret society.[6] Several Ottoman and German agents were among the radicals involved in Husaini's network, such as Shakib Arslan and Abbas II Helmy Bey.[7] Husaini already possessed ideological legitimacy to lead a jihadist movement. He studied at al-Azhar University in 1911, and a year later he attended Rashid Rida's *Dar ad-Da'wa wa'l-Irshad* (the School of Proselytism and Guidance). Husaini's religious training and access to the World War I Islamist cabal allowed him to be granted the organizational, theological, and clerical authority to cofound the apparatus.

2 Ali Ashmawi, *At-Tarikh as-Sirri,* 8.
3 Ibid., 32.
4 Mitchell, *The Society of the Muslim Brothers*, 30.
5 Al-Jazeera (Doha), December 28, 2003.
6 Rubin and Schwanitz, *Nazis, Islamists, and the Making of the Modern Middle East* (Yale University Press), 88.
7 Ibid.

Husaini's Islamic Congress was an offshoot of the Islamic Institute in Berlin, which he established with Arslan in 1927.[8] He followed the same modus operandi of the founders of the Makassed Foundation and Islamic Ethics Association, and he hijacked representation of the Muslim community in Germany in the 1920s. He also controlled the only mosque in Berlin-Wilmersdorf.[9] The Islamist policy of controlling mosques is a critical strategy that has been successful against targeted Muslim communities. Husaini established the General European Islamic Congress as the Jerusalem branch of his General Islamic Congress, which eventually morphed into the present-day *Munazzamat at-ta'awun al-Islami*, the Organization of the Islamic Cooperation (OIC). The international organization has a permanent delegation to the United Nations and European Union and consists of fifty-seven member states.

In 1931, Husaini hosted a meeting of 132 delegates from twenty-two countries "to mobilize support for Palestinian Arabs against Zionists, the meeting was also part of al-Husaini's larger scheme to become the Muslim world's leader."[10] Husaini's plan succeeded, and he became the most instrumental regional figure in the Islamic Awakening movement at the time. Banna supported Husaini's efforts and sent him a letter during this meeting: "The entire Islamic world appreciates your good jihad, and your wise decision in calling for this blessed conference." In his letter, Banna made anti-Semitic comments in his suggestion to combat "Jews fighting the Islamic idea with their gold," and he asked Husaini to establish a regional fund to funnel monies into Palestinian activism. Banna's infamous paranoia also appeared in the letter when he urged the mufti to "weed out those with sick hearts, ulterior motives, and questionable pasts."[11]

---

8 Ibid., 81.

9 Ibid., 83.

10 Ibid., 84.

11 The Official Muslim Brotherhood Encyclopedia "Hassan al-Banna wa'l-wa'l-wa'l-Qadia al-Falastininia," https://ikhwanwiki.com/, accessed May 9, 2020.

In 1933, Banna emulated Nazis and fascists by utilizing teenagers to advance his mission. He created a militia under the benign-sounding banner of Ranger Squads that trained young men and teenagers for combat and jihad. Banna said, "the Brotherhood aims to practice sports [which are] influenced by the idea of Islamic jihad and to fulfill its aims."[12]

It is commonly believed that Muslim Brotherhood terrorism began in the 1940s, but the first organized terrorist attack committed by Banna's squads was against Egypt's native Coptic Christian community in July 1933. Banna's youth wing was mobilized to riot and attack Coptic Christian priests, businesses, and homes. This organized jihadist attack was led by Muhammad al-Ahmadi al-Zawahiri (1887–1944), then-head of al-Azhar University and paternal grandfather of the current leader of al-Qaeda Ayman al-Zawahiri.

Zawahiri became the first Egyptian from Arabian tribal origins to head al-Azhar when he assumed this position in 1929. He established an association called the *lagnat muqawamat at-tansir* (Evangelism Resistance Committee). He formed the group with Brotherhood leader Mustafa al-Maraghi (1881–1945). Maraghi was the earliest head of their Propagation of the Message section, and an al-Azhar theologian. The committee included militants from the Muslim Brotherhood, Islamic Ethics Association, Young Muslim Men Association, and other Islamist entities.[13] This jihadist coalition considered Coptic Christians to be guilty by association with Western Christians for sharing their faith.[14] Jihadist riots resulted in the burning of Christian-owned homes and businesses and physical assaults on many priests.[15]

During the Brotherhood's third general conference in March 1935, Banna changed the name of his jihadist cell to *nizam al-jawala*

12 Banna, *Mudhakkirat*, 125.

13 Zawat Irfan al-Maghribi, *Hay'at Kibar al-Ullama' 1911-1961* (Cairo: Al-Hay'a al-Misriyya al-Amma l'al-Kutub, 2012), 398.

14 Khalid Na'im, *Tarikh Jam'iat Muqawamat at-Tansir 1933-1938* (Cairo: Nahw Tala'i' Islamiyya Wa'iyya, 1987), 30.

15 Ibid., 30–2.

(Rover Scouts Order or Division). The third general conference was instrumental. It was the first time that the Brotherhood publicly acknowledged they were a jihadist group.[16] They gave special attention to the Rover Scouts, and the Guidance Office issued an order to conscript every able-bodied Brotherhood member to join the scouts.[17]

In 1935, the Secret Apparatus officially launched the Rover Scouts Division as a joint project between Banna and Husaini, adopting the structure of a modern terrorist group. While speaking about the Secret Apparatus during an interview with al-Jazeera, Muslim Brotherhood cofounder Farid Abdul Khaliq said:

> The initial discussion [about the Secret Apparatus] was with the mufti Amin al-Husaini, as he was the direct leader of the cause and he shared [our] understanding of Islam and its requirements. Muslims have to support each other to fight occupation. Together they strategized this idea and they considered each other to be partners in [implementing] it, and the same happened with [leaders] who proceeded them. We need to be able to confront gangs and *tanzimat* [armed groups] with their ilk… the idea was born as a result of a brainstorming between him [Banna] and Amin al-Husaini.[18]

This correspondence between Banna and Husaini likely occurred through a delegation sent by Banna to hold a secret meeting with Husaini and another al-Azhar University jihadist, Izz ad-Din al-Qassam (1882–1935), in August 1935. His delegation included two of

16 Abdul Azim Ramadan, *Al-Ikhwan al-Muslimin w'at-Tanzim as-Sirri,* The Official Muslim Brotherhood Encyclopedia, https://ikhwanwiki.com/, accessed May 1, 2020.

17 Ahmad Adu Kamal, *Al-Nukat Fawq al-Horuf* (Cairo: Al-Zahra li al-I'lam al-Arabi, 1989), 61.

18 Al-Jazeera (Doha), December 28, 2003.

Banna's most trusted members of the Guidance Bureau, his brother Abdul Rahman and his secretary, Muhammad As'ad al-Hakim.[19]

In British Mandate of Palestine, Nazi agents had better outcomes for their propaganda campaigns against Jews, and by 1936 swastika flags were widely accepted among its Arab population.[20] After Banna's delegation met with Husaini and Qassam, the Brotherhood sent jihadists to engage in terrorist activities during the Arab revolt (1936–1939), which later became known as the "Great Revolt." In 1949, the Egyptian magazine *Dar al-Fikr al-Islami* (the House of Islamic Thought) published an interview with Husaini in which he said:

> The Muslim Brotherhood was involved in the war in Palestine from the beginning, they publicized for war and they personally engaged in its jihad, they provided weapons and ammunition ... they continue serving this cause through [sacrificing] themselves and their efforts and everything in their capacity till the end.[21]

In April 1936, Husaini founded the Arab Higher Committee. In his memoir, Secret Apparatus leader Mahmoud Assaf stated Banna was secretly involved with its founding, that he was "supplying arms for the committee," and providing Husaini with Brotherhood fighters. Assaf said Banna rented a villa in Cairo where they "established a secret radio station" for the committee. This radio station exclusively broadcast jihadist propaganda for Husaini and refrained from transmitting anything relating to the Muslim Brotherhood. The Brotherhood still uses this strategic propaganda tactic.[22] The group still follows the model of adopting grievances and causes to create dissidence and division in their targeted societies that they can exploit.

19 Ahmad Mahmoud Karima, *Al-Islam wa-Firaq Mu'asira* (Cairo: Maktabit Jazirat al-Ward, 2017), 171.

20 Bensoussan, *Jews in Arab Countries,* 303.

21 Sabbagh, *Hakikat at-Tanzim al-Khas.*

22 Mahmoud Assaf, *Ma' al-Imam ash-Shahid Hassan al-Banna* (Cairo: Iqra' for Publishing and Distribution, 1993), 138.

THE MUSLIM BROTHERHOOD SCOUTS

The Rover Scouts division still operates in many countries, including the United States. Its main objectives are to (1) provide preliminary paramilitary training for juveniles and young adults; (2) teach operatives to spread their message and recruit new members; (3) test the blind obedience of new Brotherhood members; (4) pay monthly membership fees to the Guidance Office and; (5) select militants to eventually join adult battalions of the Secret Apparatus.[23]

By the autumn of 1937, Banna developed *kata'ib ansar Allah* (Battalions of the Supporters of God) for older jihadists who were selected from the Scouts. The practice of training children and teenagers in sports to equip them to become jihadists in battalions is still practiced in the Middle East and most nations where Brotherhood operatives reside—including the US. On January 27, 2015, the Muslim Brotherhood issued a statement on its official website, IkhwanOnline.com, where it explicitly stated that the Rover Scouts form Secret Apparatus battalions:

> The founding imam [Banna] was keen on establishing "scouts teams" as an exhibition of decency and discipline to establish the "Special Order" which prominently displays [our] power. Imam al-Banna trained the jihad brigades which he sent to Palestine to fight the usurping Jews, and the second [General] Guide, Hassan al-Hudaybi, restored the "Special Order" to drain the occupying British [forces]....[24]

The statement continued to incite jihad and martyrdom:

23 Banna, *Mudhakkirat*, 125, 308, 309; "Al-Qawanin wa'l-wa'l-wa'l-Lawa'eh al-Idareyya li-Jama'at al-Ikhwan al-Muslimin," The Official Muslim Brotherhood Encyclopedia, https://ikhwanwiki.com/, accessed June 20, 2020.

24 "Risala ila Sufuf al-thuwar: wa-A'idu," The Official Muslim Brotherhood website, https://www.ikhwanonline.com/article/220195, January 27, 2015.

> [Banna] said: "A nation which excels in its industry of death, and knows how to die an honorable death, God grants it a decent life in this world and eternal bliss in the hereafter; what has weakened and humiliated us is the love of life and hatred of death, prepare yourselves for great work and be keen to die to be granted a dignified life.... Beware that a dignified death will provide us absolute bliss, may God grant us and yourselves the honor of martyrdom for His sake."

At the end of this proclamation for jihad, the Brotherhood asserts that "tactical force is the only thing that is effective," and they are on the path of a "long and uncompromising jihad" in which they "seek martyrdom."

The vast majority of Brotherhood Rover Scouts divisions are covert, but this author uncovered one of their cells in the United States. The New Jersey Muslim Brotherhood Rover Scouts is headed by self-proclaimed member of the Muslim Brotherhood Hani Elkadi.[25] He engaged in unusual behavior for a covert division and posted numerous pictures of the Brotherhood scouts on his Facebook account over the span of several years.[26] These pictures depict Elkadi leading and training juveniles in a fashion similar to the Boy Scouts of America. But he is a Brotherhood operative, which raises legitimate concerns that this could be a juvenile camp to train future jihadis.

In 2016, Elkadi posted Brotherhood scout pictures on his Facebook account and captioned them saying, "we need to revive the scouts, great work with young men, [may] Allah burn you Sisi."[27] Elkadi's

25 Farahat, "Islamists with Direct Ties to Terrorists," 8–10.

26 Hani Elkadi, Facebook, www.Facebook.com/Hani.Elkadi/posts/10151936794171218, April 6, 2014; Hani Elkadi, "'Ayzin neraga' al-Kashafah tani," Facebook, www.Facebook.com/Hani.Elkadi/posts/10153740257961218, September 9, 2016; Hani Elkadi, "Dawrah fi al-majal al-Kashafi," Facebook, www.Facebook.com/Hani.Elkadi/posts/10154694508136218, August 16, 2017.

27 Hani Elkadi, "'Ayzin neraga' al-kashafah tani," Facebook, www.Facebook.com/Hani.Elkadi/posts/10153740257961218, September 9, 2016.

comment combining the New Jersey Brotherhood scouts with his wish for God to burn the Egyptian president indicates that the scouts may be more similar to the Brotherhood's juvenile jihadist training program than to the American Boy Scouts. Brotherhood operative Sa'id Abbasy is a trainer in the New Jersey Muslim Brotherhood scouts with Elkadi.[28] He circulated the Brotherhood's 2015 jihad proclamation on his social media account, which tied the scouts to jihadist battalions.[29]

Currently, the scouts' type of training and level of concealment in training juveniles varies depending on their location and the country where the training occurs. While almost all scouts' military training camps are clandestine, one of their militias was uncovered and provided a glimpse into the Brotherhood's modern military training for teenagers and university students. The Muslim Brotherhood has almost full control over al-Azhar University. Al-Azhar has its own Brotherhood scouts and military brigade, known in Egypt as *Militiat al-Azhar* (Al-Azhar Militias). Operatives of the militia dress in black and wear black balaclavas during their military training. This covert cell was exposed when an anonymous source leaked pictures and videos of its martial arts training inside al-Azhar to Egyptian media in 2006.[30]

These activities are a direct result of Banna's jihadist ideology that officially manifested in 1938. He merged the essence of crime, totalitarianism, and jihad into a comprehensive project, which he called *sina'at al-mawt* (the Industry of Death). Banna explained his Industry of Death project in an essay published under the same title in *al-Nazir* magazine. In 1946, Banna republished the article under the title *fan al-mawt* (the Art of Death), where he said:

---

28 Ibid.

29 Said Abbasy, "wa-A'idu ba'a wa-A'idu" Facebook, www.facebook.com/said.abbasy/posts/10203558560505622, January 28, 2015.

30 "Militiat Talabat Jami'at Al-Azhar," YouTube.com, https://www.youtube.com/watch?v=1ADu5c4-kqk, May 29, 2012.

> Death is an art, sometimes a beautiful art despite its bitterness, it might even be the most beautiful of arts if it is created by the hands of a masterful artist. The Qur'an honorably presented it to its believers and compelled them to cherish and love it more than others love life … Muslims will not be saved from their reality unless they adopt the Qur'an's philosophy of death and embrace it as an art, a truly beautiful art.[31]

Banna publicly launched his battalions with an essay titled *al-manhaj* (The Methodology), which he updated the same year and republished under the title *risalat at-ta'alim* (The Teachings Manifesto).[32] On the cover of its first edition, Banna subtitled it, "My doctrine to the brothers of the battalions." This essay became the group's manual for their "industry of death."

He began the essay by saying, "This is my message to the jihadist brothers of the Muslim Brotherhood who believe in the nobility and sanctity of their idea and their sincere determination to live by it, or die for it." In this document, he confirmed the group's five principles: "God is our goal, the Prophet is our model, the Qur'an is our law, jihad is our path, and martyrdom is our aspiration."[33]

Banna presented the essay at the Muslim Brotherhood's fifth conference in 1938, where he defined his organization's philosophy, "We believe that the laws and teachings of Islam are a total system complete unto itself as the final arbiter of life in this world and the hereafter … Islam is a doctrine and a creed, a nation and a nationality, a religion and a state, spirituality and labor, a Qur'an and a sword."[34]

---

31 Al-Nazir (Cairo), September 26, 1938; Hassan al-Banna, "Fan al-Mawt wa-Thaman al-Hayyat," The Muslim Brotherhood Official Website, https://www.ikhwanonline.com/, December 6, 2020.

32 Banna, "Risalat at-Ta'alim".

33 Ibid.

34 Ali Muhammad Jarisha, "Al-Mabade' al-Khamsa," The Official Muslim Brotherhood Encyclopedia, https://ikhwanwiki.com/, accessed January 11, 2021.

During the conference, Banna also laid out ten conditions for *bai'a* stating, "our *bai'a* system has ten pillars, memorize them."[35] These ten pillars were understanding, sincerity, labor, jihad, sacrifice, obedience, consistency, altruism, brotherhood, and trust.

Banna performed several experiments to test the endurance and allegiance of individuals whom he accepted as members. He always asked the same question of new recruits, which revealed Banna's paranoia and lack of trust in his own enterprise. He asked, "If there was a coup inside the Brotherhood that eliminated Hassan al-Banna, would you still continue to work for the organization?"[36] Banna often talked about himself in the third person, and this question was intended to determine whether new members were more loyal to him or his group. Banna worried that he would be betrayed, and his paranoia would later be justified, when he was devoured by the "industry of death" he created.

The motto of the Secret Apparatus is *al-iman, al-kitman, wa-kathrat al-maran* (faith, concealment, and excessive training).[37]

The Muslim Brotherhood's initiation rites convey the depth of occultist elements in the group. The *bai'a* process for the Secret Apparatus is different than the one performed for the Brotherhood's General Apparatus.

The oath of allegiance for the Secret Apparatus is given after a Muslim Brotherhood member has been entrusted to carry out terrorist and jihadist activities. The initiation rite starts when the recruit arrives at a secret location and utters a code word to gain entry to their dwelling. Once inside, he is escorted into a bright room where a masked or hooded man tells him he is "selling his soul to Islam."[38] The individual is later taken into a pitch-black room and seated on the floor. After his eyes acclimate to the darkness, he sees a table with

35 Banna, "Risalat at-Ta'alim."
36 Assaf, *Ma' al-Imam ash-Shahid*, 62.
37 Sabbagh, *Hakikat at-Tanzim al-Khas.*
38 Kherbawy, *Sir al-Ma'bad*, 222.

a gun on top of a Qur'an and the leader of the Secret Apparatus standing in front of him, also wearing a hood. The recruit is then ordered to put his right hand on the gun and the Qur'an and told to pledge allegiance to the Secret Apparatus and dedicate himself to the victory of Islamic *d'awa*.[39]

The level of self-sacrifice of Secret Apparatus members is displayed through their willingness to die upon the orders of a man whom they do not know, although sometimes conscripts recognize the leader's voice. Secret Apparatus leader Mahmoud Assaf recalled that during his initiation rite, he recognized the voice of Saleh Ashmawi and identified him as the head of the apparatus at the time.[40] Assaf and others would later reveal the names of Secret Apparatus operatives who became heads of government, lawmakers, clergy members, and ministers. Sabbagh also revealed the Apparatus members' slogan: *kun fid'iyyan* (be a martyr).[41]

In 1940, Banna invited five members of the Brotherhood to draft a program for the Secret Apparatus. These five individuals were Saleh Ashmawi, Husain Kamal ad-Din, Hamid Sharit, Abdul Aziz Ahmad, and Mahmoud Abdul Alim. Banna designated Ashmawi to be the leader of the Secret Apparatus. He ordered the men to prepare a detailed study of jihad in Islam from the perspective of the Qur'an, Sunna, and Islamic history. He also told them to train Secret Apparatus members in military combat and test their members' unconditional obedience.

THE INTELLIGENCE APPARATUS

The Muslim Brotherhood established an Intelligence Apparatus from the day Banna founded the organization, and it still operates as a unit within the Secret Apparatus. It is headed by Secret Apparatus leaders who are also members of the Brotherhood's Guidance Office.

39 Assaf, *Ma' al-Imam ash-Shahid,* 154–5.
40 Ibid., 155.
41 Sabbagh, *Hakikat at-Tanzim al-Khas.*

When Banna founded the Secret Apparatus, it was separate from the Guidance Office. This structure changed in modern times, and the Secret Apparatus has been the governing body of the Muslim Brotherhood since Mustafa Mashhour (1921–2002) became its leader in 1971.

According to Secret Apparatus documents seized from Mashhour in 1948, the Intelligence Apparatus directs "guerrilla warfare, and its gangsters are called the Scout Guards."[42] The document lists some of the group's objectives, such as "exhausting the enemy's forces and inflicting the greatest losses upon them through assassinations, destroying their infrastructure and barracks, and plundering their weapons." According to an Egyptian police report and court documents from 1948, "the intricate intelligence body… plotted to overthrow the government."[43]

The Intelligence Apparatus division spies on both supporters and opponents of the Muslim Brotherhood. It also infiltrates and internally subverts political parties, militaries, intelligence agencies, media, educational systems, governmental and nongovernmental organizations, and other influential groups. It currently operates in every nation where Brotherhood members are active. Secret Apparatus leader Ali Ashmawi said:

> The Brotherhood are consistently keen on information gathering and surveillance, they always take pride that they have an intelligence apparatus capable of gathering and analyzing information. They spy on everyone, on parties, organizations, governments, and [intelligence] agencies, each member in [every] position is a spy for the group, every [government] employee, every working man, continuously sends

---

42 Dar al-Fikr al-Islami, *Qadiat Siarat al-Jeep,* The Official Muslim Brotherhood Encyclopedia, https://ikhwanwiki.com/, accessed May 15, 2020.

43 Ibid.

> the secrets of his trade or occupation to the leadership of the group, even every detective and police officer does the same for his leadership within the group, they have adopted this behavior since their founding, they are spying on communists, on Wafd [party]… The Brotherhood [also] implanted their operatives in communist organizations in Egypt.[44]

Ali Ashmawi's statements are corroborated by Secret Apparatus operative and lifelong Brotherhood leader Mahmoud Assaf. In his memoir, Assaf narrated a conversation he had with al-Azhar University scholar and Brotherhood operative Sayyid Sabe', also known as *mufti ad-damm* (the Bloody Mufti) for issuing fatwas ordering assassinations. Assaf states that the mufti told him:

> We gathered intelligence on all leaders, politicians, intellectuals, writers, and artists, whether they were enemies or supporters of the Brotherhood. Their information was delivered to me to archive it and review it whenever one of these individuals requested to meet ustadh Banna, or if the imam had to meet them for any other reason. I would provide him with this information so he would be aware of it while communicating with the individual in question.[45]

Secret Apparatus leader Ahmad Adil Kamal said the Brotherhood's Intelligence Apparatus "penetrated political parties and other institutions." [46] Kamal cited one successful example of the Brotherhood's infiltration of the Young Egypt Society militia, when the Brotherhood's spy As'ad as-Sayyid Ahmad reached a leadership position in the "iron guard," the intelligence and terrorism organs of Young Egypt.

44 Ali Ashmawi, *Al-Tarikh as-Sirri,* 74.
45 Assaf, *Ma' al-Imam ash-Shahid*, 152-3.
46 Ahmad Adil Kamal, *Al-Nukat Fauq al-Huruf* (Cairo: Al-Zahra, 1989), 162–7.

This infiltration pressured the group's leader to change the name of his party in 1940 to *al-Hizb al-Watani al-Islami* (The Nationalist Islamic Party).[47]

Another example of successful infiltration in the 1930s took place when the Secret Apparatus assigned one of its operatives, Faraj al-Najar, to infiltrate the Egyptian Communist Party in Gharbia district. Al-Najar ultimately became the party's Secretary General.[48]

The Intelligence Apparatus division has its own chief, deputy, secretariat, operations division, and units dedicated to investigating different groups.[49] This division directly interacts with the heads of the battalions. When addressing his battalions, Banna said:

> Create a Brotherhood cell in every street, in every town, [create] a Qur'anic battalion in every city, a Muhammadan banner in every alley, preach your values … form the battalions, the night armies defeat the morning ones … the Muslim Brotherhood's message is totalitarian.[50]

Banna's message to the Brotherhood still endures. His instructions for infiltration and the stealth work of "night armies" have made it easy for its members to operate undetected in the vast majority of organizations they penetrate.

During Banna's lifetime, the identities of most Brotherhood spies remained secret until 1948, when it was revealed that Brotherhood operatives had reached influential and leadership positions in several political parties through infiltration. These historic patterns of infiltration are repeated today by the Muslim Brotherhood's modern Intelligence Apparatus.

47 Heyworth-Dunne, *Religious and Political Trends in Modern Egypt* (Washington), 30.
48 The Muslim Brotherhood Official website, "Faraj al-Najar,", https://ikhwanonline.com/, September 6, 2018.
49 Ahmad Adil Kamal, *Al-Nukat Fauq al-Huruf,* 162.
50 Muhammad al-Amin bin ash-shaikh bin Mzid, "Al-Ikhwan al-Muslimin min an-Nash'a illa al-Hal," The Official Muslim Brotherhood Encyclopedia, https://ikhwanwiki.com/, accessed January 1, 2021.

MUSLIM BROTHERHOOD OFFICERS

Another critical Secret Apparatus division is the Muslim Brotherhood Officers. This division currently operates in many countries. It is one of the most destructive units within the Brotherhood, as it subverts its targeted nations' armies from within.

The Brotherhood attempts to infiltrate every profession and trade, but their main focus remains on police, intelligence agencies, and militaries. The Brotherhood's Officers division became their most prolific in Egypt. The next chapters confirm that this division still exists in the Egyptian army and probably within several armies in the West.

In August 1936, Egypt signed a Treaty of Alliance with the United Kingdom that terminated the British military occupation of Egypt and restricted the presence of the British army to the Suez Canal for a duration of twenty years. The evacuation of the British military significantly decreased the size of the Egyptian army. Prime Minister Mustafa al-Nahhas Pasha (1879–1965) decided to negate the decrease of army personnel by allowing all social classes to join the Royal Military Academy, which had been limited to aristocrats since 1882.

This permitted Islamists to join the army and gave Banna a wider audience. He created a subdivision in the Secret Apparatus called *dubat al-ikhwan al-muslimin* (the Muslim Brotherhood Officers). The Brotherhood's Officers division oversaw *qism al-wahadat*, which literally translates to "the units division," in reference to "Police Units Division." It is responsible for the infiltration and recruitment of police officers, and it was headed by police officer Salah Shadi (1921–1989). This division also remains operational.

From 1942 until 1954, the Secret Apparatus had both a civilian deputy and a military one. While technically the first civilian deputy of the Secret Apparatus was Saleh Ashmawi, the civilian wing of the apparatus didn't have a clear mission until it was headed by Mahmoud Abdul Halim in 1938.[51] In July 1941, he departed Cairo for profes-

51 Mahmud Abul Halim, *Ahdath Sana'at at-Tarikh* (Cairo: Dar ad-d'wa,1994) 1: 261.

sional reasons and assigned the position to Abdul Rahman al-Sendi (1918–1962). Sendi had a lifelong relationship with Muhammad Abdul Hakim Amer (1919–1967), who would later become the vice president of Egypt from 1956 to 1967. Sendi's grandfather was originally a slave from Sindh province and was owned by Amer's grandfather. Amer's family eventually freed the Sendis, and they continued to work for Amer's family until Sendi's death. Amer was also a member of the Muslim Brotherhood's Officers unit.[52]

The civilian leadership is responsible for the intellectual, theological, strategic, and decision making at the governing levels of the Secret Apparatus. The Brotherhood Officers division was originally subordinate to the civilian leadership, and it was tasked to blindly execute operations and obey orders. This structure is similar to the German Communist Party (KPD), which was also adopted by the Nazi Party. Their "secret apparatus was initially subdivided into two sections, the *Nachrichtendienst* (Intelligence Services or the N-Group) and the *Militärdienst* (Military Service or M-Group). The former was responsible for 'special political tasks' and the latter for the organization of the movement's armed uprising."[53] In 1933, the Nazis dismantled the KPD and its secret apparatus, but they continued to enforce its model in the Nazi party. Similarly, the Muslim Brotherhood's Secret Apparatus civilians are the N-Group, and the Brotherhood Officers are the M-Group.

The exact date of the founding of the Brotherhood Officers division is unknown, but it can be traced back to the recruitment of Major Mahmoud Labib (1882–1951), who was the head of the Brotherhood's Officers unit and the military deputy of the Secret Apparatus.[54] He was responsible for the recruitment and infiltration unit, which targeted the Egyptian military, and he also oversaw military operations and

52 Anadolu Agency (Istanbul), June 10, 2012.

53 Mike Dennis, *The Stasi: Myth and Reality* (Milton Park: Routledge, 2014), 29.

54 Salah Abdul Fattah al-Khaldi, *Sayyid Qutb min al-Milad ila al-Istishhad* (Damascus: Dar al-Qalam, 2010), 287.

smuggling weaponry from the army to the Muslim Brotherhood.[55] Labib grew up in a fundamentalist family. In November 1915, he partook in the Senussi jihadist campaign against British soldiers in as-Sallum, a village located near the Egyptian/Libyan border on the Mediterranean Sea. Labib joined the order of Senussi, which is named after the militant Libyan imam Ahmad Sharif as-Senussi. Senussi was closely associated with Enver Pasha.

Labib was another protégé of the World War I Islamist cabal. His jihadist activities were not limited to Sallum, and he travelled to fight in Libya in 1915. During the same year, he was sentenced to death by a British court for his role in jihadist operations in Libya. Labib escaped to Turkey until he relocated to Germany in 1922. During his stay in Germany, Labib continued his Islamist activities and the Muslim Brotherhood claimed he "protested against the British alongside Hitler."[56] He relocated to Cairo in 1924, after the Egyptian government pardoned him. Upon his return to Egypt, Labib joined the pan-Arab pan-Islamic Hizb al-Watani (National Party). In 1936 Labib retired from the military and joined the Muslim Brotherhood in 1938. Labib became Banna's most important asset for his contacts among Islamists inside the army.

In 1940, an unknown military officer invited Banna to dinner at a military compound, where Banna met the future president of Egypt, Anwar al-Sadat (1918–1981).[57] Banna's initial attempt to recruit Sadat didn't succeed, but in 1942, he co-opted him. Sadat had a secret Islamist militia inside the army, and Banna convinced him to join his apparatus after he showed Sadat his private a cache of arms to demonstrate his preparedness for jihad.[58] The Brotherhood also recruited military officer Muhammad Naguib (1918–1984), who eventually

55 Hassan Ashamwi, *Hasad al-Ayam*, The Official Muslim Brotherhood Encyclopedia, https://ikhwanwiki.com/, accessed April 20, 2021.

56 The Official Muslim Brotherhood Encyclopedia, "As-Sagh Mahmud Labib Mu'sis Tanzim al-Dubat al-Ahrar," https://ikhwanwiki.com/, accessed January 1, 2021.

57 Anwar al-Sadat, *Asrar al-Thawra al-Misriya* (Cairo: Dar al-Hilal, 1957), 45–7.

58 Sadat, *Asrar al-Thawra al-Misriya*, 65–7.

would become Egypt's first president after the Brotherhood's Officers coup d'état in 1952.[59]

Another important Brotherhood recruit was military officer Abdul Mon'eim Abdul Ra'ouf (1914–1985), who was already a full-fledged jihadist. As a teenager, Ra'ouf established the militant Islamic confraternity "the Invisible Hand." His group conducted several terrorist attacks against British personnel, including detonating a bomb at the house of Sir Percy Lyham Loraine, the British High Commissioner to Egypt from 1929 to 1933.[60]

After Nahhas Pasha allowed all classes of society to enter the military, Ra'ouf joined the army in 1936. In June 1941, Ra'ouf and one of his colleagues stole a military aircraft to transport General Aziz al-Masri to join jihadist Rashid Kilani in Iraq. They failed to fly the aircraft, were arrested, and remained incarcerated until May 1942. Ra'ouf was released from prison and allowed to return to the military. While waiting at a military office to get reinstated, he came across a Muslim Brotherhood magazine that intrigued him, and he joined the group the same year.[61] In his memoir, Ra'ouf wrote that during a discussion with Labib in 1943, they decided to "propagate the Brotherhood's message within the Egyptian army to create a seed for an Islamic populist military," and to "provide the Brotherhood with military training."[62]

Ra'ouf and Labib's mission to infiltrate and subvert the Egypt army succeeded when they recruited their most dangerous operative, then-officer Gamal Abdel Nasser. After two failed attempts to join the Royal Military Academy because of his juvenile criminal activi-

59 Husain Hamouda, *Asrar Harakat ad-Dubat al-Ahrar wa'l-wa'l-wa'l-Ikhwan al-Muslimin*, The Official Muslim Brotherhood Encyclopedia, IkhwanWiki.com, accessed April 20, 2021.

60 The Official Muslim Brotherhood Encyclopedia, "Al-Ustadh al-Mujahid Abdul Mon'eim Abdul Ra'ouf Basim Abu al-Fadl," https://ikhwanwiki.com/, accessed January 1, 2021.

61 Ibid.

62 Abdul Mon'eim Abdul Ra'ouf, *Arghamt Farouk ala at-Tanzul an al-Arsh*, The Official Muslim Brotherhood Encyclopedia, https://ikhwanwiki.com/, accessed February 1, 2021.

ties, Nasser was finally accepted in March 1937. In 1932, Nasser witnessed rioters physically engaging with Egyptian police, and though he said he "didn't know the reason they were protesting," he joined the riot and threw a rock at a police officer.[63] He was arrested and, afterward, he learned he had been protesting with the Young Egypt militia, which he joined upon his release from prison. Nasser's early rejections by the military academy became a source of his rage and class envy that infused his rhetoric.

In October 1942, Ra'ouf invited Nasser to attend the Muslim Brotherhood's weekly Tuesday meeting. Nasser complied, and he joined the Brotherhood. His code name in the Brotherhood was Zaghloul Abdul Kadir.[64] He became more active within the group in 1944 when the first Officers Family cell was officially created by seven operatives under the leadership of Labib.[65] The members of this cell were Gamal Abdel Nasser, Kamal ad-Din Husain, Abdul Mon'eim Abdul Ra'ouf, Husain Ahmad Hamouda, Sa'd Tawfik, Salah Khalifah, and Khalid Mohieddin. The cell's first official assignment was to perpetrate a widespread anti-Semitic wave of terrorism across Egypt.

In 1945, the Brotherhood Officers, Young Egypt, and Young Men's Muslim Association held anti-Jewish riots across major Egyptian cities. On Balfour Declaration Day, November 2, 1945, these Islamist mobs pillaged, destroyed, and burnt Jewish property, including an Ashkenazi synagogue. Islamist violence during the riots was also perpetrated against "Coptic, Greek Orthodox, and Catholic institutions…as well as shops owned by foreigners. Some 500 businesses were looted, 109 of these belonged to Jews."[66] These mass terrorist attacks in Cairo resulted in the death of a police officer and

63 Arabic translation of David Morgan's Interview with President Gamal Abdel Nasser, Sunday Times, June 18 1962, The Official Website of Gamal Abdel Nasser, http://nasser.bibalex.org/, accessed February 4, 2021.

64 Muhammad Naguib, *Kuntu Ra'isan li-Misr* (Cairo: Al-Maktab al-Misri al-Hadith, 1984), 167.

65 Salah Abdul Fattah al-Khaldi, *Sayyid Qutb min al-Milad ila al-Istishhad*, 288.

66 Norman A. Stillman, *The Jews of Arab Lands in Modern Times* (New York: The Jewish Publication Society, 1991), 142–3.

hundreds injured. The wave of terror in Alexandria claimed "six lives, five of them were Jewish, and another 150 persons were injured."[67] On Christmas Eve 1945, they also bombed the British Club. In 1948 they bombed several Jewish homes in Cairo and many Jewish-owned businesses and cinemas.[68] They also bombed trains in Sharqiya and Isma'ilia, including the King George Hotel. The Brotherhood continued a series of bombings into the 1950s.[69]

The government offered to bear the expenses for rebuilding the ruined synagogue, and failed to hold Banna accountable for the widespread destruction. The government's weak response encouraged them to expand their jihadist activities.

Soon after the anti-Jewish riots, Labib asked Banna to have all members of the Muslim Brotherhood "become organized militarily and receive training in guerilla warfare."[70] Banna agreed to Labib's request and since then most able-bodied members of the Muslim Brotherhood receive militant physical training prior to their acceptance as active members.

In 1946, the seven members of the Brotherhood Officers cell pledged allegiance to Sendi, the civilian deputy of the Secret Apparatus. They showed they were worthy of the position by bombing eight police stations in December 1946. Ra'ouf exposed the initiation ritual in his memoir. He said the members of the Brotherhood Officers cell were ordered to visit an apartment in civilian clothes, knock on its door and say the code: "[Is] the Hajj present?"[71] They were later escorted individually to a dark room where a man covered in a bedsheet asked, "Are you ready to sacrifice yourself for Islamic *da'wa*?" They all answered affirmatively. Ra'ouf adds that the man took their

---

67 Ibid., 143.

68 Mitchell, *The Society of the Muslim Brothers*, 66.

69 Farouk Taifour, "Al-Juz' al-Rabi': al-Ikhwan w'at-Tanzimat as-Sirriya," Egyptian Institute for Political and Strategic Studies, https://eipss-eg.org/, February 24, 2016.

70 Ra'ouf, *Arghamt Farouk ala at-Tanzul an al-Arsh*.

71 Ibid.

hand, placed it on a gun and a Qur'an and said: "Those who divulge our secret have only one penalty, and that is the penalty for treason."

After they pledged their allegiance, they realized that the anonymous man was Sendi, who told them he was head of the Secret Apparatus, "which is an armed clandestine entity, composed of men who sold themselves to God, and they're ready to die for truth and freedom."[72] The Muslim Brotherhood's and Islamists' definition of truth of freedom is contrary to the Western definition.

THE MUSLIM BROTHERHOOD'S SECRET GUIDE

The denial of the existence of the Secret Apparatus by Western Middle East experts has caused a significant and deadly setback in the field of counter-terrorism. It has helped clandestine leaders of terrorist groups and offshoots of the Brotherhood to operate with impunity. The fact that the Secret Apparatus still exists within the Muslim Brotherhood is foreign to the vast majority of Middle East experts in the West; hence, the proposition that there is also a *murshid sirri* (Secret Guide) is breaking news to those in the field. But according to the Muslim Brotherhood's own leaders, the position has always existed and still exists within the organization. Moreover, the Secret Guide is currently the actual leader of the Muslim Brotherhood and not its public figurehead, who technically acts as a public relations figure and is generally filled by a former jihadist. The Secret Guide often assumes the position of Chief Deputy of the General Guide.

Several Brotherhood leaders have revealed the existence of a Secret Guide. According to their former leader Mukhtar Nouh, the group has maintained a Secret Guide since its founding. The Secret Guide operates in parallel to the General Guide, and he is the head of

72 Ibid.

the Secret Apparatus.[73] During the author's interview with Tharwat al-Kherbawy, he said, "the existence of a Secret Guide was inevitable." Kherbawy added that the first Secret Guide was Ahmad Sukari, until his resignation in 1947. Following Sukari, the Secret Guide was Abdul Rahman al-Sendi until his arrest in 1948.

WAS AMIN AL-HUSAINI A SECRET GUIDE OF THE MUSLIM BROTHERHOOD?

This is a new proposition derived from this author's analysis of historic and theological elements within the Muslim Brotherhood. Several indicators suggest the likelihood that Husaini acted as the Secret Guide after the imprisonment of Sendi. His "deep involvement" with the Muslim Brotherhood was among the main reasons to why the Egyptian government considered him to have broken the tradition of political asylum in Egypt by 1951.[74] It is possible that Husaini operated as a Secret Guide and the head of the Secret Apparatus from 1948 until 1951.

The first of these indicators stems from the fact that he cofounded the Secret Apparatus with Banna. There has never been a founder or cofounder of the Muslim Brotherhood nor any of its divisions who was not in a leadership position within the group. The second reason for this possibility is that Husaini acted as the General Guide. Not only did he have an office inside the clandestine organization's headquarters, but also he had the power to make decisions restricted to the Guide, such as monitoring the group's internal elections.

According to Sa'id Ibrahim al-Husaini, an Islamist and relative of Amin al-Husaini, during the Brotherhood's internal elections in

73 Al-Watan News (Cairo), September 6, 2020.

74 Nazi War Crimes Disclosure Act, Document Number: 51966ec8993294098d50a495, Freedom of Information Act Electronic Reading Room Central Intelligence Agency, https://www.cia.gov/readingroom/docs/HUSSEINI%2C%20AMIN%20EL%20%20%204_0136.pdf, accessed May 1, 2021.

January 1948, the mufti sent his relative and al-Azhar University-trained jihadist, Sheikh Hassan Abu as-Sa'ud (1896–1957), to monitor the Muslim Brotherhood's internal elections. He also stated that as-Sa'ud turned their headquarters into "a military camp."[75]

Hassan Abu as-Sa'ud was also a Nazi collaborator. He was captured by allies in 1945 in Berlin, but he was able to flee, and he eventually resided in Cairo until his death.[76] The fact that the Mufti had the power to assign a delegate to monitor elections carried out by the Muslim Brotherhood Guidance Bureau confirms that he had organizational superiority above the governing body—a privilege restricted to the General Guide.

The third indicator that the Mufti was the Secret General Guide can be deduced from a historic incident mentioned in a CIA memorandum.[77] The document stated that in 1951, the "Mufti has combined the forces of the Moslem [sic] Brotherhood with his own terrorists." The memorandum states that the Mufti's decision to merge Palestinian and Egyptian terrorists was intended to "sabotage the Trans-Arabian pipeline." The author of the memorandum was not convinced of the motive for the merge and wrote that it "may be questioned since there appears to be no proof that the Israelis are receiving oil from Sidon [in Lebanon]." The author cited a more compelling reason stating the "Trans-Arabian Oil Co. has recently presented $25,000 for the relief of the Arab refugees." The author's suspicions of the reasons provided to him for the union of terrorist forces is reasonable. The decision to combine terrorist forces was attributed to the Mufti. His authority to command the Brotherhood's military forces is also only reserved to Brotherhood's Guide.

---

75 Sa'id Ibrahim al-Husaini, "Min Mudhakirati Am 1948," Arab Studies Institute, https://www.jadaliyya.com/, accessed April 8. 2021.

76 Palestinian Academic Society for the Study of International Affairs (PASSIA), "Abu al-Saud, Hassan," http://www.passia.org/, accessed April 8, 2021.

77 Central Intelligence Agency, Freedom of Information Act Electronic Reading Act, Nazi War Crimes Disclosure Act, Document Number: 51966ec8993294098d50a510, https://www.cia.gov/library/readingroom/docs/HUSSEINI%2C%20AMIN%20EL%20%20%204_0160.pdf, accessed April 2, 2020.

Following the union of Palestinian and Egyptian terrorists, King Abdullah bin al-Hussein was assassinated on July 20, 1951, by a member of Husaini's *al-jihad al-Muqadas* militia. According to another CIA memorandum,[78] "the Mufti's complicity" in the assassination of King Abdullah "was immediately inferred from the identity of the assassin, Shukri Ashou, a member of the Jihad Mukadas, an extremist Arab organization created by the Mufti in 1948."

The fourth reason the Mufti could have been the Secret General Guide is that he had the power to assign roles and leadership positions among the heads of the Muslim Brotherhood. According to another CIA memorandum, during the Islamic Congress in Karachi in 1952, Husaini accused Banna's son-in-law, Sa'id Ramadan (1926–1995), of "embezzling a large sum of money which had been subscribed in Pakistan for the benefit of the Ikhwan cause in Egypt."[79] Following this accusation, the Mufti assigned Secret Apparatus leader Saleh Ashmawi to formally represent the Brotherhood in the next Muslim Congress.

While it doesn't appear that any other Middle East expert has suggested the Mufti could have been the Secret Guide of the Muslim Brotherhood, the facts mentioned here could lead to this conclusion. The patterns of involvement and influence of the Mufti inside the group could be used as reference when investigating and trying to identify current clandestine heads of the apparatus.

The Mufti's leadership of the Secret Apparatus possibly ended after the Second General Guide, Hassan al-Hudaybi, restructured the apparatus and assigned Yusuf Tal'at (1914–1954) to its leadership. He did this in an attempt to rid the apparatus of known figures after the group's internal split between the Brotherhood Officers and the civilian leadership of the Secret Apparatus. Due to Hudaybi's duplicity, cautious approach, and conflict with Nasser, it is likely he headed

78 Ibid.

79 Central Intelligence Agency, Freedom of Information Act Electronic Reading Room, Nazi War Crimes Disclosure Act, Document Number: 51966ec7993294098d50a41a, https://www.cia.gov/readingroom/docs/HUSSEINI%2C%20AMIN%20EL%20%20%205_0091.pdf, accessed April 8, 2021.

the Secret Apparatus from 1951 to 1954. There are mainstream Brotherhood accounts of him acting as the group's Secret Guide for six months prior to officially becoming the leader of the group. Until 1973, the General Guide was operationally superior to the head of the Secret Apparatus. Since 1973, this equation has been reversed.

CHAPTER SIX

THE ART OF DEATH

Muslim Brotherhood's Past and Present Terrorism Methodologies

"Death is an art, a truly beautiful art."

—Hassan al-Banna[1]

THE MUSLIM BROTHERHOOD'S EXTERIOR FAÇADE engages in dissimulation and concealment, effectively hiding its legacy of terrorism. Both the public and covert apparatuses exist to empower the organization's theological obligation of the "permeance of jihad." While terrorism is generally utilized as a tool, in the case of the Brotherhood is also an objective in itself, and one of the main reasons for their existence. The Brotherhood has succeeded in terrorism tactics, whether they personally directly engaged in them or executed them through proxy jihadists organizations.

The 1940s and 1950s marked the Muslim Brotherhood's advancement of violent strategies that became the foundation for modern Islamic terrorism. During that time, the Brotherhood Officers combined their formal military training with covert jihad. According to Gamal Abdel Nasser's recruiter, the training program of Brotherhood Officers had four main requirements (1) translating literature to edu-

1 Hassan al-Banna, "Fan al-Mawt wa-Thaman al-Hayyat," The Muslim Brotherhood Official Website, https://ikhwanonline.com/, December 6, 2020.

cate them on "lessons that should be learned" about "gang warfare;" (2) frequently relocating the location of their secret meetings in dwellings owned by members of the Brotherhood; (3) practicing operations and strategies on sand tables; and; (4) writing articles and giving lectures to the civilian wing of the apparatus.[2]

Banna didn't just order political and religious assassinations to advance his cause and fulfill what he perceived as his religious obligation; he also used them as a tool for vengeance. When Banna ran for parliament in Ismai'ilia and failed to win the election, he retaliated by sending a Secret Apparatus operative, who was also a member of the pan-Arab Watani Party, to assassinate Egyptian Prime Minister Ahmad Maher Pasha on February 24, 1945.[3]

The Brotherhood's terrorist attacks escalated after Maher Pasha's assassination. Following the German surrender, French authorities placed Amin al-Husaini under house arrest while he awaited possible conviction before an international tribunal. But the Mufti fled to Cairo using the fake passport of Ma'ruf ad-Dawalibi, an Islamist member of the Syrian embassy staff in Paris.[4]

Husaini's presence in Cairo was instrumental for Islamic agitation. His military and political experience with Hitler was useful for the Muslim Brotherhood. Ibn Saud pressured King Farouk to accept the Mufti's presence in Egypt.[5] King Farouk must have been aware that the Mufti was accused of being responsible for the extermination of Jews in Europe, yet Farouk conceded to Ibn Saud. His decision to harbor Husaini would eventually contribute to his overthrow and assassination.

2 Ra'ouf, *Arghamt Farouk ala at-Tanzul an al-Arsh*.
3 *.Al-Youm as-Sabi'* (Cairo), August 9, 2019.
4 David G. Dalin, John F. Rothmann, Alan M. Dershowitz, *Icon of Evil: Hitler's Mufti and the Rise of Radical Islam* (New York: Random House Publishing Group, 2008), 79.
5 Central Intelligence Agency, Freedom of Information Act Electronic Reading Room, Nazi War Crimes Disclosure Act, Document Number: 51966ec7993294098d50a366, https://www.cia.gov/readingroom/docs/HUSSEINI%2C%20AMIN%20EL%20%20%20%201_0004.pdf accessed February 29, 2021.

Banna gave his most famous assassination order to Sendi in a coded fashion typical of organized criminal groups in the age of recorded surveillance utilized by both Egyptian and British police at the time. Banna wanted Judge Ahmad Khazindar killed after Khazindar incarcerated terrorists from the Brotherhood and Young Egypt militia for bombings targeting British citizens and various facilities across Egypt. Banna told Sendi, "[May] God relieve us from him and his ilk."[6] This prompted Sendi to send two Brotherhood operatives to kill Khazindar on March 22, 1948.

Khazindar was on his way to court to sentence Brotherhood members accused of bombing a cinema in Cairo when the Brotherhood operatives shot him dead. While they were fleeing the crime scene, two terrorists threw a bomb at pedestrians chasing them but the perpetrators were still caught. The assailants were Mahmoud Zinhum and Banna's personal assistant, Hassan Abdul Hafez. Zinhum said that he overheard Banna saying that "Khazindar deserves to get killed," which he understood to be an assassination fatwa.[7] The police questioned Banna following the arrest of the murderers. He confirmed that he knew Hafez, but denied prior knowledge of the assassination plot.

This was the first time Banna betrayed his operatives by claiming he wasn't aware of an assassination plan. Banna's pattern of betrayal of his jihadists would eventually become the most likely reason for his own assassination.

On December 4, 1948, the Brotherhood murdered Cairo's chief of police, Selim Zaki, by throwing a bomb at him. On December 28, they murdered Egypt's then-former Prime Minister Mahmoud Fahmi al-Nuqrashi for declaring his plan to outlaw the Muslim Brotherhood four days after Zaki's assassination.

The decision to ban the Brotherhood was due to two major investigations. The first was the one known as *al-aidun min Gaza* (the

6 Yusuf al-Qaradawi, *Ibn al-Qaraiya* (NP/ND), 1: 301.
7 Ali Ashmawi, *At-Tarikh as-Sirri*, 27.

returnees from Gaza), a reference to Brotherhood operatives who were among troops who fought against Israel from November 1947 until Israel's victory in 1949.

King Farouk was a weak man, he was more a socialite than a politician. He allowed Islamists to drag him into a failed war against Israel, which ultimately became a contributing factor in his overthrow and demise.

After Brotherhood operatives returned from Gaza, they settled in a terrorist training camp in Cairo headed by then-Secret Apparatus operative Mahdi Akef (1928–2017), who later became the seventh leader of the Muslim Brotherhood. The aim of that camp was to create a paramilitary, every bit as trained, armed, and funded as the Egyptian army. Many of them were arrested, which created fractures inside the Secret Apparatus.[8] The Brotherhood's military intended to perpetrate a coup d'état and establish an Islamic state, and they were "filled with hostility against King Farouk."[9]

The second reason for the government's decision to outlaw the Brotherhood was the discovery of the Secret Apparatus, which followed an incident and prompted an investigation known as *qadiat as-siara al-jeep* (the case of the Jeep automobile).

THE CASE OF THE JEEP AUTOMOBILE

The existence of the Secret Apparatus was discovered because of Subhi Salim, an alert police officer in Cairo. The incident was similar to one took place in the United States in August 2004, which also uncovered the Muslim Brotherhood's Secret Apparatus in North America.

On November 15, 1948, Salim spotted a Jeep automobile without license plates carrying several passengers, boxes, and crates. The

8 "Al-Ikhwan al Muslimun w'as-Sa'i ila as-Sulta," The Official Muslim Brotherhood Encyclopedia, https://ikhwanwiki.com/, accessed March 20, 2020; "Daqiqat Hiwar ma' Tharwat al-Kherbawy Hawl Asrar Khafiyya," YouTube.com, July 21, 2019.

9 Ibid.

widespread wave of Brotherhood bombings across Egypt prompted the officer to approach the suspicious vehicle after it stopped in front of a house, later discovered to belong to a member of the group. Salem ordered the individuals to exit the vehicle, which prompted them to abandon the Jeep and escape. According to the police and court documents, upon searching the automobile, police found a cache of explosives and weapons including Gelignite, also known as blasting gelatin; Pentaerythritol tetranitrate (PETN); six rolls of ignition fuse; three rolls of detonating cord; tens of bombs; a Sten submachine gun and three boxes of magazines; twenty-seven handguns; hundreds of bullets; four daggers; electric detonators; six clocks; a land mine; a black mask; and numerous documents.[10]

The large arms cache exposed the magnitude of the danger of the Brotherhood, but the government was more disturbed by the "plan to burn Cairo," which was also found among the documents.[11] The Brotherhood's plot to burn Cairo eventually would come to fruition on January 26, 1952, when Islamists set fire to forty cinemas, thirteen large hotels, sixteen clubs, ninety-two bars, countless restaurants, cafés, banks, stores. The offenders first bombed many fire departments to prevent them from responding to the burning city.[12] The perpetrators have never been officially identified, but the 1948 documents detailed the Secret Apparatus' plan to set Cairo ablaze, so it is very possible that the Secret Apparatus' civilian and Brotherhood Officers divisions were involved.

This could explain why the government under Gamal Abdul Nasser didn't identify the perpetrators. It almost certainly was due to his culpability in the event through his Brotherhood Officers cell. Another indication of the Brotherhood's involvement was that the facilities burned were all cultural, modern, and cosmopolitan. Prior to

10 Dar al-Fikr al-Islami, *Qadiat Siarat al-Jeep.*

11 "Daqiqat Hiwar ma' Tharwat al-Kherbawy Hawl Asrar Khafiyya," YouTube.com, July 21, 2019.

12 "Film Wastha'eqi, Hariq al-Qahira," YouTube.com, July 23, 2020.

the burning of Cairo, Brotherhood Officers had smuggled weapons from the Egyptian military to Banna, who hoped to arm ten thousand jihadists to carry out terrorist attacks in both Egypt and Israel.[13]

Two of the escaped passengers from the Jeep automobile, Ahmad Adil Kamal and Tahir Imad ad-Din, were eventually caught. While searching for the other passengers, the police stopped a suspicious individual, Mustafa Mashhour, the Secret Apparatus operative who would eventually become the fifth General Guide of the Muslim Brotherhood. When he was apprehended, Mashhour carried a briefcase containing documents that referred to the Secret Apparatus.

Police searched Mashhour's residence and arrested several members of the Brotherhood, including Secret Apparatus leader Mahmoud as-Sabbagh, the owner of the Jeep. Among the documents found in the vehicle were the Secret Apparatus' internal bylaws, handwritten by Sabbagh. The bylaws are called *qanoun at-takwin*, which translates to the "law of formation." The unusual title could be explained by the Brotherhood's continuous tactic of using vague and coded language when they discuss militant activities. The Secret Apparatus is sometimes called "the formation" in the Brotherhood's literature.

While the complete internal bylaws of the Secret Apparatus remain secret, some of its articles were released during the government's lawsuit against the Brotherhood. The first article in the bylaws mentioned the structure of the Islamic army of the Secret Apparatus:

> The army has three divisions: the chief, the command, the staff and soldiers. The command unit consists of a council of ten people whose task is to study the methods of implementation of the decisions issued by the chief. [This unit is also responsible for] issuing statements which all its members coauthor. [It is also tasked with] researching obstacles facing the imple-

13 Assaf, *Ma' al-Imam ash-Shahid*, 140.

> mentation of the orders of the council. The duty of this council is to fully supervise the conditions of soldiers and to guarantee the strength of their morale, through studying the reports provided on each individual or each group, and demanding clarifications if the reports neglect some aspects. The council's mission is to enforce a strong spiritual program for soldiers which includes oral narration of stories of [Islamist] heroes and their adventures. The council liaisons with the chief and provides him with all the information he needs. Each of the ten members of the command council must be ready to assume leadership of the apparatus at any time.[14]

The publicly available articles from the bylaws of the Secret Apparatus reveal two critical facts. First, the terrorism recruitment technique of oral incitement for jihad through inspirational stories is so critical to the survival of the apparatus that it was mentioned in the first article. Originally devised by the Assassins, the Brotherhood revived and spread the terror recruitment technique and continued to advance it until it reached the modern state of what Islamist call *al-jihad al-ilectroni* (cyber jihad), which is covered in the next chapters.

The second compelling element in the first article of the bylaws is the mention of clandestine troops at time of peace.[15] The forthcoming information has never been presented to a Western audience, and it provides irrefutable evidence from the Muslim Brotherhood's own words that their militants pretend to sever ties with the main organization while forming and operating terrorist offshoots.

---

14 Sabbagh, *Hakikat at-Tanzim al-Khas.*

15 Ibid.

SECRET APPARATUS SOLDIERS DURING PEACE

The Muslim Brotherhood is more dangerous during a time of peace than when involved in direct warfare. Their reliance on concealment allows them to recruit and engage in covert and subversive political and military activities. Both historically and in modern times, when the Muslim Brotherhood is not directly involved in military action against a targeted nation, they still have a clandestine jihadist army ready for combat.

A candidate for recruitment for a Brotherhood-operated militia, whether under its direct leadership or a proxy organization, must have specific qualifications and undergo a special process. An existing member of the Islamic military can nominate a candidate for recruitment to the militia's leadership and provide reasons why they believe the nominee would be beneficial for their jihadist group. They are required to include a status report on the individual's health, social and financial statuses, level of education, intellect, and religious and political inclinations. An applicant's approval depends on the leadership's decision based on an extensive study of these elements, combined with the potential conscript's "absolute belief" in the Brotherhood's mission.[16]

A Brotherhood-operated terrorist group elects an emir only under strict conditions. The promotion to emir, or head of a terrorist group, "increases the individual's responsibility and doesn't exclude him from fulfilling his prior duties as a member." He is required to militarily train his jihadists and guide them "according to the guidelines he is assigned." This indicates the level of involvement of the Muslim Brotherhood leadership in the internal operational workings of a jihadist group.[17]

The emir establishes a terrorist cell's policies and directs their missions. The emir must provide a monthly report to the Secret Apparatus

16 Ibid.
17 Ibid.

leadership, and communicate to them suggestions and ideas on how to utilize his jihadists. The emir reports every detail about the lives of his jihadists, such as marriages, illnesses, or hardships. This allows the Brotherhood to be aware of weaknesses, where a terrorist can be pressured, blackmailed, or bribed. The emir is tasked with communicating with the leadership any decisions, investigations, or penalties levied against jihadists.

Members of the Secret Apparatus and its terrorist offshoots must learn how to manufacture and operate various types of weapons, detonators, and explosive devices. Sabbagh said, "It is not limited to the theoretical study on how to dismantle and clean different types of weapons and different types of bombs. It is a requirement to train in using weapons and explosives."[18]

The Secret Apparatus' chief position was canceled in the 1940s and replaced by a "technical committee" of five members. That number is subject to increase depending upon the circumstances and is under the direct leadership of the head of the apparatus. According to Sabbagh, "This committee is responsible to organize jihadists during peace and war."[19] It is also tasked to oversee detailed studies and analysis of modern weaponry and to study all the types of challenges that face Brotherhood soldiers, including their psychological state, level of obedience, and readiness for jihad.

According to Sabbagh, there are three types of Brotherhood militants. The first type of soldier is not associated with the Muslim Brotherhood's public apparatus and is required to be "completely and entirely" separated from the public group. This type of soldier is responsible for the most dangerous terror operations. The second type of militant is not entirely separated from the public apparatus but receives the highest levels of military training and is exclusively utilized for public warfare. The third type is the Secret Apparatus militant who is allowed to join the General Apparatus but only after he

18 Ibid.
19 Ibid.

has completed his role in a terrorist group and has completely severed ties with the terrorist he was previously affiliated with.[20]

Sabbagh said the Brotherhood is keen to recruit "as many operatives as possible" to join the first type of membership. These members are urged to keep secret meetings with Brotherhood leaders to a minimum, to be able to pretend that the member has indeed severed ties with the official Muslim Brotherhood body. Sabbagh added that even "his friends and family" should be tricked into thinking that he is no longer a member of the Muslim Brotherhood.[21]

The leadership of a Secret Apparatus-operated terrorist group is composed of ten clusters, each of which comprises five terrorists. Among the five members is a leader who reports to the technical committee. The ten clusters are responsible for the secret oversight of the activities of a second level of subordinate groups composed of twenty jihadists. The third level of clusters includes eighty jihadists, and they are subordinates to the second level of jihadists. Sabbagh said that these jihadists clusters can "eternally replicate."[22]

During a terrorist group's dormant period of temporary nonviolence, only eight leaders from the Secret Apparatus are allowed to communicate with the leaders of other proxy terror groups. Those eight members remain anonymous to the other proxy jihadist group members in case they "were arrested by the enemies and tortured, they cannot reveal identities of individuals whom they do not know."[23] The next chapters will disclose facts proving that these Secret Apparatus stratagems remain functional.

---

20 Ibid.
21 Ibid.
22 Ibid.
23 Ibid.

HASSAN AL-BANNA'S BETRAYAL OF THE SECRET APPARATUS AND HIS ASSASSINATION

While there isn't evidence the Egyptian government assassinated Banna, there exists consensus in the West that the government was responsible. However, there is evidence to suggest Banna was murdered by his own jihadist group.

The government was deeply disturbed by the weapons and documents seized from the Jeep automobile. During a raid on one of the Brotherhood's offices, the government confiscated 165 bombs from a single location.[24] This prompted a wide investigation into the Brotherhood's terrorism division. During the investigation, Nuqrashi Pasha outlawed the Muslim Brotherhood in a military tribunal on December 8, 1948. Nuqrashi was assassinated twenty days later when Abdul Majid Husain shot him. Nuqrashi's assassin became a major player in exposing that Banna was aware of the Secret Apparatus' terrorism activities, and Banna became the main suspect in the assassination case.

On January 13, 1949, in an attempt to destroy evidence, a Brotherhood operative tried to bomb the Attorney General's office inside the courthouse where the Jeep automobile case was being tried. An employee of the courthouse became suspicious of an unattended briefcase and threw it into the street before it detonated. The perpetrator, Shafik Anas, was arrested, and he confessed to following the orders of the leaders of the Secret Apparatus. Anas's confession directly implicated Hassan al-Banna.

Following the bombing incident, the government brokered a deal with Banna to identify members of the Secret Apparatus and the locations of their offices, weapons caches, and radio station. In return, Banna was promised prosecutorial immunity for the terrorist attacks

24 Al-Wafd (Cairo), December 14, 2013.

in which he was implicated. Prominent attorney and statesman Mustafa Mar'i initiated negotiations with Banna though journalist Mustafa Amin. Several Secret Apparatus leaders, including Sabbagh and Ahmad Adil Kamal, confirmed Banna's negotiations with the government.[25]

Banna agreed to publicly disavow terrorism, dismantle his Secret Apparatus, and reveal the identities of its operatives to police. But first, he had to publicly denounce the apparatus' operatives, excommunicate them from Islam, and publicly admit he would cooperate with the government.[26]

Banna issued a statement titled "They are Neither Brothers Nor Muslims," which was drafted by Mustafa Amin. Banna renounced the court bomber and other Brotherhood terrorists, saying, "The perpetrator of his horrible crime and other similar ones can never be Brothers nor Muslims…the people will cooperate with the government which is keen on their safety and its peace under the rule of the glorious king [who is] ardent on destroying this dangerous phenomenon."

Banna added that he wished the government would strip the terrorists of their citizenship. This statement became Banna's death sentence. Perhaps Banna's infamous paranoia was psychological projection stemming from his knowledge that under pressure, he himself would betray his own jihadists. When Banna asked each member of his group whether his allegiance lay with him or his group, he may have been wondering whether they were willing to die for him or for the Brotherhood's mission. Banna knew those were separate causes. Were they willing to die to save him, or kill him to protect themselves?

Nuqrashi Pasha's assassin confessed to Banna's knowledge of the assassination plot. In his memoir, Sabbagh said that Banna was practicing dissimulation when he issued this statement because "war is

25 Sabbagh, *Hakikat at-Tanzim al-Khas*; Ahmad Adil Kamal, *Al-Nuqat fawq al-Huruf*, 298; Daqiqat Hiwar ma' Tharwat al-Kherbawy Hawl Asrar Khafiyya," YouTube.com.

26 Ibid.

deceit" and if Nuqrashi's assassin was aware of this, "he wouldn't have confessed about his accomplices."[27]

After Banna publicly offered his assistance to the government, he feared the Secret Apparatus would kill him for his betrayal. According to Kherbawy, journalist Muhammad Hassanin Haikal was present during the meeting between Banna and Mustafa Amin, who edited Banna's statement. Kherbawy said that Haikal told him that Banna "was scared" when Amin included excommunication from Islam in the statement. During this meeting, Banna also was asked to provide the names of all the members of the apparatus. He asked the government for time to gather his thoughts on the matter.[28]

Banna later made another fatal mistake when he confided in his friend and Secret Apparatus operative Farid Abdul Khaliq, who remained a Brotherhood leader until his death in 2013. According to Abdul Khaliq, Banna met him a "few days before his death" and asked him for his help to find a way out of this crisis that could "preserve the strength of the Muslim Brotherhood and its members."[29]

Another Secret Apparatus leader, Abdul Aziz Kamel—who later became the Minister of Awqaf (Islamic endowments) and al-Azhar Affairs from 1967 to 1974, until Sadat appointed him Deputy Prime Minister—stated that days before Banna's death, he was scared and remorseful for creating the Secret Apparatus.[30] Banna said, "and this is why God created remorse."[31]

Banna decided to give up his jihadists and save himself. This is why many Secret Apparatus operatives viewed Banna's statement not as an act of dissimulation but rather an act of treason, which is punishable by death according to their oath of alliance. Until today, Banna's state-

---

27 Sabbagh, *Hakikat at-Tanzim al-Khas*.
28 "Daqiqat Hiwar ma' Tharwat al-Kherbawy Hawl Asrar Khafiyya," YouTube.com.
29 The Official Muslim Brotherhood Encyclopedia, "Murja'at al-Ikhwan: Matha Uqssad Biha," https://ikhwanwiki.com/, accessed May 31, 2020.
30 Assaf, *Ma' al-Imam ash-Shahid*, 154.
31 Al-Musawar 4484-4489, 2010, 27.

ment continues to create controversy among the Brotherhood, and their modern apologists use it to whitewash the group's bloody history.

While the leader of the Secret Apparatus said that Banna was practicing dissimulation when he said, "They are Neither Brothers nor Muslims," Americans such as Muslim Brotherhood apologist David D. Kirkpatrick used this statement to support the factually incorrect claim that the Muslim Brotherhood is not a violent group.[32] The government arrested many Muslim Brotherhood operatives involved in numerous acts of terrorism, including the head of the civilian wing of the apparatus, Sendi. While he was in prison, Sendi was visited by Secret Apparatus operatives, including Muhammad al-Laithi, who was known in the group by the code name al-Assad. During his visit with Sendi and another Brotherhood operative, Sayyid Fayez, Laithi told them, "We have a sick cow, do we slay it or treat it?" Sendi told him, "Where I come from we slay sick cows."[33]

Laithi was in a prime position to be aware of Banna's plot against the apparatus. He was also the secretary of Saleh Harb Pasha, the president of the Young Men's Muslim Association and a retired military general involved in Banna's negotiations with the government. It's possible Laithi heard Banna was about to snitch on them. This worried Laithi, especially because he had been previously accused by the government of being involved in the assassination of Maher Pasha in 1945 but was acquitted due to lack of sufficient evidence.

On February 12, 1949, Laithi created a ruse to lure Banna to his death. Laithi went to Banna's house and told him Saleh Harb Pasha needed to see him. Banna agreed to go and took with him documents containing the names of members of the Secret Apparatus. His brother-in-law accompanied him. They went to Harb's office and discovered that there was no meeting. Harb confirmed this during the investigation of Banna's assassination. Banna gave the documents to

32 David D. Kirkpatrick, "Is the Muslim Brotherhood a Terrorist Group?" *New York Times*, April 30, 2019.
33 "Daqiqat Hiwar ma' Tharwat al-Kherbawy Hawl Asrar Khafiyya," YouTube.com.

an employee of Harb's office, Abdul Karim Mansour. When Banna and his brother-in-law left, Laithi offered to get them a taxi. When they entered the vehicle, two individuals shot at Banna, Mansour, and Banna's brother-in-law. According to Kherbawy, Banna recognized his assassins and attempted to chase them before he collapsed and died.[34]

Laithi later gave the police the license plate number of the automobile the assassins used to escape. The license plate was registered to Cairo's Chief of Police. It is highly unlikely that the chief of police and head of the criminal investigations unit would use his own personal vehicle if he was involved in Banna's assassination. That night, the documents Banna had given Mansour disappeared.

Following Banna's death, future Brotherhood General Guide Mahdi Akef visited Sendi in prison and informed him of Banna's death, saying, "We slayed the cow."[35] Sendi later said that during Laithi's initial visit to him in prison, he thought that Laithi was talking about an actual cow and not about Banna. It's implausible that Sendi thought Laithi was indeed visiting him in prison to discuss cattle. Sendi, who once took a coded order of assassination from Banna to kill Nuqrashi Pasha, gave his own.

The Muslim Brotherhood maintains the fictive narrative that the Egyptian government assassinated Banna, but Banna's death and the disappearance of the documents about the Secret Apparatus protected Brotherhood terrorists and resulted in the destruction of Egypt's modernized society, culture, and political system. It also enabled King Farouk's deposition after the Muslim Brotherhood perpetrated the 1952 coup d'état. This could have been avoided if the government's deal with Banna had been successful.

Banna's younger brother, Gamal al-Banna (1920–2013), was a communist during his childhood and teenage years. He never believed in the Muslim Brotherhood's ideology, and he found them criminal

34 Ibid.
35 Ibid.

and reprehensible. He also expressed his moral support of this author's former political party and political views. In 2003–2004, Gamal al-Banna often visited the house of the party's leader, Mohsen Lotfi as-Sayyid, where he hosted a weekly cultural gathering for Egyptian intellectuals. During one of the meeting, this author asked Gamal al-Banna if the Egyptian government killed his brother. He closed his eyes and shook his head, signaling "no." His nonverbal reaction was unusual for the outspoken and friendly Banna, who often enjoyed indulging in expansive dialogues.

Hassan al-Banna's son, Ahmad Saiful Islam al-Banna (1934–2016), also did not believe that the government assassinated his father. In 2008, he said the official Brotherhood narrative about his father's death was false and King Farouk was "innocent" of killing his father.[36] Several individuals, such as Kherbawy, personally spoke to Banna's son, who said the government did not kill Banna, and that he knew the identity of his assassin but could not share it. Banna's sister, whose husband witnessed Banna's death and was injured in the attack, also stated that the government did not assassinate him.[37]

Secret Apparatus operative and Brotherhood leader Muhammad Naguib said in 2008 that neither the government nor King Farouk killed Banna. He added that the Muslim Brotherhood "doesn't want to discuss the matter any further nor investigate the mysterious death of Banna."[38]

According to the police investigative report into Banna's death, which Kherbawy displayed on Egyptian television, Mar'i said in his statement, "He [Banna] was worried about his safety, he was afraid and terrified. He was always with his armed brother [Abdul Basit al-Banna], he was afraid of the terrorists in his party."[39]

---

36 *Al-Youm as-Sabi'* (Cairo), October 4, 2020.
37 "Daqiqat Hiwar ma' Tharwat al-Kherbawy Hawl Asrar Khafiyya," YouTube.com.
38 Al-Arabiya (Dubai), February 21, 2008.
39 "Daqiqat Hiwar ma' Tharwat al-Kherbawy Hawl Asrar Khafiyya," YouTube.com.

The police report continued, "Mar'i's statement is confirmed [by an incident] when Banna's armed brother was stopped by the police while he was circling the house of Saleh Harb during the sheikh's [Banna] negotiation with Mustafa Mar'i. When the sheikh was asked why he was taking such security measures, he said, "so you know that I am serious when I tell you that you're not the only ones threatened by this danger, it also threatens me." The report further stated the "danger facing the government is the same danger he faced, and it is the terrorists of course. The sheikh was complaining that they no longer obeyed him."

On September 25, 1949, Attorney General Muhammad Azmi Beik accused thirty-three members of the Muslim Brotherhood of a violent attempt to overthrow the government, along with numerous other terrorism and murder charges. It wasn't until March 17, 1951, that several Brotherhood leaders were convicted and imprisoned, including Sabbagh, Mashhour, and Sendi.

After Banna died, the Brotherhood disagreed for a year and half about who would become his successor.[40] The power struggle was between the Propagation of the Message section, which was controlled by al-Azhar University scholars, and the Secret Apparatus' civilian leadership. The division was finally settled, and Hassan al-Hudaybi officially became Banna's successor on October 17, 1951. As a leader in both the Secret Apparatus and the public organization, Hudaybi adopted a pattern of doublespeak to which the Brotherhood still adheres. On November 23, of the same year, Hudaybi falsely claimed the Muslim Brotherhood didn't have battalions, while the group officially engaged in jihad in the Suez Canal.[41]

40 "Ala fil-Fitna Sakatou," YouTube.com, June 29, 2014.
41 Mitchell, *The Society of the Muslim Brothers,* 90.

TERRORISM METHODOLOGY UTILIZED AND/OR INTRODUCED BY THE MUSLIM BROTHERHOOD TO ISLAMIC GUERILLA WARFARE

The Officers division was the most effective terrorism unit within the Secret Apparatus, and its leaders have admitted to being the first to utilize modern means of indiscriminate mass murder for Islamic jihad.

Secret Apparatus leader Ali Ashmawi discussed the Muslim Brotherhood's introduction of Vehicle-Borne Improvised Explosive Devices (VBIEDs) to Islamic jihad. Ashmawi said, "It was introduced by the [Police] Units Division leader Salah Shadi. This occurred during the month of Ramadan in Jewish quarters in Cairo on June 5, 1948, and also on July 18, 1948, in the same location. The vehicle bomb killed a number of bystanders."[42]

VBIEDs are still utilized by Islamic terrorist groups, including the Muslim Brotherhood's Secret Apparatus. In recent times, the most prominent assassination carried out by the Brotherhood in this fashion was the murder of Egypt's Prosecutor General, Hisham Barakat (1950–2015). Barakat was assassinated on June 29, 2015, by a VBIED. The assassination revealed previously unknown information about the modern Brotherhood's terrorism apparatus, which will be explained in the next chapters.

Suicide belts or suicide vests were a method first used by the Chinese during the Second Sino-Japanese War (1937–1945). The Brotherhood exported this terror methodology, making it religiously acceptable for jihadists to commit suicidal terrorist attacks utilizing improvised explosive devices strapped to their persons.

Ashmawi said, "The Brotherhood created the suicide belt in 1954." The original mission in which a suicide belt was utilized was during an attempt to assassinate Gamal Abdel Nasser after his fallout with the

42 Ali Ashmawi, *At-Tarikh as-Sirri*, 61.

Brotherhood. While the mission failed, the idea of using the suicidal improvised explosive survived, and its use continues to be advocated by leaders of the Muslim Brotherhood.[43] In 2015, Qaradawi said, "Suicide bombings are one of the greatest types of jihad."[44]

Fatwa assassinations are another Brotherhood homicidal tool. While religious edicts ordering assassination have been a popular method of eliminating dissidents and enemies throughout both Islamic and non-Islamic history, the Muslim Brotherhood has utilized them in a modern fashion. Fatwas ordering murders are more similar to contract killings than to traditional historic religious tribunals in which theocratic state-sanctioned murders typically occurred.

Many mainstream terrorism experts and academics claim that "the Muslim Brotherhood renounced terrorism," and Brotherhood apologists such as CNBC's news associates claim that the Brotherhood "renounced violence in the 1970s."[45] The truth is the opposite.

Banna's style of assassination fatwas never stopped, and it continues today. For example, in 1954, the Brotherhood attempted to assassinate Gamal Abdel Nasser, and in 1965 they attempted to murder him again. In 1977, the Brotherhood terrorist militia *at-Takfir wa'l-Hijrah*, kidnapped and killed Muslim scholar and Minister of Endowments and Islamic Affairs Muhammad Husain al-Zahabi. In 1981 Muslim Brotherhood militants killed Egyptian President Anwar al-Sadat, also based on a Brotherhood fatwa.

In 1992, a terrorist killed Egyptian secular intellectual and scholar Farag Fouda, justified by a Brotherhood assassination fatwa for his writings. That fatwa was issued by the Brotherhood-controlled al-Azhar University, along with *al-Gama'a al-Islamiyya* terror theologians. Brotherhood theologian Muhammad al-Ghazaly testified in court on behalf of the assassin, stating he wasn't "involved in mur-

---

43 Ibid.

44 Al-Arabiya News (Dubai), June 9, 2017.

45 Nadine El-Bawab, "Branding the Muslim Brotherhood a Terrorist Organization Could Rattle US Allies in the Middle East," *CNBC News*, May 8, 2019.

der, but in the application of Allah's law against apostates of Islam."[46] Islamists view taking the life of a human being who disagrees with them as a form of ritual sacrifice and not murder.

These are only few of many examples of high-profile assassinations based on Brotherhood religious edicts known in the Middle East as "blood fatwas." Among the most recent was their fatwa ordering the assassination of Prosecutor General Hisham Barakat. That fatwa was issued through the Propagation of the Message Section currently operating under Qaradawi's International Union of Muslim Scholars. It was delivered on May 18, 2015, by New York City-based Muslim Brotherhood imam and jihad agitator Akram Kassab, who ordered the assassination by publicly stating it was a "religious duty, a necessity, and revolutionary dream" to "get rid" of judges and officials who support the Egyptian government in its war against the Muslim Brotherhood.[47]

Close-quarters combat (CQC) is the "physical confrontation between two or more opponents. It involves armed and unarmed and lethal and nonlethal fighting techniques that range from enforced compliance to deadly force."[48] Unarmed techniques are hand-to-hand combat, and armed techniques are "applied with a rifle, bayonet, knife, baton, or any weapon of opportunity."[49]

While this is the most common fighting tactic throughout human history, the Muslim Brotherhood started to utilize this tactic when they first attacked Coptic Christian homes, churches, and businesses in July 1933.[50] Till today the Muslim Brotherhood attacks Coptic Christian churches in the same manner; for example, from 2011 to 2013, the Brotherhood attacked, destroyed, and burnt seventy-three

46 Al-Bawaba News (Cairo), June 8, 2020.
47 Al-Diar (Lebanon), July 1, 2015.
48 Jack Hoban, *U.S. Marine Close Combat Fighting Handbook* (New York: Skyhorse Publishing, 2010), 21.
49 Hoban, *US Marine Close Combat Fighting Handbook*, 21.
50 Khalid Na'eem, *Tarikh Jam'iat Muqawamat at-Tansir (1933-1938)* (Cairo: Nahw Tala'i' Islamiyya Wa'iyya, 1987), 30.

churches and 212 Coptic Christian homes and business, and killed and injured numerous victims.[51]

The Brotherhood also utilize CQC strategy against police stations and military complexes in Egypt and across the world. The most famous recent Brotherhood CQC terrorist attack is the Kerdasa massacre. Kerdasa is a town in Giza, located near the Giza Plateau. On August 14, 2013, Muslim Brotherhood terrorists attacked Kerdasa Police Station, resulting in the death of seventeen officers including the warden, his deputy, investigations assistants, and civilians.[52]

The instructions for this massacre can be traced to the Secret Apparatus bylaws and documents that police found in the possession of Brotherhood leader Mustafa Mashhour in 1948. According to the Secret Apparatus documents, "the general plan of attack on authority…can be implemented through destroying police and military vehicles, bombing police stations, murdering officers, and destroying energy and water power plants, destroying fire departments, disrupting telephone services, bombing railroads and trains, bombing major roads and bridges, destroying public transportation."[53]

Secret Apparatus terrorists took control of the police station during combat that lasted for six hours. The attack was gruesome, and the torture and desecration of officers' bodies was filmed and published online by the Brotherhood. One horrific video showed bloodied and tortured Police Brigadier Muhammad Gabr begging for water, and female Brotherhood terrorist Samia Shanan forcing him to drink acid until he died.[54]

Other videos depicted Brotherhood members dragging mutilated bodies of police officers in the streets and parading them around. After destroying the police station, the Brotherhood set it on fire. This

51 Al-Youm as-Sabi' (Cairo), August 19, 2013.

52 Al-Watan News (Cairo), April 17, 2021.

53 Dar al-Fikr al-Islami, *Qadiat Siarat al-Jeep,* The Official Muslim Brotherhood Encyclopedia, https://ikhwanwiki.com/, accessed May 15, 2020.

54 Al-Youm as-Sabi' (Cairo), April 17, 2021.

terrorist attack would later lead the author to discover critical information about the Muslim Brotherhood's relationship with al-Qaeda and their involvement in trafficking terrorists worldwide.

These acts of terrorism are only part of the Muslim Brotherhood's real threat. The infiltration of Egyptian and other militaries has been and still is one of the most destructive acts in the group's activities. The devastating consequences of the history of infiltration of the Egyptian army should be viewed as a cautionary tale while attempting to identify current patterns the Brotherhood employs in targeting Middle Eastern, Arab, and Western militaries.

MUSLIM BROTHERHOOD POLITICAL MARRIAGES AS A TOOL OF INFILTRATION AND STRATEGY OF COLLATERAL

Being a member of the Muslim Brotherhood is not akin to having a professional position or an affiliation in a political party. It is a cultist affiliation that extends to the operative's family members. Muslim Brotherhood members are only allowed to marry into other Muslim Brotherhood families. It is prohibited to marry outside the Muslim Brotherhood, with rare exceptions. This process is known within the organization as *al-zawaj al-bi'y*, which literally translates to "conservational marriage."[55] This is another awkward term the Brotherhood uses to conceal its ideological components. This practice is also known in the organization as *mashru' al-bait al-muslim*, the Muslim household project.[56]

The Brotherhood's organizational dominance extends to the most intimate personal decisions when it comes to marriage. Not only are Brotherhood operatives required to marry other members of the

55 Ali Ashmawi, *At-Tarikh as-Sirri*, 7.

56 Jamal Fathi Nassar, "Al-Watan wa'l-wa'l-wa'l-Muattana fi-Fikr al-Imam al-Banna," The Official Muslim Brotherhood Encyclopedia, accessed June 6, 2021.

group, but they must marry from a family that is similar to their hierarchy within the group. A Brotherhood Secret Apparatus official has to marry a female relative of another; a lower-level soldier also marries the female descended or relative of another. This practice guarantees a level of allegiance and commitment to secrecy that goes beyond mere organizational affiliations. It also provides them with a plausible explanation to conceal their organizational affiliations.

Former Muslim Sisterhood operative Intissar Abdul Mon'im said that female children or teenage girls who are born into Muslim Brotherhood families or are recruited from a young age are referred to as *zahra* (flower) within the group. A zahra's "mission is to be wed to a *shibl* [cub]," which is the Brotherhood term for male juveniles.[57]

Ashmawi discussed the Brotherhood's marriage practices in the context of its importance for clandestine networking. He said that their marriage system allows them to "utilize their family and marriage relationships as a very important cover for their communications."[58]

Maintaining a marital relationship with a spouse is also regulated by the group. For example, the Muslim Brotherhood ordered its operative Fawzi al-Gazzar to divorce his wife after she privately criticized a Brotherhood leader. He refused, and he ended up losing his business after he was socially ostracized from his community.[59]

There are numerous examples showing that Brotherhood operatives not only marry other Brotherhood members but also have to match their ranking in the organization. For example, former Brotherhood Guide Mahdi Akef was married to Mahmoud Ezzat's sister, Wafa' Ezzat. Mahmoud Ezzat's sister Fatima was married to Mahmoud Amer, a former head of the Brotherhood's Executive Bureau. Mahmoud Ghozlan, official spokesman of the Muslim Brotherhood and a member of the Constituent Assembly, is mar-

57 The Reference Institute (Paris), "Al-zawaj al-bi'iy," September 6, 2018.
58 Ali Ashmawi, *At-Tarikh as-Sirri*, 7.
59 "Tharwat al-Kherbawy Daif Tony Khalifah Sirri Jidan," YouTube.com, April 19, 2014.

ried to Khairat al-Shater's sister.[60] Sayyid Qutb's sister was married to Secret Apparatus leader Kamal as-Sananiri.

In February 2012, Egyptian journalist Hamdi as-Sa'id Salem uncovered the incestuous relationship between Islamists and the Mubarak regime.[61] Salem listed a series of marriages that confirmed the social institution was exploited by both by Mubarak's regime and the Brotherhood during their own political marriage.

These marriages included (1) the niece of Salafi jihadist Muhammad Hassan is married to State Security Lieutenant Rami Kiwan; (2) Brotherhood leader Selim al-Awa's brother is married to the sister of Major General Mohab Yammish, who was also a commander in the Egyptian military and a member of Egypt's Supreme Council of Armed Forces (SCAF); (3) Issam Sharaf was the Prime Minister of Egypt from March 2011 to December 2011 and brother of former Muslim Brotherhood General Secretary Ibrahim Sharaf. One of their brothers is married to Makarim ad-Dairy, a prominent Muslim Sisterhood leader, former Member of Parliament candidate, and professor at al-Azhar University.

When marriage isn't utilized to provide access and cover to nefarious affiliations, professional relationships often become the next level. For example, Brotherhood sheikh, terrorism propagandist, and Islamic State supporter Muhammad Abdul Maksoud is the brother of Major General Adil Abdul Maksoud who was the assistant to Habib al-Adly, Mubarak's Minister of Interior from 1997 to January 2011.[62]

The Muslim Household Project is a successful strategy that provides some prosecutorial immunity for both parties. When either party yields political power of the other, the family ties become a deterrent against attempts to use the legal system to settle disputes or hold a party responsible for crimes they may have committed.

60 Al-Masriyyun (Cairo), April 4, 2013.
61 Al-Hiwar (Berlin), February 25, 2012.
62 Masrawy (Cairo), October 26, 2016; *Al-Youm as-Sabi'* (Cairo), January 13, 2020

CHAPTER SEVEN

MILITARIZING ISLAM

The Muslim Brotherhood's Coup d'État of 1952, the Secret and Public Guides from 1973 to 2013

"Al-Azhar [University] is a practical tool which can create a psychological awakening to serve our aim for political and military upheaval."
—Muslim Brotherhood leader and al-Azhar scholar MUHAMMAD AL-GHAZALI[1]

THE MUSLIM BROTHERHOOD WENT THROUGH three major organizational developments. These are known in Muslim Brotherhood literature as *ta'sis*, which literally means founding. The first took place when Banna officially established the group in 1928. The second is what the Brotherhood calls *at-ta'sis al-thani* (the second founding), which officially took place in the 1970s and was based on the teachings of its principal theologian, Sayyid Qutb. The deviations from their traditional model occurred in the second founding, which tried to negate the problems the Brotherhood faced after the crisis within the Secret Apparatus between military and civilian leaderships that began in the 1950s. The third founding, or *at-ta'sis al-thalith*, took place from 2013 to 2016, and many of its details remain a mystery. The conditions which led to the Muslim Brotherhood's first massive institutional crisis resulted in the organization's second

1 Muhammad al-Ghazali, *Kifah ad-Din* (Cairo: Maktabit Wahbah, 1991), 233.

founding, which also was fraught with secrecy, disinformation, and widely accepted fallacies in its historic narrative.

The Muslim Brotherhood's Officers' 1952 putsch needs to be carefully reexamined. Not only is its historic event saturated with misinformation and disinformation, but the Brotherhood's ritualistic repetition of history has compelled them to replicate the same patterns today. Following the first Muslim Brotherhood Coup d'état in 1952, they modified the Secret Apparatus. The patterns of infiltration, subversion, and control they employed against targeted nations should identify their behavioral patterns against their current targets. They still regurgitate the same strategies of the 1940s and 1950s.

During that era, the most dangerous operative of the Brotherhood Officers was Gamal Abdel Nasser. Nasser was a totalitarian dilettante who adopted far-left-wing ideologies. During his membership in the Young Egypt Society, Nasser was schooled in pan-Arab nationalism, Islamism, socialism, anti-Semitism, xenophobia, and fascism. These values of the Young Egypt Society, combined with the clandestine jihadism he practiced in the Secret Apparatus, ultimately became his blueprint when he revolted against Egypt's modernized society under the guise of fighting British occupation. Nasser could have preserved the nation's civilization and heritage when the British evacuated Egypt, but his war against Egypt's modernized and cosmopolitan society was fiercer than his war against the British occupation, which he used as a convenient excuse to strip the country of its freedoms.

Nasser's brother, Adil Abdel Nasser, and Egyptian intellectual and screenwriter Wahid Hamid both said that Nasser was once a member of the Egyptian Communist Party, and his alias at the party was "Maurice."[2] While Nasser was not intellectually sophisticated like other chameleons in history, such as Nasir ad-Din at-Tusi, Nader Shah, and Afghani, Nasser's eloquence served him during his Islamist and leftist propagandistic endeavors.

2 Al-Fagr News (Cairo), June 13, 2017; *Al-Youm as-Sabi'* (Cairo), June 29, 2017.

Nasser had pledged allegiance to Sendi when he was in charge of the Secret Apparatus' civilian wing. This positioned Nasser and Brotherhood Officers as subordinates to the civilian leadership—but Nasser had other plans.

After Banna's assassination, the government arrested additional Brotherhood operatives and among them was the head of the Brotherhood Officers, Mahmoud Labib. The power vacuum allowed Nasser to step in. Brotherhood operative Muhammad Adawi stated in his memoir that following Labib's arrest, "Nasser proposed to the Brotherhood the idea of changing the name of their division to the Free Officers" instead of the Brotherhood Officers because "the affiliation with the Brotherhood will bring unwarranted attention, prosecution, and [legal] pursuits against them."[3] Nasser also suggested they temporarily relax the Brotherhood Officers requirement of Islamic fundamentalism when joining the apparatus until the Brotherhood perpetrated a coup d'état, and could later "cleanse" their ranks of moderate Muslims after they seized power.[4]

A few Brotherhood Officers refused, but Nasser's plan proceeded. This may have constituted the first time a Muslim Brotherhood body operated under a different banner.

On October 8, 1951, Egyptian Prime Minister Nahhas Pasha, who had grown closer to Islamists, announced the government unilaterally had abrogated the 1936 Anglo-Egyptian Treaty. This was the treaty that resulted in the evacuation of British troops from all of Egypt, except from the Suez Canal. It also compelled the government to augment the army with recruits from all classes of society and allowed Nasser and many of his cabal to serve in the military. The Anglo-Egyptian Treaty was scheduled to expire in 1956, which supposedly would have ended the British government's control over the Suez Canal Company, but the Muslim Brotherhood couldn't afford to wait

3 Muhammad Adawi, *Haqa'iq wa Asrar*, The Official Muslim Brotherhood Encyclopedia, https://ikhwanwiki.com/, accessed April 22, 2021.

4 Ibid.

until the British troops fully evacuated Egypt in 1956. They would lose their justification for carrying out a putsch and seizing power.

On July 23, 1952, Muslim Brotherhood Officers perpetrated a coup d'état under the banner of the Free Officers and overthrew the Egyptian monarchy, its capitalist economic system, and its constitution.

Generally, after a coup d'état, the actual perpetrators do not immediately seize power. It is often preferable to install a puppet ruler for various reasons, such as to absorb the first waves of challenges, shocks, reactions, and to take blame for the chaos that ensues before the actual culprit emerges. The member on which both the Secret Apparatus' civilian and military leadership agreed upon was Brotherhood Officer Muhammad Naguib.[5]

On June 18, 1953, the monarchy was officially abolished, and the Muslim Brotherhood installed Naguib as president of the new republic. According to Anwar al-Sadat, the news that Naguib was chosen to become "the leader of the people" was delivered to him in his house by Nasser, before Naguib was even aware of the putsch.[6] Sadat frequently portrayed Naguib as a gullible man who was completely oblivious to what was happening around him.[7] Naguib was chosen for important reasons. He was an ideologue and a believer in the Brotherhood's mission, and he was also in the army. Naguib was famous for advocating for the transfer of power from the coup's Revolutionary Command Council to "civilians."

Both historically and in modern times, when a member of the Muslim Brotherhood discusses "civilians" in a political contest, he is almost certainly not talking about citizens outside the military institution, but they use the term in reference to the Secret Apparatus' civilian wing or the public Brotherhood organization. Naguib frequently met with Brotherhood leaders. In his memoir, he stated that

5 Husain Hamouda, *Asrar Harakat ad-Dubat al-Ahrar wa'l-wa'l-wa'l-Ikhwan al-Muslimin.*.
6 Anwar Al-Sadat, *Kisat al-Thawra* (Cairo: Dar al-Hilal, 2015), 60–1.
7 Ibid., 58.

the Muslim Brotherhood's civilian leadership believed the putsch was perpetrated "on their behalf."[8]

Immediately, the Brotherhood Officers began implementing fascistic socialist policies, and they followed the classic path of tyranny, which traditionally takes place in three main stages (1) disarming citizens and outlawing the ownership of all kinds of firearms; (2) prohibiting freedom of speech, press, and assembly; and (3) abolishing most property rights through government seizure of lands, business, and countless private dwellings, and/or through enforcing high taxation. As the country turned into a prison, Nasser released all Muslim Brotherhood terrorists from prison.

Under Naguib's presidency, Nasser frequently consulted the Brotherhood's Guidance Bureau when forming the new government, and most of his ministers were Brotherhood leaders.[9] Nasser was uncomfortable with Naguib's allegiance to the civilian wing of the Secret Apparatus, and he forced him to resign on February 25, 1954. Two days later, he reinstated him after the Brotherhood rioted on Naguib's behalf.[10]

On November 14, 1954 Nasser placed Naguib under house arrest, which did not end until 1970. Brotherhood Officers started to consolidate their power through terror, and Nasser's prisons were filled with classic liberals, secularists, capitalists, communists, artists, aristocrats, and human rights activists. The Officers' main war was with their ideological enemies, the secularist and capitalists of the Free Constitutionalists Party.

On March 29, 1954, the new revolutionary jihadists marched in the streets of Cairo protesting against the country's liberty, rule of law, modernity, civility, peaceful transition of power as well as rational and science-based education. They chanted, "Down with the Constitution,

---

8 Muhammad Naguib, *Kuntu Ra'isan,* 166–7.

9 Ibid., 167.

10 Ahmad Salama, "Muhammad Naguib wa-Ilaqatahu bil-Ikhwan al-Muslimin," The Official Muslim Brotherhood Encyclopedia, https://ikhwanwiki.com/, accessed April 20, 2021.

Down with Freedom, Down with Democracy, and Down with the Educated." These slogans were broadcast on the radio at the time.[11]

The Brotherhood Officers and their civilian counterparts were dismayed by Egyptian education that taught children logic and critical thinking, evidence-based decision making, philosophy, science, evolution, different languages, and history.

While the Brotherhood was rioting to end all forms of civilization in the country, Egyptian classic liberals desperately attempted to offer the Officers an alternative. In 1955, Friedrich August von Hayek was invited to speak at the fifty-year anniversary of Banque Misr, which was originally known as Crédit Foncier Égyptien. At the bank, Hayek delivered four speeches entitled "The Political Ideal of the Rule of Law," which later inspired his book, *The Constitution of Liberty*. Nasser responded to Banque Misr's invitation to Hayek and his speech by nationalizing the bank.

Egyptian education at the time didn't equip the Brotherhood and their ilk to recruit from educated segments of society. Nasser wanted a type of education that produced slaves or tyrants, and he chose Brotherhood Officer Kamal ad-Din Husain (1921–1999) for the job. Husain became Minister of Education from 1954 to 1959. His credentials were limited to being an avid believer in the Muslim Brotherhood's mission, and he was later a successful propagandist for terror theologian Sayyid Qutb. He successfully publicized the Muslim Brotherhood values in the Egyptian army and recruited officers to join the group. From the mid-1950s, Husain was an ardent devotee of Qutb, and once said that he "believes in everything Sayyid Qutb said in his book, *Milestones*."[12] Nasser banned educated men from enrolling in the military until 1956.[13]

11 "Shahid Ala al-Asr – Murad Ghalib – al-Halaqa al-Thania," YouTube.com, December 28, 2008.

12 Ahmad Salama, "Kamal ad-Din Husain wa Ilaqatahu bil-Ikhwan al-Muslimin," The Official Muslim Brotherhood Encyclopedia, https://ikhwanwiki.com/, accessed May 28, 2021.

13 NBC News (New York), February 6, 2009.

Nasser took advantage of Nazis fleeing the Nuremberg trials, and he hired Nazi war criminals to aid in the ideological subversion of Egypt. Those criminals included Paul Joseph Goebbels's advisors.[14] One of those advisors, Dr. Johann von Leers, also known as Omar Amin, was Goebbels's specialist on the "Jewish question." Another was Alfred Zingler, also known as Mahmoud Saleh, the director of the anti-Semitic Institute for the Study of Zionism, founded in Cairo in 1955.

Egypt continued to be a Nazi haven until the death of the last known Nazi resident in Egypt, Aribert Heim, in 1992. Heim was also known as "Dr. Death" and "the Butcher of Mauthausen." He killed and tortured inmates by various methods, including injecting toxins into the hearts of his victims. Heim committed his crimes in Mauthausen concentration camp. He fled to Egypt in 1963, and his name was on a 1967 list of twenty-six former Nazis believed to be hiding in Egypt at that time.[15] Heim converted to Islam and called himself Tarek Farid Husain. In 2009, Nazi hunters exposed that Egypt had harbored Heim until his death in 1992. In 2012, a court in Baden-Baden confirmed that Heim had died in Egypt in 1992.

Nazi war criminals helped Nasser and the Muslim Brotherhood dismantle the Egyptian education system and ideologically subvert the country. This mission was one of the most successful Brotherhood operations, and the current government of President Abdel Fattah al-Sisi is still struggling to reverse the damage those Brotherhood policies inflicted on the country.

14 Bat Ye⊠or, *Eurabia* (New Jersey: Fairleigh Dickinson University Press, 2005), 42.
15 "Hasrian: Al-Fariq Awal Muhammad Fawzi Shahid ala al-Asr," YouTube.com, November 30, 2016.

THE MUSLIM BROTHERHOOD'S SECOND FOUNDING

Incorrect historic narratives can have dire consequences on modern policy. Falsifying history, whether out of ignorance or for ideological, political, or financial reasons, has a direct impact on reality. The following example demonstrates how a single historic fact has been misrepresented by an expert in the United States who propagated false historic narratives that serve to advance the Brotherhood. In 2012, Middle East expert Steven A. Cook wrote an article titled "Debunking Three Myths About the Muslim Brotherhood," in which he said:

> Observers often point to the fact that Sayyid Qutb and Ayman Zawahiri were Muslim Brothers to confirm the group's violent tendencies. In the case of Zawahiri, he had a brief flirtation with the Brothers in his teens, though it is unclear whether he was actually a member of the organization. Zawahiri was arrested in 1966 (at the age of 15) for being a Brother, but it is more likely that he was part of a vanguard that split from the mainstream Brotherhood in the late 1950s and 1960s. This vanguard was a radical faction that followed Sayyid Qutb—a Brother and an intellectual architect of jihadism—and whose members wanted to engage in a direct confrontation with Nasser and the Egyptian state. Although the Brotherhood's Supreme Guide, Hassan al Hudaybi, tolerated the vanguard for a time, the two factions ultimately fell out over doctrinal issues as well as over al Hudaybi's desire to seek an accommodation with the leaders of the Egyptian regime.[16]

16 Steven A. Cook, "Debunking Three Myths About the Muslim Brotherhood," *The Atlantic*, June 28, 2012.

This section of Cook's argument is refuted by Muslim Brotherhood members' own words. It is true there was a split within the Muslim Brotherhood, but it was between the Secret Apparatus' civilian and military wings over power—not ideology.

Soon after the 1952 coup d'état, Muslim Brotherhood Guide Hassan al-Hudaybi understood that Nasser would not transfer power to the group's civilian wing. Nasser demanded that Hudaybi fully incorporate the Secret Apparatus into his new regime's security structures. Hudaybi declined Nasser's demand and sacked his loyalists from its helm, including Nasser's friend and head of the civilian apparatus, al-Sendi.[17]

In September 1954, Hudaybi again rebuffed Nasser's demand to dissolve the apparatus and refused to refrain from publicly criticizing his policies.[18] While Hudaybi was claiming he had dissolved the Secret Apparatus, he was actually restructuring it with his loyalists who included Sayyid Qutb.

According to the head of the Police Units Division in the Secret Apparatus, Salah Shadi, Hudaybi was "persuaded by Sayyid Fayez to reform the apparatus by getting rid of its leaders who are known to the government." Shadi added that this needed to be done, "or the secret order would lose its value and become public."[19] Shadi also confirmed that Hudaybi had faked the apparatus' death by "announcing that this order no longer exists in the organization."[20] This constituted the split within the Muslim Brotherhood and planted the seed of what would later become known in the group as the *Second Founding*.

After Hudaybi removed Nasser's supporters, he established the Brotherhood militia, known as *Tanzim 54* (the Group or Order of 1954). Hudaybi assigned jihadist Yusuf Tal'at, also known as, "the

17 Muhammad Hamid Abu al-Nasr, The Official Muslim Brotherhood Encyclopedia, "Haqiqat al-Khilaf baina al-Ikhwan al-Muslimin wa-Abdel Nasser," https://ikhwanwiki.com/, accessed May 28, 2021; "Tharwat Kherbawy: Abdel Hakim Amer lahu Dawr fi Kashf Jarimat Muhawalat Ightial Gamal Abdel Nasser," YouTube.com, January 22, 2019.

18 Abu al-Nasr, "Haqiqat al-Khilaf baina al-Ikhwan al-Muslimin wa-Abdel Nasser."

19 Salah Shadi, *Safahat min At-Tarikh*, 79.

20 Ibid.

desert lion" and "the lover of martyrdom," as the new head of the Secret Apparatus.[21]

Following the restructuring of the apparatus, Sayyid Fayez was murdered on November 20, 1953, with his nine-year-old brother, when someone delivered a dynamite bomb to his house. While no one was officially charged with the murder, it is widely accepted within the Muslim Brotherhood that Sendi was behind it.

Hudaybi formed his new militia based on the vision of Sayyid Qutb. In 2003, Muslim Brotherhood operative and Sayyid Qutb biographer Muhammad Tawfiq Barakat mentioned in his book that Hudaybi famously said about Qutb, "The author of *In the Shade of the Qur'an* speaks truths that [shall] not be doubted."[22] Barakat said Hudaybi "deeply trusted" Qutb that he assigned him the "leadership of The Propagation of the Message Section," and he became the editor of "the Muslim Brotherhood magazine."[23]

Steven A. Cook's claim that Hudaybi "tolerated" Qutb's wing is inaccurate. Both Hudaybi and the current Muslim Brotherhood group are *the* Qutb vanguard. Cook's so-called division over "doctrinal issues" is also another one of his incorrect claims. The fact is, Hudaybi handed Qutb control of the group's "doctrinal issues" when he gave him full control of the Brotherhood's propaganda division and newspaper. The Muslim Brotherhood still requires its members to read Qutb's literature as a part of their ideological training, and the following evidence will demonstrate that Hudaybi officially assigned Qutb to the leadership of the Secret Apparatus.

Hudaybi also restructured the Brotherhood's public organization and installed his supporters in the Guidance Bureau. Some Middle East experts whitewash the Muslim Brotherhood's history surrounding the assassination attempt of then-Prime Minister Gamal Abdel Nasser.

21 The Official Muslim Brotherhood Encyclopedia, "Yusuf Tal'at Assad as-Sahara' w-Ashiq ash-Shahad," https://ikhwanwiki.com/, accessed May 29, 2021.

22 Muhammad Tawfiq Barakat, *Al-Jouz' al-Thani: Sayyid Qutb wa Qiadatahu lil Tanzim,* https://ikhwanwiki.com/, accessed May 29, 2021.

23 Ibid.

Cook said, "There is, of course, the allegation that the Brothers were behind the attempted hit on Gamal Abdel Nasser in October 1954, but there continue to be questions whether the would-be assassin, Mahmoud Abdel Latif—who was a member of the Brotherhood—was working on behalf of the Islamists or another group intended to discredit the Brotherhood."[24]

Cook's conspiracy theory is debunked by Muslim Brotherhood members. According to Secret Apparatus leader Ali Ashmawi, members of the clandestine order were instructed in October 1954 to "avoid official Muslim Brotherhood gatherings." Their militants were told by one of their leaders, Kamal as-Sananiri (1918–1981) that their conflict with Nasser rose to the degree of "holy jihad" and they were ordered to stay in contact with him as the "orders will be issued at any moment" to assassinate Nasser.[25] Ashmawi added that they were ready and well trained for "battle assembly," which is a military training for individual and unit readiness. In the event of mobilization of Secret Apparatus units, they should be prepared to deployment within fifteen minutes.[26] On October 26, 1954, Muslim Brotherhood operative Mahmoud Abdul Latif fired eight shots at Nasser while he was giving a speech in Alexandria.

The Brotherhood's argument about Nasser was not about whether they should kill him, but when. Ashmawi dismissed another conspiracy theory that posited Nasser could have faked the incident by saying he knew Nasser, and he "wasn't going to gamble with his own life," in such a manner.[27]

Secret Apparatus leader Hindawi Dwidar gave Latif the hasty order to assassinate Nasser. According to Ashamawi, Latif was a well-trained soldier, but he was a "simpleton who only followed orders."[28]

24 Cook, "Debunking Three Myths About the Muslim Brotherhood," *The Atlantic*, June 28, 2012.
25 Ali Ashmawi, *At-Tarikh as-Sirri,* 114.
26 Ibid.
27 Ibid., 116.
28 Ibid.

After the attempt to assassinate Nasser, many members of the Muslim Brotherhood were arrested, including Qutb and Hudaybi. While officially and publicly the second founding of the Muslim Brotherhood was launched by Hudaybi in 1973, its first seed began when he gave Qutb control of the ideological wing of the group and leadership of the Secret Apparatus.

Nasser's assassination attempt is known in Egyptian history as *hadith al-Manshiyya* (the Manshiyya incident) in reference to the name of the square in Alexandria where Nasser gave his speech. The Manshiyya incident constituted the Muslim Brotherhood's first crisis. It is always described as a clash between the Muslim Brotherhood and Nasser's socialist regime, but a more accurate description would portray it as a conflict between the military and civilian wings of the Secret Apparatus.

The assassination attempt did not stop Nasser from believing in the group's mission. Combined with his lust for power, Nasser appears to have believed he was the one to fulfill Banna's true vision, and not the civilian clique. This is confirmed by the fact that he continued to stack his regime with members of the Muslim Brotherhood. Nasser even assigned the former German-Ottoman jihad project spy Sheikh Khidr to the leadership of al-Azhar University in Cairo, in September 1952. Khidr lasted in that position for only two years, and he resigned after Nasser asked him to condemn the Muslim Brotherhood following his assassination attempt.

On February 12, 1954, a few months before the Manshiyya incident, Nasser visited Banna's grave with Muhammad Naguib, Anwar al-Sadat, and Banna's brother, Abdul Rahman. In front of Banna's grave, Nasser and his companions renewed their pledge of allegiance to Banna. Nasser said, "As God is my witness, I will uphold his values and wage a jihad on their behalf."[29]

29 *Tahrir Magazine* (Cairo), February 16, 1954; Al-Arabiya (Dubai), December 4, 2008.

In 1955, several Muslim Brotherhood leaders departed Egypt to Europe and elsewhere in the Middle East, where they officially established the International Apparatus. The Secret Apparatus remained without formal leadership from late 1954 until Hudaybi's release from prison a year later. In 1957, Hudaybi assigned Ali Ashmawi the leadership of the apparatus.[30]

According to Qutb's student and lifelong member of the Secret Apparatus Ahmad Abdul Majid (1933–2012), during the summer of 1964, he and other members of the apparatus met with Qutb and asked him to officially become emir of the Secret Apparatus. Majid stated that Qutb agreed under two conditions. First, he demanded information on how each member of the apparatus was to be evaluated and monitored, especially since they were scattered across different cities. Second, Qutb required Hudaybi to grant him permission before he accepted the role as head of the Secret Apparatus. Qutb said, "I do not do anything without his guidance, and I have to be granted his permission before I start working with you."[31] Majid said that these were the exact words uttered by Qutb, and he added that Qutb provided Hudaybi with a memorandum for his plans and he was granted the Guide's approval.[32]

Under Qutb's leadership, the Secret Apparatus founded *Tanzim 1965*. They tasked it with executing terrorist attacks, including assassinating then-President Gamal Abdel Nasser.

Qutb's official leadership of the apparatus was terminated with his arrest on August 9, 1965, and he was executed on August 29, 1966.[33] Qutb remains the spiritual leader of the Muslim Brotherhood, a fact

30 Ahmad Abdul Majid, *Al-Ikhwan wa Abdel al-Nasser al-Kissa al-Kamila li Tanzim 1965*, The Official Muslim Brotherhood Encyclopedia, https://ikhwanwiki.com/, accessed May 10, 2021.

31 Majid, *Al-Ikhwan wa Abdel al-Nasser al-Kissa al-Kamila li Tanzim 1965*.

32 Ibid.

33 Ahmad Abdul Majid, *Al-Ikhwan wa Abdel al-Nasser al-Kissa al-Kamila li Tanzim 1965*, The Official Muslim Brotherhood Encyclopedia, IkhwanWiki.com, accessed May 10, 2021.

not known by those who rely on Islamist and Muslim Brotherhood disinformation for their opinions and analysis. Qutb, or the "emir of terror" as he is known in Egypt, is the main figure behind the modern Muslim Brotherhood.

MUSLIM BROTHERHOOD SECRET AND PUBLIC GUIDES FROM 1973–2013

Since 1976, the Muslim Brotherhood's de facto ruler has been the head of the Secret Apparatus, and the General Guide position has been relinquished to a retired jihadist. This formula remains today. Prior to officially becoming the group's General Guide, Hassan al-Hudaybi operated as the Secret Guide for six months before he publicly assumed the position.[34] Under Hudaybi's leadership, the Brotherhood decentralized the Secret Apparatus' operations and leadership. Hudaybi was more cognizant than Banna of the danger the apparatus poised to him, and he never fully yielded its leadership to one person. Hudaybi ran simultaneous terrorist groups under ostensibly different banners.

While standard practice since the group's inception, according to Kherbawy, the term "Secret Guide" appeared for the first time in the public apparatus in 1973. Kherbawy said during his interview with the author:

> After Hudaybi's death five leaders of the Secret Apparatus met. They were Mustafa Mashhour, Helmi Abdul Mejid, Husni Abdul Baqi, Ahmad Hasanain, and Ahmad Almalt. They decided that Helmi Abdul Mejid (1919–2013) would become the Secret Guide because of his professional position as vice president of the [government-owned company] *al-Muqaweloun*

34 "Al-Mustashar Hassan al-Hudaybi al-Murshid al-Thani lil Ikhwan al-Muslim," The Official Muslim Brotherhood Encyclopedia, https://ikhwanwiki.com/, accessed May 1, 2021.

> *al-Arab* [The Arab Contractors]. Mejid's position allowed him close access to policy makers. He accepted to be the head of the group under the condition of secrecy.

Mejid was also one of the founders of Faisal Islamic Bank in Egypt, which was investigated in the 1990s in the US for possible terror financing links. Kherbawy added that the idea of having a single clandestine leader caused many issues for the group and compelled them to revert to the earlier model of having both.

While the organization has two leaders today, the General Guide became primarily a public relations position, and the actual decision-making remains mostly in the hands of the Secret Guide. This has been the standard practice since the Muslim Brotherhood's third General Guide, Omar al-Tilmisani (1904–1986). When Tilmisani assumed his position in 1973, he was initially called the "Public Spokesman," but after the Muslim Brotherhood was widely criticized by its members for their failed attempt at concealment, they gave Tilmisani the title "General Guide" in 1976.

It's commonly and falsely stated that during the leadership of Tilmisani, the Secret Apparatus was dismantled. While some experts do believe that Tilmisani was genuine in his intention to dismantle the apparatus, it's hard to believe that he was gullible enough to assume that giving leadership positions to operatives from Qutb's 1965 militia wasn't the equivalent to allowing them to resume the terror apparatus, for which they repeatedly expressed support. Under Tilmisani's leadership, they restructured the Secret Apparatus to guarantee more violence and secrecy.

Mustafa Mashhour was the Muslim Brotherhood's head of the Secret Apparatus under Tilmisani and also the de facto head of the public organization.[35] Secret Apparatus member and former member

35 Hussam Tamam, *Tahawulat al-Ikhwan al-Muslimin* (Cairo: Maktabat Madbuli, 2010), 33.

of the Consultative Assembly as-Sayyid Abdul Sattar al-Miliji, also known as As-Sayyid Abdul Sattar, swore allegiance to Mashhour in 1975. Sattar said many Brotherhood jihadists involved in Qutb's 1965 militia—especially Mustafa Mashhour and Ahmad Hassanain—proposed the idea "of reestablishing the Secret Apparatus with the notion that its head acts as the actual Guide, with the presence of a sham Guide to divert the attention of intelligence agencies."[36] Some protested his suggestion, but Mashhour went forward with his plan.

While Tilmisani's public operation of the Brotherhood was practically government-sponsored and Tilimisani was a close friend of Sadat,[37] this only encouraged and expanded the group's clandestine branch. Sattar accurately described Mashhour, saying he was the man who turned secrecy into "a tool, an aim, a philosophy, and a behavior."[38]

After President Gamal Abdel Nasser's death on September 28, 1970, his vice president and fellow Brotherhood Officer Anwar al-Sadat succeeded him on October 15, 1970. In 1971, Sadat released all Brotherhood jihadists from prison and began to call himself *al-ra'is al-mu'min* (the believer president). During the same year, he introduced Shari'a law to the Egyptian constitution. The second article of the constitution Sadat introduced was "Islam is the religion of the state, Arabic is its official language, and the principles of Islamic Shari'a are a principal source of legislation."

In 1979, Sadat turned the Muslim Brotherhood into a parliamentary parastatal opposition. This resulted in turning Egypt into a constitutional theocracy by amending the second article for Shari'a to become *the* principal source of legislation instead of *a* principal source.

Transforming the Muslim Brotherhood into a parliamentary parastatal opposition created the common Western mistake of tying elec-

36 As-Sayyid Abdul Sattar, *Tajrubati ma' al-Ikhwan min ad-d'wa ila at-Tanzim as-Sirri,* The Official Muslim Brotherhood Encyclopedia, https://ikhwanwiki.com/, accessed June 9, 2021.

37 Ibid.

38 Ibid.

tion charades with public opinion under dictatorships. From 1952 until 2013, most state organs were decorative structures to give the country a superficially modern guise.

In 1976 Sadat installed Secret Apparatus operative and al-Azhar University sheikh Salah Abu Isma'il (1927–1990) in the parliament. Isma'il was once arrested for his role in the Brotherhood's assassination attempt of Gamal Abdel Nasser.[39] He resumed his work within the Secret Apparatus and was involved with several Brotherhood operated militias, such as the Egyptian Islamic Jihad. Isma'il is widely credited as the major player in turning Egypt into a constitutional theocracy after Sadat gave him a parliamentary position.[40] He is also the father of Muslim Brotherhood and al-Qaeda propagandist Hazem Salah Abu Isma'il, who ran for president in Egypt in 2012.

Under both Sadat and Tilmisani, the relationship between the government and the Muslim Brotherhood changed into one of cooperation that went as far as collaborative governance. Contrary to common narratives, this remained the defining relationship between the Muslim Brotherhood and the Egyptian government until 2013.

After Tilmisani's death in 1986, Mashhour and his Secret Apparatus cabal declared him the next General Guide of the Brotherhood. But per the General Apparatus' bylaws, the position had to be filled by the oldest member of the Guidance Bureau. To avoid an internal rift within the organization, Mashhour decided to abide by the rules. He continued to be the head of the Secret Apparatus and allowed Muhammad Hamid Abu al-Nasr (1913–1996) to become the General Guide.[41]

Several Brotherhood leaders, including Tharwat al-Kherbawy and As-Sayyid Abdul Sattar, said al-Nasr was "intellectually limited" and suffered from age-related health issues when he took the position.[42]

39 Muhammad al-Majzub, *Ulama' wa-Mufakirun Ariftahum* (Riyadh: Dar ash-Sherouk, 1992) 2: 144.

40 SWI Swissinfo (Switzerland), October 20, 2005.

41 As-Sayyid Abdul Sattar, Tajrubati ma' al-Ikhwan min ad-d'wa ila at-Tanzim as-Sirri, The Official Muslim Brotherhood Encyclopedia, https://ikhwanwiki.com/, accessed June 9, 2021.

42 Ibid.

From 1973 to 1996, Mashhour headed the Secret Apparatus and was the Brotherhood's Secret Guide until he officially became the group's fifth General Guide following Nasr's death on January 20, 1996. Mashhour elevated specific operatives to key leadership positions, many of whom eventually would become the most influential leaders of the Brotherhood across the world. These included Khairat al-Shater, Muhammad Morsi, Mahmoud Ezzat, and Muhammad Badie.[43]

Between the late 1960s and the early 1970s, Khairat al-Shater was recruited to join the Muslim Brotherhood by two operatives in the 1965 militia, Sabri Arafa and Muhammad al-Adawi.[44] After Anwar al-Sadat's assassination on October 6, 1981, Shater and several Brotherhood members fled to Arab and European countries. Shater escaped to Saudi Arabia and headed to Europe to study but decided to work in other trades instead. This launched Shater's shady and mysterious career in which he eventually became the Muslim Brotherhood's financial facilitator.

Shater is often described as a Brotherhood strategist, but his role was mainly as human resources director for the group's International Apparatus. Shater's forte was his ability to assign operatives roles based on their strengths. He was also responsible for the International Apparatus' propaganda training unit until his arrest on July 5, 2013. He was also the head of the Muslim Sisterhood section in the International Apparatus. Shater assigned the leadership of the section to his wife, Azza Ahmad Tawfiq, and his daughter, Aisha, after he was arrested.[45]

Muhammad Morsi (1951–2019) was probably recruited to join the Muslim Brotherhood during his compulsory draft in the Egyptian army from 1975–1976. He joined the Brotherhood immediately upon completion of his military service. Mosri's consistent elevation in leadership positions within the Brotherhood reveal he was inten-

43 Kherbawy, *Sir al-Ma'bad*, 99.
44 Al-Masry al-Youm (Cairo), May 8, 2012.
45 Al-Wafd (Cairo), February 2, 2020.

tionally chosen to fulfill specific roles where he operated more as a faithful soldier than as a leader.

Morsi suffered all his life from epilepsy, which was poorly treated in Egypt's rural Sharqiya governorate. In 2012, the official website of the Muslim Brotherhood stated that Morsi had received a temporal lobectomy surgery at a hospital in Sharqiya, but they later deleted the article from their website and said Morsi's 2008 surgery was to remove a benign brain tumor. It is not clear exactly when Morsi received his lobectomy surgery, but during his presidency he was mentally impaired to a noticeable degree. Morsi hardly spoke English, yet the Egyptian government granted him a scholarship to study in the United States. He received a PhD in materials science from the University of Southern California in 1982. This begs the question of how and why Morsi received a PhD in the United States while suffering from mental impairment and barely speaking English. In 2012, Morsi became the first civilian Brotherhood operative to be installed as president.

Another of Mashhour's prominent operatives was one of the most powerful men in the Secret Apparatus. Born in 1944, Mahmoud Ezzat joined the Muslim Brotherhood in 1962, and he was an operative in Qutb's Militia of 1965. He was imprisoned with Qutb, then released in 1974. In 1975, he completed his medical studies and worked as a professor at the University of Sana'a in Yemen in 1981, a year after he became a member of the Brotherhood's Guidance Bureau. Some Muslim Brotherhood sources state that Ezzat received a PhD from a British University in the early 1980s.[46] This pattern is similar to Morsi's. While Ezzat is an intelligent man, he hardly spoke English. This could have been part of their mission when Brotherhood was openly recruiting and fundraising for al-Qaeda with the blessing of Middle Eastern, Arab, American, and European governments.

46 Al-Araby (London), August 29, 2020.

Mashhour also selected Muhammad Badie to work in the Secret Apparatus. Born in 1943, Badie joined the group when he was a teenager and was recruited to join *Tanzim 1965*. Badie received his degree in veterinary medicine from Cairo University in 1965. He continued to operate inside the Brotherhood's clandestine apparatus until he became the group's eighth General Guide in 2010.

Apart from Ezzat and Badie, several influential Brotherhood operatives came out of Qutb's *Tanzim 1965*, such as Ibrahim Munir, the current Acting General Guide of the Egyptian Muslim Brotherhood and the Secretary General of the International Apparatus. These men were recruited by Qutb's close affiliate, Sheikh Abdul Fattah Isma'il, who was executed with Qutb in 1966.[47]

Mashhour was the most dangerous man in the Muslim Brotherhood's history due to his activities in franchising the Brotherhood terrorism model. When he became the General Guide, he relinquished his position as head of the Secret Apparatus to another Brotherhood leader, Hassan al-Hudaybi's son, Ma'mun al-Hudaybi (1921–2004), who became head of the Secret Apparatus and the Secret Guide. As-Sayyid Abdul Sattar said that the same cycle had been "repeated and when Ma'mun al-Hudaybi became [Mashhour's] deputy he also became the de facto leader."[48] In 1992, Ma'mun al-Hudaybi famously said, "we are proud of the Secret Apparatus and it brings us closer to God."[49]

After Mashhour died in 2002, Ma'mun al-Hudaybi became the sixth General Guide until he died two years later. As soon as he became the official leader, he severed his role as the Secret Guide. After al-Qaeda's September 11, 2001, terrorist attack, the Secret Apparatus dynam-

47 Al-Masry Al-Youm (Cairo), February 11, 2010.
48 As-Sayyid Abdul Sattar, Tajrubati ma' al-Ikhwan min ad-d'wa ila at-Tanzim as-Sirri, The Official Muslim Brotherhood Encyclopedia, https://ikhwanwiki.com/, accessed June 9, 2021.
49 Al-Bawaba News (Cairo), December 3, 2016.

ics changed, and the pattern of succession of the Secret Apparatus' leadership was modified to add another level of secrecy.

In January 2004, Secret Apparatus operative and Qutb's associate Muhammad Mahdi Akef became the General Guide of the Muslim Brotherhood. Akef's seniority and familiar face helped the Brotherhood ease national and international concerns about the group. Akef's leadership was similar to Muhammad Hamid Abu al-Nasr's. Both men struggled with age-related illnesses, and it allowed the Secret Apparatus to become more powerful and more mainstream within the group. During a conversation with Kherbawy, he said:

> After Mashhour's death in 2002, Khairat al-Shater and Mahmoud Ezzat started to reestablish the Secret Apparatus with the purpose of making it mainstream within the organization. They assigned Muhammad Kamal the leadership of this apparatus under the direct supervision of Ezzat.

While Akef was the General Guide, Mahmoud Ezzat was the leader of the Secret Apparatus and true head of the Muslim Brotherhood.[50] Muhammad Kamal (1955–2016) was a member of the Guidance Bureau and one of the most powerful leaders of the Secret Apparatus.

Kherbawy said Kamal was publicly scrutinized for the first time after pictures and videos of al-Azhar militia martial training were leaked to the press in 2006. In 2010, the Brotherhood performed a political stunt perhaps intended to modify the group's public image by faking democracy. They decided to elect the General Guide as opposed to assigning him the job based on age and seniority. This resulted in the assignment of retired jihadist Muhammad Badie as the eighth General Guide of the group, in January 2010. While the Secret Apparatus was led by Ezzat and Kamal, Shater was the actual leader of the public General Apparatus and the Egyptian branch of

---

50 "Tharwat al-Kherbawy Daif Tony Khalifah Sirri Jidan," YouTube.com, April 19, 2014.

the International Apparatus until the Egyptian revolution against the Muslim Brotherhood in 2013.

CHAPTER EIGHT

BLOOD SACRIFICE

The Muslim Brotherhood's Coup d'État of 2011 and their Third Founding

"The ummah which yearns to live [eternally] has to all die because it is yet to sacrifice its blood for the hereafter."

—Hassan al-Banna[1]

FROM 1952 TO 2012, EACH of Egypt's transitions of power resulted from a coup d'état by officers belonging to the Muslim Brotherhood. Presidents Muhammad Naguib, Gamal Abdel Nasser, President Anwar al-Sadat, Muhammad Morsi, and even President Hosni Mubarak all came out of the Muslim Brotherhood.

Mubarak's affiliation with the Brotherhood is supported by individuals both inside and outside of the group. In 2018, Tharwat al-Kherbawy revealed that Mubarak joined the Brotherhood when he was in high school, prior to joining the Military Academy in 1944.[2] Kherbawy added that Mubarak was not a leader in his cell, but he did become a member and even received a membership card in the organization's division in Kafr Masilha village. At the time, the Brotherhood

1 Al-Ikhwan al-Muslimin daily newspaper (Cairo), May 21, 1948; "Hadith Iza'i Nader l'al-Imam al-Banna," The Official Muslim Brotherhood Encyclopedia, https://ikhwanwiki.com/, accessed June 22, 2021.

2 Al-Bashayer (Cairo), May 4, 2018.

issued membership cards. Kherbawy also stated that Mubarak didn't go far in the organization and didn't succeed in their selection criteria.[3]

In 2019, a member of an overt al-Azhar coalition group for the Brotherhood, Imam Farouk Musahil, said on their official Facebook page, "Mubarak's father sent him to his uncle Mr. Abdul Aziz, who was the head of the Department of Education in al-Minufiyyah governorate and a member of the Muslim Brotherhood's Guidance Bureau. Mubarak's father told Abdul Aziz that he wishes to enlist his son in the Brotherhood."[4]

While Musahil and Kherbawy both agree that Mubarak's family attempted to enroll him in the group, Musahil said that the Brotherhood refused to accept Mubarak because he was "dumb." It is highly unlikely this occurred, as the Brotherhood conscripted both educated and uneducated teenagers, regardless of their educational or intellectual levels. While the relationship between Mubarak and the Muslim Brotherhood was ambiguous when he was a teenager, it became well-defined when he became the president of Egypt on October 14, 1981.

THE MUSLIM BROTHERHOOD'S PARASTATAL OPPOSITION

The common narrative in the West is that the Brotherhood was an opposition group under Mubarak's regime, but it was actually government-sponsored fake opposition. While Brotherhood leaders feigned victimhood during their communications with Westerners, the government was subsidizing their businesses across Egypt. The Salafi movement received its orders from Mubarak's State Security Investigations Service, and Islamists took control of almost all state-

3 Ibid.

4 Rabitat Ulama wa-Du'at Europe did al-Inqilab fi Misr, "L'al-Tarikh Farouk Musahil," Facebook, October 31, 2019, www.Facebook.com/Amuac1/posts/736441066832080/.

run educational institutions. The Brotherhood also controlled Egypt's theocratic legislative branch at al-Azhar University as well as the vast majority of professional unions.

Mubarak's regime's arrangement with the Muslim Brotherhood was similar to the Saudi-Wahhabi pact. In 1744, Muhammad ibn Abdul Wahhab fled from Medina to al-Diriyya, where he requested protection from Muhammad bin Saud al-Muqrin. They charted a theocratic pact and swore an oath to uphold Wahhab's religious edict, when Wahhab said, "You are the settlement's chief and wise man. I want you to grant me an oath that you will perform jihad against the unbelievers. In return, you will be imam, leader of the Muslim community and I will be leader in religious matters."[5]

This was almost precisely the arrangement between Sadat and the Brotherhood, and between Mubarak and the Brotherhood as well. After Sadat deviated from this arrangement through the peace treaty with Israel, on March 26, 1979, Muslim Brotherhood militants assassinated him.

Mubarak was less ideological than Sadat, and he was known to have "never read a single book in his entire life."[6] But he still believed he would be able to dominate and manage the world's most sophisticated jihadist transnational crime syndicate. Mubarak was armed with the audacity of profound ignorance, the rigidity of the peasantry, and a lust for power. Mubarak's regime, like many other governments, employed Islamists as mercenaries to carry out the government's national and international criminal biddings. Islamists, on the other hand, were happy to oblige because they almost always win this equation.

Mubarak's regime awarded a significant amount of government contracts to Muslim Brotherhood businessmen, who became multimillionaires under his financial oligarchy. Among them were

---

5 Madawi al-Rasheed, *A History of Saudi Arabia* (Cambridge University Press, 2011), 16.
6 Al-Watan (Cairo), May 15, 2012.

Khairat al-Shater, Hassan Malik, and hundreds of other lesser-known Brotherhood leaders, such as Khalid Uda.[7] The Brotherhood also ran a vast money-laundering operation headed by Safwan Thabit, the head of Juhayna Food Industries, and Sayyid as-Suwirki, the owner of department stores across Egypt.[8] These contracts provided a legal cover for Mubarak's regime funding of the Brotherhood and their militant offshoots.

While it wasn't a secret in Egypt that the Brotherhood was a parastatal entity, that characterization was somehow lost in translation when it made it to Western experts and commentators. In July 2005, Brotherhood General Guide Mahdi Akef publicly and officially pledged the Islamic oath of allegiance given to a caliph to Mubarak adding, "We support President Mubarak's presidential candidacy, and I wish to meet him."[9]

Yassir al-Hudaybi, a former leader of the Muslim Brotherhood's Freedom and Justice and Party (FJP), confirmed in an interview in January 2012 that the Brotherhood "officially gave *bai'a* to Mubarak and his son Gamal in 2005."[10] Former Egyptian First Lady Suzanne Mubarak also worked with the Brotherhood on numerous cultural projects, and she often attended and cosponsored their events.[11]

The Salafi jihadist movement, which also is consistently and often inaccurately considered a separate entity from the Muslim Brotherhood, gave its oath of allegiance to Mubarak as well. Salafi jihadist leader Tal'at Zahran admitted, in January 2012 that they gave *bai'a* to Mubarak. He also confirmed at the time that Salafists were willing to give *bai'a* to Field Marshal Hussein Tantawi, or any other Muslim president who upholds the basics of Islamic jurisprudence.[12]

7 "Khairat al-Shater wa-Qadiat Salsabil," The Muslim Brotherhood Official Encyclopedia, The Official Muslim Brotherhood Encyclopedia, https://ikhwanwiki.com/, accessed June 10, 2021.
8 Al-Arabiya (Dubai), December 13, 2020.
9 Akher Sa'a (Cairo), July 20, 2005.
10 Al-Masry al-Youm (Cairo), January 1, 2012.
11 "Tharwat al-Kherbawy Daif Tony Khalifah Sirri Jidan," YouTube.com, April 19, 2014.
12 "Shaikh Salafi: Tazwir al-Intikhabat Wajib Shar'i," YouTube.com, January 4, 2012.

The end of the rule of Mubarak on February 11, 2011, was expected. Almost every major governmental department was controlled or infiltrated by the Brotherhood. Mubarak avoided his predecessors' fate as his rule didn't end with his death. This was probably because he ran a massive blackmail and extortion operation through his infamous Chairman of State Information Services, Minister of Information, and Secretary General of the National Democratic Party, Muhammad Safwat al-Sherif (1933–2021).[13] Even Mubarak's wife, publicly threatened to publish thirty hours of sex tapes from sitting Arab and Egyptian politicians if her husband was found guilty during his trial in 2011.[14]

Mubarak's state television constantly streamed Salafi jihadist recruitment videos and television shows. Al-Qaeda-affiliated terrorists, recruiters, and propagandists appeared daily on Egyptian television networks, such as *al-Rahma*, *an-Nas* and *Iqra'*. These shows openly advocated for the genocide of Jews, Christians, atheists, homosexuals, and moderate Muslims.

Among the most prominent Salafi jihadists under Mubarak's regime was Muhammad Hassan. Hassan admitted on an-Nas television station that he was directed by Mubarak's State Security Investigations Service. In December 2011 Hassan said, "[Islamic] clergymen and [state] security are in the same camp." Hassan added that he was "ordered" and directed by Mubarak's security apparatus on where, when, and what to preach, during his jihadist sermons. He also said that the Salafi jihadist movement and state security reciprocated "love and cooperation." He added, "I have my religious vision and they have their security vision, when they decline a specific action, I concede." Hassan said the link between Salafists and state security

---

13 Al-Jazeera (Doha), April 16, 2011.
14 El Fagr (Cairo), July 27, 2011.

"should never be severed." He also bragged that he operated with impunity and was never harassed by law enforcement.[15]

Under Mubarak's regime, the government provided state sponsorship for the Brotherhood's terrorism recruitment through state-owned television networks. It also went further and his regime sponsored terrorism internationally. Hassan was a prolific terror recruiter. He often gave private sermons to terrorists and suicide bombers before they carried out terrorist attacks in Gaza using Paltalk Messenger.[16]

It is commonly and falsely accepted in the West that the Brotherhood was banned under Mubarak's regime. During a speech in April 2011, Khairat al-Shater admitted that under Mubarak's regime, "the group was openly and widely operating all over Egypt, from Cairo to every governorate and every village with all the [Brotherhood's] structure and divisions." Shater added that their wave of infiltrating every aspect of Egyptian society was briefly interrupted in the early 1990s. Shater said that prior to the early 1990s, while "they didn't have absolute liberty," they still enjoyed "freedom to some extent with few restrictions."

Shater later said that Mubarak's regime shift was due to several reasons. Shater attributed one of them to Algeria's Islamist *Front Islamique du Salut* (FIS), which supposedly won a fifty-five percent majority in Algerian municipal and provincial elections on June 12, 1990. Mubarak's relationship with the Brotherhood changed for another reason that Shater omitted. In 1992, the regime discovered the Brotherhood was still operating the Secret Apparatus.

In his speech, Shater also discussed a strategy that Islamist regimes consistently and historically utilized to stifle dissent:

15 An-Nas television network, (Cairo), December 12, 2011; "Muhammad Hassan Unafiq Am ad-Dawla," YouTube.com, December 12, 2011.

16 Archived video of Sheikh Muhammad Hassan giving a inspirational speech to a jihadist in Gaza prior to carrying out a terrorist attack, accessed February 15, 2022, https://archive.org/details/yt-1s.com-2-360p.

> He [Mubarak] begun a systematic technique—which he learned from Imam Ahmad in Yemen. It is the method of capturing hostages. For Imam Ahmad to control tribes which he feared their dissent, he would take from every tribe the favorite son of the head of the tribe as a hostage in his palace. This guaranteed that the tribe would remain submissive out of fear for its son. So Mubarak implemented this rule on a relatively wider scale.

Shater was referring to Ahmad bin Yahya Hamidaddin (1891–1962), who reigned in Yemen from 1948 to 1962. But Shater was mistaken. This old strategy of taking collateral was mainly utilized by the Ottomans. Their most famous hostage was Vlad III or Vlad Drăculea, commonly known as Vlad the Impaler.

In 1442, Vlad and his younger brother Radu were sent to the court of Sultan Murad II as collateral to guarantee that their father wouldn't attempt to militarily stop Murad's colonialization of Europe. In the case of Vlad III, the strategy backfired. He was able to study and absorb the Ottoman stratagems of war, including mimicking their most brutal and common form of execution—impalement. The Ottomans employed the gruesome technique as late as the twentieth century during the Armenian genocide. The Ottoman impalement pole was so heavily utilized against Egyptians that it is still part of common colloquial Egyptian. For example, when faced with an adversity, Egyptians often say, "I received a *khazou*," the Arabized word for the Turkish term for impalement pole, *kazığa oturtmak*.

While Shater might have been aware that the practice of collateral hostage-taking was mostly an Ottoman practice, he chose to attribute it to Imam Ahmad instead, since the group is currently propagating for the revival of the Ottoman Caliphate under the rule of Recep Tayyip Erdoğan—they are working to establish the same style of caliphate that trained the man who inspired Bram Stoker's *Dracula*.

Shater admitted to having relative freedom in Egypt, which allowed them to penetrate major institutions in the country. While the relationship between Mubarak and the Muslim Brotherhood slightly changed in 1992, Mubarak continued to allow them to openly recruit terrorists on state-run television. For example, Brotherhood leader Safwat Hegazy daily propagated means of torture and murder according to the Brotherhood's theology.

The group did not just operate freely, they dominated the country. This was confirmed by the Brotherhood's interim General Guide Mahmoud Ezzat after his arrest on August 28, 2020. The government released a few seconds of Ezzat's debriefing. When an intelligence agent asked him about what his group's idea of success was, Ezzat said, "My idea of success is to return to [our] status prior to the revolution" in reference to the 2011 coup d'état. That was an admission that they were not persecuted under Mubarak and allowed to freely operate their public and clandestine apparatuses.[17]

Former Brotherhood leader and member of the Guidance Bureau Mukhtar Nouh explained Ezzat's statement, "Under President Mubarak, the Muslim Brotherhood controlled two-thirds of the country's political decision making." He added that "eighty percent of government institutions and unions were dominated by the Muslim Brotherhood. Even the legislative branch, if they [Mubarak's regime] wanted to pass a legislation which the Brotherhood would object to, they had to pass it secretly and swiftly…They were the power behind decision making prior to 2011."

Nouh also said that when Brotherhood operatives were imprisoned under Mubarak's regime, "it was to facilitate a form of dialogue between them and the regime. Even the manner, the identities, the timing, and the treatment of [prisoners] was coordinated [between the regime and Brotherhood] and sometimes with the knowledge of the Secret Apparatus." Nouh provides an example of the last case against

17 MBC Masr television network (Cairo), May 24, 2021.

the Muslim Brotherhood under Mubarak's regime, which was known as the Unions Case. He said it was orchestrated by the Brotherhood. Nouh added, "It was the golden age."

MUSLIM BROTHERHOOD'S 2011 COUP D'ÉTAT

Under Mubarak's police state, engaging in protests was often punishable with prison, torture, kidnapping and, sometimes, death. The January 25, 2011, protests were popular only after tanks trolled the streets with banners saying *yasqut Hosni Mubarak* (Down with Hosni Mubarak). A few days after the protests began, the military issued a statement that said, "The demands of the protestors were legitimate." This was an admission of a coup d'état.[18]

This author witnessed the plan to depose Mubarak. In 2006, the Muslim Brotherhood Officers unit inside the Egyptian army assigned one of its operatives, a physician and colonel in the army, to forcibly attend the Liberal Egyptian Party meetings and their gatherings at the house of Egyptian classic liberal celebrity and the late close friend of the author, Muhammad Nouh (1937–2012). In Egypt, where it was illegal to own firearms, the Brotherhood Officer almost always sat in the meetings with his gun on the table aiming toward the author and her colleagues. He would sometimes jokingly pretend to fire his gun at the party members, and he often grabbed it whenever someone offended him. He was assigned to record our discussions and report their content to the leaders of his Brotherhood Officers Unit.

Perhaps it's due to the Brotherhood's collective narcissism, but their operatives frequently divulged secrets. The colonel fit their typical psychological profile. He boasted about his closeness to leaders of the military, and in the fall of 2009 he revealed the information about a "coups d'état that will be called a revolution" in a very detailed account that eventually took place in 2011.

---

18 Al-Arabiya (Dubai), January 31, 2011.

Since 2002, the author had been anticipating a coup d'état against Mubarak as he publicly groomed his youngest son, Gamal, as his successor. Gamal was a civilian backed by an empire of corruption, and he did not have direct ties to the Brotherhood. It was highly unlikely for someone with his resume to be allowed to replace an oligarchy of Brotherhood Officers. The prospect of turning Egypt into a Mubarak family kingdom was opposed by all segments of Egyptian society.

As soon as the former Tunisian President Zine El Abidine Ben Ali was deposed by a Muslim Brotherhood coup d'état—euphemized as a revolution on January 14, 2011—the author realized that the ripple effect of the Muslim Brotherhood Officers coups across the Middle East was in motion.

On January 25, 2011, on Egypt's Police Appreciation Day, a few activist groups decided to protest police brutality. On January 27, that same colonel called the author and said, "This time, we are coming and you will call it a revolution."

He had always been offended when the author called the Brotherhood Officers' 1952 movement a coup d'état and not a revolution. The author asked him if they thought about the consequences of empowering people by making them believe they had broken the police state and deposed Mubarak. He was startled by the thought, as they never considered it. When the author asked him what would happen after Mubarak was deposed, he said, "The Sudanese model. Field Marshal Tantawi is Egypt's Suwar ad-Dahab. We will hand over the rule to civilians." When a member of the Muslim Brotherhood Officers uses the term "civilians," they are referring to the civilian wing of the Secret Apparatus and not random civilians.

THE SUDANESE MODEL

Sudan was the first country to be openly and directly ruled by the Muslim Brotherhood. The Sudanese model became more relevant after it was emulated during Brotherhood upheavals, euphemized as the "Arab Spring."

The former president of Sudan, Omar al-Bashir, seized power in the 1989 coup d'état, and became the first member of the Muslim Brotherhood to publicly and officially rule a country. Bashir seized power through the Sudanese Brotherhood's National Congress Party (NCP), formerly the National Islamic Front (NIF). He was assigned the presidency of Sudan after the Brotherhood's coup d'état toppled Gaafar Nimeiry on April 6, 1985. Field Marshal Abdel Rahman Suwar ad-Dahab led the coup and it later inspired his Egyptian counterpart. It is not known whether Field Marshal Muhammad Hussein Tantawi was a member of the Muslim Brotherhood or not, but it is most probable given the fact that he carried out a coup d'état on their behalf in Egypt on February 11, 2011.

Al-Bashir was not only the first public Muslim Brotherhood member to become president, but he also became the first sitting president to be indicted by the International Criminal Court (ICC) for genocide, war crimes, and crimes against humanity. It is estimated that Bashir's regime killed between five hundred thousand and two million people and displaced another four million. Bashir's rule and crimes against humanity were aligned with the Brotherhood ideology and methods of governance, and his policies as president were dictated by the Brotherhood's International Apparatus.

During an interview in 2013, Kherbawy said:

> The Sudanese people need to be aware that their political leaders are working against their interest as they are obliged to offer their absolute loyalty and obedience to the International Apparatus of the Muslim Brotherhood. Omar al-Bashir is a member of the Brotherhood and I met him in Egypt between 1993 and 1994 when he visited the Guidance Bureau … The General Guide at the time, Muhammad Hamid

> Abu al-Nasr, told him "It's good that you seized power, it is a good omen that will rule Egypt as well."[19]

Kherbawy is highly credible, and his statements are supported by the International Apparatus' ideology, bylaws, and the Brotherhood's own words.

The details of the inner workings of the military conspiracy to topple Mubarak were also apparent in WikiLeaks' Hillary Clinton emails regarding Egypt during this period. One of those emails discusses how military officials forced Mubarak to step down, and some of them used the term "coup d'état" to describe the toppling of Mubarak.

UNITED STATES DEPARTMENT OF STATE LEADERSHIP BRIEFED ON THE MUSLIM BROTHERHOOD CONSPIRACY TO MURDER CHRISTIANS IN 2011

Secretary of State Hillary Clinton supported the Muslim Brotherhood's rise to power in Egypt, even after learning they planned to murder Coptic Christians. An email chain released by WikiLeaks confirmed that Clinton was briefed on a conspiracy between the Brotherhood and the former head of the Egypt's Supreme Council of Armed Forces (SCAF), Field Marshal Muhammad Hussein Tantawi, to besiege, attack, and kill Egyptian Coptic Christians.

On November 23, 2011, Sidney Blumenthal sent Secretary Hillary Clinton an email titled "H: Intel. Secret Offer to EL Baradei/Muslim Brotherhood-Army Alliance," which she received and forwarded to her aide, Jacob Sullivan.[20] This email callously discussed a murderous conspiracy against the indigenous Coptic community.

19 "Omar al-Bashir Odu fil-Tanzim ad-Dawli l'al-Ikhwan al-Muslimin," YouTube.com, August 25, 2013.

20 Hillary Clinton Email Archive, "H: Intel. Secret Offer to EL Baradei/Muslim Brotherhood-Army Alliance," WikiLeaks.org/clinton-emails/emailid/12843, November 23, 2011.

According to Blumenthal's sources, SCAF and the Brotherhood admitted their role in the October 9, 2011, massacre of Coptic Christians, where twenty-eight people were killed for peacefully protesting religious persecution. The massacre took place in front of the Maspero building, the headquarters of the Egyptian Radio and Television Union. That state-run media outlet routinely incited its audience to engage in violence against Christians, Jews, Bahai's, Shi'ites, moderate Muslims, and anyone who wasn't a fundamentalist Sunni Muslim.

In the email to Clinton, Blumenthal stated, "According to knowledgeable individuals, Badie [then-General Guide of the Brotherhood] and the other leaders of the [Muslim Brotherhood] MB are also extremely concerned over the growing violence in Cairo. They note that during recent attacks against the Coptic Christian community in Egypt, the MB and the SCAF worked discreetly to ensure that the military and security forces did not intervene forcefully to protect the Copts as they were besieged by Islamist groups."

Blumenthal later continued: "In this discussion Subhi Saleh, a lawyer and former Member of Parliament, who served as the MB delegate to the March 2011 constitutional commission, pointed out that discussions between the MB and the SCAF regarding the Copts had been relatively simple, because both sides were not concerned about the fate of the Coptic Christian community."

After Clinton received this information about the plan to target Christians, she continued to support and praise the Brotherhood's seizure of power, saying, "We stand behind Egypt's transition to democracy. This is not only the right thing to do. It is in our interest as well."[21]

In the same email, Blumenthal wrote that his sources in police and military intelligence indicated the demonstrations would continue,

21 Jason Devaney, "Document: Hillary Praised, Supported Muslim Brotherhood Member Morsi," *Newsmax Media*, October 13, 2016.

"even in the face of deadly force." Blumenthal continued, "Tantawi has informed the MB leadership that the Army and security forces will use increasingly aggressive measures to counter the demonstrators." That is a clear admission that the Islamist military under SCAF was involved in killing protestors. Blumenthal added: "(Source Comment: Some Egyptian political figures—including some senior military officers—are referring to this change of leadership as a military coup, while others see it as the regime—and the Army—preserving their positions of leadership under a system put in place by Mubarak's mentors, Gamal Abdel Nasser and Anwar al-Sadat, during the 1952 officers revolt against King Farouk. Some younger army officers are calling for a 'Turkish solution,' where the Army takes power in a crisis, acting as the guarantor of civilian democracy.)"

Hillary was given intelligence that the Muslim Brotherhood and the fundamentalist SCAF leadership claimed responsibility for political murders and intended to continue killing innocent civilians in the process of carrying out a coup d'état, and yet she continued to support this action.

After Hillary received the details of the conspiracy, more Christians were brutally murdered and displaced. More than 161 Christian buildings were attacked, and seventy-three churches were burned or vandalized.[22] One unprecedented attack was openly carried out by both Egyptian security forces and the Muslim Brotherhood against Cairo's St. Mark's Cathedral, in April 2013.[23] They attacked the church with bombs and set it on fire while mourning Christians gathered for the funeral of four Christians killed by rioting Brotherhood militants.

Following the January 25 coup d'état, it became apparent SCAF was almost certainly a Muslim Brotherhood Officers cell. SCAF's first

22 "For Egypt's Christian Churches, Western Media With Their Lies Help Islamists," PIME Asia News,, August 19, 2013; Ahmed Rushdi, "Harq 73 Kanisa wu 212 min Mumtalakat al-Aqbat Hasilat Unf al-Ikhwan hata al-An," Mubtada (Cairo), August 20, 2013.

23 Gary Lane, "Video: Egyptian Security Forces Attack Cairo Cathedral," *The Christian Broadcasting Network* (Washington, DC), accessed June 1, 2018.

action after toppling Mubarak was to celebrate by inviting Qaradawi to give the first speech in Tahrir Square, on February 18, 2011.

By March 2011, SCAF had facilitated the return of three thousand jihadists and convicted terrorists to Egypt from Afghanistan, Chechnya, Bosnia, Somalia, and Iran.[24] Among these terrorists was Muhammad al-Islambuli, the brother of President Anwar al-Sadat's assassin, Khalid al-Islambuli.[25] During the same month, SCAF pardoned many terrorists operating worldwide, and released numerous jihadists from prison.

On March 19, 2012, the Supreme Military Court issued an acquittal for Muhammad al-Islambuli, Muhammad al-Zawahiri (the brother of al-Qaeda's leader), Sayyed Imam al-Sharif, (also known as Dr. Fadl), and Abdul Qadir bin Abdul Aziz, a cofounder of al-Qaeda, its former Mufti, and leader of its governing council.[26]

Among the terrorists freed by SCAF was another of Sadat's assassins, Abbud al-Zummar. Following his release, he publicly supported al-Qaeda and its operatives—whom he had been associated with since he officially began his Islamist activities. In January 2012, al-Zummar said, "I welcome Ayman al-Zawahiri's return to Egypt with his head held high."[27] During his interview with *al-Watan* newspaper, al-Zummar said that he considered "al-Qaeda to be a patriotic segment of society," and added that he doesn't mind if they officially "operate in Egypt as long as they are peaceful."[28] Along with other al-Qaeda and al-Gama'a al-Islamiyya convicted terrorists, Zummar founded the political party *Hizb al-Bina' w'at-Tanmiya* (Construction and Development Party) and installed his cousin Tarik al-Zummar, who was also involved in Sadat's assassination, as the Chairman of the party.

---

24 Al-Masry Al-Youm (Cairo), March 31, 2011.
25 Ibid.
26 Al-Masry Al-Youm (Cairo), March 19, 2012.
27 Al-Ahram (Cairo), January 27, 2012.
28 Al-Watan News, (Cairo), November 16, 2012.

SCAF leadership openly expressed its fundamentalism. For example, in March 2011, Army General Hassan al-Roueini, the Commander of the Cairo military at the time, criticized Egyptian protestors' opposition and fears from Egyptian Salafi jihadist preachers and said, "We are Salafists."[29]

Roueini was right. SCAF continued to prove their fundamentalism with a jihadist attack on October 9, 2011, when they perpetrated the Maspero massacre. On that day, SCAF jihadists shot and executed peaceful Christians and ran them over with military vehicles, killing twenty-eight and wounding hundreds of peaceful protestors rallying against religious discrimination and genocidal incitement against Christians on Egypt's governmental television.

While the protests were ongoing, the government's television proved protestors right by calling upon Egyptian Muslims to head to Maspero to fight the Christian "sons of dogs."[30] The military leaders who were responsible for deploying armored vehicles and armed officers to murder protests were the former Armed Forces Chief of Staff Sami Anan, the Salafist General al-Roueini, and the former Chief of SCAF, Muhammad Hussein Tantawi. Islamist soldiers in the military blocked the path of protestors and fired into the civilian crowd. Four armored vehicles drove into the crowd, crushing protesters under their wheels. Specific dissidents were targeted for assassination that day, such as classic liberal Coptic Christian human rights activist Michael Mos'aad.

The Muslim Brotherhood coup d'état of 2011 installed the mentally impaired Muhammad Morsi as president on June 30, 2012, after a sham election. It is inconceivable that SCAF, a fundamentalist Islamist body that murdered citizens in front of television cameras, would respect their votes in an election. The process of peaceful transition of power does not exist outside the confines of the Western defi-

29 "Al-Liwa' qa'id al-Mantika al-Markaziyya Yaqul Kuluna Salafiyyn," YouTube.com, May 22, 2011.

30 "Al-Television al-Masri Yuharid al-Masriyyin ded al-Aqbat," YouTube.com, October 10, 2011.

nition of the rule of law. Under different circumstances, democracy is merely a convenient word to describe the despotic action of mob rule.

Under SCAF's leadership, the military subsidized both the Muslim Brotherhood and Salafi political parties during the parliamentary elections held between November 28, 2011, and January 11, 2012. SCAF's "slush fund totaling millions of dollars in the form of 'walk around' money, clothing and food giveaways that enabled hundreds of local chapters of Islamist political organizations to buy votes."[31] SCAF established "political 'action committee' bank accounts to funnel an underground supply chain of financial and commodity support" to the Muslim Brotherhood and Salafi political parties.[32]

Despite the fraudulent electoral process, Morsi still lost the election to his opponent, Ahmed Shafik, but Morsi was still appointed to the presidency.[33] While Islamists consistently fake a belief in democracy when they speak to Westerners, they describe the democratic process as "criminal" and "infidel" and "rigging it is a religious duty" when they discuss the process in Arabic.[34]

The choice to install Morsi as president was a detriment to the Brotherhood, SCAF, and Islamists in Egypt and across Middle East. The Brotherhood might have selected Morsi because he could be manipulated due to his limited mental capacity and the fact that he was a prison escapee who wasn't even legally eligible to run for public office.

On January 28, 2011, Hamas terrorists and Brotherhood militants attacked several prisons in Egypt, including Wadi al-Natrun prison. They killed forty-six prisoners and officers and kidnapped four policemen. They broke out thirty-four Muslim Brotherhood operatives

---

31 National Review Online, December 6, 2011; Daniel Pipes and Cynthia Farahat, "Egypt's Sham Election," December 6, 2011, https://www.meforum.org/4628/egypt-sham-election.

32 Ibid.

33 Ibid; 24; Daniel Pipes and Cynthia Farahat, "Don't Ignore Electoral Fraud in Egypt," January 24, 2012, https://www.meforum.org/4632/egypt-electoral-fraud.

34 Al-Masry Al-Youm (Cairo), June 7, 2015.

from prison and thousands of terrorists and criminals.[35] Morsi was among the prisoners who escaped from Wadi al-Natrun prison, and while he was on the run, he called al-Jazeera television and reported that he had escaped from prison with other Brotherhood operatives.[36]

In 2011, SCAF and the Muslim Brotherhood openly flaunted their relationship with al-Qaeda, under both the interim presidency of Muhammad Hussein Tantawi and his Brotherhood successor after he was installed as president on June 30, 2012.

MUSLIM BROTHERHOOD'S SLAUGHTERHOUSES AND BLOOD SACRIFICE

Protests against Mubarak's regime involved numerous Muslim Brotherhood acts of violence. Many of their operatives publicly engaged in acts of terrorism, including Egyptian actor Amr Waked, who appeared in Hollywood movies with celebrities such as Scarlett Johansson. Waked is almost certainly affiliated with the Muslim Brotherhood, since he was caught on video with Brotherhood operative illegally interrogating a kidnapped and beaten man during protests in 2011.[37]

Waked interrogated the victim inside the Brotherhood-owned Safir Travel Agency in Tahrir Square, which they turned into a torture cell. The Brotherhood committed atrocities inside this office against people who protested them or against citizens whom they suspected were police officers. In 2013, several Brotherhood leaders bragged during television interviews about kidnapping and torturing civilians and police officers at Safir Travel Agency and other locations.

---

35 "Mukalamat Morsi ma' Al-Jazeera Akib Hirubahu min as-Sijn fi 2011," YouTube.com, May 16, 2015.

36 Ibid.

37 "Amr Waked Yusawir Ta'thib fi-Sharikat Safir al-Ikhwaniyya," YouTube.com, January 23, 2014.

Former Member of Parliament and Brotherhood leader Mahmoud Khodair was arrested in November 2013 after he boasted during a television interview about kidnapping a man whom they suspected was a police officer in 2011.[38]

The victim, attorney Osama Kamal, was bound and tortured for three days with other victims. The Brotherhood released Kamal's torture video to terrorize their opponents. Kamal said Brotherhood leadership personally tortured him in different ways, including electrically shocking his genitals. He identified two former Brotherhood Members of Parliament, Hazim Farouk Mansour and Mohsen Radi, who represented the Brotherhood's Freedom and Justice Party.[39]

Mansour's face can be clearly seen in the torture video. Kamal also identified Brotherhood leaders Muhammad al-Beltagi and Safwat Hegazy. He named Brotherhood journalist and al-Jazeera commentator Ahmed Mansour among his torturers, and in 2015 Mansour was sentenced in absentia to fifteen years in prison for his role in the torture.[40]

Safwat Hegazy proudly boasted about torturing Kamal in an interview with al-Jazeera, saying, "We have done the impossible to make him confess [that he was a police officer], and that's why I was sure he was a police officer. No one can endure what was done to this man if they weren't trained to undergo such hardship."[41] In 2013, Hegazy was arrested following the interview while trying to flee to Libya. Both Hegazy and Khodair were sentenced to fifteen years in prison for the kidnapping and torture of Kamal.

The Brotherhood also leaked a video that featured actor Amr Waked participating in acts of terrorism at the Safir Travel Agency. A short clip showed Waked holding a video camera and filming his interrogation of a man they had kidnapped and appeared to have

38 Veto Gate Online News (Cairo), November 26, 2013.
39 "Video al-Ta'thib al-Mutaham fih al-Ikhwan," YouTube.com, May 26, 2012.
40 Al-Youm as-Sabi' (Cairo), June 20, 2015.
41 "Ta'thib al-Ikhwan al-Muslimin li Osama Kamal," YouTube.com, July 7, 2012.

been beaten. The terrorized man kept saying, "I swear I am with you," as Waked angrily questioned him about his name, his job, and why he was in Tahrir Square. The victim said his name was Ibrahim Muhammad Ibrahim and that he worked in a restaurant. The victim also pleaded, "I am here for the Brotherhood, my colleagues," before the video stopped.

In 2014, an Egyptian attorney filed a complaint with Egyptian Attorney General Hisham Barakat—before the Brotherhood assassinated Barakat a year later—accusing Amr Waked of involvement in torture.[42] But Waked wasn't brought to justice, possibly due to his international popularity and Hollywood connections. Waked is widely despised in Egypt since his appearance in the disturbing video. He is often referred to in Egyptian mainstream media as "al-Hamsawi Amr Waked," a derogatory term that associates him with the Hamas terrorist organization.

Waked became famous in Egypt in 2001 with a propaganda movie called *Ashab wala Business* (are we friends or business [acquaintances]). The movie glorified suicide bombings in Israel. He played the role of a suicide bomber called *Jihad.* Waked also acted with George Clooney in 2005 in the movie *Syriana*, with Scarlett Johansson in *Lucy* in 2014, and in the movie *Geostorm* in 2017.

After toppling Mubarak's regime, many Brotherhood leaders publicly bragged about their engagement in acts of terrorism. But more importantly, they also confessed to the existence of the Secret Apparatus. Brotherhood renowned cleric Safwat Hegazy admitted in an interview with al-Jazeera that they had a secret military apparatus, and it was working with the Islamists in the army during the protests.[43] Hegazy said they worked with the military while the Brotherhood abducted and tortured individuals from Tahrir Square whom they suspected were "thugs" or state security police officers.

---

42 Al-Bawaba News (Cairo), April 12, 2014.
43 Al-Jazeera TV (Cairo), August 14, 2011.

In a series of televised interviews with al-Jazeera, Osama Yassin, a minister in former President Mohammed Morsi's cabinet, revealed that *al-Firqat 95* (the 95 Brigade) still exists and engaged in terrorism in Egypt in 2011.[44] The 95 Brigade was a terrorism cell of the Secret Apparatus that was created in 1995 by Khairat al-Shater and Mahmoud Ezzat.[45] According to Yassin, the 95 Brigade engaged in the abduction, beating, and torture of "thugs" and threw Molotov cocktails at their opponents. Brigade operatives were implicated in the killing of anti-Brotherhood protestors. For example, in March 2014 two Brotherhood operatives were sentenced to death after an online video clip showed them killing a teenager by throwing him from a building.[46]

After the Muslim Brotherhood officially seized power in 2012, they became openly jihadist. The group installed torture and murder tents or camps across Egypt, where they abducted, tortured, and murdered protesters and sometimes random civilians. These camps were known in Egypt as *salakhanat al-ikhwan* (the Brotherhood slaughterhouses). These torture camps resulted in mass protests during Morsi's brief presidency, demanding the Brotherhood shut down its "slaughterhouses."[47]

Among those who were kidnapped and tortured in one of the camps was Egyptian Ambassador to Venezuela Yehya Najm. He was randomly kidnapped from the street and tortured in December 2012. During an interview with Ambassador Najm, he appeared bloodied and severely bruised. He testified that the room where he was held captive and tortured with forty-nine other people was "like a Nazi camp."[48] Najm said there were military and police officers guarding these tents, and they took orders from Muslim Brotherhood leaders

44 Al-Jazeera TV (Cairo), November-December 2011.
45 Al-Wafd (Cairo), January 11, 2013.
46 Al-Arabiya (Dubai), March 29, 2014.
47 Al-Masry Al-Youm (Cairo), April 6, 2013.
48 Cynthia Farahat, "CairoGate: Egyptian Diplomat Survives MB Torture Says 'It was like a Nazi camp,'" cynthiafarahat.com. December 9, 2012.

who tortured and mutilated victims.[49] The Ambassador said that a female Brotherhood physician was also involved in his torture and repeatedly stomped on him and other victims with her shoes when they asked her to help them. Najm reported that there was a child among the victims with several stab wounds. He also said he watched while Brotherhood leaders tried to "mutilate the hand" of one of their victims.[50]

When the number of kidnaped victims exceeded the capacity of a tent, the victims were transported to the Central Security Forces prison, where Brotherhood leaders made final decisions on whether to release them or continue to hold them captive.[51] Najm was among the lucky victims who were released from the prison, perhaps because as an Ambassador, his assassination might have invited international attention. Widespread, indiscriminate torture and murder carried out by the Brotherhood resulted in mainstream opposition to the group. Most Egyptian families, whether Muslim or non-Muslim, know someone who was murdered or tortured by the Brotherhood. They also had plans for mass extermination in Egypt of not just Christians but Muslims too.

THE MUSLIM BROTHERHOOD'S BLOOD SACRIFICE

The plan to mass murder Muslims was not a tactic applied only to their opponents or simply to promote mass fear. Mass extermination of Muslims is a doctrinal necessity for the Brotherhood. Hassan al-Banna's eschatological doctrine demanded that the whole Muslim ummah be annihilated and presented as a blood sacrifice, which he called *daribat ad-dam* (the blood tax). In the Brotherhood's ideology,

49 Ibid.
50 Ibid.
51 Ibid.

the blood tax is a ritual sacrifice that must be presented to God for penance, and it will be the only way they could be granted immortality and resurrection in the hereafter.

In 1947, the Muslim Brotherhood established an Islamist coalition called *Haiy'at Wadi al-Nile li-Inqaz al-Quds* (Nile Valley Authority to Save Jerusalem).[52] This entity operated a radio station that agitated for jihad while teaching and indoctrinating its listeners in the Muslim Brotherhood's philosophy. On May 20, 1948, Banna gave an interview on the radio station that was transcribed and published the following day in the *Jaridat al-Ikhwan al-Muslim al-Yawmiyya* (The Daily Muslim Brotherhood Newspaper) under the title "The Price of [After] Life."[53]

During the interview, Banna elaborated on his genocidal philosophy stating, "it is strange that the price of [eternal] life is loving death, and there is no other price for it except this." Banna believed that any expression of "loving life is a death omen, and the [Muslim] nation which strives to collectively exist in the hereafter has to all die." Banna believed that loving life was a deadly sin that prevented Muslims from entering paradise. He believed Muslims could only go to heaven if they "shed their blood as tax for [loving] life." Banna said that blood sacrifice was not only a price for eternity in paradise but also the "price of victory and the price of dignity." Banna quoted a statement attributed to the Prophet of Islam: "If I could, I would kill for Allah, then get revived to kill again, then revived to kill again." While the historic accuracy of this statement is disputed, Islamists fully believe in its legitimacy.[54]

Sayyid Qutb continued Banna's doctrinal principle that all Muslim who aren't members in jihadists groups are infidels and deserve to get

52 Islam Tawfiq, "Al-Murshid al-Am: al-Banna Sahib Ro'ya," The Muslim Brotherhood Official Website, https://ikhwanonline.com/, February 12, 2010.

53 Jaridat al-Ikhwan al-Muslim al-Yawmiyya (Cairo), May 21, 1948; "Hadith Iza'i Nader l'al-Imam al-Banna," The Official Muslim Brotherhood Encyclopedia, https://ikhwanwiki.com/, accessed June 22, 2021.

54 Ibid.

killed. In his book *Milestones*, Qutb stated that those who "call themselves Muslims are not Muslims," and he considered "societies which claim to be Islamic" to be "non-Islamic."[55] Qutb believed that there is only one legitimate form of Islamic nation, which he referred to as *dar al-Islam* (House of Islam, or Nation of Islam) where, "an Islamic state is established and dominated by Shari'a and its penal code, and where Muslims only ally with each other." Any other system is considered *dar harb* (a Nation or House of War), "which a Muslim's relationship with, should be confined to warfare."[56]

While it is widely known that the Muslim Brotherhood believes in the extermination of all non-Muslims, it is not common knowledge that they also consider all Islamic nations houses of war, and the vast majority of its Muslims are infidels whom they believe should all be killed.

The concept of human ritual sacrifice, which they call the "blood tax," is dominant in the group's doctrine. Banna's and Qutb's ideas lived on through Mustafa Mashhour. In 1995, Mashhour published "Jihad Is The Way," in which he discussed the concept of ritual self-sacrifice through jihad as the ultimate goal of members of his group and the only means by which one can attain "absolute bliss."[57]

The application of the Brotherhood's doctrinal concept of blood ritual sacrifice includes killing and being killed for their cause. The widespread terror under the Brotherhood's brief leadership instigated mass dissent against the group, and resulted in the largest anti-terrorism rally in history. Tens of millions of Egyptians took to the streets to protest the Muslim Brotherhood on the first anniversary of the inauguration of Muhammad Morsi on June 29, 2013. The 1952 coup d'état was perpetrated by a limited group of Brotherhood military officers and had the backing of only a miniscule population of mili-

55 Sayyid Qutb, *Ma'alim fi al-Tariq* (Beirut: Dar al-Shorouk, 1979), 91.
56 Sayyid Qutb, *Ma'alim fi al-Tariq*, 137.
57 Mustafa Mashhour, Al-Jihad huwa as-Sabil, The Official Muslim Brotherhood Encyclopedia, https://ikhwanwiki.com/, accessed April 22, 2021.

tants. The mass protests of Morsi involved the majority of Egyptian society who revolted against the Muslim Brotherhood.

The Brotherhood lost control of government institutions, because only a minority of army and police are now affiliated with the Secret Apparatus. The mass protests were a national revolution against the Brotherhood and everything it represented. Under the Brotherhood's leadership, the country headed toward civil war between Islamists inside and outside the government and the rest of the Egyptian population.

In August 2012, Muhammad Morsi appointed General Abdel Fattah al-Sisi, then-head of military intelligence, as Minister of Defense. Sisi was widely expected to serve the Brotherhood's agenda, given the fact that he was a leader in an Islamist army under the Brotherhood's control. More importantly, Sisi was related to Muslim Brotherhood cofounder Abbas as-Sisi.[58] But al-Sisi decided to spare the country from an inevitable civil war by overthrowing the unlawful presidency of Morsi. On July 3, 2013, Morsi was forced to resign his position because he faced civil disobedience and had lost control over the majority of the country's government organs, including the army and intelligence agencies.

Egypt later suffered a wave of Brotherhood terrorism. The most prominent of these terrorist attacks was known in Western media as the "Rabi'a sit-in protest," which described the Muslim Brotherhood taking over a neighborhood in Cairo from June 28 to July 14. Brotherhood operatives and members of other terrorist groups blocked roads surrounding the Nasr City neighborhood and turned it into an armed militant camp where they engaged in torture, murder, and kidnapping.

58 Al-Watan News (Cairo), August 2, 2012.

THE MUSLIM BROTHERHOOD'S THIRD FOUNDING

On August 20, 2013, the Egyptian government arrested Public Guide Muhammad Badie on terrorism charges, and he was sentenced to life in prison. Following his arrest, Secret Apparatus leader Mahmoud Ezzat became the Acting General Guide. On June 14, 2021, Egypt's highest civilian court upheld the death sentence for twelve Muslim Brotherhood leaders for their roles in various terrorist attacks across the country. These included the Brotherhood Mufti Abdul Rahman al-Bar, former Brotherhood Member of Parliament Muhammad al-Beltagi, and former Brotherhood Minister in Morsi's regime, Osama Yassin. While Ezzat was acting as the interim Guide, he went into hiding from Egyptian police until his arrest.

After the government dispersed the Rabi'a militant camp, the Brotherhood continued their asymmetrical warfare. Ezzat's interim leadership left the group split into two camps. It is important not to fall into the trap of projecting assumptions on the nature of their rift. The fracture in the organization was not over ideology but rather regarding which strategy to utilize in implementing the ideals they shared. One camp believed in maintaining the current structure of operating two façades, a public and secret one. The other vanguard believed that maintaining this structure had failed and the group's false public narrative regarding nonviolence had damaged the morale of the Secret Apparatus jihadists engaged in terrorism.

THE OLD GUARD

The first camp is the Brotherhood's old guard. The Brotherhood's elderly leadership were a group of comfortable parastatal opposition figures living under regimes that either sponsored them or allowed them to operate with impunity, while they carried out their clandestine, gradual revolutionary project against these governments. After the Egyptian crackdown on their national and international empire, they became refugees and émigrés.

The old guard's leader from 2013 to 2020 were Mahmoud Ezzat, and its current spokesman is the London-based Ahmed Ibrahim Munir Mustafa, also known as Ibrahim Munir. Munir is currently the Acting General Guide of the Egyptian Muslim Brotherhood. He is also the Secretary General of the International Apparatus and Spokesman for the Muslim Brotherhood in the West. Munir's role is to sell shallow rhetoric to Westerners about the Brotherhood, and he does not have much organizational power. Munir's function doesn't go beyond being one of the retired jihadists of Qutb's *Tanzim 1965*.

THE KAMAL VANGUARD

The second camp is known as the Kamal Group, Kamal Vanguard, or *al-Kamaliun* (the Kamalists), named after Muhammad Kamal. The vanguard comprises of the younger generation of Brotherhood jihadists and older operatives, such as Yusuf al-Qaradawi. It incorporates the International Apparatus within chapters in the West.

The Kamalists believe that the Brotherhood should openly operate as a militant organization similar to the structure of Hamas. With many Secret Apparatus leaders in prison, Kamal took full control of the military wing and assigned Yassir Abdul Mijid Mihriz to be the Secret Apparatus' spokesman. Mihriz operated with the code name Muhammad Muntasir.

From July 2013 to mid 2015, Kamal established *al-lajna al-idaria al-ulliya* (the Supreme Administrative Committee) to act as the governing body of the Secret Apparatus.[59] The committee operated the terror apparatus' *lijan al-amaliyat al-mutaqadima* (the Progressive

59 The Supreme Administrative Committee, "Bayan al-Lajna al-Idariya al-Ullia l'al-Ikhwan bi-Sha'n al-Azma ad-Dakhiliyya l'al-Jama'a," https://ikhwanonline.com/, December 18, 2015.

Operations Committee or POC), also known as *al-lijan al-naw'iyya* (Qualitative Committees).[60] The names of these committees are intentionally vague and awkward, as they are responsible for plotting, funding, and carrying out terrorist attacks.

The Supreme Administrative Committee announced its launch on December 18, 2015, in a press release titled *Bayan al-Lajna al-Idaria al-Ulliya l'al-Ikhwan bi-Sha'n al-Azma ad-Dakhiliyya l'al-Jama'a* (The Proclamation of the Supreme Administrative Committee Regarding the Internal Crisis in the Organization). This proclamation was written by the group's Spokesman, Muntasir, and it was published on the Kamalist vanguard's official website, IkhwanOnline.net.[61] The Kamal Vanguard considered Muntasir and not Munir as the actual spokesman of both the Secret Apparatus and General Apparatus.[62]

The proclamation was also published on the Muslim Brotherhood's official website, IkhwanOnline.com. It stated:

> To the masses of our brothers and sisters, the offspring of the blessed Muslim Brotherhood across the earth, the loyal sons of the ummah who await Allah's victory, and an imminent conquest which will depose tyrants squatting on its chests, [the Supreme Administrative Committee] is [the] forefront of the bereaved whose blood was shed to elevate truth, and [represents] the lions behind the bars of injustice and oppression, [to] our rebellious sisters who are awaiting vengeance from criminal aggressors, [to] the rebellious jihadists in the streets and the public squares who comprehend the [jihadist] means of victory, those chased and on the run everywhere, to those we say, God will help us.

---

60 Bawabat al-Haraqat al-Islamiyya (Cairo), December 20, 2016.

61 The Supreme Administrative Committee, "Bayan al-Lajna al-Idariya al-Ullia l'al-Ikhwan bi-Sha'n al-Azma ad-Dakhiliyya l'al-Jama'a," https://ikhwanonline.com/, December 18, 2015.

62 Ibid.

The document stated that Muntasir was the actual spokesman of the Brotherhood, and added, "We call upon everyone to work hard and exert effort in resisting the brutal coup, and we urge the revolutionaries not to be distracted and focus on the revolution, and we call upon the Brotherhood abroad to be our support and back their brothers through prayer, funds, in addition to their other obligation in the fields of jihad."

The same day the Kamal Vanguard issued this announcement, the American Muslim Brotherhood chapter responded by accepting the Supreme Administrative Committee's demands. New York City-based Muslim Brotherhood spokesman Mahmoud Elsharkawy accepted the legitimacy of the Kamal Vanguard and vowed to uphold it. Elsharkawy operates in the United States under the Muslim Brotherhood front organization, Egyptian Americans for Freedom and Justice (EAFAJ).

On his official Facebook page, Elsharkawy said:

> God Almighty has willed that the Muslim Brotherhood organization go through a path of rebirth. A year and half ago, it started to follow the path of Hamas. I think the third founding of the Muslim Brotherhood has publicly emerged today, which means that the banner of jihad will topple any other. The resistance will strike the forts of tyrants. The desire of our youth to raise the banner and refuse submission was heeded. Now, it is time for the early great leaders and mentors to leave the leadership of the field of revolution to the youth who have not abandoned it.[63]

Prior to this official announcement of his support for the vanguard, Elsharkawy and the American Brotherhood chapter had already been publicly supportive of the Secret Apparatus' Progressive

63 Mahmoud Elsharkawy's Facebook Account, www.facebook.com/mahmoud.sharkawy.7, accessed July 4, 2021; Farahat, "Islamists with Direct Ties to Terrorists." 11-3.

Operations Committee (POC) and the terrorist organizations they created. Among the militias established by the POC was Hasm. On January 14, 2021, the US Department of State designated Hasm a Foreign Terrorist Organization.[64]

Hasm was involved in several terrorist attacks. For example, on August 5, 2016, they attempted to assassinate former Grand Mufti of Egypt Ali Gom'a. On September 29, 2016, they placed a Vehicle-Borne Improvised Explosive Device (VBIED) to attempt to murder Zakaria Abdul Aziz, senior secretary to the country's top prosecutor. While Aziz was not harmed in the attack, several pedestrians were injured. Ten days later, Hasm perpetrated a terrorist attack at the Giza Plateau that killed six police officers.[65] On April 11, 2019, Hasm executed another VBIED terrorist attack outside the National Cancer Institute in downtown Cairo, killing twenty people and injuring forty-seven.[66] These are only a few examples of numerous similar attacks.

Hasm worked closely with Islamic State, and several of its members appeared in Islamic State propaganda videos. One of the most famous Hasm cells embodied Kamal's vision. The case is known in Egypt as the *khaliat Arab Sharkas* (the cell of Arab Sharkas). The cell is named after an Arabia tribe situated in Qalyubiyya governorate, located in the Nile Delta region. Members of the Muslim Brotherhood's youth wing from the Arab Sharkas tribe operated Hasm and were fully supported by the American Brotherhood chapter.

On May 17, 2015, Elsharkawy called for jihad and praised the Arab Sharkas terrorist cell on his Facebook page, saying:

> Oh revolutionaries, let's revive the absent obligation, let's revive jihad, if the criminals are persistent in the

64 United States Department of State, Terrorist Designations and State Sponsors of Terrorism Foreign Terrorist Organizations, www.State.gov/Foreign-Terrorist-Organizations, accessed July 4, 2021.

65 Lizzie Dearden, "Cairo Bombing: Hasm Movement Claims Responsibility for Explosion that Killed Six Near Giza Pyramids," *The Independent*, December 9, 2016.

66 Reuters Staff, "Twenty Dead as Car Explodes Outside Cairo Hospital," *Reuters*, August 4, 2019.

> path of killing young people and carrying out executions. Where are we—myself included—from our pact with Allah? The path of the believers is not easy. We all know that, for it is not laden with roses. Truth requires force, so be the force. Your knowledge is power, your money is power, your time is power, your prayer is power. The resistance pains them and shakes their world and you know it. Let's start surprising them. We should be initiators and not reactionaries. By God, by God, they are weak, submissive and they are terrified of you. Our initiative should be well-calculated and well-studied, let's avoid any impulsive actions that can do more harm than good and lead to more losses than gains. Revive faith in your hearts, and know that Allah will bestow victory upon his soldiers. Our martyrs are blissful in heaven. By Allah we ask that we should join them, not turning away in flight.[67]

Elsharkawy followed his statement with the hashtag *#Arab_Sharkas* and *Shouhad'a_Arab_Sharkas_Fi'l_Janaah* (Arab Sharkas martyrs are in heaven).

On May 18, 2015, Elsharkawy posted a tribute to the Arab Sharkas terrorist cell on his public Facebook page, writing that the group "revives in us the meaning of jihad." On February 3, 2016, Elsharkawy posted a picture of Secret Apparatus/Hasm terrorist Abdul Rahman Sa'id, who was featured in an Islamic State propaganda video, calling him a "martyr" and a "hero."[68] Elsharkawy posted pictures featuring letters he wrote in gold ink, Qur'anic verses with the names of Arab Sharkas terrorists who were executed in Egypt.[69]

---

67 Mahmoud Elsharkawy's Facebook Account, accessed July 4, 2021; Farahat, "Islamists with Direct Ties to Terrorists," 11.
68 Al-Bawaba News (Cairo), May 5, 2015.
69 Farahat, "Islamists with Direct Ties to Terrorists," 13.

Elsharkawy is also an activist in local New York City politics. He has posted several pictures of himself with New York Mayor Bill de Blasio, a politician Elsharkawy supported in the election campaign. Elsharkawy also posted a picture of himself dining with former Republican Congressman John Faso.[70]

The next pages will reveal that Elsharkawy is one of many examples of Brotherhood operatives associated with the Kamal Vanguard who wield power in the United States.

70 Ibid.

CHAPTER NINE

THE VANGUARDS OF ORGANIZED INVASION

The Creation of the International Apparatus and the Role of Al-Azhar University in Transnational Terrorism

"All our vigilance has to be directed toward establishing a solid Qaeda of pure believers"

—Omar Abdel Rahman, the Blind Sheikh[1]

THE MUSLIM BROTHERHOOD WAS FOUNDED as an Egyptian organization, but its members view it as a stateless international entity because of their theological belief that nation-states should not exist. Syrian Brotherhood leader and member of the International Apparatus' Guidance Bureau Sa'id Hawwa (1935–1989) described the world's partition into nation-states as an "infidel international structure which entirely conflicts with the organization."[2]

The Muslim Brotherhood exists to implement an Islamic caliphate, and it fights national sovereignty around the world. The International Apparatus initially emerged as another organ of the Egyptian Secret

1 Omar Abdel Rahman, *Mawqif al-Qur'an min Khusumahu* (Cairo: Masr al-Mahrousa Publishing House, 2006), 21–2.

2 Sa'id Hawwa, *Al-Madkhal ila-Da'wa al-Ikhwan al-Muslimin* (Cairo: Maktabat Wahabah, 2006), 171.

Apparatus, but it now operates as a clandestine unit disembodied from any specific nationality yet with powerful representation in the Middle East and the West.

Some Muslim Brotherhood apologists even deny the existence of its core mission by claiming each of the Muslim Brotherhood chapters has "complete operational independence" where they engage in "reshaping" and accommodating "the Brotherhood's ideology and tactics to fit into non-Muslim majority societies."[3] The core mission of the International Apparatus is the exact opposite, according to its bylaws and the words and actions of its operatives and leaders. Whether out of ignorance or nefarious motivations, Muslim Brotherhood propagandists claim chapters are independent to distance Brotherhood members in the United States from openly violent Middle Eastern and African branches.

Since the Muslim Brotherhood is a clandestine organization, the overwhelming majority of its members keep their group affiliation secret. Only a few operatives advertise their membership, and they do so in compliance with the Brotherhood's rules and regulations to fulfill specific roles. The International Apparatus is the body that hosts Secret Apparatus leaders worldwide. It is directly involved in founding and sometimes operating transnational terror groups. The International Apparatus is not only responsible for franchising terrorism worldwide. Equally important is its political machine, which propagates specific narratives to aid their covert and overt missions.

In 1983, Secret Apparatus leaders established *al-Markaz al-Ilmi l'al-Behuth w'ad-Dirasat* (Scholarly Center for Research and Studies), or *Ma'bad*. The aim of the center was to network among Muslim Brotherhood members who infiltrated academia in Egypt. As-Sayyid Abdul Sattar led the unit. The center was established as a limited liability company to give a "legal and logical" cover for their clandestine

3 Editorial, "The Opportunities Arising from Designating the Muslim Brotherhood as a Terrorist Organization," *European Eye on Radicalization*, May 10, 2019.

communications.[4] The center was successful in utilizing the classic Islamist pattern of operating nongovernmental organizations to provide cover for their activities, and they branched out internationally.

The International Apparatus' political and militant missions are based on Sayyid Qutb and Abul A'la al-Mawdudi's (1903–1979) definition of *hakimiyya* (Islamic theocracy), which recognizes neither nations nor borders. The myth of independent chapters is refuted by the Brotherhood's own words, their philosophy toward nation-states, and their definition of citizenship. This notion is deeply ingrained in their mentality, and it explains why President Gamal Abdel Nasser renamed Egypt and removed its name *Misr* for the first and only time in the country's history and called it the United Arab Republic from 1957 to 1971 during its short alliance with Syria which only lasted till 1961. Nasser wanted to become a caliph and rule the region.

THE VANGUARDS OF ORGANIZED INVASION

The Secret Apparatus calls the covert operators in their international subversive mission *Talai' al-Ghazw al-Mu'ad*: the Vanguards of Organized Invasion (VOI), or Vanguards of Organized Conquest.[5] This International Apparatus cell was led by Ahmad Abdul Mejid (1933–2012), Khairat al-Shater, and Hassan Malik. In the early 1980s the cell operated under the guise of a company they called Salsabil, sometimes spelled Salsabeel. Its first branch was established in London in 1983 and Shater and Malek franchised it across Europe, Egypt, the Kingdom of Saudi Arabia, Kuwait, and Yemen.[6] Salsabil

4 As-Sayyid Abdul Sattar, *Tajrubati ma' al-Ikhwan min ad-D'wa ila at-Tanzim as-Sirri,* The Official Muslim Brotherhood Encyclopedia, https://ikhwanwiki.com/, accessed June 9, 2021.

5 Ibid.

6 The Official Muslim Brotherhood Encyclopedia, "Khairat al-shater wa-Qadiat Salsabil," www.IkhwanWiki.com, accessed June 10, 2021; As-Sayyid Abdul Sattar, *Tajrubati ma' al-Ikhwan min ad-d'wa ila at-Tanzim as-Sirri*, The Official Muslim Brotherhood Encyclopedia, https://ikhwanwiki.com/, accessed June 9, 2021.

was an import/export company that traded in a wide array of products including food, beverages, and computers. The International Apparatus, under the guise of Salsabil, was led by clandestine operatives in every country where it operated.

In 1982, the VOI had evolved into the *Maktab al-Irshad al-Alami* (International Guidance Bureau).[7] Among the most prominent ideological leaders in the VOI was Sa'id Hawwa. He was recruited to join the Muslim Brotherhood in 1954 when he was still in high school. While he was studying Shari'a law at Damascus University, he became a protégé of Mustafa al-Siba'i, the Brotherhood Guide in Syria at the time. Hawwa succeeded Siba'i in the leadership of the Syrian wing of the Brotherhood and was among its most prominent leaders from 1978 to 1982. In 1982, he left the leadership of the local group to become a member of the International Guidance Bureau until 1984 and again from 1984 to 1987.[8]

Hawwa was among the most important clandestine leaders in the Muslim Brotherhood's International Apparatus and a prominent recruiter for al-Qaeda.[9] During his international ventures for the Brotherhood, he traveled to recruit jihadists and promote their rhetoric in the Kingdom of Saudi Arabia, Qatar, Kuwait, the United Arab Emirates, Iraq, Jordan, Egypt, Pakistan, the United States, and Germany.[10] When Hawwa recruited jihadists, they had to study his Muslim Brotherhood manifesto, titled *Al-Madkhal ila Da'wa al-Ikhwan al-Muslimin* (Introduction to the Muslim Brotherhood Call). In his book, he followed in the footsteps of his ideological predecessors and limited the definition of "Muslim" to only those who were active members in the Brotherhood.[11]

---

7 Ash-shaikh al-Imam Sa'id Hawwa, "Ash-shaikh Sa'id Hawwah: Bitaka Shakhsiyya," www.SaidHawwa.com, October 21, 2010.

8 Ibid.

9 Ibid.

10 Abdullah al-Aqeel, "Ad-Da'iyya al-Mujahid Sa'id Hawa," The Official Muslim Brotherhood Encyclopedia, https://ikhwanwiki.com/, accessed June 20, 2021.

11 Sa'id Hawwa, *Al-Madkhal ila-Da'wa al-Ikhwan al-Muslimin*, 172.

The Salsabil company operated with impunity in Egypt under President Mubarak's regime until 1992. On February 5, 1992, Egyptian State Security Investigations Service (SSIS) searched its offices and seized its computers and documents. The police arrested Khairat al-Shater, Hassan Malek, Mahmoud Ezzat, and others. The head of the SSIS unit investigating Salsabil was Colonel Rif'at Qumsan. This investigation was known in Egypt as "the Salsaibil case."

Police seized a document about the Secret Apparatus and another titled *ghazw Misr*, "The Conquering of Egypt." The Egyptian government released parts of the document that focused on propaganda tactics similar to the Explanatory Memorandum, which the FBI uncovered in Virginia in 2004. The Egyptian document reveals that while its author is Egyptian, Brotherhood members view themselves as outsiders on a colonial expedition. This outlook is deeply ingrained in the Brotherhood.

Former Brotherhood leader Mukhtar Nouh, the Brotherhood's attorney in the Salsabil case, said that al-Shater's "biggest mistake was discussing the Secret Apparatus in a document on his computer. Which is why officer Rif'at Qumsan was able to identify the apparatus in the Salsabil case."[12] The investigation led to the arrest of Shater, Malek, and fifty-four other members of the apparatus, but they were all released after making a deal with Mubarak's regime.

The Conquering of Egypt document also detailed the Brotherhood's strategy of infiltrating Egyptian military intelligence. The Brotherhood later proved they succeeded in this strategy. For example, Major General Abbas Mukheimar, the army officer assigned to oversee the purge of officers with Brotherhood or other Islamist affiliations from the army under President Mubarak's regime, was himself a member of the Brotherhood.[13] Tharwat al-Kherbawy said he was confident the Muslim Brotherhood Officers cell is still opera-

12 Akhir al-Nahar, "Liqa' Mukhtar Nouh," YouTube.com, June 1, 2015.
13 *Al-Quds Al-Arabi* (London), September 3, 2012.

tional inside the army.[14] It's highly likely that his statement applies to most armies in countries where the Brotherhood operates.

The Brotherhood copied the USSR's international apparatus' stratagems, and several of the twenty-one conditions of the Comintern. In Brotherhood literature, the International Apparatus is often referred to as *al-Nizam al-Alami* (the international order), and it is also known as *al-Jihaz ad-Dawli* (International Apparatus). Similar to the Comintern, the Brotherhood is always "prepared for transition to illegal conditions," which is clear from their description of their military preparations during the time of peace. Also, like the Comintern, the Brotherhood requires "a secret apparatus even where a party may operate openly."[15] The group's persistent requirement for secrecy and concealment has benefited their mission around the globe.

The International Apparatus' mission in the West has two façades: an overt one, which operates Islamic front organizations, Islamic schools, and mosques; and a covert operation, which handles funds, and partially or fully operates terrorist groups or cooperates with them.

The apparatus evolved through several stages over several decades. The Brotherhood's international activities can be traced to 1931, when Amin al-Husaini established the World Islamic Congress' secret society in Jerusalem. This Congress included several prominent jihadists who were involved with the Muslim Brotherhood, such as the founder of the Islamic Ethics Association, Sheikh Abdul-Wahhab al-Naggar.[16] During his stay in Cairo, Banna was close to Naggar, whose trip to Jerusalem is considered by the Brotherhood to mark the beginning of their involvement in international "active jihad."[17]

During the summer of the same year, Naggar led a delegation of young Islamists from several organizations, including the Muslim Brotherhood, on a trip to Mandatory Palestine, Syria, and Lebanon.

14 Kherbawy, *Sir al-Ma'bad*, 183.
15 Attorney General v. Communist Party, Reports on the Subversive Activities Control Board, 273, https://play.google.com/books/reader?id=UiUrAQAAMAAJ&pg=GBS.PA272.
16 Al-Risala (Cairo), January 12, 1941.
17 Ibid.

The trip aimed to connect them with Islamists from these countries. In 1934, Naggar took his Islamist youth mission to connect with Islamists from Turkey.[18]

Early signs of Banna's expansionist vision included his delegation to Husaini in 1935 and their involvement in the 1936–1939 Great Revolt in Mandatory Palestine. In the Brotherhood's duplicitous fashion, parallel to the Brotherhood's jihad in the Great Revolt, their ideological wing promoted their values internationally. The first head of Banna's Propagation of the Message section, Mustafa al-Maraghi, organized an official al-Azhar campaign in India in 1936. This movement aimed to "study the state of Indian lower castes prior to attempting to convert them to Islam."[19] The Brotherhood studied the conditions of Indian Muslims to establish a rapport with them. During the same year, Banna travelled for hajj to Saudi Arabia, where he met with Ibn Saud. Banna asked him to grant him permission to establish a branch of the Brotherhood in Saudi Arabia. Ibn Saud declined, so Banna reverted to clandestine proselytism in Arabia and used the hajj to circulate his propaganda.[20]

Sheikh Maraghi's trip to India in 1936 regurgitated the Ottoman-German strategy of mobilizing al-Azhar as a tool for political agitation and international jihad under the guise of promoting religion. This suggests Maraghi was one of the founding fathers of the International Apparatus.

Utilizing al-Azhar for transnational terrorism and political agitation may have led to the University's involvement in founding al-Qaeda and their pioneering the practice of cyber jihad. The involvement of al-Azhar allowed the Brotherhood to propagate covert jihad in Saudi Arabia and other nations by assigning Brotherhood operatives to work in education in targeted nations. The Secret Apparatus has adopted this strategy across the world, including in the United

---

18 Ibid.
19 Ibid.
20 Okaz (Riyadh), December 23, 2018.

States, where confirmed Brotherhood operatives and convicted terrorists are involved in education.

During the third Shura Council meeting in 1935, Banna presented a list of fifty demands to all Muslim rulers, leaders, judges, heads of Islamic organizations, and Islamist public figures. The demands covered means for Islamizing every aspect of life. He urged leaders to abolish their political systems and parties and establish a universal Islamic caliphate to rule the world.[21] Several of the fifty demands were fulfilled by Gamal Abdel Nasser, Anwar al-Sadat, and Mubarak.

The most important demands were abolishing political parties, Islamizing education, and injecting Shari'a law into the Egyptian constitution. This turned Egypt into a constitutional theocracy where the legislative branch is unofficially controlled by al-Azhar University clergy who are involved in drafting or vetting laws prior to parliamentary approval. This system remains in place today.

The International Apparatus is responsible for implementing Banna's rules worldwide. The first Brotherhood cells outside Egypt were officially formed in Mandatory Palestine in 1937, when they created Brotherhood clans and assigned their chiefs.[22] The Brotherhood also operated the clandestine Islamic Ethics Association society in Palestine from 1943–1944.[23] In 1947, Banna assigned his son-in-law, Sa'id Ramadan (1926–1995), to officially establish the Muslim Brotherhood's office in Gaza. Amin al-Husaini requested that King Abdullah I of Jordan place Ramadan in his government, but he only served for one or two months. With the help of Husaini, Brotherhood offices were established across Mandatory Palestine and Transjordan.

Ramadan became instrumental in creating the International Apparatus in the West, and he began with Germany. It wasn't a diffi-

21 Ali Abdul Halim Mahmud, *Wasa'il at-Tarbiyya*, 71–5.

22 "Tarikh al-Ikhwan al-Muslimin fi Falastin," The Official Muslim Brotherhood Encyclopedia, https://ikhwanwiki.com/, accessed May 20, 2021.

23 Ra'fat Fahd al-Morra, *Al-Harakat wa'l-wa'l-wa'l-Quwah al-Islamiyya fi al-Mujtama' al-Falastini fi Lebanon* (Markaz al-Zaituna, 2010), 18.

cult task. Max von Oppenheim's policy of unleashing "Muslim fanaticism that borders on insanity" was adopted by Gerhard von Mende (1904–1963), who reinstated the policy of using jihadist mercenaries against the Soviets, just like his predecessors used them against the British. In 1941, Mende was hired by then-Reich Minister of the Occupied Eastern Territories Alfred Rosenberg. Mende was "fully briefed on the planned genocide of Jews at March 6, 1942, follow-up meeting of the Wannsee Conference since he would help implement that policy in the Caucasus."[24]

Mende also worked with Amin al-Husaini.[25] Despite his resume, Mende was still funded by West Germany's government to continue his research to help them implement their policies of mobilizing Muslim against communists. By the late 1950s, Germany was a hub for spies recruiting Islamist émigrés—including Muslim Brotherhood operatives escaping Nasser's regime after his failed assassination attempt. The most important of the Brotherhood immigrants was Sa'id Ramadan. His proximity to Banna gave him organizational power over his peers.

The CIA's American Committee for Liberation (Amcomlib) in Munich began to replicate Mende's mission and even collaborated with him at some point.[26] In his book *A Mosque in Munich: Nazis, the CIA, and the Rise of the Muslim Brotherhood in the West*, Ian Johnson suggested the CIA worked with Ramadan. Johnson wrote, "West German intelligence stated plainly in separate reports that the United States had secured Ramadan a Jordanian passport, allowing him to flee to Europe, while Swiss intelligence claimed that he was a US agent."[27]

But as it is almost always the case, Muslim Brotherhood spies ended up operating as double agents. While Mendes and Ramadan's

---

24 Rubin and Schwanitz, Nazis, *Islamists, and the Making of the Modern Middle East* (Yale University Press), 147.

25 Ian Johnson, *A Mosque in Munich: Nazis, the CIA, and the Rise of the Muslim Brotherhood in the West* (Boston: Houghton Mifflin Harcourt Trade, 2010), 112.

26 Ibid., 90.

27 Ibid., 131–2.

CIA handlers might have believed that they were using Islamists, the Muslim Brotherhood's plan was more farsighted. Ramadan also used the CIA but better. In the late 1950s Ramadan met with then-Prince Faisal bin Abdulaziz al-Saud (1906–1975), and he convinced him to help "establish Islamic centers in major European cities with the aim to Islamize them."[28] Prince Faisal would become king and the world's most important patron of jihadist agitation before others followed suit.

Ramadan toured Europe with his personal assistant, the Syrian-born Ali Ghaleb Himmat. Himmat played a secretive role most of his life. Born in 1938, he joined the Muslim Brotherhood branch in Syria when he was a teenager. The Muslim Brotherhood's Syrian branch was formed by Mustafa al-Siba'i, who was recruited by the Brotherhood in 1930 while he was studying at al-Azhar University in Cairo. Mustafa al-Siba'i joined the group and returned to Syria to lead their office from 1946 to 1961.

After joining the Brotherhood, Himmat visited Cairo in 1950, where he befriended Ramadan. When the attempt to kill Nasser failed, they both fled together and traveled to several countries, including Saudi Arabia, Syria, and Lebanon, before traveling to Europe in 1956. In 1961, they cofounded the Islamic Center in Munich, as a Muslim Brotherhood front group. The Brotherhood assigned Himmat as head of the group's unit, managing their refugees abroad.

In May 1947, the Muslim Brotherhood held a multinational conference in Pakistan. The conference was formally attended by representatives from three of the organization's sections; the al-Azhar dominated Propagation of the Message section, the Liaison with the Islamic World Section (currently the International Apparatus), and the Students section. The conference's mission was to dominate Muslim-majority countries. It had representatives from Tunisia, Lebanon, Syria, the Kingdom of Saudi Arabia, and other countries.[29]

28 "Dr. Said Ramadan: As-Sikirtair ash-Shakhsi l'al-Imam al-Banna," The Official Muslim Brotherhood Encyclopedia, https://ikhwanwiki.com/, accessed May 21, 2021.

29 Bawabat al-Haqat al-Islamiyya (Cairo), August 26, 2019.

The first public establishment of the International Apparatus was in 1963 when the Guidance Bureau established the *Maktab at-Tanzim bain al-Aqtar al-Arabiyya* (Inter-Arab Coordination Office).[30] The office operated from the Islamic Center in Munich, which the Brotherhood referred to as the *Markaz al-Amaliyat* (Operations Headquarters).[31] The Islamic Center in Munich franchised the Muslim Brotherhood's wings worldwide, including their branch in the United States. The Brotherhood admits that the operation of the Islamic Center of Munich was aborted only after the September 11, 2001, attacks against the United States.[32] Prior to the attack, the center coordinated between Muslim Brotherhood leaders and jihadists from al-Qaeda. Himmat was also accused of funding al-Qaeda.[33]

THE STRUCTURE THE INTERNATIONAL APPARATUS

The 1980s witnessed a significant revival of the International Apparatus. The International Apparatus was officially formed in 1963 but as a single office without a well-defined mission or massive structure. The apparatus fully emerged on the international scene almost two decades later. The announcement of the inauguration of the revised International Apparatus took place on July 29, 1982, under the leadership of Mustafa Mashhour.

Abdullah Yusuf Azzam (1941–1989) is commonly referred to as the Father of Global Jihad, but the title more fittingly describes Mustafa Mashhour, who was known in the Brotherhood as the "iron

30 Nahda Media Institute, "Al-Ikhwan al-Muslimin fi-Asr Mubarak," The Official Muslim Brotherhood Encyclopedia, https://ikhwanwiki.com/, accessed July 3, 2021.

31 Ibid.

32 Ibid.

33 Ian Johnson, *A Mosque in Munich*, 188.

man" of the Secret Apparatus.[34] He was the one responsible for the structure of modern terrorist organizations.

On September 5, 1981, one month prior to the assassination of then-President Anwar al-Sadat, Mashhour escaped to Kuwait and then fled to Germany, where the Brotherhood's Secret Apparatus had a strong presence. Mashhour reestablished his apparatus with several leaders, including Kamal as-Sananiri, one of the masterminds of Nasser's assassination attempt of 1954; Ahmed al-Malt, one of the terrorists imprisoned by the government in the case of the Jeep automobile and the deputy of the three General Guides: Omar al-Tilmisani, Muhammad Hamid Abu al-Nasr, and Mustafa Mashhour.

The third major Secret Apparatus operative who cofounded the new International Apparatus with Mashhour was Ahmed Hassanein, who had previously cofounded the Secret Apparatus with Banna. Other leaders of the Secret Apparatus also were involved in reestablishing the International Apparatus. Their first mission was to build a heavily regulated unit with strict guidelines and to "restructure the Brotherhood's scattered entities around the world to fuse them together into one organization."[35]

The 1982 Muslim Brotherhood bylaw amendments clearly defined the purpose for the International Apparatus. The introduction to the International Apparatus section of the bylaws states, "The Muslim Brotherhood everywhere are one organization united by *da'wa* and [these] bylaws."[36]

Articles forty-three to forty-seven of the bylaws lay out the rules that govern every member of the Brotherhood. These articles explicitly bind Brotherhood members to the laws and regulations dictated by

34 Ahmad Ban, *Al-Ikhwan al-Muslimin wa Mihnat al-Watan w'ad-Din* (Cairo: Mahrusa Publishing, 2015), 53.

35 Nahda Media Institute, "Al-Ikhwan al-Muslimin fi-Asr Mubarak," The Official Muslim Brotherhood Encyclopedia, https://ikhwanwiki.com/, accessed July 3, 2021.

36 "La'hat 1982," The Official Muslim Brotherhood Encyclopedia, https://ikhwanwiki.com/, accessed July 3, 2021.

the General Guide, the Guidance Bureau, and the Shura Council. The mythology propagated by Brotherhood apologists that each chapter has "complete operational independence" is refuted by these articles.

The apparatus has its own Shura Council, comprising at least thirty leaders, a number subject to increase. Each Shura member is a representative of a country where the Brotherhood operates. They are chosen by their local General Apparatus' Shura Council and Brotherhood leaders in each nations. Local Shura Councils are aided by a local Executive Office. Each level of this operation must be approved by the Brotherhood's main public apparatus leadership, represented in the General Guide and the Guidance Bureau. The local Guidance Office of each country is prohibited from exercising any major political activities without the permission of the General Guidance Bureau.[37]

Since the Muslim Brotherhood is a clandestine organization, it operates through front groups in every country. Front groups are controlled by each country's Secret Apparatus branch. Each country has its own clandestine General Guide and a Secret Guide for both legal and/or illegal activities.

According to the Brotherhood, their nongovernmental organizations and think tanks are all "centralized institutions governed by a Guide for International Apparatus and a Guidance Bureau for the International Apparatus."[38] The General Guide for the International Apparatus' Guidance Bureau consists of thirteen members; eight from the geographic region where the Guide resides, and five from other major international regions where the apparatus operates. The General Guide of the International Apparatus is also the Secret Guide of the Muslim Brotherhood. This leadership mechanism was instigated by Mustafa Mashhour, who assumed both positions at the same time.

37 Ibid.
38 Ibid.

HIGHLIGHTS IN THE BYLAWS OF THE INTERNATIONAL APPARATUS

The 1982 bylaws have three major requirements.[39] First, all Muslim Brotherhood leaders in every country where they operate "must abide by the decisions of the General [Apparatus'] leadership, represented by the General Guide, the General Guidance Bureau, and the General Shura Council." These entail "commitment to the articles in these bylaws," including conditions and degrees of membership. It is also mandatory to operate a local Shura Council alongside the Executive Office, which is headed by a General Supervisor. The first section of the bylaws also obliges each Brotherhood member to abide by the Brotherhood's "understanding of Islam derived from the Qur'an and Sunnah and represented in the twenty principles [of the International Apparatus]."[40]

The bylaws also state that it is obligatory to abide by "the compulsory methodology of restructuring members in the manner mandated by General Apparatus' Shura Council." The document stressed the required commitment to the Muslim Brotherhood's "policies and positions toward public matters which are decided by the General [Apparatus'] Guidance Bureau and Shura Council prior to taking any major political decision."

The second major requirement of the 1982 bylaws states the clandestine General Guide in any nation "should consult with/and concur" the General Apparatus' leadership decisions regarding important local dealings that can affect the group in another country.

The third section of the bylaws allows a narrow margin of operational autonomy where the local clandestine leaders are allowed to work with "complete freedom" strictly in logistic matters, which do not have any bearing on the Brotherhood's operation in any other

39 Ibid.

40 Walid Shalabi, "Waqafat ma' al-Usul al-Ishrin," The Official Muslim Brotherhood Encyclopedia, https://ikhwanwiki.com/, accessed January 15, 2021.

country. The second restriction on this freedom is "conditioned by the chapter's obligation to abide by the general public opinions and positions, as well as methodologies legitimized by the General [Apparatus] to fulfill its mission and values depending on the chapter's circumstances and [operational] state." The Brotherhood defines complete freedom as, "everything which relates to the group's plan toward its targeted region, the activities of their sections, its [plans] for expansion, its views on local issues."[41] All decisions taken by a local chapter must be detailed in an annual report submitted to the General Supervisor who is tasked with sharing it with the General Apparatus' leadership.

In September 1991, International Apparatus leaders met in Istanbul. The head of the International and Secret Apparatuses was Mustafa Mashhour, who operated with the code name Abu Hani. During the meeting, Mashhour presented a document titled *Reassessing the Past Stage of the International Apparatus.* The document analyzed the International Apparatus operation since Mashhour reestablished it in 1982. It was divided into five sections: (1) the ideology of the apparatus, (2) objectives, (3) methodology, (4) mistakes during the prior decade, and (5) suggestions and recommendations.[42]

Currently, the International Apparatus is directed from Brotherhood enclaves in the United States, Qatar, Turkey, and several European nations. The heads of the apparatus in each country are clandestine, but they can be identified through specific markers that will be revealed in the next pages.

41 "La'hat 1982," The Official Muslim Brotherhood Encyclopedia.
42 Al-Bawaba News (Cairo), March 21, 2018.

AL-AZHAR UNIVERSITY'S ROLE IN SPREADING TRANSNATIONAL JIHADISM

The appointment of former Ottoman-German agent Khidr as the Grand Imam of al-Azhar University in 1952 began the trend of installing jihadist agitators and Muslim Brotherhood leaders into positions of power. Khidr's successor, Abdul Rahman Taj (1896–1975), continued this agenda during his leadership at al-Azhar, and the Brotherhood's control of the university remains until today.

This author discovered the involvement of two Islamic institutions, al-Azhar University and the Council of Senior Scholars in the Kingdom of Saudi Arabia, in the founding of terrorist groups through a seemingly legitimate path. Future terrorists and jihadists conceal their terrorism manifestos as master's and PhD theses in both institutions. While the Saudi institution recently halted this practice, its Egyptian counterpart is adverse to reform. These are the only state-run institutions that the author was able to uncover evidence implicating them in this practice, but it's possible that other Islamic universities around the world are involved in the practice of legitimizing and providing material support to terrorist groups through this mechanism. Both al-Gama'a al-Islamiyya and al-Qaeda's founding document and manifestos were approved in this manner.

Yusuf al-Qaradawi was instrumental for clandestine proselytism inside al-Azhar University. Qaradawi was a known operative inside the Secret Apparatus, and he was among the Brotherhood operatives imprisoned in 1949. He was imprisoned again with the Secret Apparatus cell that attempted to assassinate Nasser in 1954 and again in 1963. Every time the government arrested Qaradawi, he was only imprisoned for few months before he was released to resume jihadist agitation.

Qaradawi was most active at al-Azhar, where he had studied since childhood. After he received his diploma from al-Azhar in 1953, he taught Arabic at al-Azhar while he resumed his post-graduate Islamic studies. He received the al-Azhar equivalent of a master's degree in 1960, and in 1973 he received the equivalent of a PhD from al-Azhar with Excellence and First-Class Honors.

During Qaradawi's two decades of activism at al-Azhar, he was involved in three different Muslim Brotherhood sections: the Propagation of the Message; Liaison with the Islamic World, where he was responsible for Syrian Islamists; and the Students section, where he was the head of al-Azhar's Brotherhood's Students division.[43]

The Brotherhood implemented specific demands inside al-Azhar. Qaradawi said these demands were: (1) teaching the English language; (2) allowing students with al-Azhar high school diplomas to join other universities and the military academy; (3) opening an al-Azhar section for women; (4) opening a higher education department and hiring adjunct professors; (4) reevaluating the curriculum and school books; and (5) giving special attention to restructuring the students' behaviors.

Qaradawi organized several riots and protests inside al-Azhar until most of these demands were fulfilled by Khidr in 1953. Qaradawi said that when Khidr was the Grand Imam of the University, he was "extremely welcoming" to Qaradawi's demands.[44] According to Hamas and Brotherhood leader Ahmad Yussef, "The openness of Sadat in the 1970s encouraged many young men from various Arab countries to flee to al-Azhar to receive master's and doctorate degrees." Yussef named several jihadists, and among them was Abdullah Azzam.

The Muslim Brotherhood employs al-Azhar University to successfully recruit transnational terrorists. Some of the world's most brutal jihadists received their formal religious training there. Al-Azhar has thousands of affiliated mosques, schools, learning centers, and uni-

---

43 Yusuf al-Qaradawi, "Al-Halqa al-Ula: Ma ba'd al-Jami'a," The Official Muslim Brotherhood Encyclopedia, https://ikhwanwiki.com/, accessed June 1, 2021.

44 Ibid.

versities around the world, such as the Islamic American University in Michigan in the United States, which removed its formal association with al-Azhar University in Cairo from its website after the author uncovered the association and wrote about it in an article in 2017.[45] This university was under the leadership of Egyptian-American Brotherhood operative Muhammad Sultan (also spelled Mohamed Soltan).[46]

In 2018, President Sisi's advisor, Ahmad Okasha, said, "The Brotherhood infiltrated al-Azhar." He added that it was unconstitutional for the university to offer non-Islamic studies such as medicine and engineering, which are restricted to Muslims only and prohibited for Christians.[47] The University is funded by Egyptian taxpayers, while it militarizes its students and turns them into jihadists.

Many infamous terrorists received their theological jihadist training at al-Azhar. Those include Amin al-Husaini; Boko Haram leader Abubakar Shekau; Muhammad Salim Rahal, founder of the al-Gama'a al-Islamiyya branch in Jordan; Afghan politician and former mujahideen commander Abdul Rasul Sayyaf; Burhanuddin Rabbani, Afghan politician and president of the Islamic State of Afghanistan from 1992 to 2001; Taliban commander Mawlawi Qassim Halimi; Abu Osama al-Masri, emir of the Islamic State in Sinai; and Muslim Brotherhood leader and Islamic State supporter Wagdi Ghoneim. These are only few examples of numerous terrorists who received their formal training at al-Azhar.

In 2015, the Egyptian government released data showing that 297,000 students were studying at al-Azhar University in 2013 and 2014.[48] In 2015, there were 39,000 foreign students at al-Azhar. All

45 Cynthia Farahat, "Is al-Azhar University a Global Security Threat?" *American Thinker*, www.AmericanThinker.com, August 23, 2017.

46 *USA Today*, April 11, 2015, https://www.usatoday.com/story/news/world/2015/04/11/michigan-muslims-sentenced-egypt/25661551/.

47 Al-Misriyun (Cairo), June 4, 2018.

48 Al-Wafd (Cairo), November 16, 2015; Al-Youm as-Sabi' (Cairo) October 12, 2015.

these students were taught the theological legitimacy of inflicting pain upon infidels through different means, including cannibalizing them.

In 2016, Muslim reformer and attorney Ahmed Abdu Maher exposed that al-Azhar University was teaching its high school students cannibalism in several texts. Among them was a book entitled *Al-Iqna' fi Hal Alfaz abi Shuja'* (Convincing Arguments in Solving the Expressions of Abi Shuja').[49] This book teaches Muslim students that it is "permissible to consume the flesh of a dead human if there wasn't any other type of meat available" but under strict conditions. For example, "if the deceased was Muslim," and the cannibal is an infidel, "then it is forbidden due to the honor of Islam."[50] The book also states that in case of famine, it is permissible for a human being to consume parts of their own bodies. The "Muslim is allowed to murder an apostate and eat him, [as well as] kill [an infidel] warrior, even if they are a child or female. It is permissible to eat them because they are not [granted] protection."[51]

In 2015, *Al-Youm as-Sabi'*, an Egyptian newspaper, published an investigative report about the curriculum at al-Azhar University. On the treatment of non-Muslims, the report quotes a section of the book that states, "To preserve oneself from the evil of an infidel, any Muslim can gouge their eyes out, or mutilate their hands and legs, or sever one arm and one leg."[52]

Also according al-Azhar, "If a Muslim apostates [from Islam] he should be imprisoned and given the choice to repent. If he doesn't repent he should be killed." The incitement for murder goes beyond leaving the religion, al-Azhar also teaches its students that "Any

49 Shams ad-Din Muhammad ash-Shirbini, *Al-Iqna' fi Hal Alfaz Abi Shuja'* (Cairo: Al-Azhar ash-Shareif Kita' al-Ma'ahid Al-Azharia l'al-Kutub, 2016), 55–7; Al-Arabiya (Dubai), March 10, 2016.

50 Al-Arabiya (Dubai), March 10, 2016.

51 Ibid.

52 Farahat, "Is Al-Azhar University a Global Security Threat?"; Al-Youm as-Sabi' (Cairo), November 26, 2014.

Muslim is allowed to kill a fornicator, a warrior, or a [Muslim] who misses prayer, even without permission of the [ruling] imam."[53]

The current Grand Imam of al-Azhar University, Ahmed al-Tayeb publicly advocated for the theological legitimacy of domestic violence against women in February 2022.[54] Al-Azhar's celebrity scholar Abdullah Rushdi went as far as advocating for bonded slavery, sex trafficking, and pedophilia. He stated that having sexual intercourse with a kidnapped slave "is not rape." Rushdi is also known for encouraging randomly sexually assaulting women as punishment for not observing Islamic clothing.[55]

These examples explain why numerous Egyptian public figures and intellectuals have called for a terrorism investigation into al-Azhar University. For example, Egyptian historian Sayyid Al-Qemany called upon the Egyptian government to designate al-Azhar University as a terrorist organization.[56]

DID AL-AZHAR UNIVERSITY PLAY A ROLE IN FOUNDING AL-QAEDA?

Omar Abdel Rahman, also known as the Blind Sheikh, died in federal prison in 2017, but the ideological tradition he created endures. It is well known that Rahman was the ideological founder of al-Qaeda and al-Gama'a al-Islamiyya. This author discovered that Rahman received direct institutional support and theological legitimization from al-Azhar University. Moreover, al-Azhar could be directly involved in the founding of al-Qaeda. The Blind Sheikh was the most influential theologian for Sunni militant groups over the past fifty years. While Rahman is dead, his violent teachings remain at al-Azhar.

53 Ibid.
54 Al-Jazeera (Doha), February 1, 2022.
55 Rahma Hajja, "Bahith Islami: As-Sabiy Ja'iz," Irfa' Sawtak website, September 10, 2019, www.irfaasawtak.com; Masrawy (Cairo) June 7, 2020; Al-Watan (Cairo), February 24, 2020.
56 "Sayyid Al-Qemany: Na'mal Jahidin ala Idrag Al-Azhar ka-Mu'asasa Irabiyya," YouTube.com, February 24, 2016.

Rahman is infamous for his 1995 conviction for conspiring to levy a terrorist war against the United States.[57] Rahman was also convicted for the 1993 World Trade Center bombing, as well as for additional bombing plots, and for planning political assassinations. Rahman's notoriety originally came after issuing a fatwa that resulted in the assassination of President Sadat. He was also the emir of al-Gama'a al-Islamiyya.

Rahman was the godfather of Islamic jihad. His vast network included Arab-Afghan terrorists involved in anti-Soviet jihad, such as Osama bin Laden and al-Zawahiri, and it also included Afghani warlord Gulbuddin Hekmatyar. Rahman was the head emir of the Egyptian Islamic Jihad terrorist organization. A year after al-Qaeda's September 11, 2001, terrorist attacks against the United States, al-Jazeera television aired a video of bin Laden in which he demanded the release of Omar Abdel Rahman from prison.

In 1971, al-Azhar University granted Rahman a PhD with the highest honors. Omar Abdel Rahman's doctoral thesis was titled, *Mawkif al-Qur'an min Khusumahu* (The Position of Qur'an from its Adversaries). It was published in Cairo in 2006 by Masr al-Mahrousa Publishing House, and it remained on the market for only forty-eight hours before it was banned by al-Azhar for its damning content, which implicated the university in transnational terrorism.

In his thesis, Rahman discussed the theological approach to non-Muslims, according to fundamentalist Sunni interpretation of chapter nine of the Qur'an. In five chapters, Rahman strictly relied on major theologians to make his case for global jihad and the fundamentalist Sunni approach to what he theologically defined as "adversaries." Rahman's definition of adversaries encompasses all non-Muslims and Muslims who are not members of organized Sunni jihadist groups.

The first two chapters were dedicated to arguing for the annihilation of Jews and Christians. In his first chapter, "The Final Position from Polytheists: Islam or Murder," Rahman explained that

57 Andrew C. McCarthy, "Omar Abdel Rahman, the 'Blind Sheikh,' Is Dead," *National Review*, February 18, 2017.

the polytheists are Christians, Jews, and all non-Muslims. Over hundreds of pages, he elaborated on ways to humiliate, torture, and kill non-Muslims.[58]

His second chapter was entitled "The Relationship of Muslims with their Adversaries from the People of The Book," which also refers to Jews and Christians. Rahman concludes that they all have to be murdered after they have been thoroughly humiliated and tortured.[59]

In his third chapter, "The Relationship of Muslims with Their Hypocritic Adversaries," Rahman attacks all Muslims who are not engaging in warfare, and by chapter five, he declares that all non-combatant Muslims are infidels who should also be exterminated.[60] Rahman wrote, "The whole ummah is an army, God is keen and diligent to cleans the army from elements of sedition and discord. If the army in Islam is the whole nation, then cleansing it is cleansing the ummah."[61]

Rahman's genocidal manifesto is most likely the founding document for al-Qaeda and al-Gama'a al-Islamiyya. He repeatedly mentioned both groups by name. It is not a coincidence that after he wrote his dissertation, two terrorist groups were created bearing the same names. In his thesis, Rahman repeatedly refers to "al-Qaeda," (the Foundation or the Base). He described al-Qaeda as the solid foundation, the pure foundation, and the faithful foundation. Rahman focused on the concept of al-Qaeda in his introduction, and the fourth and fifth chapters of his thesis. In the introduction, he mentions the word "al-Qaeda" twenty-five times. He described it as "the first al-Qaeda" as the first faithful, theologically pure group of jihadists. He called them the early friends and followers of the Prophet of Islam, theologically known as *muhajiroun wa'l-ansar* (the emigrants and sup-

---

58 Omar Abdel Rahman, *Mawqif al-Qur'an min Khusumahu* (Cairo: Masr al-Mahrousa Publishing House, 2006), 55–143.

59 Ibid., 225–347.

60 Ibid., 505

61 Ibid., 682.

porters), who established what Rahman called the "first Islamic State," in 622 AD.

In his thesis introduction, Rahman discussed his definition of al-Qaeda:

> First, all our vigilance has to be directed toward establishing a solid base of pure believers. Those who only get stronger in the face of burning crisis. They must be carefully prepared with deep religious doctrine, to make them strong and vigilant. They must be conscientiously aware of the risk of horizontal expansion, before there are guarantees of the foundation of a pure, solid, conscientious base. Horizontal expansion before the establishment of a base, is a true risk that would threaten the existence of any organization, that doesn't follow the path of the first da'wa in this respect, and doesn't put into consideration the Godly tactical nature of the Prophet's first group.[62]

Rahman's warning against "horizontal expansion" is a tactical one, which he elaborated upon in his fourth and fifth chapters. In those chapters, he laid out in great detail the guidelines on how to establish and operate what he referred to as "organized combat in Islam." He wrote an intricate plan for funding, mobilizing resources, recruiting jihadists, providing them military training, details of the military training, gathering intelligence, and finally, strengthening the morale of fighters. Rahman's plans for Islamic jihad, as laid out in his thesis, is adhered to by al-Qaeda and other modern terrorist groups today.

These are only few of many examples which suggest that Rahman's dissertation is the founding document for al-Qaeda and other terrorist groups. It is the first document to mention the group's name. Rahman was also the spiritual mentor for al-Qaeda founders Osama

62 Ibid., 21–2.

bin Laden and Abdullah Azzam. In the late 1980s, after traveling to Afghanistan, Rahman fought alongside bin Laden in the Afghan war against the Soviets, and he became the leader of the international arm of al-Qaeda.

The Blind Sheikh couldn't have created this massive wave of transnational terrorism without al-Azhar. The institution where he was indoctrinated since his childhood later provided him with the ideological authority he needed, by awarding him a PhD for his terrorist manual with the highest honors. This shouldn't be viewed as an isolated incident, given the fact that one of the al-Azhar scholars who granted Rahman his PhD was Mohammed Sayyed Tantawi, the Grand Imam of al-Azhar until 2010.[63]

Al-Azhar continues to recruit notorious terrorists to teach them how to rape, decapitate, humiliate, enslave, and cannibalize infidels and moderate Muslims.

63 Al-Jazeera (Doha), March 1, 2006.

CHAPTER TEN

FRANCHISING TERROR

The Muslim Brotherhood's Role in Establishing Transnational Terror Groups and the Secret Apparatus Operation Under Different Banners

"We will only be victorious with terrorism and horror, we should never be morally defeated when they call us terrorists; yes we are terrorists."

—Mustafa Mashhour, Fifth General Guide of the Muslim Brotherhood[1]

MUSLIM BROTHERHOOD SHEIKH MUSTAFA MARAGHI utilized al-Azhar University for jihadist activities in the 1930s, and their militant operation significantly expanded in the 1960s when the Brotherhood started operating proxy terrorist organizations under different banners. The Secret Apparatus' bylaws state that they seek to recruit "as many members as possible" to operate in its terror groups. These operatives are ordered to restrict secret meetings with Brotherhood leadership to a minimum and pretend not to have ties to the official public organization. Even a jihadist's own "friends and family" are deceived into thinking he is no longer a Brotherhood operative. This secrecy has helped the Secret Apparatus operate international terrorist entities.[2]

1 Al-Masry Al-Youm (Cairo), August 19, 2018.
2 Sabbagh, *Hakikat at-Tanzim al-Khas*.

These terror groups are organized into hierarchical clusters, with each level subordinate to its seniors. These clusters can "eternally replicate."[3] Hudaybi's strategy of operating terrorist organizations under separate banners created a pattern similar to cancerous cell division, where the primary tumor is the Secret Apparatus, and the metastatic spurs are the rest of the modern jihadist groups.

After Qutb became the emir of the Secret Apparatus, he founded the clandestine militia of 1965 with the intention for it to assassinate Gamal Abdel Nasser. A Secret Apparatus internal rift led one of its operatives, Mourad al-Zayyat, to inform the police about the existence of the militia and its mission.[4] The government arrested Qutb and other Brotherhood members. Qutb's execution led to the Brotherhood's practice of operating militias under different banners. Doing so was not a foreign premise to the group. The Brotherhood Officers had changed their name to the Free Officers to create the illusion that they were a separate unit. Qutb was dead, but the Brotherhood carried on his vision and Nasser's regime sponsored the same ideas, which twice attempted to kill him.

The Secret Apparatus bylaws list three types of Brotherhood militants. The first type of soldier is not associated with the Brotherhood's public apparatus and is required to be "completely and entirely" separated from the public group.[5] This clandestine soldier is responsible for the most dangerous operations, which allowed the Secret Apparatus to run many terrorist organizations utilizing clandestine proselytism and covert jihad.

There are discrepancies regarding the dates on which these groups were established. Sometimes these organizations operated for nearly a decade before they are discovered. The most famous terrorist organization established and operated by the Muslim Brotherhood is Hamas. It was founded in 1987, in the Palestinian territories. The

3 Ibid.
4 Ali Ashmawi, *At-Tarikh as-Sirri*, 21.
5 Sabbagh, *Hakikat at-Tanzim al-Khas.*

second article of the Hamas charter stated, "The Islamic Resistance Movement is one of the wings of Muslim Brotherhood in Palestine." In March 2014, Egyptian terrorism expert Abdel Rehim Ali aired on his television show a leaked phone call from Egyptian intelligence between Khairat al-Shater and Ismail Haniyah, then-Prime Minister of the Palestinian National Authority. In the call, Shater confirmed his organizational allegiance to Hamas by saying he was "constantly praying for every one of its leaders and members for victory and full political dominance."[6]

Hamas is the most famous of these Secret Apparatus terror groups, and it became a model into which the Kamal Vanguard aspires to transform and replicate in all Brotherhood chapters. While the Brotherhood founded many terrorist organizations, the forthcoming examples demonstrate a pattern of behavior that indicates their terroristic intent.

Sometimes, when a Secret Apparatus-operated terrorist cell is uncovered by law enforcement it changes its name. This strategy is also common in Brotherhood front corporations and nongovernmental organizations. The upcoming examples of Brotherhood-operated jihadist entities demonstrate the chameleon nature of their terrorism apparatus and show how it has eluded police and drained law enforcement resources. Whether out of ignorance, treason, or conspiracy, intelligence and foreign political departments' leadership in many countries have perpetuated the myth that the Secret Apparatus is no longer operational and that known terrorist groups are organizationally separate from the Muslim Brotherhood. Both myths are dangerously false.

The Secret Apparatus Operation Through Excommunication and Emigration

Among the Secret Apparatus operatives who were imprisoned with Qutb were two al-Azhar University trained brothers, Sheikh Abdul

6 "Tasrib Mukalamat Khairat al-shater wa Ismail Haniyah," YouTube.com, March 13, 2014.

Fattah Isma'il and Sheikh Ali Isma'il. Abdul Fattah was executed with Qutb, but his brother, Sheikh Ali Isma'il, briefly operated the civilian wing of the Secret Apparatus from inside prison with another infamous Secret Apparatus operative, Shukri Mustafa (1942–1978), in the late 1960s.

After Shukri Mustafa was released from prison in 1971, he publicly led civilian militants under the auspices of the Secret Apparatus. Mustafa adopted a different name for the Secret Apparatus cell to distance Brotherhood leaders from direct jihad and avoid Qutb's fate.[7] Shukri Mustafa called his group *Jama'at al-Muslimin*, also known as *at-Takfir wa'l-Hijrah*.

In 1978, Shukri Mustafa and several members of his group received death sentences for murdering the Minister of Islamic Aqwaf (endowments), Sheikh Muhammad Husain al-Zahabi, a year earlier. Jama'at al-Muslimin was one of the earliest modern terrorist groups covertly established and operated by the Secret Apparatus.

THE SECRET APPARATUS OPERATION THROUGH THE MILITIA OF THE MILITARY TECHNICAL COLLEGE

Following the Brotherhood's ritualistic repetition of history, Hudaybi and every leader of the General and Secret Apparatuses maintained a variation of the N-Group/M-Group structure. Hudaybi's civilian wing ran Excommunication and Emigration, but he needed to also revamp their Brotherhood Officers cell. While Excommunication and Emigration was still operational in prison, several Brotherhood operatives outside prison were frustrated by the lack of organized Islamic jihad.

Brotherhood operative Sheikh Talal al-Ansari (1942–2012) gave important testimony, recorded by Brotherhood operative Abdullah

7 Tharwat al-Kharbawy, *Sirr al-Ma'bad,* 68–9.

Serour in Alexandria in 1968. Serour said, "Five members pledged to revive the Muslim Brotherhood."[8] Those members were Muhammad Basyouni, Talal al-Ansari, Hamid ad-Difrawi, Rifa'i Serour, and then-Lieutenant Colonel Yehya Hashim. Serour said that this group also included Ayman al-Zawahiri.[9]

The militia was headed by Yehya Hashim, and it was known as the Militia of the Military Technical College (*Tanzim al-Faniyya al-Askaria*). Sometimes the Brotherhood referred to this militia as *Tanzim Shabab Muhammad* (the militia or Group of Muhammad's Youth). It was a highly secretive Brotherhood Officers cell, but according to Serour, the cell communicated and coordinated with Shukri Mustafa's group.[10]

The most dangerous operative of the five wasn't its leader, Hashim, but the al-Azhar-trained Sheikh Rifa'i Serour (1947–2012). Serour is referred to in Muslim Brotherhood literature as a "secretive creature" and the "man for clandestine missions."[11] Rifa'i Serour was Ayman al-Zawahiri's recruiter and intellectual leader.[12] He remained involved with al-Qaeda until his death in 2012. After he died, al-Zawahiri mourned his death by describing him as his "beloved brother, comrade, and friend" stating he had "learned so much" from him.[13],[14] Also following Serour's death, the website Islam Way mourned his death, describing him as an "invisible holy [man]."[15] IslamWay.net is a Muslim Brotherhood-run terrorist recruiting website whose founder once worked for Google LLC.

---

8 Ibid., 20–21.

9 Ibid., 21.

10 Ibid., 69.

11 *Elaph* (London), September 11, 2003.

12 Ibid; Transcript of Ayman al-Zawahiri speech, "Cairo and Damascus: Gates to Jerusalem," As-Sahab Media, September 2012.

13 Ibid.

14 "Aza' al-Doctor Ayman al-Zawahiri fi Sadikahu as-Sahikh Rifa'i Serour," YouTube.com, October 26, 2012; Al-Bawaba News (Cairo), June 16, 2016.

15 Islam Way website, "Rifa'i Serour al-Rabani al-Khafi," https://ar.islamway.net/, February 24, 2012.

In 1973, Saleh Sariyya (1936–1976) headed the militia of the Military Technical College. Sariyya was the Jordanian-born Muslim Brotherhood leader in Iraq and cofounder of the Palestinian Liberation Front, which was designated as a terrorist organization by the United States. He was involved in the murdering and looting properties of Iraqi Jews. When he arrived in Egypt, he visited Hudaybi's house and gave Hudaybi his oath of allegiance. He also met with Zaynab al-Ghazali (1917–2005), who harbored Sariyya in her house for six months.[16] Ghazali was a female Brotherhood operative and former head of the Muslim Sisterhood, which operated out of the Brotherhood's headquarters under the name the Muslim Women's Association. She is often portrayed by Western Middle East experts as "feminist."[17]

The Brotherhood Officers' Military Technical College terror cell included Ayman al-Zawahiri. Its members pledged the Islamic oath of allegiance to Hudaybi, who instructed them to communicate with him only through Talal al-Ansari.[18] Their main goal was to carry out a coup d'état, like the one perpetrated by Nasser. The group's affiliation with Hudaybi was confirmed by another militia member, Sheikh Yassir Sa'ad, who said the Brotherhood's General Guide gave his blessing to the new Brotherhood Officers militia.[19]

The militia aggressively recruited jihadists from the Military Technical College. On April 18, 1974, Sariyya, along with eighteen other jihadists, perpetrated a terrorist attack at the college in hopes of controlling it. The group planned a coup d'état, but the government stopped it and prosecuted the involved terrorists in a case known as *qadiat kulliat al-faniyya al-askariya* (the case of the Military Technical

16 Al-Watan (Cairo), September 3, 2012.
17 Susan Mumm, ed., *Religion Today: A Reader (Religion Today: Tradition, Modernity and Change),* (Routledge, 2002), 38.
18 Sorour, *Min al-Naksa ila al-Mashnaqa,* 67.
19 Al-Watan (Cairo), September 3, 2012.

College). In 1976, Sariyya was sentenced to death and executed with several of his cell members. Many others were sentenced to prison.

THE SECRET APPARATUS OPERATION THROUGH THE EGYPTIAN ISLAMIC JIHAD ORGANIZATION

Most historians and Middle East experts believe that the Egyptian Islamic Jihad Organization, or *Tanzim al-Jihad*, was founded in 1980, but it was actually formed over a decade earlier. In the late 1960s, al-Azhar University scholar and Brotherhood Secret Apparatus leader Rifa'i Serour recruited al-Zawahiri when he was still in his late teens. Serour's effectiveness compelled the Brotherhood to make him a recruiter for teenage jihadists.

Brotherhood leader and journalist Gamal Sultan said about Rifa'i Serour in 2012, "He was attractive to young men which made him a necessary ideological transit throughout the [modern] history of the Islamic movement. Every Islamist from the late 1960s to this day has encountered Rifa'i, especially those in Salafi and jihadist movements."[20] Sultan said Serour specifically targeted high school students and typically "spent two to three years" indoctrinating them before they were assigned to a jihadist organization or role in the public apparatus. In 2012, Serour's student and Brotherhood youth wing leader Hossam al-Bukhari said Serour was the "extension of Sayyid Qutb."[21]

In the mid-1960s, he recruited three high school students, Ulwi Mustafa, Isma'il Tantawi, and Nabil al-Bura'i. These young men, along with Serour and al-Zawahiri, established *Jama'at al-Jihad* (al-Jihad Group).[22] The group officially pledged allegiance to al-Hudaybi.[23] This cell also operated within the Militia of the Military Technical College.

20 An-Nas Television Station (Cairo), March 6, 2012.
21 Ibid.
22 Al-Watan (Cairo), August 13, 2012.
23 Sorour, *Min al-Naksa ila al-Mashnaqa,* 67.

Serour remained obsessed with waging jihad against Coptic Christians all his life. He became infamous in 1966 after he issued a fatwa, known in Egypt as *fatwa al-istihlal* (entitlement edict), a religious ruling stating it was halal (Islamically permissible) to raid and plunder Christian-owned jewelry stores.[24] His fatwa became a standard practice by Muslim Brotherhood terrorists and their off-shoots in Egypt.

The fatwa's most recent application occurred on April 19, 2021, when Islamic State terrorists ritually sacrificed sixty-two-year-old Coptic jewelry store owner Nabil Habashi.[25] Islamic State streamed the execution on their channel on the Telegram instant messaging software application.[26] According to Sky News Arabia, Islamic State terrorists also streamed the execution of two other individuals, but the report didn't name them.[27] Among the most prominent Brotherhood leaders to publicly defend the Egyptian Islamic Jihad group was another Secret Apparatus sheikh, Salah Abu Isma'il.[28]

Probably in 1978, Abbud al-Zummar joined Egyptian Islamic Jihad and became the head of its military apparatus. Zummar was the ideal candidate for recruitment according to the Brotherhood's standards. He fits every stereotype and criterion of a man ripe for jihadist conscription. Born in 1947, Zummar had a fundamentalist upbringing. His uncle Ahmad al-Zummar was a member of the Free Officers, and he died in 1973 during the Arab-Israeli Yom Kippur War, also known as the October War. He grew up in Kerdasa neighborhood, a hub for Brotherhood terrorism training and recruitment since the 1940s. He joined the military academy in 1965, and in 1967 he joined military intelligence.

In his free time, Zummar enjoyed killing cats by using them for target practice. After he was released from prison by SCAF's regime,

24 Elaph (London), September 11, 2003.
25 Ibid.
26 Ibid.
27 Ibid.
28 Al-Majzub, *Ulama' wa-Mufakirun Ariftahum*, 141.

he said during an interview that he "regrets" killing cats.[29] It is not exactly known when he joined Egyptian Islamic Jihad, which operated under the umbrella of al-Gama'a al-Islamiyya, but he was recruited[30] by Muslim Brotherhood and al-Azhar Sheikh Ibrahim Ezzat. Ezzat played a significant role in recruiting terrorists during the 1970s and 1980s, and he is referred to in Brotherhood literature as one of their *al-a'lam al-akhfiah* (concealed figures).[31]

Ezzat also recruited President Anwar al-Sadat's other assassin, Khalid al-Islambuli, as well as Muhammad Atif, also known as Abu Hafs al-Masri, (1944–2001). [32] Atif eventually became one of the founders of al-Qaeda and one of Osama bin Laden's two deputies, the other being Ayman al-Zawahiri. Atif was bin Laden's military chief, and his resume is similar to Zummar's. When Atif was recruited by Ezzat, he was working as a police officer.[33] Ezzat was also the founder of the Egyptian branch of *Tablighi Jama'at* (Society of Preachers) or in Arabic, *at-Tabigh w'ad-Da'wa*. Ezzat frequented Kerdasa, where he recruited several jihadists including Zummar.

The group revived ideologically in 1980, after its leader, Muhammad Abdul Salam Faraj (1951–1982), published his manifesto *Jihad: The Neglected Obligation*. Faraj was initially ideologically influenced by Sayyid Qutb's writings. During the 1970s Faraj was recruited by another of the Brotherhood's concealed figures, Sheikh Ibrahim Salama.[34] Salama is also credited for recruiting Brotherhood jihadist Ahmad Abu Shadi.[35]

---

29 Al-Bawaba News (Cairo), June 12, 2016.

30 Al-Bawaba News (Cairo), June 12, 2016.

31 The Official Muslim Brotherhood Encyclopedia, "Ibrahim Izzat," https://ikhwanwiki.com/, accessed June 1, 2021.

32 Al-Bawaba News (Cairo), June 12, 2016.

33 Al-Jazeera (Doha), June 3, 2015.

34 Ibrahim bin Salih al-Ayyid, "at-Takfir ind Jama'at al-Unf al-Mu'asira," Namaa for Research and Studies Center, https://nama-center.com/, accessed July 2, 2021.

35 The Muslim Brotherhood Official Website, "Zikrayyat Ramadaniyya ad-Da'ia al-Mujahid Ahmad Abu Shadi," https://ikhwanonline.com/, April 24, 2020.

THE SECRET APPARATUS OPERATION THROUGH AL-GAMA'A AL-ISLAMIYYA

In the early 1980s, the Egyptian Islamic Jihad officially operated under the leadership of al-*Gama'a al-Islamiyya or al-Jama'a al-Islamiyya*, the Islamic Group (IG). The organization later publicly became a branch of al-Qaeda. On August 5, 2006, Ayman al-Zawahiri announced in a video aired on al-Jazeera that the leadership of al-Gama'a al-Islamiyya had joined al-Qaeda. He stated, "The Islamic nation is rejoiced by [our] unification with this great sect under the leadership of Muhammad Shawqi al-Islambuli."[36] While al-Zawahiri only made the announcement in 2006, al-Gama'a al-Islamiyya has always been a branch of al-Qaeda.

The group's spiritual leader, Omar Abdel Rahman, has potentially been a leader of the Muslim Brotherhood since at least the late 1960s. Major General Fouad Allam said the first time Egyptian police noticed Rahman was in 1968, when he travelled to Saudi Arabia to meet Sa'id Ramadan. Allam said that during this trip, Ramadan gave Rahman $20,000 to deliver to Abdul Moneim al-Busatti, the head of the Brotherhood's Secret Apparatus in Faiyum. Rahman delivered only $15,000 and kept the rest to himself.[37]

It's commonly and falsely stated in the West that al-Gama'a al-Islamiyya emerged as a reaction to the Muslim Brotherhood's public renouncement of terrorism in the early 1970s.[38] Throughout the Brotherhood's history, every time the Muslim Brotherhood publicly renounced violence, it engaged in clandestine jihadist actives under a different banner. Western experts fall for this tactic every time.

36 Al-Jazeera (Doha), August 5, 2006.
37 Rif'at al-Sa'id, *Ash-Shaikh al-Musalah Hassan al-Banna* (Cairo: Kutub Arabiya, 2012), 198.
38 Gilles Kepel, *Muslim Extremism in Egypt: The Prophet and Pharaoh* (University of California Press, 1985), 125.

The newly named entity is usually founded by the same individuals, carrying out the same type of activities, and publicly regurgitating the same narratives, but somehow, experts and academics manage to fall for the deception. Incredibly, even when the entity retains the same name, operatives, ideological references, and rhetoric, Western academics still argue it's an unrelated group. Perhaps the most glaring example of this is al-Gama'a al-Islamiyya. Similar to the Muslim Brotherhood's official organization, this group successfully managed to create vast conflicting narratives about almost every aspect of its operation.

Al-Gama'a al-Islamiyya is another name for the Muslim Brotherhood's terrorism apparatus. Initially the Egyptian group borrowed the name from *Jamaat-e-Islami* (Islamic Group), which was founded by Indo-Pakistani theologian Abul A'la al-Mawdudi. Mawdudi officially established his organization in 1941. His group became the inspiration for the name of the new Brotherhood terrorism apparatus. Mawdudi launched his group with a speech titled "The Methodology of an Islamic Coup d'État," which he gave on September 12, 1940, at the Aligarh Muslim University in India. The speech has been translated into many languages and circulated among Islamists worldwide. It was first translated and published in Arabic in Egypt in 1946.

Prominent Syrian Islamist Muhammad al-Majzub said, "if one attempts to contemplate which organization influenced the other," the Muslim Brotherhood or Jamaat-e-Islami, it will not be known due to "the identical" ideological nature of Mawdudi and Qutb. He added that it is hard to "completely decide who is the influencer and who is the influenced."[39]

The Brotherhood's youth wing began operating under the banner of al-Gama'a al-Islamiyya, where they successfully recruited numerous terrorists and controlled student unions in most major universities.

---

39 Muhammad al-Majzub, *Ulama' wa-Mufakirun Ariftahum*, 2: 15.

According to Brotherhood leader Abul'ila Madi, by 1977, they were able to control student unions at twelve universities.[40]

Brotherhood students replicated their parent organization's configuration of family clusters. Each university family cell was led by a consultative assembly and emir. They were all under the leadership of *al-emir al-am* (the General Emir), who was also known as *Emir Umara' al-Gama'a al-Islamiyya* (the emir of emirs of al-Gama'a al-Islamiyya).[41] The actual head of the group was the Blind Sheikh, Omar Abdul Rahman who mentioned the group in his 1971 dissertation. In 1979, Rahman issued a fatwa declaring President Sadat an infidel, after Sadat signed the Camp David Accords on September 17, 1978, establishing peace between Egypt and Israel.

In 1980, Muhammad Abdul Salam Faraj's relationship with the Brotherhood landed him a job at the administrative office of Cairo University. During the same year, he met Zummar. Faraj suggested combining his Egyptian Islamic Jihad and al-Gama'a al-Islamiyya to its then-leader, Karam Zuhdi (1952–2021). Zuhdi agreed and merged both entities. He created a consultative assembly for the group, composed of eleven jihadists. Faraj was the head of the assembly, and Omar Abdul Rahman was its emir.[42]

Among the group's main leaders was Jordanian terrorist Muhammad Salim Rahal. Rahal joined Egyptian Islamic Jihad in 1970 while studying at al-Azhar University. In 1981, the Egyptian government deported him to Jordan after they suspected him of engaging in terrorist activities. In Jordan, he officially established a new branch in 1984. After establishing the group, Rahal set fire to his own office and murdered his father for being an infidel. Rahal and his family were originally members of Hizb ut-Tahrir.[43]

40 Al-Bawaba News (Cairo), July 26, 2015.

41 Ibrahim bin Salih al-Ayyid, "At-Takfir ind Jama'at al-Unf al-Mu'asira," Namaa for Research and Studies Center, https://nama-center.com/, accessed July 2, 2021.

42 Ibid.

43 Ibid.

On September 5, 1981, Sadat addressed the Egyptian parliament, equated al-Gama'a al-Islamiyya with the Brotherhood, and expressed regret for having released Brotherhood operatives from prison. Sadat said, "That is no difference between al-Gama'a al-Islamiyya and the Muslim Brotherhood, they are one and the same."[44]

Sadat was right. On October 6, 1981, al-Gama'a al-Islamiyya assassinated Sadat during an annual parade to celebrate the military crossing of the Suez Canal and the seizure of part of the Sinai Peninsula from Israel at the beginning of the Yom Kippur October War. In conjunction with the assassination, al-Gama'a al-Islamiyya committed numerous terrorist attacks, and sixty-eight policemen and soldiers were killed by terrorists.[45]

In 1982, five terrorists involved in Sadat's assassination were sentenced to death and executed, including Faraj, Islambuli and three assistants. Omar Abdel Rahman was found not guilty after his theological argument, justifying why Sadat should have been executed, convinced the Islamist judge. Rahman's infamous testimony was later published and is still circulated among jihadists.

Since Sadat's death there have been assumptions about Mubarak's involvement in his assassination, and speculations that the death sentences were never carried out continue to circulate. March 17, 2011, Sadat's daughter, Roukaya, claimed on Egyptian television that she saw Islambuli with her "own eyes" at a Saudi hotel in 1996 and he panicked when he saw her. Roukaya filed a complaint with the attorney general, in which she accused Mubarak of complicity in Sadat's assassination and asked for the reopening of the investigation into her father's murder—but her complaint was ignored.[46] Other members of Sadat's family have also implied the military was involved in Sadat's

---

44 "Al-Sadat Yatahadath an al-Gama'a al-Islamiya wa'l-wa'l-wa'l-Ikhwan," YouTube.com, May 9, 2012.

45 Marc Sageman, *Understanding Terror Networks* (University of Pennsylvania Press, 2004), 34.

46 Al-Youm as-Sabi' (Cairo), March 18, 2011; Misr News (Cairo), March 21, 2011.

assassination. One such accusation, by Talaat Sadat, his nephew and a former Member of Parliament, led to his incarceration for a year in military prison, in 2006, for defaming the military.[47]

Zummar was incarcerated for Sadat's death. At the time he was head of al-Gama'a al-Islamiyya's military apparatus, which operated under Egyptian Islamic Jihad. It is typically the case that, when a head of a terrorism group or unit is incarcerated, his position is given to other leaders or his deputies. Ayman al-Zawahiri replaced Zummar, and has been the group's actual leader since 1982. This information first became public during one of Egypt's most important terrorism investigations, known as "the Returnees from Albania" in reference to the defendants who committed acts of terrorism after they finished a jihadist campaign in Albania. The case was tried in Egyptian military court between February and April 1999. The case documents and investigation revealed that al-Gama'a al-Islamiyya, Egyptian Islamic Jihad, and al-Qaeda were all one entity. After Egyptian police arrested one of its leaders, Ahmad Ibrahim al-Naggar, he fully cooperated and gave information that explained the relationship between these groups.[48]

THE MUSLIM BROTHERHOOD INTERNATIONAL APPARATUS OPERATING UNDER THE BANNER OF AL-GAMA'A AL-ISLAMIYYA

In Egypt, the Muslim Brotherhood concealed their operation under the banner of al-Gama'a al-Islamiyya, but they did the opposite in other countries. From the late 1940s and 1950s, the Muslim Brotherhood's reputation in the Middle East significantly deteriorated due to their

47 Jano Charbel and Michael Slackman, "Egypt Sends Sadat's Nephew to Prison for Defaming Military," *New York Times*, November 1, 2006.
48 Al-Bayan (Dubai), February 12, 1999.

involvement in widespread terrorism, including Nasser's assassination attempt in 1954. This compelled the Brotherhood hide their clandestine *da'wa* mission behind different names. In Lebanon and Tunisia, Islamism was almost nonexistent beyond a small minority of jihadists, so they adopted a different name.

In 1964, the Brotherhood appointed its Palestinian leader, Abdullah Muhammad Abu Izza, to travel to Lebanon and study at the American University in Beirut. They assigned him to organize Brotherhood operatives in Syria and Lebanon under the leadership of the Palestinian entity.[49] During the same year, Izza established the Brotherhood's first branch in Lebanon under the name *al-Jam'a al-Islamiyya*. The difference between the Egyptian group and other branches is that the word is pronounced *Gama'a* (Group) in Egypt and *Jama'a* elsewhere in the Middle East.

Izza succeeded in his mission to organize them under the leadership of the Palestinian branch, and he assigned Syrian Brotherhood leader Issam al-Attar as head of the transnational body in Lebanon. The Lebanese branch falsely propagated to Westerners that they were independent from the violent Egyptian branch of al-Gama'a al-Islamiyya, but the Lebanese branch of the Brotherhood has been operating as a jihadist terrorist organization since its public launch in 1978. Al-Qaeda terrorist Abdullah Azzam was personally involved in overseeing the military training of their youth wing.[50] Currently, the Lebanese branch is led by Azzam Ayoubi, and his deputy and representative in Lebanese parliament is Imad al-Hout.

In April 1972, Muslim Brotherhood operatives, including Rached Ghannouchi, the leader of the Ennahda Movement in Tunisia established the first official Muslim Brotherhood branch and named it *al-Jama'a al-Islamiyya*. In 1981, they changed its name to *Harakatu il-Itijah al-Islami* (The Movement of Islamic Tendency), which later

49 Ra'fat Fahd al-Morra, *Al-Harakat wa'l-wa'l-wa'l-Quwah al-Islamiyya fi al-Mujtama' al-Falastini fi Lebanon* (Markaz al-Zaituna, 2010), 19.
50 Ibid,. 47–50.

called itself *Harakat Ennahda*. It's often translated as "the Renaissance Movement," but since it's a Muslim Brotherhood group, the term "renaissance" is a benign expression that conceals the mission of Islamic Awakening.

The initial founding in 1972 was known as *Ijtima' al-Arba'in*. It is an awkward code that translates to "the assembly of the forties." It is not known whether "the forties" is a reference to the number of individuals attending the conference, to the revival of the May 1940 conference in Pakistan, or both. During a meeting in Tunisia, the attendees fully adopted the mission of the Brotherhood, but according to Tunisian Brotherhood leader Abdulfattah Mourou during an interview on al-Jazeera, they "didn't openly" propagate it.[51]

As with all Muslim Brotherhood chapters in the world, the Tunisian branch operated a Secret Apparatus. Mourou said their Secret Apparatus was first discovered in 1980 after the arrest of Secret Apparatus leaders Salah Karker and bin-Issa al-Maddani, who had a 2,000-page document about their jihadist apparatus. They vowed to dismantle the apparatus, but the government rediscovered it again in 1987.[52] This led to the arrest of several Brotherhood operatives in 1992. Mourou said even after the Brotherhood's Secret Apparatus invited him to be one of their leaders, in 2005 and 2006, he preferred to be in the group's public division.[53]

During his interview series with al-Jazeera, Mourou confirmed that after the release of many members of the Muslim Brotherhood after the 2010 coup d'état, they still operated a Secret Apparatus. While Ghannouchi was celebrated in the West and dubbed by *Foreign Policy* magazine as one of their "Top 100 Global Thinkers" in 2011, he was still operating a Secret Apparatus, and his published works in

51 Al-Jazeera Television Network (Doha), April 19, 2015.
52 Ibid.
53 Ibid.

Arabic praised jihadist movements, calling them a "revolution against tyranny and exploitation." [54]

In October 2018, Tunisian police investigated Ghannouchi's Ennahda party for operating a Secret Apparatus militia that may have been involved in the assassination of two national figures, Shukri Bel'id and Muhammad al-Barahmi, for their opposition to Ennahda.[55]

AL-QAEDA AND THE MUSLIM BROTHERHOOD

The Brotherhood played a pivotal role in the Soviet-Afghan war, which lasted for almost a decade, from 1979 to 1989. The civil war that followed resulted in over a million deaths in Afghanistan, due to foreign terrorists' migration and vast amounts of weapons and funding pouring into Afghanistan and Pakistan from across the world. Al-Qaeda was originally founded as *Maktab al-Khidamat* (MAK), the Services Bureau, also known as *Maktab Khidamat al-Mujahidin al-Arab* (the Services Bureau of Arab jihadists), and the Afghani Services Bureau. The 1980s and 1990s were the most important decades for the Brotherhood militarily.

The Brotherhood facilitated the migration of fighters from across the Middle East to Afghanistan and Pakistan. They were officially in charge of running recruitment jihadist services through MAK offices and branches in almost every country in the Middle East. In 1984, Brotherhood leader Abdullah Yusuf Azzam established the MAK office in Jordan.[56] Azzam's philosophy helped establish and organize the Muslim Brotherhood's "global jihad" movement, which earned

---

54 Foreign Policy, November 28, 2011; Rached Ghannouchi, *Min Tajrubat al-Haraka al-Islamiyya fi Tunis,* The Official Muslim Brotherhood Encyclopedia, https://ikhwanwiki.com/, accessed June 1, 2021.

55 Raseef 22 (Tunisia), October 8, 2018.

56 Farouk Taifour, "Hal Kharajat Daesh min Rahm Fikr al-Ikhwan al-Muslimin?" Egyptian Institute for Political and Strategic Studies, Cairo, https://eipss-eg.org/.

Azzam the alias, "The Father of Global Jihad." [57] Azzam's Brotherhood philosophy and training equipped him to export terrorism around the world. While at face value these offices were established to migrate jihadist mercenaries to fight the Soviet Union, the equally important mission of MAK was to replicate previous models of parastatal entities created to deploy terrorists internationally.

The first modern form of this practice was with the Ottoman-German trained jihadists deployed to fight against the Triple Entente. The second time was when the Mufti of Jerusalem deployed jihadists to fight among Nazi troops, and the third was in 1948 when the Brotherhood settled jihadists in Lebanon, which inevitably caused the Lebanese civil war, where they waged jihad against the country's Christian and Jews from 1975 to 1990. The fourth major manifestation of this strategy took place on October 23, 1979, in Washington DC, during the "covert action" meeting which unleashed the joint CIA-Arab jihadist propaganda and militant campaign creating worldwide terrorism hitherto.[58]

One of the many devesting consequences of the CIA-Arab jihad coalition, resulted in the creation of al-Qaeda. In 1985, when three Muslim Brotherhood leaders, Abdullah Azzam, Osama bin Laden (1957–2011), and Ayman al-Zawahiri, founded MAK in Pakistan, which morphed into al-Qaeda. All three MAK leaders were members of the Muslim Brotherhood and continued their affiliation with it after founding al-Qaeda.

In 2012, al-Zawahiri released a video in which he stated that bin Laden was a member of the Muslim Brotherhood. Al-Zawahiri also said the Brotherhood's objections to bin Laden's travel for jihad in Afghanistan was to avoid embarrassing the Saudi government with Russia, if a Saudi royal like bin Laden were captured in battle.

57 The Official Muslim Brotherhood Encyclopedia, "Ra'id al-Jihad al-Islami Abduallah Azzam," https://ikhwanwiki.com/, accessed June 1, 2021.

58 United States Government Publishing Office, Foreign Relations of the United States, 1977–1980, Volume XII, Afghanistan, Document 76.

Al-Zawahiri also stated that the Brotherhood ordered bin Laden to remain in Lahore, Pakistan, with al-Gama'a al-Islamiyya, who would be in charge of delivering funds and aid needed by jihadists in Afghanistan. Zawahiri said, "After sheikh [bin Laden] started to become well known due to several successful battles, sheikh Mustafa Mashhour, may he rest in peace, the General Guide of the Muslim Brotherhood, visited bin Laden in Peshawar, and told him, *come back to your Brothers, they are more worthy of you.*"

Al-Zawahiri claimed bin Laden's affiliation with the Brotherhood was severed after he disobeyed Mashhour, but that narrative was discounted by more credible sources. During an interview in 2014, Tharwat al-Kherbawy said:

> Osama bin Laden was a [member of the] Muslim Brotherhood's Saudi branch, as well as Ayman al-Zawahiri, he was also a member of the Saudi Brotherhood. Osama bin Laden asked Mustafa Mashhour to grant him permission to travel for jihad to Afghanistan, Mustafa Mashhour didn't grant him permission, and said, 'I will inform you how you can go, and who will go with you,' and how the international apparatus, founded by Mashhour will facilitate this process. But bin Laden didn't follow the orders of Mashhour and he took a group of people and traveled to Afghanistan, and started his jihad there. A leader of the Muslim Brotherhood in Saudi Arabia communicated with Mashhour telling him they request the dismissal of Osama bin Laden from the Brotherhood, because he didn't follow the orders and traveled without the permission of the leadership in Egypt, but Mashhour declined and said, 'No, he left his brothers to go to his brothers, he will never be dismissed.'

> Osama bin Laden was never sacked out of the Muslim Brotherhood.[59]

According to Emirati terrorism expert Issa Muhammad al-Omairi, Khalid Sheikh Mohammed, the mastermind of the September 11, 2001, terrorist attack, was a known member of the Muslim Brotherhood. So was one of the planes' hijackers, Mohamed Atta.[60]

THE MUSLIM BROTHERHOOD NORMALIZING RELATIONS WITH AL-QAEDA

In 2012, the relationship between the Muslim Brotherhood and al-Qaeda became official and public after Egypt's 2011 coup d'état. Muhammad Morsi stacked his regime with Islamists and their relatives. He appointed Ayman al-Zawahiri's first cousin, Muhammad Rifa'a at-Tahtawi, as head of his Presidential Office. According to Major General Mohsen Hefzi, then-secretary to the minister of interior, Tahtawi was "sharing every single detail" taking place in Morsi's office with his cousin, Zawahiri. Hefzi also said that he intercepted many calls between Morsi and Zawahiri.[61]

From mid-2011 to late 2012, Ayman al-Zawahiri gave a series of speeches titled *Rislat al-Amal wa'l-Bishr li-Ahluna fi Misr* (A Message of Hope and Good Tidings for Our People in Egypt). The title of the series clearly expressed his approval of developments in Egypt. The eleventh episode was titled *al-Qahira wa-Dimishq Bawabatuna ila al-Quds* (Cairo and Damascus are Our Gates to Jerusalem). The three-hour episode aired in early September 2012 on al-Qaeda's as-Sahab Media Center, which transcribed the episode and circulated it among the Muslim Brotherhood on social media.

59 Al-An Television (Dubai), April 20, 2014.
60 Al-Bayan (Dubai), October 22, 2019.
61 Al-Youm as-Sabi' (Cairo), November 21, 2013.

During the speech, Zawahiri expressed his dismay at the Salafi movement for not "unifying with the Muslim Brotherhood" in their "aim to establish Shari'a law." While it was predominantly targeted at Egypt, he also addressed all Islamists in the Middle East. In his speech, al-Zawahiri said, "I call upon Muslims to hold hostage the citizens of nations which waged war against Muslims, neither our captives nor sheikh Omar Abdel Rahman will be freed without force, it is the only language they understand."

Zawahiri's statements prompted a coordinated terrorist attack against two United States government facilities in Benghazi on September 11, 2012. Terrorists attacked the American diplomatic compound, resulting in the torture and death United States Ambassador to Libya J. Christopher Stevens and US Foreign Service Information Management Officer Sean Smith. Terrorists also attacked the CIA annex and killed two contractors, Tyrone S. Woods and Glen Doherty.

The attack was attributed to the terrorist group Ansar al-Shari'a. The *New York Times* published a lengthy report by David D. Kirkpatrick, which stated, "Months of investigation by The *New York Times*, centered on extensive interviews with Libyans in Benghazi who had direct knowledge of the attack there and its context, turned up no evidence that al-Qaeda or other international terrorist groups had any role in the assault."[62]

Republican Representative and Chairman of the House Intelligence Committee Mike Rogers disagreed, "It was very clear to the individuals on the ground that this was an al-Qaeda-led event." Congressman Rogers was correct. Ayman al-Zawahiri ordered the attack, and it was carried out by both Ansar al-Shari'a and the Muslim Brotherhood.

Ansar al-Shari'a is an offshoot of al-Qaeda. The group was founded in 2012 by al-Qaeda to operate in Libya under the leadership of Tharwat Salah Shehata, also known as Abu al-Samah. Shehata was

62 David D. Kirkpatrick, "A Deadly Mix in Benghazi," *New York Times*, December 28, 2013.

born in Egypt in 1960, and he was the head of the intelligence division in Egyptian Islamic Jihad.[63] He was implicated in Sadat's assassination and other terrorism cases in Egypt. In 2012, al-Qaeda relocated Shehata to Libya after he was released from prison in Ankara.[64] According to former al-Gama'a al-Islamiyya leader Nabil Na'eem, Shehata is the most important figure in al-Qaeda after Ayman al-Zawahiri.[65] On April 8, 2014, Egyptian media reported that the government finally arrested Shehata.

During the Benghazi terrorist attack, jihadists uploaded numerous videos to YouTube. One video depicted a mob approaching the besieged American compound. In the video, a man approached the compound and told the terrorists in the dialect of Upper Egypt, "*mahadish, mahadish yermi, Dr. Morsi ba'atna*"—"no one, no one shoots, Dr. Morsi sent us." The words "*mahadish yermi*" (no one shoots) are characteristically spoken in Egyptian Arabic, while Libyans from Benghazi would say, "*matirmi*" (don't shoot). Dr. Morsi refers to then-Egyptian President Mohamed Morsi. The name Morsi is Egyptian, and does not exist in any other Arabic-speaking country.

Egyptian media demanded an explanation from Morsi's regime on why his name was mentioned by jihadists during the attack.[66]

On July 30, 2013, former Egyptian State Security Intelligence officer and television commentator Ahmad Moussa reported on his television show that the Egyptian government had identified one of Ambassador Stevens's assassins, and that he was harbored by the Muslim Brotherhood. Moussa said that the assassin was an al-Qaeda operative named Mohsen Al-Azazi, and the Egyptian government found his passport at Khairat al-Shater's house on July 5, 2013.

---

63 Al-Bayan (Dubai), February 12, 1999.
64 An-Nahar (Cairo), April 8, 2014.
65 Ibid.
66 Cynthia Farahat, "Benghazi Terrorists: 'Dr. Morsi Sent Us'," *Front Page Magazine*, May 31, 2013.

Moussa also stated that Azazi was present at the Rabi'a mosque terrorist attack with Brotherhood lead cleric Safwat Hegazy and Muhammad El-Beltagi, then-general secretary of the Muslim Brotherhood's Freedom and Justice Party (FJP).[67] Moussa addressed then-US ambassador Anne Patterson (in absentia) on his show, "Ambassador Stevens was killed in Benghazi, and you know who killed him, the US administration knows who killed him, and you know how he was killed and it was a major strike against the US administration, and all of you." He continued, "Ask the Muslim Brotherhood to hand Azazi to US authorities...and of course they will not, as he is there to wage terrorist attacks against Egyptian citizens, as he hides protected in Rabi'a, among killers with massive amounts of weapons.... Why doesn't the Muslim Brotherhood, which you often praise, hand him to you?"

While President Barack Obama was spreading false propaganda that the attacks were caused by a Coptic Christian man who published a blasphemous YouTube video, which few people had viewed, Libyan and Egyptian intelligence painted a different story.

On November 26, 2013, an Egyptian newspaper published segments from a Libyan intelligence report about the Benghazi terrorist attack.[68] According the report, the arrested terrorists said, "Muhammad Morsi, Safwat Hegazy, and Sheikh Hazem Salah Abu Ismail were the masterminds behind the attack on the American consulate." The report added that the "plan intended to only kidnap the Ambassador and not kill him, to swap him with Sheikh Omar Abdel Rahman." The report stated this information was retrieved from the confessions of six Egyptian terrorists arrested from Ansar al-Shari'a in Libya.

The report was written by Libyan General Muhammad Ibrahim Sharif, then-head of the Libyan National Intelligence Services. The report confirmed Azazi was involved in the attack, and as well as

---

67 Cynthia Farahat, "Is Muslim Brotherhood Working Together with Amb. Chris Stevens' Assassin?" *Fox News*, August 12, 2013.

68 Al-Mogaz (Cairo), November 26, 2013.

Muhammad Jamal Abu Ahmad,[69] the head of an al-Qaeda cell known as Muhammad Jamal Network (MJN). MJN was designated a terrorist group by the US Department of State in 2013. But the Obama administration still maintained the narrative that the attack was caused by a YouTube video. Muhammad Jamal was among the terrorists broken out of prison in January 2011 with Muhammad Morsi.[70]

After the ouster of Morsi from power, Zawahiri continued his support for the Brotherhood. For example, in 2013, Zawahiri issued a videotaped statement on Morsi's behalf, in which he criticized Egyptian Salafi jihadists for not formally joining the Muslim Brotherhood's Freedom and Justice Party to help it uphold Shari'a law. Al-Zawahiri stated, "I was pained to see secularists criticize the Muslim Brotherhood." In the same video, al-Zawahiri called for open jihad against the Egyptian military.[71]

In another statement, Zawahiri criticized Morsi for having played politics with opponents, but eventually prayed for his release while he was facing trial for inciting the killing of regime opponents and for espionage for foreign militant groups including Hamas, Hezbollah, and Iran's Revolutionary Guard Corps.[72] Zawahiri said, "I ask Allah to free you from prison, and give you the strength you need and fill your heart with faith to uphold his law."[73]

---

69 Siobhan Gorman And Matt Bradley, "Militant Link to Libya Attack," *The Wall Street Journal,* October 1, 2012.

70 Al-Mogaz (Cairo), November 26, 2013.

71 "Ta'kib ash-Sheikh Ayman al-Zawahiri ala Azl Morsi wa-Tahdid al-Jaish," YouTube.com, July 5, 2013.

72 "Ayman al-Zawahiri Yuwajih Risalat Itab li-Morsi wa-Yad'u Allah an Yafuku Anahou," YouTube.com, February 11, 2014; Erich Follath, "Political Stability Eludes Polarized Egypt," *Der Spiegel* (Hamburg), July 29, 2013.

73 "Ta'kib ash-Sheikh Ayman al-Zawahiri ala Azl Morsi wa-Tahdid al-Jaish," YouTube.com, July 5, 2013.

THE MUSLIM BROTHERHOOD CONNECTION TO JAMA'AT AT-TAWHID WA'L-JIHAD AND ISLAMIC STATE

It is commonly believed that *Jama'at at-tawhid wa'l-Jihad* (Organization of Monotheism and Jihad) was founded in 1999 by Jordanian terrorist Abu Musab al-Zarqawi (1966–2006). While al-Zarqawi was the face of the organization, the group's founding can be traced to the Muslim Brotherhood's MAK office in Jordan, which recruited Zarqawi. Al-Zarqawi later founded Jama'at at-tawhid wa'l-Jihad in 1999 after being mentored by Jordanian Muslim Brotherhood leader Abu Muhammad al-Maqdisi. Al-Zarqawi introduced the gruesome trend of video decapitations when he beheaded American freelance radio-tower repairman Nick Berg in 2004.

In 2005, the Arabic newspaper *Elaph* interviewed al-Zarqawi's recruiter, Abdul Majid Ibrahim al-Majali, also known as Abu Qutaiba al-Urduni.[74] Al-Majali was also a member of the Muslim Brotherhood. He was a driver in the Jordanian army and fought with bin Laden in Pakistan and Afghanistan in the 1980s. In the interview, Majali stated he met al-Zarqawi in 1988 when he was in charge of running the MAK office in Jordan.

After Zarqawi's death, his group operated under the banner of *ad-Dawla al-Islamiyya fil Iraq wa'l-Sham* (The Islamic State of Iraq and the Levant), also known as the Islamic State of Iraq and Syria (ISIS), or Islamic State (IS), and Daesh. Not only was the Brotherhood responsible for recruiting al-Zarqawi, but they also recruited the terrorist leader of Islamic State. In 2014, al-Arabiya news aired a video interview with Yusuf al-Qaradawi, in which he justified global terrorism and admitted that Islamic State leader Abu Bakr al-Baghdadi was a member of the Muslim Brotherhood.[75] Several Brotherhood

---

74 Elaph (London), July 18, 2005.
75 Al-Arabiya (Dubai), October 14, 2014.

leaders publicly announced their support for Islamic State, among them Sheikh Wagdi Ghoneim, residing in Qatar and Turkey. In 2014, Ghoneim issued a statement in support of Islamic State condemning the war against them.[76]

THE SECRET APPARATUS OPERATION THROUGH THE VANGUARDS OF CONQUEST

Talai' al-Fateh (Vanguards of Conquest) was founded in 1993 by Muslim Brotherhood leaders and operated outside Egypt. The group adopted its name from the Brotherhood's International Apparatus cell, the Vanguards of Conquest or Invasion. It was established by Egyptian jihadists operating in Sudan, Somalia, and Yemen. Prior to its founding, the Brotherhood's Syrian branch operated a terrorist cell under the same name in 1966.[77]

According to Egyptian jihadist Nabil Na'eem, the Syrian Vanguards of Conquest, also known as *at-Tali' al-Muqatila*, (The Fighting Vanguards) were "funded by Saddam Hussein."[78] It perpetrated several terrorist attacks in Syria, the most prominent of which was the Aleppo Artillery School massacre, where fifty to eighty Alawi cadets were murdered by Brotherhood terrorists on June 16, 1979.

Hani al-Siba'i was the main founder of the 1993 Vanguards. Born in 1960, Siba'i joined the Muslim Brotherhood under the leadership of Omar al-Tilmisani and Mustafa Mashhour.[79] He studied law in Egypt and specialized in defending jihadists. He joined Egyptian Islamic Jihad in the 1970s and recruited several militants for training in Afghanistan. Siba'i fled to the United Kingdom after the assassination of President Sadat and was granted refugee status in 1998.

76 Al-Youm as-Sabi' (Cairo), September 16, 2014.
77 DAAL Research and Media Center, (Cairo) June 26, 2019.
78 Nabil Na'eem, "Madrassat al-Fattah al-Ikhwaniah," The Reference Institute (Paris), October 20, 2019.
79 Al-Arabiya (Dubai), October 1, 2017.

He still resides in the UK and continues to freely recruit terrorists. Siba'i was the preacher and possibly the recruiter of Islamic State's Mohammad Emwazi, also known as "Jihadi John." Emwazi appeared in several Islamic State decapitation videos.[80]

The second founder was Ahmad Basuni Dwidar (1956–2007). He was recruited by the Brotherhood while he was a college student. In the 1980s, he joined Egyptian Islamic Jihad. In 1990, he trained in Afghanistan, where he became a sniper and an expert on improvised explosives. In 1992, he briefly went to Egypt and resumed his clandestine jihadist activities. In 1993, he relocated to Sudan and cofounded the Vanguards of Conquest terrorist group. In 1995, he relocated to Yemen and worked for the government's Ministry of Education while he continued to operate his jihadist group. At the time, Ayman al-Zawahiri was also in Yemen, where the group's headquarters was located.[81] In 1997, the Vanguards of Conquest officially merged with al-Qaeda.[82] In 2006, their al-Qaeda cell merged with Jama'at at-tawhid wa'l-Jihad.

THE MUSLIM BROTHERHOOD AND AL-AZHAR UNIVERSITY'S ROLE IN RADICALIZING AFGHANS

Jihadists have always targeted Afghanistan for its landlocked geographic position and its mountainous terrain. It provided a perfect training ground for jihadist groups. It was natural for the Brotherhood's Liaison with the Islamic World section, in collaboration with al-Azhar University in Cairo, to target Afghanistan. They recruited Afghan Islamist Harun Mujaddidi when he attended a Brotherhood conference in Cairo in 1948. This launched a collaboration among the Brotherhood, al-Azhar, and Islamists in Afghanistan to send young

80 The Sun (London), August 28, 2016.
81 Ash-sharq al-Awasat (London), August 9, 2007.
82 Ibid.

Afghans for ideological indoctrination at al-Azhar. This provided students with ideological legitimacy when they returned to Afghanistan.

Issam Daraz, a former Egyptian military leader, Brotherhood operative, and Osama bin Laden's close associate for almost a decade, wrote, "Afghan jihadists told me that those who travel to study at al-Azhar, return to Afghanistan to be received with festivities and people travel across the country to welcome them back and request their advice…they even consider them holy men." Daraz added that "Afghan jihadists consider themselves one of the intellectual streams of the Muslim Brotherhood, they declare this and they are very proud of this affiliation. They consider the Brotherhood movement the leading movement for everyone who operates within the field of jihad."[83]

By the 1950s, the Brotherhood flooded Islamic madrassas in Afghanistan with jihadist literature of Sayyid Qutb, Banna, and Mawdudi, and founded a clandestine entity inside the country. Qatar-based Syrian Brotherhood leader, al-Qaeda operative, and head of al-Jazeera television network's Pakistan office Ahmad Muaffaq Zaidan wrote an extensive study on the roots of the Taliban as an offshoot of the Muslim Brotherhood. Zaidan is currently on the US government's terrorism watch list.[84]

Zaidan categorized the Brotherhood's founders of the jihadist groups in Afghanistan as the "older" and "younger" leaders, who played a pivotal role in the founding of the Taliban. At the forefront of the "older" guard was the official head of the Brotherhood's chapter in Afghanistan, Ghulam Mohammad Niazi (1932–1978). Following Niazi's return to Afghanistan in 1958, after studying at al-Azhar, Niazi became the dean of Shari'a College at Kabul University and later became the president of the university.[85]

---

83 Issam Daraz, Al-Aidun min Afghanistan, The Muslim Brotherhood Official Encyclopedia, https://ikhwanwiki.com/, accessed September 25, 2021.

84 The Intercept (Washington DC), May 8, 2015.

85 Ahmad Muaffaq Zaidan, *Sayif Afghanistan at-Tawil: Min al-Jihad ila al-Imara* (Dar Lebanon, 2021), p. 15.

Many Afghan Islamists followed Niazi's footsteps and traveled to study at al-Azhar. Among the jihadists recruited by the Brotherhood at al-Azhar was Burhanuddin Rabbani (1940–2011). He was among the Islamists who translate Sayyid Qutb's works into Persian. He returned to Afghanistan in 1968 and founded the Muslim Brotherhood's wing under the banner of *Jamiat-e Islami Afghanistan* (Islamic Society of Afghanistan). Rabbani was the President of Afghanistan from 1992 to 2001. Rabbani ruled Afghanistan in accordance to the Brotherhood's philosophy of governance, which turned into the transnational terrorism training camp that led to many atrocities including September 11, 2001, attack against the US.

Zaidan said the leader of the "younger" Brotherhood jihadists, who played a role in advancement of jihad in Afghanistan, was another terrorist recruited at al-Azhar, the warlord Abdul Rasul Sayyaf. Jamiat-e Islami became an influential jihadist coalition, which included Gulbuddin Hekmatyar, who briefly served as the Prime Minister of Afghanistan in the 1990s. Al-Azhar also contributed to indoctrinating Taliban leaders who weren't formally members of the Brotherhood, such as Mawlawi Qassim Halimi.

The Brotherhood's Afghani chapter utilized Islamic madrassas to raise a generation of jihadists. The most important of these schools was *Darul Uloom Haqqania*, established in 1947 in Akora Khattak, Khyber Pakhtunkhwa province, in northwestern Pakistan. That jihadist school attracted many Brotherhood lecturers, including Sayyaf. The Shari'a department at Kabul University and Haqqania jihadist school were among the two major bodies that produced student jihadists in Afghanistan.

Egyptian and Arab Brotherhood leaders also played a significant role in the military training of Afghan jihadists. While Osama bin Laden, Zawahiri, and Abdullah Azzam were the most famous, lesser-known Brotherhood leaders also engaged in atrocities in Afghanistan. Among them was Secret Apparatus operative and leader in al-Gama'a al-Islamiyya Rifa'i Taha. Brotherhood leader, jihadist, and 2012 Brotherhood presidential candidate Abdel Moneim Aboul Fotouh also engaged in jihadist activities in Afghanistan. Fotouh appeared in numerous leaked videos training Afghan terrorists.[86] Yet, he was dubbed by the *BBC* and the *New York Times* as a "moderate Islamist." Calling an Islamist a "moderate Islamist," is like calling a World War II German war criminal a "moderate Nazi." This kind of oxymoron can only exist in a pro-jihadist propaganda machine.[87] Other Brotherhood terrorists who fought in Afghanistan were Qutb's brother-in-law, Kamal as-Sananiri, and Guidance Bureau member Kamal al-Hilbawi.

Through Brotherhood-run MAK offices across the Middle East, the Brotherhood sent numerous Arab and Egyptian fighters for jihad. The most active MAK officers were in Egypt, Pakistan, Sudan, Jordan, and Saudi Arabia. These terrorists were known as *al-Afghan al-Arab* (Arab Afghan) who also had the Brotherhood's Afghans in their camp.

THE TALIBAN AND AL-QAEDA

Jihadist school students officially created the Taliban, which is Pashtu for "students." It was established in September 1994 by Mullah Omar (1959–2013) in his hometown in the southern Afghan province of Kandahar. The first mention of the Taliban appeared in 1987. The militia was called "Taliban brigades" under the leadership of Lala Balch, who was killed during the Soviet-Afghan war.[88]

It's not clear whether Mullah Omar borrowed the name from the original Taliban group, or whether his militia was part of it. But Omar was also a student at Haqqania jihadist school. The difference between the Taliban and al-Qaeda is ethnicity. While Omar adhered

86 "Sada Elbalad: Abdul Moneim Aboul Fotouh Yusharik al-Irabiyyn," YouTube.com, November 21, 2015.

87 "Top Challenger in Egypt Vote Is an Islamist, and Moderate," *New York Times*, March 14, 2012; Yolande Knell, "Egypt Candidate: Moderate Islamist, Abdul *Moneim Aboul Fotouh,"* *BBC News*, April 13, 2012.

88 Ahmad Muaffaq Zaidan, *Sayif Afghanistan at-Tawil*, 363.

to the slightly less radical orthodox Hanafi school of jurisprudence and al-Qaeda adheres to the more militant Hanbali one, there is a general consensus between the two schools regarding the jurisprudence of war.

The second distinction is that al-Qaeda is a coalition of predominantly Arab, as well as transnational fighters, but the Taliban belong to the Pashtun ethnic group. After Osama bin Laden returned to Afghanistan from Sudan in May 1996, he became close with Mullah Omar. Zaidan was an associate of both bin Laden and Omar. Zaidan said that after bin Laden's return to Afghanistan, he "gave his oath of allegiance to Mullah Omar." This effectively made the Taliban the secret leader of al-Qaeda. Zaidan also stated that Mullah Omar was aware of bin Laden's plans to attack the World Trade Center in New York City in 2001. He said Omar wasn't fully on board, because he believed that the "priority should be to [first] stabilize the Islamic emirate and the Afghani Islamic government." Zaidan added that while Omar wasn't in full agreement, he still ended up "approving" the attack.[89]

The strong organizational bond between al-Qaeda and the Taliban was not severed by the death of bin Laden nor by the death of the Mullah Omar. Omar's death created a power struggle within the Taliban over whether they should have peaceful relations with the government of then-President Muhammad Ashraf Ghani Ahmadzai. The head of the camp that advocated for coexistence with the Afghani government was Taliban leader Mullah Akhtar Mohammad Mansour. In July 2015, Mullah Aktar officially became the Taliban chief after Mullah Omar's family declared him the legitimate successor. Following this announcement, Ayman al-Zawahiri pledged his allegiance to Mansour.[90]

89 Alkhalij Online (Riyadh), January 8, 2015.
90 Arabi 21 (Istanbul), August 2, 2015.

The second camp that opposed coexistence or working with the Afghan government was Taliban's senior military commander Abdul Qayyum Zakir, also known as Abdullah Ghulam Rasoul and Abdul Qayyum. Abdul Qayyum was originally detained by the United States at Guantanamo Bay detention camp, but he was returned to Afghan custody and released in 2009. In August 2021, Abdul Qayyum became the Taliban's Deputy Defense Minister.

One would imagine that President Obama's administration would favor Mansour, the lesser of two evils who would essentially be easier to defeat, but the Obama administration killed Mansour in a drone strike in May 2016. Following Mansour's death, the Taliban appointed Hibatullah Akhundzada as its chief and Zawahiri renewed his allegiance to the new chief.[91] Akhundzada is the current head of the new Islamic Emirate of Afghanistan. The Taliban is the official leadership of al-Qaeda and other jihadist groups in Afghanistan. Currently, the man in charge of security in Kabul is Khalil Haqqani, who has had a $5 million bounty on his head and is a potential member of al-Qaeda.

The claim that there is a real distinction between al-Qaeda, Taliban, the Haqqani Network, and Islamic State in Khorasan province (ISKP, also known as ISIS-K), is a form of counterintelligence aimed at the West.

ISLAMIC STATE IN THE KHORASAN PROVINCE AND THE BAD TERRORIST/ WORSE TERRORIST MYTHOLOGY

ISKP was directly formed from *Tehrik-i-Taliban Pakistan* (TTP), the Pakistani branch of the Taliban. It was officially launched after a meet-

91 "Al-Qaeda chief pledges allegiance to new Taliban leader," YouTube.com, June 11, 2016.

ing of senior Taliban commanders on December 13, 2007, but the core cell of jihadists had been operational since 2002.[92]

TTP was based in South Waziristan and headed by Baitullah Mehsud, who was killed two years after its formation. TTP was created as an alliance of five different militant groups, with the goal of uniting Taliban factions that operated in North-West Frontier Province (NWFP). According to a report from The Jamestown Foundation:

> Its [TTP] spokesman, Maulvi Omar, a shadowy figure using a fake name, claimed that 27 Taliban factions operating in the Federally Administered Tribal Areas (FATA) were part of the movement. Nobody was surprised when Baitullah Mehsud, amir of the Taliban in the territory populated by the Mehsud Pashtun tribe in South Waziristan, was named as leader of the TTP. He was the most powerful among the Pakistani Taliban commanders and it was natural that he would lead the organization.[93]

TTP leadership was represented by five Shura council members, collectively known as the "Wana Five," named after the capital of South Waziristan. The first member was Maulvi (also spelled Mawlawi) Javed Karmazkhel, who represented *Lashkar-e-Jhangvi* (army of Jhangvi), the militia of the anti-Shi'a political party of *Sipah-e-Sahaba Pakistan* (Guardians of the Prophet's Companions in Pakistan).[94]

---

92 Hassan Abbas, "A Profile of Tehriki-i-Taliban Pakistan," Belfer Center for Science and International Affairs archived web page, https://web.archive.org/web/20170101073222/http://belfercenter.ksg.harvard.edu/publication/17868/profile_of_tehrikitaliban_pakistan.html, accessed March 5, 2022; Zaffar Abbas, "Pakistan's Undeclared War," *BBC,* achieved web page, https://web.archive.org/web/20080915111021/http://news.bbc.co.uk/2/hi/south_asia/3645114.stm, September 10, 2004.

93 Rahimullah Yusufzai, "The Impact of Pashtun Tribal Differences on the Pakistani Taliban," The Jamestown Foundation *Terrorism Monitor* 6, no. 3 (February 11, 2008).

94 Imtiaz Gul, *The Al Qaeda Connection: the Taliban and Terror in Pakistan's Tribal Areas* (New Delhi: Penguin Books Viking, 2009), 250.

The second figure was Taliban commander Nek Muhammad, who was later replaced by Haji Omar. Haji Omar was one of Mullah Omar's deputies in Afghanistan until the Taliban was toppled in late 2001, and he represented *Hezb-e Islami Khalis* (Islamic Party of Khalis), which was named after jihadist teacher Mohammad Yunus Khalis. The party is currently headed by Haji Din Muhammad, also known as Azizullah Din Muhammad, who was the governor of Kabul Province from 2005 to 2009. He was also involved in the alleged peace and reconciliation process between the Afghan Government and the Taliban, and is acting as the deputy of High Council for National Reconciliation—while still affiliated with the party represented in the founding of TTP. Haji Omar was later joined by his brother, Haji Sharif Khan.

The third individual is Maulana Abdul Aziz. Aziz is an infamous Pakistani terror preacher, known as The Religious Godfather of the Punjabi Taliban. He is a cofounder of the TTP, and on September 19, 2021, he declared his support and allegiance to the Taliban in Afghanistan by hoisting their flag on his Islamic madrassa in Pakistan.[95]

The fourth Wana leader was Mawlawi Muhammad Abbas, who represented the Islamic Movement of Uzbekistan (IMU). He was killed in 2012. The fifth member is Noor Islam, who appeared in a *CNN* interview on July 26, 2021, and declared his full support to the Afghan Taliban. Noor also vowed to fight the Pakistan government on behalf of the Afghan Taliban.[96]

The Pakistani government has sheltered the TTP since its inception. The Wana Five signed a peace deal with the Pakistani government, where they pledged to halt attacks in Afghanistan, stop attacking the Pakistani military, and cease harboring foreign militants. But

95 *Hindustan Times*, September 19, 2021, https://www.hindustantimes.com/world-news/afghan-taliban-flags-hoisted-in-islamabad-seminary-police-registers-case-101632059329425.html.

96 654. "Pakistani Taliban Leader Reacts to Afghan Gains After US Withdrawal," YouTube.com, July 26, 2021.

during an interview in August 2006, Haji Omar stated his intention to continue sending jihadists to Afghanistan and to continue fighting stating, "America and its friends including Britain, France and Germany have toppled our Islamic government in Afghanistan. We have started jihad against them." Omar added, "When Afghanistan will be free, we will go after them in Iraq. When Iraq will be free, we will go after them in Lebanon. In every country where they are being brutal, we will try to do jihad against them."[97]

TTP was and continues to be sheltered by the Pakistani government. TTP is also closely associated with al-Qaeda. In 2004, Pakistan accused the Wana Five of sheltering al-Qaeda terrorists in Waziristan. In response, the Wana Five reportedly offered to surrender. Brigadier Mahmood Shah, chief of security for the tribal regions, said local lawmakers met with Nek Muhammad, Haji Sharif, Maulana Abdul Aziz, Maulvi Abbas, and Haji Noor Islam. According to the South Asia Terrorism Portal (SATP):

> Five tribesmen accused of sheltering al-Qaeda terrorists surrendered to the Pakistan army at a tribal council. The five men from the Zalikhel tribe turned themselves in before a council and also reportedly pledged loyalty to Pakistan in return for clemency. The ceremony occurred at a Madrassa (seminary) in Shakai, 20 kilometers north of Wana, in South Waziristan. "We give amnesty to these people in return for their pledge of brotherhood and loyalty," said Peshawar Corps Commander Lt Gen Safdar Hussain. "I congratulate Nek and his colleagues on their courageous decision.

97 *Frontline*, Interview with Haji Omar, October 3, 2006.

> You are our brothers and your allegiance pledge is exemplary."[98]

Since its founding, Pakistan has always been a state sponsor of terrorism. It's inconceivable to actually believe that there is a real difference between ISKP, TTP, the Taliban, and al-Qaeda. The only tangible distinction is their names. It is impossible for Afghanistan to have operated as a jihadist training playground without the support of Pakistan. Pakistan is not the only state sponsor of terrorism. It is also joined by "Sultan" Recep Tayyip Erdoğan in the league of terrorism-sponsoring nations.

THE MUSLIM BROTHERHOOD'S NEO-OTTOMAN SULTAN RECEP TAYYIP ERDOĞAN

Since 2013, and perhaps as early as 2003, the clandestine head of the International Apparatus is also the General and Secret Guide of Muslim Brotherhood, which no longer has its headquarters in Egypt. The Brotherhood's paradox is that both its successes and detriments stem from the group's inescapable ideological and ritualistic repetition of history. During crisis, they place themselves in a narrow chaotic gray area where they struggle to maintain the balance between public and clandestine façades and operations.

When the Brotherhood was faced with crisis during its second founding, they gave Omar al-Tilmisani the title "Public Spokesman," from 1973 to 1976, while the actual leader was the Secret Guide. Today, the Brotherhood engages in the same behavior. The group currently calls its public leader, Ibrahim Munir, the "Acting General Guide of the Egyptian Muslim Brotherhood" and the "Secretary

98 South Asia Terrorism Portal (SATP), "Federally Administered Tribal Areas (FATA) Timeline–Year 2004," https://www.satp.org/satporgtp/countries/pakistan/waziristan/timeline/2004.htm, accessed October 1, 2021.

General of the International Apparatus." The term "secretary" indicates that there is an *actual* leader.

The Kamal Vanguard is not only an Egyptian reaction to the mass rejection of the Muslim Brotherhood in its country of origin but an international one among the ranks of the Brotherhood worldwide. Currently, the international Kamal Vanguard is trying to revive the Ottoman Empire under the leadership of Brotherhood leader and Turkish President Recep Tayyip Erdoğan. Numerous indicators suggest Erdoğan is the General and Secret Guide of the Muslim Brotherhood and also the head of its International Apparatus.

The Muslim Brotherhood didn't just raise him to the highest levels of leadership; Brotherhood Mufti al-Qaradawi bestowed upon him Islamic sacred kingship and officially declared him a Sultan. On April 23, 2016, the Muslim Brotherhood held an international conference titled *Shukran Turkiyya* (Thanks Turkey), and it served as Erdoğan's inauguration ceremony as caliph.[99] The conference presenter launched the event saying, "Thanks Turkey…this celebratory event with different Arab and Muslim communities, we gather in Istanbul the previous capital of Islam and the current capital of Islam, and the future capital of Islam."

During the conference, Qaradawi took the stage and said:

> Thanks Turkey, we came here to present our gratitude to Turkey. Turkey, this great nation which served Islam throughout its history with endless services. Turks today have risen to defend Islam, no one can deny the stance of this great Sultan, known to the people as Recep Tayyip Erdoğan. Who can resist this great Sultan? The Sultan of Muslims, the Sultan of the ummah who defends the Muslim nation with absolute force, under the banner of Islam, under the ban-

99 Al-Jazeera (Doha), April 23, 2016.

> ner of Qur'an, under the banner of Sunnah, under the banner of the creed, under the banner of Shari'a, under the banner of loyalty and morality ... He strives and sacrifices to stand against tyrannical forces, telling them no, with all his strength he says no. On behalf of millions on behalf of 1.7 billion Muslims, the nation of Islam worldwide.

After the Brotherhood's religious edict declared Erdoğan a Sultan, they held numerous events to propagate on his behalf. For example, at a press conference on December 10, 2016, Qaradawi said, "I swear to God I am telling the truth, the man who carries the burden of the Islamic nation everywhere is Recep Tayyip Erdoğan, the Islamic nation should support him. Our Brothers in Qatar are by his side, and we are behind them and we have their back."

Following Erdoğan's inauguration, Islamist media outlets began to refer to Turks as "Ottomans." History repeated itself, as if Islamists were stuck in an endless vortex of repetition.

The old clandestine Islamic Ethics Association was reestablished in Lebanon on May 4, 2007, in the Lebanese hub of clandestine proselytism in Tripoli in Northern Lebanon.[100] The group is a Muslim Brotherhood front organization and was reestablished by Muhammad Rashid Mikati, who was also involved in establishing the Muslim Brotherhood branch in Lebanon.[101]

In 2018, the Islamic Ethics Association publicly revealed that it continues to uphold its intention to revive the Ottoman Empire through several projects. On March 18, 2018, the Turkish newspaper *Ahval* published an article titled "A Desire to Develop the Ottoman

100 Faculty of Law and Political and Administrative Sciences, "Jama'at Makarim al-Akhlaq al-Islamiyya," www.legiliban.ul.edu.lb, May 4, 2007.

101 "Muhammad Rashid Mikati," The Official Muslim Brotherhood Encyclopedia, https://ikhwanwiki.com/, accessed June 10, 2021.

Relationship Between Turkey and Lebanon: [through] a Research Institute in Tripoli." The article stated:

> The Lebanese nongovernmental [Islamic] Ethics Association, in cooperation with the Turkish Cultural Center in Lebanon, established the Ottoman Studies Center in Tripoli, in northern Lebanon. During the celebration held for this occasion, the founders of the center issued a statement to Turkish media where they stressed that Ottoman documents and manuscripts are among the most important elements of the concealed strength of Turkey after it has taken a solid step to reach international dominance.[102]

The article also stated that Serhat Koçkurt, a representative of Turks in the Middle East, said they had established a "Turkish language department in the Lebanese University," which will "teach students the modern Turkish and Ottoman language." The president of the Islamic Ethics Association, Mikati, stated, "The aim of opening the center is to restore the relationship between Lebanon and Turkey in this field, and to restore the Ottoman relations which prevailed in the past." In 2017, the Islamic Ethics Association opened a branch in the Kingdom of Saudi Arabia, which is most probably operating as a Muslim Brotherhood front group. The other Lebanese clandestine entity, the Makassed Foundation, also began propagating on behalf of the Ottomans. For example, in 2012, they hosted an event at their school in honor of the Bloody Sultan Abdul Hamid II.[103]

---

102 Ahval (Istanbul), March 18, 2018.
103 Turkiyya Al-An (Istanbul), October 5, 2017.

ERDOĞAN SPONSORS TERRORISM

Under Erdoğan's leadership, Turkey became the command-and-control center for Islamic terrorism. Turkey's sponsorship of terrorism has expanded with the help of Egyptian Secret Apparatus operatives who fled to Turkey after Muhammad Morsi was deposed.

Turkish journalist Burak Bekdil said, "Turkey became known as a 'jihadist highway' that transported Islamist fighters from across the globe to the Levant."[104] The Brotherhood certainly contributed to this. The apparatus is fully operational in Istanbul, where the regime provides them with a haven for recruiting terrorists, smuggling jihadists in and out of Turkey, and plotting international terrorist attacks.

Muslim Brotherhood television networks operating from Turkey constantly stream terrorism incitement against Egypt, the Kingdom of Saudi Arabia, the United Arab Emirates, and Israel. For example, the Mekameleen television network, which is operated by Brotherhood jihadists, openly incites terrorism. In January 2015, Brotherhood commentator Muhammad Naser said, "kill his [President al-Sisi's] officers. I am telling you on live television kill his officers. I want to tell the wives of every officer, your husband will be murdered. If not today, it will be tomorrow, or after tomorrow. He will be killed." Naser also threatened the families of police and military personals and said that he has "information" that the Brotherhood started "stalking... their children, their wives, and their relatives and the second wave [of terrorism] will be inside the homes of officers." He also threatened that they will kidnap their children.[105]

An incident on January 16, 2019, revealed several key pieces of information about the Secret Apparatus operation in Turkey. On this day, Muhammad Abdul Hafiz, an Egyptian Muslim Brotherhood convicted terrorist and member of the Kamal Vanguard, arrived at

---

104 Burak Bekdil, "Turkey: Jihadist Highway Revisited," The Begin-Sadat Center for Strategic Studies (BESA Center), https://besacenter.org, December 6, 2019.

105 Mekameleen Network (Istanbul), February 2, 2015.

Istanbul Atatürk Airport with a fraudulent visa from Mogadishu on his Egyptian passport. After detaining him for few hours, Turkish airport police deported him to Egypt.

This incident caused an uproar inside the Muslim Brotherhood that ensued an online fight between the two camps of the organization, the Secret Apparatus' Kamal Group and public leadership. They secretly recorded each other's conversations and shared them on their social media accounts. Brotherhood youth wing operative Abdul Rahman Salih published a recorded conversation with the Brotherhood's counsel in Turkey, Mukhtar al-Ashri. Ashri said, "In short, what happened with Muhammad Abdul Hafiz is that he agreed with some of the young people here from the Kamal Group, that he would pay them and they would facilitate his entry."

They released another recording in which convicted terrorist and Brotherhood leader Saber Abdul Fetouh revealed the name of the leader of the Secret Apparatus terrorism operations in the Kamal Group. Fetouh said, "Dr. Muhammad Ghozlani called me asked me about Muhammad Abdul Hafiz." Fetouh continued saying that during talks with Turkish authorities regarding this incident, they "asked which wing does Hafiz belong to, they asked [whether he] is Ikhwan, [Egyptian Islamic] Jihad, or Gama'a Islamiyya?" Fetouh said, "because I was contacted by Dr. Muhammad Ghozlani, I said that he was Jihad."

This conversation understandably caused a lot of confusion among analysts in the Middle East. At face value, it seems that they are three different entities, but they are all operating under the wider umbrella of the Muslim Brotherhood but with different roles. Muhammad Nasr Ghozlani, who is identified as a leader of Egyptian Islamic Jihad, is also a leader in the Muslim Brotherhood's terrorism apparatus. Under Morsi's presidency, Ghozlani was working in his regime, and his official title was *al-mab'uth al-ri'asi li-muhawarat al-jihadiyin* (the Presidential Liaison to Communicate with Jihadists).[106]

106 Madrass (Cairo), October 27, 2012.

Ghozlani is from a large Brotherhood family from Kerdasa, and he was one of the perpetrators of the horrific Kerdasa police station massacre.[107] He still resides in Turkey, where he is responsible for the transport of terrorists from and to Turkey. On his public Facebook page, Ghozlani repeatedly glorified Muhammad Kamal and the Kamal Group, and he posted several pictures of himself beside posters of Kamal. This behavior is consistent with the leaders and members of the Kamal Vanguard.[108]

In an interview in 2015, Egyptian Major General Rif'at Qumsan said, "We shouldn't be fooled with names [of terrorist organizations] such as Daesh, Nusrat al-Haq, Nusrat al-Islam, Hamas, and others. They are all one. We can say the Brotherhood is the frame that cloaks all these organizations, whether they are so-called peaceful like Jamaat at-tabligh w'ad-Da'wa or as their most violent organizations such as al-Qaeda, Tanzim al-Jihad, and Daesh."[109]

Stating that the Muslim Brotherhood has denounced terrorism is a myth exclusively propagated to their Western targets. No Arabic-speaking nation is under this impression. If the Brotherhood were to give up violent jihad, it would be mean the leaders had dismantled the organization, because the Muslim Brotherhood would lose its legitimacy and its sole reason for existence.

According to the Brotherhood's own standards and internal bylaws, there are ten constants in their organization's *bai'a* process. The fourth of these constants is violent jihad and martyrdom, which the Brotherhood states is an obligation of every individual Muslim, as well as the collective obligation of their organization.

107 Al-Watan (Cairo), February 16, 2015.

108 Archived picture from Muhammad al-Ghozlani's public Facebook page, "Screenshot of Mohammed al-Ghozlani's public Facebook page holding a sign that features Mohammed Kamal," Archive.org, February 7, 2019.

109 Al-Nahar (Cairo), June 9, 2015.

CHAPTER ELEVEN

SALAFISTS AND SHI'ITES

The Muslim Brotherhood's Alliance with Iran

"Taqiyya is my religion and the religion of my forefathers"[1]

—JA'FAR AS-SADIQ

DISPUTES BETWEEN THE MUSLIM BROTHERHOOD and Iran have compelled the majority of experts to focus on their conflict rather than their commonality. Cooperation between the Muslim Brotherhood and Iran grew through three major stages, during which Shi'a jihadists and Sunni Brotherhood jihadists created a foundation that Banna used to fulfill Nader Shah's two-century-old dream. The first stage of the cooperation project took place during Hassan al-Banna's lifetime. The second stage occurred during the Iranian revolution in 1978; and the third stage of their relationship was their formal alliance after Egypt's 2011 coup d'état.

The death of Rashid Rida in 1935 marked a significant transformation in the Brotherhood's relationship with Shi'ites. Islamists steadfastly pushed the unity narrative, but Rida eventually gave up his proximity project due to his relationship with Ibn Saud, whom he viewed as the legitimate caliph. Rida may not have seen the need to

1 Ismail al-Muzay al-Malairi, *Jami' Ahadith ash-Shi'a* (Iraq: Maktabat al-Jawadeen al-Ama, 1941), 2: 391.

maintain his dissimulation toward Shi'its after Sunnis reached their objective of a Sunni caliphate in Saudi Arabia. Rida began to change his tone in his articles in *al-Manar* magazine and attacked the clandestine *da'wa*, which he had relied upon heavily throughout his career. [2]

In his book *A'imatu ash-Share* (Imams of Evil), Tharwat al-Kherbawy concluded that Banna's proximity project remained relatively subdued until Rashid Rida's death.[3] According to Kherbawy, Rida's death emboldened Banna and the Brotherhood to have a more public and more official relationship with their Shi'a counterparts. The ideological influence Rida had on Banna was matched by an elusive Shi'ite figure, Muhammad Taqi ad-Din al-Qummi (1908–1990).[4]

Qummi was born in Iran to a religious Twelver family. His father, Ahmad al-Qummi, was a midranking scholar with the title *Hujjatu al-Islam wa'l-Muslimin* (authority over Islam and Muslims). Qummi left Iran in 1937 to tour Sunni countries and try to revive the legacy of Jamal ad-Din al-Afghani's proximity project. He visited Iraq and Lebanon, and his third destination was Cairo.

As soon as Qummi arrived in Cairo, he went directly to Banna. Typically, Qummi started his project in Cairo by targeting al-Azhar University. Banna introduced him to then-Grand Imam of al-Azhar, Muhammad Mustafa al-Maraghi.[5] Qummi proposed his project of Islamic unification to Maraghi. Maraghi accepted the idea of proximity on the premise that it potentially could convert Shi'ites to Sunnism.[6] Again, just like Qummi's ideological predecessor al-Afghani, he was able to convince Maraghi to allow him to teach the same Islamic philosophy course, which Afghani taught at al-Azhar almost six decades

2 Muhammed Rashid Rida, *As-Sunna w'ash-Shi'a* (Cairo: Dar al-Manar, 1947), 6; Anwar Mohammed Zanati, *Mawsou'at Tarikh al-Alam*, (Cairo: Kotob Arabia, 2007) 2: 143.

3 Kherbawy, *A'imatu ash-Share*, 272–275.

4 Ibid., 122–125; "Ash-shaikh Muhammed Taqi ad-Din al-Qummi, Mu'ases Dar al-Taqrib bil Qahira," IjtihadNetwork.Ir, August 23, 2015.

5 Mohammed as-Sayyid, "Sheikh Muhammad Mustafa al-Maraghi", The Official Muslim Brotherhood Encyclopedia, https://ikhwanwiki.com/, accessed February 15, 2018.

6 Kherbawy, *A'imatu ash-Share*, 124.

before him. Maraghi's close relationship with Amin al-Husaini, who was a major figure in the proximity project, made him susceptible to Qummi's propositions.[7],[8] In 1933, Husaini visited Iran and gained support from Islamist activists and the government.[9]

After Qummi visited Banna, another Shi'ite figure who would later become one of the most prominent figures in the history of Shi'ism would visit the Muslim Brotherhood's Cairo headquarters. According to Kherbawy, Khomeini visited al-Banna in 1938, in the Brotherhood's headquarters in Cairo. In his book, Kherbawy published evidence of the visit, which he found while researching old documents in the Brotherhood headquarters in Cairo in 1992.[10] Kherbawy discovered a letter sent from Saleh Ashmawi, then-editor-in-chief of the Brotherhood's *al-Nazir* magazine. The letter was sent to Secret Apparatus leader Mahmoud Abdul Halim, requesting him to ask Banna to grant Ashmawi permission to write and publish an article about Khomeini's visit, who was at the time known as Ruhollah Mustafa Musavi.[11] The letter states:

> Honorable brother Mahmoud Abdul Halim, kindly ask al-Murshid [Hassan al-Banna] about the visit of Shi'ite cleric Ruhollah Mustafa Musavi to the [Brotherhood's] headquarters. Is it acceptable to write about the details of this visit, or he prefers we don't? I myself, would like to personally write about this issue and what he [Banna] said regarding cooperation in what we agree upon, and excuse each other's differences. Anyhow, the decision is his, but I also wanted to share my opinion with you. Kindly get back to me

7 Rubin and Schwanitz, *Nazis, Islamists, and the Making of the Modern Middle East*, 88.
8 The Organization of Islamic Cooperation (OIC), OICUN.org, accessed February 19, 2018.
9 Rubin and Schwanitz, *Nazis, Islamists, and the Making of the Modern Middle East*, 88.
10 Kherbawy, *A'imatu ash-Share*, 294.
11 "Mahmoud Abdul Halim wa Kitabahu Ahdath Sana'et At-Tarikh," Islamist-Movements.com, September 19, 2016.

> soon because it should go to print next Friday. Saleh Mustafa Ashmawi.

Kherbawy recounted that the letter he discovered startled him, and he discussed it with a member of the Guidance Office and Banna's protégé, Abbas as-Sisi (1918–2004). Abbas as-Sisi was the uncle of the current Egyptian President, Abdel Fattah al-Sisi. He confirmed to Kherbawy that the Shi'a cleric Ruhollah Mustafa Musavi was indeed Khomeini. According to Kherbawy, Abbas as-Sisi said, "Ruhollah was Khomeini, may he rest in peace. He wasn't known at the time, and he also wasn't convinced of proximity between Sunnis and Shi'ites then, until the martyr Imam [Banna] met with him to try to recruit him."[12]

Khomeini had already been acquainted with radical Assassins-style militias a year prior to his visit to Brotherhood headquarters in Cairo. In 1937, he was introduced to the Muslim Brotherhood and *Fada'iyan al-Islam* terrorist group during his pilgrimage trip to the Imam Ali Shrine in Najaf in Iraq, a historic destination for the proximity project since the time of Nader Shah, 194 years earlier.[13] While in Najaf, Khomeini improved his knowledge of Arabic, and studied Sunni clandestine theological books written by Muhammad Abduh.[14]

Saleh Ashmawi letter's letter to Banna featured Rashid Rida's proximity slogan, "We cooperate in what we agree upon, and excuse each other's differences." It indicated how this idea had been deeply integrated in the Brotherhood's philosophy and operation. Ashmawi never published his article in *al-Nazir*, and it may have been ignored for more nefarious reasons. The timing of Khomeini's visit to Banna was critical. Banna was still in the process of adequately organizing his militia, and the full announcement of cooperation with Shi'ites wasn't a good strategic move while recruiting Sunni terrorists.

---

12 Kherbawy, *A'imatu ash-Share*, 119.

13 Amir Taheri, *The Spirit of Allah:* Khomeini and the Islamic Revolution, (Bethesda, Md.: Adler & Adler, 1986), 97–99.

14 Ibid.

Of this mysterious visit, one can speculate Banna swayed Khomeini, as Banna's influence on Khomeini would become apparent years later in several ways.

After World War II began, al-Qummi departed Cairo to Iran for several years. There, he met Grand Ayatollah Sayyid Hossein Borujerdi, who granted him support and encouragement for his proximity project, which could potentially convert Sunnis to Shi'ism.[15] Major militant figures in both sects, Ayatollah Borujerdi and Grand Imam Maraghi practiced dissimulation and concealment, which was at the heart of the proximity project. Each believed they could ideologically outmaneuver the other. After World War II ended, Qummi returned to Cairo "to resume a journey, conspicuously for proximity and secretly for Shi'itization."[16] Banna offered him a residency in the Muslim Brotherhood's headquarters, where they hosted numerous discussions with Sunni scholars.

In February 1947, Banna and Qummi officially cofounded their proximity organization and called it *Dar at-Taqrib bain al-Madhahib al-Islamiyya* (The Kinship House for Proximity of Islamic Schools of Thought). After establishing the organization, Qummi acted as its General Secretary and its leader.[17] Through al-Azhar University, the organization issued *Risalat al-Islam* (Islam's Mission) magazine, which was published by al-Azhar until the early 1960s. The organization is still operational, and is currently called the World Forum for Proximity of Islamic Schools of Thought (WFPIST).[18] Its headquarters is in Tehran under the leadership of Ayatollah Ali Khamenei, who reestablished it in 1990. One of the organization's main objectives, according to its official website:

15 All-Kherbawy, *A'imatu ash-Share*, 125.
16 Ibid.
17 Ibid., 126.
18 The World Forum for Proximity of Islamic Schools of Thought (WFPIST), http://taqrib.ir/fa, accessed February 15, 2018.

> Islamic unification, in terms of cooperation between followers of Islamic sects based on shared solid declared Islamic values to adopt a unified stance to accomplish the goals and best interest of the Islamic ummah. To adhere to one position toward its enemies, with respect to each other's Muslim faith, sect and rituals.[19]

According to Iranian professor and member of WFPIST Mohammad Ali Azarsab, al-Azhar University's early call for the proximity project was led by al-Maraghi.[20] Three of the scholars it recruited later became heads of al-Azhar University. They were Mohammed Shaltout, Abdul Mijid Selim, and Mustafa Abdul Razik.

In 1948, Banna took it upon himself to settle a Sunni–Shi'ite rift that started years earlier, and he used it to revive a historic Shi'ite objective. In 1944, Abi Talib al-Zaydi, a Persian Shi'ite, was beheaded by the Saudi government after he vomited during Hajj. The Saudis believed it was due to him drinking alcohol, therefore desecrating Hajj, and they killed him. The Iranians believed Zaydi was just ill and viewed the act as an excuse to threaten their participation in Hajj.

Soon after Banna and Qummi established their organization, Banna proposed an interesting resolution to the problem, which was initially proposed in the Council of Najaf by Nader Shah over two hundred years earlier. The solution was to allow Hajj to be practiced according to Islam's five sects through officially recognizing the Ja'fri sect as the fifth school of Islam. Banna published his opinion in a small pamphlet that he distributed during his Hajj trip in 1948.

Former Iranian mullah, ambassador and advisor to the Iranian Minister of Foreign Affairs Sayyid Hadi Khosroshahi—who is also a cleric trained by Khomeini and Qummi—recounted that al-Qummi's

19 "Istratijeyyt al-Magma' al-Alami l'al-Taqrib bai al-Mathaheb al-Islamiyya," http://taqrib.ir/fa, accessed February 15, 2018.

20 Mohammad Ali Azarsab, "Dar al-Taqrib bain al-Mathaheb al-Islamiyya," Azarshab.com, accessed February 15, 2018.

was impressed by Banna's proposal. Khosroshahi said the incident had a "massive effect on the unity between Muslims."[21]

During Banna's Hajj, he met with another influential Shi'ite figure, Ayatollah Abu al-Ghasem Kashani (1882–1962), who was in the process of establishing the Persian jihadist group *Majma'-e Mojahedin-e Islam* (Society of Muslim warriors) to be more "inclusive" than *Fada'iyan-e Islam* (Devotees of Islam).[22] The Fada'iyan was another terrorist group modeled after the Assassins, founded by Iranian jihadist Navvab Safavi (1923 –1955).[23] The Fada'iyan borrowed elements and terminology from the Brotherhood, who borrowed it from the Assassins. For example, the leader of Fada'iyan was also called *murshid* (Guide), like their Brotherhood counterparts. The Fada'iyan was founded in 1946, and Kashani was one of its leaders. He aimed to create a new group to advocate for nationalizing oil, which required his alliance with communist, socialist, activist lawyers, and with Members of Parliament.[24] One of Kashani's most important allies was the socialist activist lawyer Mohammad Mosaddegh, who eventually became the Prime Minister of Iran from 1951 to 1953.

Kashani's pragmatism and *taqiyya* in his alliance with communists was similar to his alliance with the Brotherhood. Kashani was impressed by Banna after he defended Shi'ites during a meeting with radical Sunni Egyptian participants in Hajj who protested Shi'ite Hajj rituals. Banna gave an infamous speech for proximity and said, "The difference between some Sunnis and Shi'ites, is that Shi'ites love the Prophet's family more than their counterparts. They should

21 Sayyid Hadi Khosroshahi, "Nazra ila al-Turath al-Fikri wa'l-wa'l-wa'l-Ijtima'i wa'l-wa'l-wa'l-Sheikh Hassan al-Banna," The Official Muslim Brotherhood Encyclopedia, https://ikhwanwiki.com/, accessed February 17, 2018.

22 Lotfallah Ajdani, "Ayatollah Kashani Khawahan Srgwny Daktar Musdq bud," TarikhIrani.ir,, accessed February 21, 2018.

23 Amir Taheri, *The Spirit of Allah*, 102.

24 Seyyed Nima Hosseini, "Ikhtilafa Navvab Safavi wa-Kashani," TarikhIrani.ir, accessed February 21, 2018.

be a role model to Egyptians [who should have] allegiance to the Prophet's family."[25]

Banna's words would be another major influence in the proximity between the two sects that would continue to influence future leaders of the Muslim Brotherhood. Mustafa Mashhour wrote a letter to Kherbawy in which he stressed the importance of upholding these values and said, "Since its inception, the Muslim Brotherhood and its great leader Hassan al-Banna urged everyone to overlook sectarian differences to unify all Muslims. In fact, this is a divine order."[26]

The Brotherhood's Shi'ite relationship went further than one would expect. Following Banna's assassination, Kashani was among those promoted by the Brotherhood for consideration to succeed as General Guide.[27] This precedent would be repeated in Iraq. In 1960, the Muslim Brotherhood branch of Iraq nominated the Shi'ite cleric, al-Sayyed Talib al-Refa'i, to head the group.[28] Refa'i rejected the position to avoid controversy, but the incident was one of several clues about the nature of the Shi'ite–Sunni relationship within the Muslim Brotherhood.

Banna's assassination in 1949 did not halt the proximity project. The General Islamic Congress became an equally powerful outlet for the project. In 1953, the General Islamic Congress meeting in Jerusalem was attended by both Sayyid Qutb and Navvab Safavi.[29] The following year, Qutb invited Safavi to Egypt, where he received a formal welcome by then- President Muhammad Naguib and his de facto vice president, Gamal Abdul Nasser. Safavi gave a speech at Cairo University, where he said, "Anyone who wants to be a true

25 Kherbawy, *A'imatu ash-Share*, 232-4.
26 Ibid., 232.
27 Ibid.
28 Rasheed al-Khayou, *Amali as-Sayyid Talib al-Refa'i*, (Dubai: Madarek Publishing House, 2012), 106–113.
29 Martin Kramer, "Anwar Sadat's Visit to Jerusalem, 1955," https://martinkramer.org, accessed February 25, 2018.. Abdel Rahim Ali, "Ikhwan Muslimoun fi Iran min al-Khomeini ila Rouhani," Islamist-Movements.com, April 17, 2014.

Shi'ite Ja'fari, should join the Muslim Brotherhood."[30] Both Qutb and Safavi would later be executed by their governments for their involvement in assassinations and terrorist activities.

The proximity project was maintained throughout the sixties predominantly by Muslim Brotherhood operatives in the leadership of al-Azhar and members and cofounders of The Kinship House for Proximity of Islamic Schools of Thought. Safavi's trip was fruitful. He also met with leaders of al-Azhar, including its then-Grand Imam, Abdul Rahman Taj. This level of cooperation between a Shi'ite militant like Safavi and one of the largest Sunni institution in the world should not come as a surprise to anyone aware of the theological basis for this cooperation. Safavi's Brotherhood invitation to Egypt opened a new historic chapter in the cooperation which continues till today. Interestingly, it would fulfill another of Nader Shah's centuries-old dream.

Among the most influential cofounders of Kinship House was Brotherhood member Sheikh Mahmoud Shaltout (1893–1963), who succeeded Taj as the Grand Imam of al-Azhar. In April 1960, Shaltout issued a historic fatwa that fulfilled a major demand of Nader Shah over two centuries earlier during the Najaf convention, when he insisted that Sunnis recognize the Ja'fari sect as a fifth school of jurisprudence. Shaltout's fatwa was titled, "The permissibility of worship through Islamic sects including the Shi'a Twelver Imamate denomination." Shaltout and al-Azhar officially recognized the Ja'fari jurisprudence of Shi'a Twelvers as a fifth school of Islam.[31]

While Shaltout's fatwa faced some pushback within the ranks of al-Azhar, the influential clerics were on board. In 1965, former head of the Faculty of Shari'a Law at al-Azhar Muhammad Abu Zahra stated that he wished al-Azhar would adhere to the Ja'fari jurispru-

30 Kherbawy, *A'imatu ash-Share*, 154.

31 Kherbawy, *A'imatu ash-Share*, 126; Nasir al-Qaffari, *Mas'alatu al-Taqrib bain as-Sunna w'ash-Sh'ia* (Riyadh: Dar Tiba, 1992) 2: 309.

dence in the matters of divorce.[32] That was a powerful indication of his support for Shi'ism at one of the most powerful Sunni institutions.

Shaltout's fatwa was the culmination of centuries of struggle to unify militants of ummah, and the fatwa still stands. During a television interview in 2013, Syrian journalist Zaina Yazigi asked the head of al-Azhar, Ahmed al-Tayeb, if he recognized the Shi'ite sect as an official fifth sect of Islam.[33] He replied, "Yes, it is officially a fifth sect of Islam." He confirmed that al-Azhar sometimes relies on Ja'fari jurisprudence.

One of the most important developments in legitimizing the Shi'ite sect by al-Azhar is their attempt to portray the conversion to Shi'ism as less of a social stigma in Egypt than it actually was. One example is the mysterious and powerful former Brotherhood leader and judge al-Demrdash al-Aqali, who later became the imam of the Shi'ites in Egypt. Born in the 1930s, Aqali held several prominent positions throughout his career. He was a judge in the Egyptian Justice Ministry, a Member of Parliament, and an advisor to Saudi Arabia's Interior Ministry in 1975. Aqali said that he converted to Shi'ism in the mid-1960s and ultimately became the imam of Shi'ites in Egypt. He traveled to Iran several times until he was prohibited from traveling there in 1988.

Aqali's ties to the Muslim Brotherhood were deeper than just ideological. He was married to Amna Nosseir. She was a distant relative of Sayyid Qutb's, a member of the Muslim Sisterhood, an al-Azhar University professor, and a member of Parliament.[34] Aqali and Nosseir divorced, but he said their divorce was due to marital disputes and not because he became a Shi'ite.[35] The fact that the Muslim Brotherhood didn't demand their divorce after his conversion suggested his conversion could have been a Brotherhood intelligence

32 Al-Bawaba News (Cairo), April 5, 2015.
33 Zaina Yazigi, Interview with Sheikh Ahmed al-Tayeb, Dubai TV, May 26, 2013.
34 Al-Wafd (Cairo), April 3, 2015.
35 Donia al-Watan News (Gaza), March 4, 2012.

operation and not real, especially since the Muslim Brotherhood persecutes and murders Shi'as who aren't party to their alliance with Shi'a jihadists. For example, on June 24, 2013, the Brotherhood attacked a group of four Shi'ites, beat them to death, and posted the video of the horrific incident online.[36]

The recognition of the Shi'ite sect had groundbreaking repercussions on the relationship between the Brotherhood and Persian militants. It greatly worked to the advantage of clandestine Islamist revolutionaries in both sects. Shaltout's fatwa and the Brotherhood's al-Azhar proximity organization created a valid framework for their cooperation, which gave institutional justification to their collaboration and communication. This has allowed them to move their cooperation into its second stage of the evolution during the Islamic revolution in Iran.

THE MUSLIM BROTHERHOOD AND THE ISLAMIC REVOLUTION IN IRAN

After Banna built a theologically and organizationally acceptable bond with Persian jihadists, his politically savvy Shi'ite counterpart, Ayatollah Khomeini, exploited it during the socio-political climate of the Iranian revolution.

Khomeini can be viewed more as a movement, not merely a cleric and politician. He was the culmination of almost a millennium-old project for unification of militant Islam. The collaboration between the Muslim Brotherhood and Shi'a militants prior to the Islamic revolution was spearheaded by the Brotherhood's Cairo office and the Brotherhood's International Apparatus, under the leadership of businessman and Muslim Brotherhood financial strategist, Youssef Nada.

The second stage of the relationship took a more formal and public nature. Prior to perpetrating the Islamic revolution, Khomeini was

36 France 24 (Cairo), June 24, 2013.

exiled in Iraq for fourteen years, until October 1978, when he was expelled by the Iraqi government. He relocated to France and stayed at the residence of Seyyed Abolhassan Banisadr (1933–2021), a left-wing Iranian politician who briefly held the presidential office in Iran following the Islamic revolution, until he was deposed by Khomeini in 1981.[37] The clandestine nature of Khomeini and the Brotherhood's activities created a mystery around the few months Khomeini spent in France and their relationship after the Islamic revolution, but several Brotherhood operatives provided testimony demonstrating the depth of the association during the Brotherhood's two official visits to Khomeini—one visit before he perpetrated the Islamic revolution and one after.

THE FIRST VISIT

During an interview with al-Jazeera in 2015, Tunisian Brotherhood leader Abdulfattah Mourou stated that he had visited Khomeini with a Muslim Brotherhood delegation in France in January 1979. It's not clear how many Brotherhood representatives were in the delegation, but Mourou said operatives from several countries were represented.[38]

Mourou mentioned the names of two Brotherhood leaders who accompanied him. The first was Islamic-Socialism activist and cofounder of the Brotherhood's al-Jama'a al-Islamiyya branch in Tunisia, Hmida Ennaifer. Ennaifer is a theologian and currently a member of the Islamic-Christian Research Group (*Groupe de Recherches islamo-chrétien*, GRIC).[39] The second representative was the Lebanese Brotherhood leader and emir of al-Jama'a al-Islamiyya in Lebanon, Faisal al-Mawlawi (1941–2011). In another interview with

37 Ahmed Mansour, Interview with Youssef Nada, Shahed ala al-Aser, Al-Jazeera Channel, https://www.aljazeera.net/, August 11, 2002.
38 Ibid., April 19, 2015.
39 The Islamic-Christian Research Group (GRIC), GRIC.ASSO.FR, Web.Archive.Org, accessed March 6, 2018.

al-Jazeera, Youssef Nada stated Rached Ghannouchi was among the delegates. Nada said Hassan al-Turabi was also present.[40]

Mourou said that meeting Khomeini was something he "greatly hoped for," and that "they were oblivious" to their sectarian difference. Mourou said he had asked Khomeini many questions, but the only question he shared in the interview was: How could they "make people love Islam?" To which Khomeini answered, "Fulfill people's needs with Islam, solve their problems with Islam." Mourou added that this was the lesson he had learned from Khomeini.

Mourou's admission is significant. This is the first known record of a variation of the Muslim Brotherhood electoral slogan, "Islam is the solution," which they used throughout the years when they ran for elections. It was potentially Khomeini's idea. Mourou said Khomeini offered them a new beginning for the history of Iran and the Muslim world.

THE MUSLIM BROTHERHOOD'S SECOND OFFICIAL TRIP TO IRAN

Shortly after Khomeini's return to Iran in February 1979, the Brotherhood Guide, Omar al-Tilmisani sent another official delegation to support him and give him an official Islamic oath of allegiance.[41] Also according to Nada, the Brotherhood delegation's private jet was the second plane to land in Tehran following the revolution.[42] The first was Yasser Arafat's.

The relationship between Palestinians and Khomeini began much earlier. According to a declassified US Department of State document, Mahmoud Abbas, the current President of the Palestinian National Authority, revealed in a 1979 interview with the Kuwaiti Arabic

40 Ahmed Mansour, Interview with Youssef Nada, Shahed ala al-Aser, Al-Jazeera Channel, https://www.aljazeera.net/, August 11, 2002.

41 Kherbawy, *A'imatu ash-Share*, 159, 287.

42 Ahmed Mansour, Interview with Youssef Nada, Shahed ala al-Aser, Al-Jazeera Channel, https://www.aljazeera.net/, August 11, 2002.

newspaper *al-Watan* that "Fatah's relationship with Iranian religious Ayatollah Khomeini began in 1968, when a Fatah delegation visited Khomeini at his place of exile in Najaf, Iraq, for the purpose of seeking the support of Khomeini and other religious leaders in Iraq for Fatah and the Palestinian cause. At the time Khomeini asserted his support for Fatah and, since then, relations between Khomeini and Fatah have been close."[43]

Nada said that he was the Brotherhood's Iran communications director and was responsible for handling the logistics of this second trip.[44] He sent his business partner, Ali Ghaleb Himmat, on his behalf. The visit included Brotherhood representatives from Malaysia, Indonesia, Sudan, Egypt, Jordan, Saudi Arabia, Turkey, Syria, and Iraq. Nada said that they all met in Islamabad in Pakistan and rented a private jet for the trip. The Iranian who handled the logistics of the trip was Ebrahim Yazdi (1931–2017). According to Nada, his relationship with Yazdi dated back to the 1970s, when Yazdi was in the United States. Yazdi later briefly became the Minister of Foreign Affairs after the 1979 revolution. Among the delegates was al-Qaeda recruiter and Syrian Brotherhood leader Sa'id Hawwa.[45]

Though Nada denied he was part of the second delegation, he said he visited Iran numerous times. Kherbawy said that the late Brotherhood leader Abbas as-Sisi told him that Nada was present at the delegation.[46] Sisi was also among the Egyptian representatives, along with Brotherhood leader Gaber Rizk al-Fouli, aka Gaber Rizk, a former accomplice of Sayyid Qutb in the assassination attempt against Nasser in 1965.

43 The Bureau of Near Eastern Affairs, "PLO/Fatah Delegation Visits Kuwait," Wikileaks Cable: 1979KUWAIT00776_e, dated: February 14, 1979, https://wikileaks.org/plusd/cables/1979KUWAIT00776_e.html.

44 Ahmed Mansour, Interview with Youssef Nada, Shahed ala al-Aser, Al-Jazeera Channel, https://www.aljazeera.net/, August 11, 2002.

45 Abdullah al-Aqeel, "Ad-Da'iyya al-Mujahid Sa'id Hawa," The Official Muslim Brotherhood Encyclopedia, https://ikhwanwiki.com/, accessed June 20, 2021.

46 Kherbawy, *A'imatu ash-Share*, 158.

During their meeting with Khomeini, the Brotherhood expressed its desire to give an official *bai'a* to Khomeini, on behalf of the Muslim Brotherhood worldwide. Gaber Rizk said:

> We would like to convey a request from your brother, the Guide Omar al-Tilmisani . He pleads that you allow the Muslim Brotherhood to establish a group in Iran, and it would be called *Jama'at ad-Da'wa wa'l-Islah* [The Call to Islam and Reformation Group]. We have a small group of Iranians here which will propagate [their message] only among other Sunnis in Iran, and never surpass them.[47]

Khomeini agreed to the request and in 1979, the Muslim Brotherhood branch in Iran was formally established. The Brotherhood Iran chapter is still operational and currently under the leadership of Abdul Rahman al-Birani. According to Iranian diplomat Abbas Khamayar, on May 14, 1979, Iran hired a communications officer in Lugano, Switzerland, thirty minutes away from Campione d'Italia where Nada resided, to handle their Brotherhood communiqué.[48] Khamayar was the former cultural attaché at the Iranian Embassy in Beirut and head of the Department of African Affairs in the Ministry of Culture and Islamic Guidance. He is currently Chairman of the Palestine Committee in the Culture and Islamic Relations Organization in Iran.[49]

The fact that ideological and organizational collaboration between the Muslim Brotherhood and the Iranian revolution compelled Khomeini to hire a communications officer based in Lugano reveals that there were more concealed layers to their semi-clandestine cooperation. Kuwaiti Islamist Abdullah al-Nafisi identified the Iranian

47 Ibid, 278.

48 Ahmed Mansour, Interview with Youssef Nada, Shahed ala al-Aser, Al-Jazeera Channel, https://www.aljazeera.net/, August 11, 2002; Abbas Khamayar, *Iran wa'l-wa'l-wa'l-Ikhwan al-Muslimin* (Beirut: Markaz al-Dirasat al-Islamiyya, 1997), 230.

49 Abbas Khamayar, The 11th Al-Jazeera Forum State Crisis and the Future of the Middle East in Doha, https://www.aljazeera.net/, April 15–16, 2017.

communications officer as Kamal Khamayaro, who later became Iran's cultural attaché to Qatar.[50]

That second trip begun a long-lasting official cooperation between the Brotherhood and Iran. According to Nada, during their meeting with Khomeini, they requested that Iran's new constitution identify as Islamic and not particularly mention the Shi'a Twelvers as the state's official religion.[51] Khomeini ignored this request.

Although Khomeini refused to give up the Shi'a Twelvers as the state's religion in the constitution, he still honored Hassan al-Banna. According to former Muslim Brotherhood member and leader of Shi'ites in Egypt Akali, Khomeini called himself "*Rahbar-e Mo'azzam-e Iran*" (Supreme Leader, or Supreme Guide) of Iran, "in honor" of Hassan al-Banna's former title and to "follow his trail in proximity" between jihadists of the two sects.[52] It could also have been in honor of the Assassin, Hassan Sabbah, the *mu'allim-i sadiq* (the truthful teacher), "the spiritual guide of men."[53]

Khomeini and the Brotherhood were able to surpass their sectarian differences and understand the value of using each other's propaganda to radicalize their bases. As a Muslim Brotherhood activist and college student in Cairo in 1979, Kherbawy and his peers studied Khomeini's book, *Islamic Government*. Mustafa Mashhour listed Khomeini's book as required reading in their military camps.[54] Kherbawy recounts that he attended one of these camps under the leadership of al-Jama'a al-Islamiyya, where Syrian Brotherhood leader Ziad Abdul Khaliq al-Suri distributed Khomeini's book among them and asked them to study it extensively.[55] Mashhour lectured them from the book and pointed

50 Ahmed Mansour, Interview with Youssef Nada, Shahed ala al-Aser, Al-Jazeera Channel, https://www.aljazeera.net/, August 11, 2002.

51 Ibid.

52 *Al-Watan* (Kuwait), November 27, 2007; Al-Arabiya (Dubai), March 22, 2015.

53 Farhad Daftary, "Hassan Sabbah," The Institute of Ismaili Studies, https://www.iis.ac.uk/, accessed July 11, 2021.

54 Kherbawy, *A'imatu ash-Share*, 155

55 Ibid., 156–7.

out similarities to Sayyid Qutb's book, *Milestones*. He said Khomeini's book and Qutb's *Milestones* both "emerged from the same nook."

Iranian Islamists also taught Muslim Brotherhood literature to their base. While in prison in the mid-1960s, Khomeini's acolyte and current Supreme Leader of Iran, Ali Khamenei, translated two of Sayyid Qutb's books, *Al-Islam wa-Mushkilat al-Hadharah* (Islam and the Problems of Civilization) and *Al-Mustaqbal li-Hadha ad-Din* (The Future of This Religion).[56] According to Kherbawy in his introduction to *Islam and the Problems of Civilization*, Khamenei wrote, "The creative chapters of this book provide a truthful view of religion. It shows how religion is a way of life, its rituals are void if they don't reflect its truth. He shows in superb style and an objective vision, that the world is heading toward our mission, and that the future belongs to this religion."[57] After Khamenei seized power in 1989, he started including Qutb's books in the curriculum of the Islamic Revolutionary Guard Corps' (IRGC) ideological-political schools.[58]

Under Khomeini's rule, Iran continued its glorification of Sunni Brotherhood terrorists. Following the assassination of Egyptian President Anwar al-Sadat, Iran named one of its streets in Tehran after one of his assassins, Khalid al-Islambuli.[59] In an attempt to improve diplomatic relations with Egypt, Iran renamed al-Islambuli street to *Intifada* (Uprising) in 2004.[60]

---

56 Karim Sadjadpour, "Sons of the Iranian Revolution," *The Atlantic*, January 9, 2017; Mehdi Khakaji, "Egypt's Muslim Brotherhood and Iran," The Washington Institute, February 12, 2009.

57 Kherbawy, *A'imatu ash-Share*, 158.

58 Ibid., 163.

59 Al-Ahram Weekly (Cairo), July 26–August 1, 2001.

60 "Tehran renames street to improve Egypt ties," *The Irish Times*, January 6, 2004.

THE MUSLIM BROTHERHOOD'S POSITION FROM THE IRAN-IRAQ WAR

On September 22, 1980, the Iran-Iraq war officially began, and it lasted until August 1988. The long history of territorial disputes was centered around Iraq's plan to annex the oil-rich Khuzestan Province. Conventional wisdom would lead one to assume the Sunni Muslim Brotherhood would side with their Sunni counterparts in the Iraqi regime. In fact, the opposite was true. The Muslim Brotherhood officially backed the Iranian regime.

The Brotherhood's position was a testament to its allegiance to the Iranian revolution. In all three of the Brotherhood's major newspapers, *ad-Da'wa*, *al-I'tisam*, and *al-Mukhtar al-Islami*, they sided with the Iranian regime.[61] According to the Muslim Brotherhood's official encyclopedia, the Brotherhood's International Apparatus' official statement to the Iraqi people in 1980 stated:

> This is not a war to liberate frail men, women, and children who are disadvantaged and trapped. The Iranian Muslim people liberated themselves from injustice and American Zionist colonialism with the heroic incredible jihad of the popular Islamic revolution, which is one of a kind in the history of humanity under the leadership a Muslim Imam, who is undoubtedly a pride for Islam and Muslims.... Kill your tyrants, this is your only chance. Relinquish your weapons and join the camp of the revolution. The Islamic revolution is your revolution.[62]

In *al-I'tisam* magazine, Brotherhood leader al-Fouli said:

61 "Al-Ikhwan al-Muslimin w'ash-Shi'a: Bain ru'ya Shar'ia wa-Mumarasa Sisasia," 7, The Official Muslim Brotherhood Encyclopedia, https://ikhwanwiki.com/, accessed April 11, 2018.

62 Ibid.

> The Iranian people are persistent in resuming the war until victory, and until the fall of [the] Ba'athist murderous regime. The spiritual and psychological incitement and lust, [the] struggle and hurling toward martyrdom among the Iranian people is unprecedented and the Iranian people are completely confident that the Iranian Islamic revolution will be victorious… Hezbollah is triumphant, but jihad and martyrdom are essential, because Allah helps those who support him.[63]

The Brotherhood's order of jihad against a Sunni ruler on behalf of a Shi'a one is an unequivocal testament to the organization's stance. The Brotherhood's priority was to support a theocratic Islamic state, even if it was ruled by Shi'ites.

In 1981, the Brotherhood toned down its rhetoric, possibly to avoid antagonizing other Sunni regimes it was allied with, and called for "discontinuing the war, which is distracting Muslim from the real battle with international Judaism, and its dangers to Islam and Muslims everywhere."[64]

After this statement, they still expressed their support for Iran. According to Kherbawy, Omar al-Tilmisani said in an interview with *Crescent Magazine* in February 1984, "I don't know of any [member] of the Muslim Brotherhood in the world who criticizes Iran."[65]

The Brotherhood's influence on the course of the war was not just propagandistic. Nada stated he attempted to intervene to solve the conflict by pressuring Saddam Hussein through King Fahd of Saudi Arabia, who funneled around 26 billion dollars to Saddam during the war.[66] Nada said he used his relationship with Giandomenico Picco,

---

63 Ibid.

64 Ibid.

65 Kherbawy, *A'imatu ash-Share*, 161.

66 Brian Washington, "Operation Desert Shield," US Department of Veteran Affairs, August 26, 2011, https://www.veteranstodayarchives.com/2011/08/26/operation-desert-shield/.

then-Under Secretary-General of the United Nations for Political Affairs, to help stop the war.

During his interview with al-Jazeera, Nada referred to Picco as a "friend" with whom he coauthored a book in 1996. Nada and his interviewer were both familiar with this mysterious book, which Nada said was about the security of the Red Sea. The absence of physical or digital copies of this book, or even its name, raises many questions. It is unclear how a man in Picco's position would coauthor a book or have a friendly relationship with Nada, who was under FBI investigation in 1996.[67] On November 7, 2001, Nada was designated as a terrorist financier by the United States Department of Treasury. In a major setback to counterterrorism measures under President Barack Obama's administration, Nada's designation was removed from the Office of Foreign Assets Control (OFAC) and Specially Designated Nationals (SDN) list.[68]

IRAN AND SUNNI MILITANT COOPERATION

According to a CIA report declassified in 2010, in 1980, Khomeini referred to Yasser Arafat's Palestine Liberation Organization (PLO) as "Iran's closest allies."[69] The relationship was far from just diplomatic. The PLO provided training to Khomeini's militias and provided him with militants during the Islamic revolution.

In 2016, the CIA declassified another document about the Iran American hostage crisis that provided an important account of the depth of the cooperation between the PLO and Tehran.[70] In 1979,

67 Douglas Farah and John Mintz, "U.S. Trails Va. Muslim Money, Ties," *The Washington Post*, October 7, 2002.

68 U.S. Department of the Treasury, "Counter Terrorism Designations; Counter Terrorism Designations Removals," February 26, 2015.

69 "CIA Report Reveals Budding Tehran-PLO Relationship in 1979," *The Jerusalem Post*, January 16, 2018.

70 Constantine Christopher Menges, "The destiny of the Middle East is being decided in Tehran," The New Republic, December 15, 1979.

professor, author, and US National Security Council and CIA intelligence officer Constantine Christopher Menges wrote an account of the Iran American hostage crisis. Menges said that the embassy was captured by "radical Marxists, Communists, and PLO-trained clergy." Menges added that "neutral visitors of the besieged embassy" reported that so-called "student leaders speak Arabic rather than Farsi to one another."

The joint military training between Sunnis and Shi'ites was common practice at the time. For example, in the late 1970s and early 1980s, the Muslim Brotherhood-affiliated Sunni Palestinian militia *Saraya al-Jihad* (The Jihad Brigade), received their improvised explosive devices training in Hizbullah camps in Lebanon.[71]

Iran still supports Sunni militancy by arming and funding Brotherhood and other Sunni terrorist groups. For example, Mahmoud Abbas, said, "Hamas is funded by Iran. It claims it is financed by donations, but the donations are nothing compared to what it receives from Iran."[72]

The Brotherhood Iranian proximity project wasn't always smooth. It did not stop Iran from adopting an aggressive stance toward Sunni proselytism in its territory. Several Sunni religious leaders were killed by the Iranian regime. In 1990, Sunni scholar Abdul Wahhab al-Khuffi, Sheikh Qadralllah Ja'afari, and others were executed for Sunni proselytism.[73]

When asked about the persecution of Sunni figures in Iran, Youssef Nada brushed it off, saying, "the incarcerations and executions are painful, but they are normal, for every revolution has its mistakes."[74]

---

71 Abdullah Issa, "Mutafigrat fi Maktab Shamir," (Gaza) Donia al-Watan, March 16, 2006; Ataf Alian Ra'edat al-Amaliyat al-Ishteshhadiyya al-Falastinyyia," (Gaza) Donia al-Watan, September 14, 2003.

72 *Asia Times*, June 11, 2019.

73 Kherbawy, *A'imatu ash-Share*, 287.

74 Ahmed Mansour, Interview with Youssef Nada, Shahed ala al-Aser, Al-Jazeera Channel, https://www.aljazeera.net/, August 11, 2002.

FRIENDS OR FOES? THE THIRD STAGE OF THE MUSLIM BROTHERHOOD AND IRAN'S COOPERATION

The Muslim Brotherhood's doublespeak toward Iran has prompted several experts to take their criticism of Iran at face value and overlook their common strategic objectives. An example of this strategy can be summarized through an incident at the Guidance Bureau. As the spokesman of the Brotherhood's International Apparatus, Youssef Nada's open and brazen support of the Iranian regime hindered Brotherhood recruitment of Salafi jihadists in the region. The Guidance Office leadership reverted to its doublespeak strategy, which is traditionally reserved for their Western targets. The Brotherhood used this tactic to recruit more Salafists. They manufactured a crisis within the Guidance Bureau to serve this goal.[75] The so-called internal dispute was between prominent Brotherhood leaders regarding the group's position toward Iran. Guidance Bureau member and former Brotherhood spokesman Mahmoud Ghozlan accused Yousef Nada of "Shi'ite proselytism" and said that Nada "doesn't represent the group."[76]

In his book, Kherbawy explained his shock over Ghozlan's statements, because the Brotherhood's kinship with Shi'ites was an integral part of its ideology and strategy since its inception.[77] Kherbawy stated that in 2010, he understood what the alleged dispute was about from information provided by Hossam Tamam, a prominent Islamist and former editor-in-chief of one of the largest Islamist websites on the internet, IslamOnline.net. Tamam told Kherbawy that the dispute was artificial. Tamam said Mahmoud Ezzat met with Salafi preacher and bin Laden supporter Yasser Burhami to bridge the public gap

75 The Official Muslim Brotherhood Encyclopedia, "Muthakirat Amin Tohsem Mawkif al-Ikhwan min ash-Shi'a," https://ikhwanwiki.com, December 15, 2010.

76 Ibid.

77 Kherbawy, *A'imatu ash-Share*, 151-2

between the two movements.[78] According to Tamam, Burhami had a problem with the Brotherhood's position toward Iran. After the meeting, the Brotherhood manufactured the dispute, and another member of the Guidance Bureau, Gom'a Amin, issued a memorandum condemning Shi'ism.[79]

This temporary change in public narrative did serve to bridge the gap between Salafist movements and the Brotherhood. Some Salafi jihadist theologians had attacked Brotherhood figures, such as Yusuf al-Qaradawi, for their support of Iran. For example, Yemeni Salafi scholar Muqbil bin Hadi al-Wadi'i wrote a book titled *Iskat al-Kalb al-Awi Yusef bin Abdullah al-Qaradawi* (Silencing the Barking Dog Yusef bin Abdullah al-Qaradawi). Several Salafists joined al-Wadi'i in attacking al-Qaradawi for his support of Hezbollah.[80]

Salafist rhetoric toward the Brotherhood changed following the release of Gom'a Amin's memorandum. The election of Muhammad Badie as General Guide of the Muslim Brotherhood in January 2010 also helped, as Badie was a well-known Salafi jihadist himself.[81] The elevation of Badie to a leadership position translated into implementing a more overt adaptation of Salafist discourse inside the Brotherhood. Muslim Brotherhood member and Salafi Sheikh Abdul Khaliq ash-Sherif used his own television show to boost his status and bridge the gap between the Brotherhood and some Salafist leaders, as well compete with the Salafists in recruiting jihadists for the Brotherhood.[82] The single issue the Muslim Brotherhood consistently supported Iran in, is its nuclear program.

While the relationship between Iran and the Brotherhood in Cairo superficially appeared to halt for a few years, the Palestinian wing of the Brotherhood maintained its public cooperation with Iran.

---

78 Al-Bawaba News (Cairo), September 30, 2014.
79 The Official Muslim Brotherhood Encyclopedia, "Muthakirat Amin Tohsem Mawqif al-Ikhwan min ash-Shi'a," https://ikhwanwiki.com, December 15, 2010.
80 Al-Jazeera (Qatar), July 29, 2006.
81 Al-Masry al-Youm (Cairo), February 11, 2010.
82 Hossam Tamam, *Tasaluf al-Ikhwan* (Library of Alexandria Publishing, 2010), 24.

On the thirty-year anniversary of the Islamic Revolution, Hamas leader Khaled Mashal gave a speech in Iran in which he glorified its regime and thanked it for its financial, military, and moral support for Hamas.[83]

In 2011, the coup d'état in Egypt proved that the Brotherhood's Iranian cooperation remained strong. One week after the fall of Mubarak's regime, Iranian newspaper *Asr Iran* announced that the Iranian regime officially invited the Muslim Brotherhood to its 24th WFPIST conference.[84] Brotherhood member of the Guidance Bureau and its representative in Europe, Kamal al-Helbawi, accepted the invitation and was accompanied by a formal delegation from al-Azhar University during his visit to Tehran. The meeting was videotaped and segments of it were posted online.

In the presence of Khamenei, al-Helbawi gave a speech at the conference, stating, "This is a first step toward our desired Islamic unity, in the light of the current political changes to the advantage of Islam and Muslims, and the sinking international [Western] supremacy led by America." [85] Al-Helbawi continued, "We have seen the fall of the Soviet Union, and I ask Allah to show us the revival of Islam and its dominance over what is left of their power, as we witness the tumbling and fragmentation of their power every day."

Al-Helbawi stated, "The Islamic Republic of Iran, and the leader Mr. Khamenei, may Allah bless him, are role models in standing up to Western supremacy and role models for the Muslim nation's revival. We [the Brotherhood] always say, we have learned from Imam al-Khomeini as we have learned from Imam Hassan al-Banna, Imam Abul A'la al-Mawdudi, and Sayyid Qutb, may they rest in peace, and we still learn from our contemporary brothers."

---

83 "Khalid Meshal fi Iran Yamdah Gumhoriat Iran al-Islamiyya," YouTube.com, July 23, 2014.

84 Asr Iran (Tehran), February 17, 2011.

85 "Kamal al-Helbawi fi Iran," YouTube,com, July 3, 2012.

Al-Helbawi continued to glorify Iranian leaders, adding, "I admire his [Khamenei's] persistence to uphold the development of the ummah, and their technological advancement has become a disturbing issue for the West…soon we also will witness a similar model incorporated in the rest of Muslim nations which will be revived in our Arab and Islamic world, after the collapse of one dictatorship after the other."

After the Brotherhood was criticized for its participation in the conference, the organization attempted to distance itself from the meeting. Brotherhood leader Saad al-Katatani stated, "Al-Helbawi went to Iran representing himself, not the organization."[86] This does not seem credible when considering two facts. First, according to the internal collectivist structure of the Brotherhood and its bylaws, members of the Guidance Bureau are prohibited from engaging in any political activity without the consent of the Bureau, or they risk dismissal from the organization.[87] Second, al-Helbawi remained a leader in the Brotherhood after his visit to Iran. Al-Helbawi did resign a year later in objection to the Brotherhood's 2012 nomination of Khairat al-Shater for president, because he favored another presidential candidate, Brotherhood theologian Selim al-Awa.

In 2013, almost a year after Morsi was installed in power, Iran's former Minister of Foreign Affairs and current advisor to Khamenei, Ali Akbar Velayati, issued a statement saying, "We and the Brotherhood are friends, we support them and of all Islamic groups, they are the closest to us ideologically."[88]

The Iranian public admission of cooperation with the Brotherhood was much deeper than just diplomatic flattery. In January 2013, the *Sunday Times* reported that Iranian spy chief and US-designated ter-

---

86 Rose al-Yusuf (Cairo), February 18, 2011.

87 "Al-La'eha al-Alamiyya li Gama'at al-Ikhwan al-Muslimin," Philipps-Universität Marburg, https://www.uni-marburg.de/de, accessed May 4, 2018.

88 Al-Arabiya (Dubai), April 4, 2013.

rorist Qasem Soleimani (1957–2020) met with Morsi's advisor Essam al-Haddad in Cairo.[89]

According to two members in the Guidance Bureau, "The Government requested a high-level meeting with Iranian officials. Iran sent Soleimani," said one official. The second official told the *Times*, "The meeting was intended to send a message to America, which is putting pressure on the Egyptian Government, that we should be allowed to have other alliances with anyone we please."

As the Commander of the Quds Force, the elite unit of Iran's Revolutionary Guard, Soleimani was there to help the Brotherhood regime build a paramilitary, similar to Iran's Basij.[90] Haddad later denied that he met with Soleimani, but the *Times*'s communiqué with two officials from the Guidance Bureau appears more credible than the Brotherhood's pattern of denying its own actions after they've been exposed. The cooperation with Iran militaristically is further confirmed by its continued supply of arms and funds to the Brotherhood's military wings in the Palestinian territories. In a speech in 2014, Abu Obeida, the official spokesperson of *Izz ad-Din al-Qassam* Brigade, thanked Iran for providing them with funds, weapons, and assorted anti-tank missiles.[91] Abu Obeida also thanked Qatar and Turkey for their support of the militia.

In 2013, Kuwaiti Islamist Abdullah al-Nafisi discussed his first-hand knowledge of the relationship between the Muslim Brotherhood regime in Egypt and Iran.[92] Al-Nafisi said that during his trip in Cairo in 2013, he met a Brotherhood official from Morsi's cabinet who attended the meeting between then-Iranian Minister of Foreign Affairs Ali Akbar Salehi and Muhammed Morsi. According to al-Naf-

89 *The Sunday Times* (London), January 8, 2013.
90 Al-Wafd (Cairo), January 11, 2013.
91 "Abu Obeida Yashkur Iran al-latti bi Sawarikh'a Hazamat Israel," YouTube.com, December 14, 2014.
92 Sada News (Riyad), https://slaati.com, accessed May 5, 2018; "Khatir Gidan—Maza Talabet Iran min Morsi Muqabil Da'am Masr Iqtisadian?", YouTube.com, March 30, 2013.

isi's contact, Salehi offered Morsi $30 billion and the following benefits: (1) normalizing relations between Egypt and Iran and exchanging embassies; (2) guaranteeing five million Iranian tourists to visit Egypt annually; and (3) providing Egypt with experts to help rebuild and resume operations in more than two thousand closed factories.

Al-Nafisi stated that when Morsi asked what they wanted in exchange for these benefits, Salehi demanded (1) giving Iran the right to manage and restore all the mosques built by the Fatimid Caliphate; (2) opening and operating two newspapers to represent Iran in Egypt; and (3) annually sending twenty thousand Egyptian students to study in Qom, Iran.

Al-Nafisi accurately noted the contrast between what Salehi offered and what he demanded: "He offered resources and demanded ideology." While Iran is ideologically and governmentally backward-thinking, its few successes are due to its reliance on dissimulation and secrecy. The statements of al-Nafisi regarding the meeting between Morsi and Salehi resemble Nader Shah's Council of Najaf in 1743, when Shah offered Sunnis a deal to retreat militarily in return for their openness to accept the Ja'fari sect.

Two centuries before Salehi's meeting with Morsi, the offer was peace for ideology, and two centuries later it was resources for ideology.

After Morsi was deposed from power in Egypt in 2013, diplomatic relations between the Brotherhood and Iran were spearheaded by Qatar with the help of the United States and the United Nations. Following President Barack's Obama 2013 announcement to provide "modest relief" of America's sanctions against Iran, Qatar and Iran established an economic free zone and expanded their existing economic relations.[93]

---

93 Barack Obama, "Statement by The President on First Step Agreement On Iran's Nuclear Program," The White House, November 23, 2013; Asharq al-Awsat (London), July 8, 2014; "The Middle East's New Battle Lines," European Council on Foreign Relations ecfr.eu, accessed March 3, 2022.

In 2014, a Muslim Brotherhood delegation consisting of Brotherhood London-based leaders Ibrahim Munir, Mahmoud Elibiary, and Youssef Nada met with the Iranian revolutionary guard to collaborate with them on the war in Yemen.[94] While one would expect a Sunni group like the Brotherhood to support the Sunni government of Saudi Arabia, the Brotherhood was actually working with the militant Zaidi group *Ansar Allah* (Supporters of God), more commonly referred to as the *Houthi* movement.

President Obama's Iran deal and his legitimation of the Muslim Brotherhood backed coups d'état across the Middle East and encouraged other American institutions to play a role in mediating relationships between Iran and Sunni Islamists. For example, in 2015, the Muslim Brotherhood regime in Qatar, in cooperation with Georgetown University's School of Foreign Service in Qatar, invited Iran's Cultural Attaché in Qatar, Mehdi Khaleqi, to join an event titled "Iran-Arab Cultural Ties." The conference took place in January 2016.[95]

It's not clear how an American institution like Georgetown University would actively mediate a relationship between the Brotherhood and Iran, which the US has designated a State Sponsor of Terrorism. It is not a coincidence that this event occurred in Qatar, a self-confessed sponsor of terrorism. During an al-Jazeera-broadcasted conference in Doha in July 2017, Qatari Minister of Foreign Affairs Muhammad bin Abdul Rahman bin Jassim al-Thani said, "As for the issue of terrorism financing, this exists in all counties in the region and it doesn't only apply to Qatar. Qatar is actually at the bottom of the list of nations implicated in this crime."[96]

After this blatant admission and numerous others, the United States has not taken any measures against Qatar, which only emboldened the dangerous Iranian coalition. In 2018, Qatar's cooperation

94 Al-Arabiya (Dubai), November 18, 2019.
95 Iran Daily News (Tehran), December 6, 2015.
96 "Wazir Kahrijiayat Qatar Ya'tarif bi Tamwil al-Irhab," YouTube.com, July2, 2017.

expanded its ambition to announce the two nations' intention to build an entity that will most certainly pose a security threat.

According to *Russia Today*, Iran and Qatar have launched an initiative to create a new platform for what they called "conflict resolution" in the region. According to the Emir of Qatar Tamim bin Hamad al-Thani, a body "like the European Union" should be formed. The Iranian Foreign Minister, Muhammad Jawad Zarif, was inspired by the example of the Organization for Security and Cooperation in Europe (OSCE).[97]

The Muslim Brotherhood and Iranian cooperation is one of the most dangerous and complicated relationships in the world of international politics, jihadism, and transnational terrorism. The Iranian millennial vision for the ideological infiltration of the Sunni militant brigade is actualized by its clandestine and equally fanatic Muslim Brotherhood counterpart.

While it's a common opinion among experts, scholars, and policy makers that the religious division between Sunnis and Shi'ites is mainly the focus of the relations, the evidence mentioned should compel readers to reexamine this stance. The real focus of security and Middle East experts in the West should center around the cooperation of radical elements and not their disputes. This crucial aspect, which is almost unanimously ignored, is due to the many philosophical and epistemological differences between the mind of the Islamist and the mind of the Westerner. While peace between Sunnis and Shi'ites is in the best interest of every sound and reasonable individual, the Islamic proximity project is one of division, bloodshed, dominance, and lust for power.

---

97 *RT Arabic*, February 28, 2018.

CHAPTER TWELVE

CIVILIZATION JIHAD OPERATION

Weaponized Muslim Brotherhood Terminology, Infiltration of American Institutions, and Terror Recruitment

"It is a Civilization Jihad Operation … The Brotherhood needs to understand that their work in America is a form of a great jihad to abolish and destroy Western civilization internally and destroying its miserable house from within by their own hands and the hands of the believers."
—The Explanatory Memorandum[1]

THE MUSLIM BROTHERHOOD IS RESPONSIBLE for establishing the vast majority of Sunni terrorism in the world. But the group's deeper threat is its vast, covert operation of infiltration, cultural and political subversion, and the recruitment of people inside academia, military, intelligence community, law enforcement, and other governmental agencies. The most damaging aspect of the Brotherhood's international Vanguards of Organized Invasion is infiltration.

Following the International Apparatus' September 1991 meeting in Istanbul, representatives from each country drafted their plans for their targeted nations. Only two of these documents were publicly uncovered from all the international chapters. The Egyptian docu-

1 The Muslim Brotherhood's Strategic Plan for America—Court document," The Investigative Project on Terrorism, Washington, DC, accessed July 12, 2021, https://www.investigativeproject.org/documents/20-an-explanatory-memorandum-on-the-general.pdf.

ment was titled *Conquering Egypt*, and the North American plan was titled *An Explanatory Memorandum: The General Strategic Goals for North America.*[2] The latter described their strategy as "long term." This is one of the most important elements in the document. Long-term strategic planning of jihadists in a country like the US is a sharp contrast to politicians' strategic goals, which generally are limited within the time frame of election cycles. Dealing with enemies who calculate their goals in decades and centuries can be hard for Westerners to compute. Even when some lawmakers do, few are willing to deal with the repercussions of this realization.

The Secret Apparatus' Explanatory Memorandum was discovered in the US in 2004, after a policeman spotted a Muslim woman taking pictures of "close-ups of cables and other features" that were "integral to the structural integrity of the" Chesapeake Bay Bridge in Maryland.[3] The woman was the wife of Ismail Selim Elbarasse, a Muslim Brotherhood operative. Elbarasse was a former board member of the Islamic Association for Palestine (IAP) and Hamas activist. He served on the Palestine Committee, created by the Muslim Brotherhood in the United States to help Hamas politically and financially.[4]

Among the documents seized by federal investigators from Elbarasse's house was the Explanatory Memorandum, which outlined the Muslim Brotherhood's strategic goals for North America. It was entered as evidence in the Holy Land Foundation (HLF) terror-funding trial in 2008. In 2009, five Brotherhood leaders were sentenced for providing material support to Hamas. This was the largest terror financing case in US history.

In the memorandum's introduction, its author said he wrote it as an answer to a question presented in the 1991 meeting, probably

---

2 Ibid.

3 "Ismail Selim Elbarasse," The Investigative Project on Terrorism, Washington, DC, https://www.investigativeproject.org/case/534/ismail-selim-elbarasse, accessed July 12, 2021.

4 Ibid.

by Mashhour: "How would you like to see the Islamic movement in North America after ten years?" As is usually the case with the Muslim Brotherhood, almost nothing is random, and every time they mention the duration of "ten years," it should be a red flag. It is also not random that the meeting of 1991 took place almost ten years after Mashhour reestablished the International Apparatus.

The Muslim Brotherhood adheres to the ideology of *dawam al-jihad* (permanence of jihad), hence its ostensibly dormant state of nonviolence against targeted nations must be revisited every decade and paralleled with what the Brotherhood called in the Explanatory Memorandum "*Amalia Jihadiyya Hadariyya*" (Civilization Jihad Operation). The document described the covert subversive operation as "sabotaging" the American "miserable house by their hands and the hands of the believers."

Neither Sunni nor Shi'ite Islamists adhere to the modern concept of nations or nationalities. According to both Shi'ite and Sunni Islamist jurisprudence, the only way they are theologically allowed to maintain a noncombatant state is during a form of *hudna* (truce) between them and non-Muslim nations. The *hudna* allows the suspension of jihad for no longer than ten years, provided that afterward, Islamists have to engage in holy war. Both fundamentalist Shi'ite and Sunni jurisprudence allows an imam to extend the duration of *hudna*, but it still must expire.

Kassim Khudair Abbas, Shi'ite Legal Adviser at the General Secretariat of the Council of Ministers in Iraq, stated in his book, "When one wonders about the legitimacy of whether Muslims can accept the non-Muslim international laws, judges, or courts, especially in conflict resolution with Muslim nations, Shari'a prohibits the arbitration of non-Muslims according to Qur'an; therefore, there is no authority which can bind a Muslims to a non-Muslim under any circumstances."[5]

The Muslim Brotherhood adopts a similar view. They adhere to the opinion on this matter of the prominent twelfth-century jurist, Ala' ad-Din al-Kasani, who is modernly referred to as the "king of jurists." The Brotherhood follows Kasani's partition of the world as *dar Islam* (nation or house of Islam), which implements Shari'a law, and *dar harb* (nation or house of war), which doesn't implement Shari'a law.[6] Kasani conditioned any form of a noncombatant state between jihadists and houses of wars with "necessity, the necessity for preparing for war... peace entails abandonment of obligatory jihad, and this is not permissible unless there it is a way to facilitate war."[7]

The condition of a noncombatant state is also limited to a duration of ten years, after which, jihad should ensue.[8] Due to these factors, it may not be coincidence that al-Qaeda's September 11, 2001, terrorist attack was ten years after the International Apparatus' September 1991 meeting in Istanbul.

MUSLIM BROTHERHOOD'S WEAPONIZED TERMINOLOGY

Secret societies and criminal syndicates rely on coded language to protect their missions. The Muslim Brotherhood has done the same. They have desecrated their own religion by weaponizing theological terminology and poisoning it with violent and terroristic definitions that are alien to the vast majority of Muslims. The Brotherhood's

5 Kassim Khudair Abbas, *Al-Imam Ali Ra'id al-Adala al-Ijtima'iyya* (Beirut: Dar al-Adawa', 2004), https://www.haydarya.com, accessed July 5, 2021.

6 "Wathiqa Takshif Wad' al-Ikhwan al-Muslimin," DAAL Research and Media Center, https://hafryat.com/ar, February 1, 2019.

7 Ala' ad-Din al-Kasani, *Bada'i' as-Sana'i'* (Beirut: Dar al-Maktaba al-Alamiyya, 1986) 7: 108.

8 Abdul Moneim Zain ad-Din, "Al-Hudna bain al-Muslimin wa'l-Adua'hum," Rashad Center for Research, Sites.Google.com/Site/RashadSTC, September 27, 2016.

coded theology is almost exclusively for jihadists, and its theologians often refer to coded knowledge in their literature as, *ilm al-khassa* (knowledge of the special [ones]) versus *ilm al-amma* (knowledge of commoners). The use of the word *khassa* in reference to those who specialized in theology dates back to legist Abu Abdullah Muhammad ibn Idris al-Shafi'i (767–820). Imam Shaf'i originally used the term *khassa* to allow leniency for Muslims who committed religious transgressions, while they were unaware of Islamic jurisprudence.[9]

It is imperative to decode the language used by the Brotherhood to avoid detection by law enforcement and other governmental and nongovernmental institutions while discussing the logistics of their covert nonviolent and violent operations. The forthcoming definitions are unknown to most Muslims, and many of these terms are rarely used by Muslims who aren't members of violent groups, with the exception of Muslim counter-terrorism experts and researchers.

The Brotherhood's common practice of concealment in use of language has significantly contributed to the organization's successful franchising of its brand of terrorism, both politically and militarily. On the political front, veiled terminology was a contributing factor in the infiltration of the US government and led to policies that supported the Brotherhood.

The Brotherhood uses words like "truth" and "freedom," as well as other semantically loaded terms that are infused with jihadist theological connotations, requirements, and instruction. The upcoming definitions are only a few examples used by the Brotherhood and other Islamists in their war on civilization and their mission of infiltration. This aspect of clandestine jihad has not been appropriately deciphered in the West. This linguistic tactic also helps the Brotherhood recruit Muslims who, like Westerners, are overwhelmingly unaware of Islamist's alternative definitions.

---

9 Abu Abdullah Muhammad ibn Idris ash-Shafi'i, *Al-Risla* (Cairo: Mustafa al-Babi al-Halabi, 1938), 478–479.

Truth (*Haq*). A rational individual would think the word "truth" is defined as a quality that conforms to facts or reality, but the Brotherhood's definition of *al-haq* (the truth) is the implementation of Shari'a law. In his essay *al-Manhaj* (The Methodology), Banna said, "the aim of the believer should be [to implement] the supremacy of Allah's religion on earth, guiding humanity to the truth, and directing them to illuminate the world with the sun of Islam."[10] In the same essay, he defined the truth as what he believes is "the true Islam" where an "ideal Islamic nation resurrects the true Islam" and builds a state "based on Qur'anic teachings and propagates the Qur'an through jihad, and sacrificing one's self and wealth for this cause." The word *haq* or *huquq* can also mean "right" or "rights," depending on the context in which it is used.

Freedom (*Huriyya*). The Brotherhood's understanding of "freedom" contradicts the meaning of the word. Brotherhood historian and former member of the Guidance Office Goum'a Abdul Aziz (1934–2015) described the classical liberal secular movement, which was adhered to by the Free Constitutionalists Party during the first half of the twentieth century, as "a morally degenerate movement attempting to secularize Egypt."[11] Aziz also described the freedom movement as "a massive wave of moral decay and filthiness," which "encourages rot in spirit, opinions, and ideas under the banner of personal liberty and individual freedom." Aziz goes on to criticize Egypt's booming film industry at the time, as an institution that promotes "Western women's whorishness and lewdness" to Muslim nations.

The Brotherhood's view of freedom and liberty is freedom from all forms of transgression against Shari'a law. The term "freedom" is frequently used by members of the Brotherhood, and it is common

10 Hassan al-Banna, "Risalat al-Minhaj," The Muslim Brotherhood official website, https://ikhwanonline.com/, accessed February 9, 2020.

11 Goum'a Amin Abdul Aziz, *Awraq min Tarikh al-Ikhwan al-Muslimin* (Cairo: Dar al-Tawi' wa'l-wa'l-wa'l-Nashr al-Islamiyya, 2002) , 23–24.

in their literature. It is also often associated with jihad. For example, in his essay titled *Ummah fi Midan al-Jihad* (A Muslim Nation in the Battleground of Jihad),[12] Banna calls upon his followers to fight on "the battleground of jihad" to "breathe the fresh air of freedom to regain violated rights and stolen glory." Another one of many examples of the frequent association between freedom and jihad was articulated by contemporary Brotherhood theologian Tawfik al-Waa'i, when he wrote, "if Muslims are granted freedom they will not chose anything but Islam, to live and die by it, and to jihad for it till death."[13]

Tyrannical Deity (*Taghut*). The Muslim Brotherhood and all Sunni terrorist groups consider the support of any system of government that isn't based on Shari'a law as a form of worshipping *taghut*. *Taghut* means "a tyrannical deity." It is the Islamic terminology denoting idolatry or engaging in an activity other than worshiping God. The expression "worshipping *taghut*" in early Islamic history was used in reference to idolatry. In modern times, the word *taghut* is exclusively used by Islamists and jihadists. The vast majority of Arabic-speaking Muslims have never used this terminology. Qaradawi's theological defined *taghut* as:

> A word derived from the term tyranny. Tyranny means the opposition to a Shari'a law ruling...*taghut* is every practice employed by a slave to oppose a [Shari'a] law, or has exceed his limit beyond worshiping, following, and obeying [God]. The taghut of every nation is everything they utilize to make decisions which aren't guided by Allah and his prophet. These are the tyrannical deities of the world, if you contemplate the status of humanity you will realize that they are closer

12 Hassan al-Banna, *Umma fi Midan al-Jihad*, Brotherhood Encyclopedia, https://ikhwanwiki.com/, accessed February 10, 2021.

13 Tawfik al-Waa'i, *Al-Ikhwan al-Muslimum Kubra al-Haraqat al-Islamiyya*, The Official Muslim Brotherhood Encyclopedia, https://ikhwanwiki.com, accessed February 10, 2021.

> to worshiping tyrannical deities than they are worshiping God.[14]

Islamists deem the act of worshiping *taghut* as a form of apostacy, which should be punishable by death. In his book *at-Taghut*, the popular Saudi mainstream Islamist Sa'id bin Ali bin Wahf al-Qahtani (1952–2018) stated that those who either adhere to or rule "by man-made laws, and tribal and *jahiliyyah* (pre-Islamic and non-Islamic practices) customs" should get "excommunicated from the religion."[15] Qahtani added that governance based on man-made law is an act "of infidelity and its transgressor deserves extreme torture."[16] This is at the core of what makes an Islamist, an Islamist. It is to implement Shari'a law and eliminate and terrorize its opponents. Muslim Brotherhood operatives both in the Middle East and in the West, often use the words "dictator," "dictatorship," and "tyranny." When Islamists use any of these terms, they mean the theological definition of tyrannical deity. Replacing the word *taghut* with modern Arabic words for "dictatorship" or "tyranny" has been a successful tool for recruitment, as the overwhelming majority of Muslims are not aware of these Islamist theological connotations.

Islamic theocracy (*Hakimiyya*). In his infamous terrorism manifesto, *Milestones*, Qutb articulated the Islamist vision of freedom, which he also defined as liberation from *taghut*. He also used the important term *hakimiyya*, which is almost never used by Arabic-speaking Muslims who aren't researchers or experts in field. It is almost exclusively used by organized Islamists and members of terrorist groups. Moreover, the vast majority of Arabic- speaking Muslims are not familiar with the word nor its definition. The Islamic, theocratic term,

14 Yusuf al-Qaradawi, *Haqiqat at-Tawhid* (Cairo: Dar al-Kutub wa'l-wa'l-wa'l-Watha'iq al-Qawmiyya, 2010), 39; Islamists often use the word *abd* (slave) in reference to any human being, as they perceive human beings as slave implements to worship God.

15 Sa'id bin Ali bin Wahf al-Qahtani, *At-Taghut* (Riyadh: Dar al-Amal, [2011]), 106–8.

16 Sa'id bin Ali bin Wahf al-Qahtani, *At-Taghut* (Riyadh: Dar al-Amal, [2011]), 106–8.

hakimiyya, was coined by Abul A'la al-Mawdudi. The word *hakimiyya* is derived from the common mainstream Arabic word *hukm*, which means both "governance" and "a ruling," depending on its usage. It is the Islamist term equivalent to the English word "theocracy."

According to Mawdudi, the Islamist doctrine of *hakimiyya* means, "supreme and absolute" legislative and political authority of Islamic jurisprudence.[17] Mawdudi added that diversion from this course "is blatant *kufr* [disbelief or infidelity]." He envisioned this system to function under what he called *al-khalifa al-jumhuriyya* (a caliphate republic), where "its citizenship is limited only to those who implement [various functions of the] caliphate."[18] This violent revolutionary doctrine was officially adopted by the Muslim Brotherhood, and they have propagated it through Sayyid Qutb and continue to publicize it.[19]

In Qutb's book, *Milestones*, he summarized his ideology when he amalgamated the Islamist concepts of freedom, *taghut*, and *hakimiyya*, and hinted about the latter's concealed meaning:

> The [righteous] way is not to free the earth from a Roman or a Persian *taghut* to hand it to an Arab one. *Taghut* is *taghut*! The Earth is Allah's and it has to be exclusively His. It can only be exclusively for Allah through unfurling the banner there is "no deity but Allah." An Arab who is knowledgeable of the connotations of his language [realizes that]: There is no *hakimiyya* but to Allah, there is no law except from Allah, there is no authority of one man over another, because all authority belongs to Allah; because "nationality" as dictated by Islam is the nationality of the creed, where

17 Abul A'la al-Mawdudi, *Tadwin ad-Dustur al-Islami* (Beirut: Mu'asassat al-Risala, 1981), 18–22.

18 Ibid., 24–5.

19 Yusuf al-Qaradawi, "'Alama Houkim Sayyid Qutb," Yusuf al-Qaradawi's official website, October 27, 2016, www.al-qaradawi.net.

> the Arab, the Roman, the Persian and all ethnicities and races are equal under the banner of Allah.[20]

This paragraph is not only important for what it reveals about the Muslim Brotherhood's political theology, but it also explains a common tool of *kitman* and clandestine proselytism when these theological terms conveniently and literally get lost in translation. Unfortunately, translations of Islamist literature are commonly encumbered by mistranslations, falsehoods, and omissions. Whether it is out of ignorance or calculated deception, translations of jihadist literature is often whitewashed, and the theological terminology and semantics are frequently mistranslated.

The most popular English translation of Qutb's terrorism manifesto is a perfect example of this problem. The English translation of *Milestones* was published in the United States by The Mother Mosque Foundation in Iowa, and it is considered by both Islamists and experts to be the most authoritative translation. Several governments around the world use it in their counter-terrorism studies. This version is blatantly mistranslated, and it is propagandistic in some respect. The Mother Mosque Foundation's version mistranslated *hakimiyya* to "sovereignty."[21] In Arabic, the word for sovereignty is *istiqlaliyya*, which is commonly used in Arabic to denote political sovereignty and independence from a foreign occupying force. This translation also ignores the fact that Qutb hinted to the "connotations" of Arabic language terms during his discussion of *hakimiyya*. Instead, the translation omitted the word "connotations" and the sentence was translated as, "An Arab with knowledge of his language." The third translation problem in this single paragraph was that it omitted Qutb's statements about the illegitimacy of the concept of nationality, where he explained that Muslim allegiance should only be to their religion and not their country.

20 Sayyid Qutb, *Ma'alim fi al-Tariq*, 24.
21 Sayyid Qutb, *Milestones* (Cedar Rapids, IA: Mother Mosque Foundation, 1981), 26.

The use of terms such as *taghut* and *hakimiyya* could be used by intelligence and law enforcement agencies to identify covert Brotherhood operatives. These are all examples from only one paragraph of one Brotherhood book.

Another example of false translation came from the Qatari-funded Brookings Institution. Brookings Institution has engaged in misinformation, or disinformation, on behalf of the Brotherhood. For example, a Brookings Institution article on their Arabic website stated that the fourth of the Muslim Brotherhood's ten *thawabet* (precepts) in its bylaws specified that "during the process of establishing democracy and relative political freedom, the Muslim Brotherhood is committed to abide by the rules of democracy and its institutions."[22] This is a bold misrepresentation of the fourth precept. According to the Brotherhood's own standards and internal bylaws, the fourth precept is violent jihad and martyrdom. It states, "*al-jihad sabiluna*" (jihad is our way), which the Brotherhood insists is an obligation of every individual Muslim, as well as the collective obligation of the organization.[23]

Justice (*Adala*)**.** The topic of justice in Islamist discourse is a complex one, as it incorporates all principles of Islamic jurisprudence. But when a Brotherhood member or an Islamist uses this term, they mean that it is the domination and governance by Shari'a law over every aspect of a human being's life, including punishing opponents of this idea by "murder, crucifixion, mutilating their limbs from opposite sides, or exile."[24]

Peace (*Salam*). This is perhaps the most abused term by the Muslim Brotherhood. It is best summarized by Brotherhood sheikh and scholar Muhammad Abdul Maksoud. In 2014, on Rabi'a tele-

---

22 Umar Ashur, "Hal Yad'u al-Ikhwan al-Muslimun fi Masr ila al-Unf as-Siyasi?" Brookings Institution Arabic website, https://www.amherst.edu/system/files/media/1357/Milestones%2520I_001.pdf, Washington, DC, July 30, 2014.

23 Muhammad Qandil, "Al-Thabit al-Rabi' al-Jihad Sabiluna," The Official Muslim Brotherhood Encyclopedia, https://ikhwanwiki.com/, accessed July 12, 2021.

24 Sayyid Qutb, *Al-Adala Al-Ijtima'iyya fil Islam* (Beirut: Dar al-Shorouq, 1995), 23.

vision, Maksoud discussed the Muslim Brotherhood riots and said, "setting police vehicles and the vehicles of thugs on fire" falls under the Brotherhood's definition of "peacefulness."[25] The Muslim Brotherhood's Research Center of Islamic Legislation and Ethics (CILE), in Doha, explained its convoluted definition of peace and how it relates to jihad. In 2017, sheikh Ali Muhammad al-Sawwa gave a speech at the center titled "The Influence of Jihad in Achieving Peace," where said that the "order of jihad using military power" is among the means "to enforce truth and peace."[26]

Empowerment or Dominance (*Tamkin*). When the word *tamkin* (also spelled *tamkeen*) is used in common Arabic discourse, it translates to "empowerment." But in the context of the Brotherhood's theological concept of *fiqh at-tamkin* (the Jurisprudence of [Islamic] Dominance), it means the full political dominance of Islamists and Shari'a law.

During Khairat al-Shater's speeches in in 2011, Shater explained the Muslim Brotherhood's goal of full establishment of Sharia law and empowering its absolute political supremacy:

> Our main mission as Muslim Brotherhood is *tamkin* to the religion of Allah of earth, regulating our lives and the lives of the people in accordance to Islam. It is building the *nahda* (revival) of the nation and its culture on Islamic basis, it's the subjugation of the people to Allah on earth, these are all synonyms with similar meanings, and that's why one of the preachers of the Brotherhood stated, the Brotherhood everywhere work on restoring Islam in its all-encompassing conception to regulate people's lives on Islamic basis, and they believed that this will only come to

25 "Al-Irahbi Muhammad Abdul Maksoud: Harq Saiarat ash-Shurta," YouTube.com, September 15, 2018.

26 Muhammad as-Sawwa, "Athar al-Jihad fi Tahqiq as-Salam," Research Center of Islamic Legislation and Ethics (CILE), February 11, 2017.

> fruition through a strong *jama'a* (Islamic group). Thus the mission is clear: restoring Islam in its all-encompassing conception to [run] people's lives; subjugating people to Allah, upholding the religion of Allah, the Islamization of life, *tamkin* to the religion of Allah.[27]

Islamic revival (*Nahda*). *Nahda* literally translates to "resurrection" or "renaissance." In the context of the Muslim Brotherhood, it is another weaponized term to conceal their agenda while communicating with Westerners. In his speech in Arabic, Shater eloquently explained that the term means "the subjugation of people on earth to Allah" and of course, the Brotherhood, as self-appointed God's military on earth, they believe they should oversee its implementation.

Saudi Brotherhood International Apparatus leader, pilot, and al-Qaeda operative Muhammad Mussa al-Sharif explained in a speech published online in June 2018 that, "The Islamic Awakening Project started operating under the term *al-Nahda* with the beginning of the International Apparatus' mission."[28]

The Tunisian branch of the Brotherhood was among the first international cells to adopt the term when they named their party *Ennahda*, which is another spelling for *al-nahda*. The ideological basis for the Nahda Project was articulated by Brotherhood scholar and terrorism theologian Muhammad al-Ghazali, whose fatwa was responsible for the assassination of Muslim Egyptian intellectual Farag Fouda. Ghazali explained that the totalitarian mission of the Nahda Project was "the unification of thought, culture, and psychology" of subjects of an Islamic State.[29] Ghazali once held the position of chairman of the Academic Council of the International Institute of Islamic Thought (IIIT), a Muslim Brotherhood front organization founded in Pennsylvania in 1981 and headquartered in Herndon, Virginia.

27 Khairat al-shaṭer "Mashrou' al-Nahda al-Islami," YouTube.com, April 24, 2011.
28 Muhammad Mussa ash-Shareif, "Qabl as-Sahwah al-Islamiyya wa-Ba'daha: Dr. Muhammad Mussa ash-Shareif," YouTube.com, June 19, 2018.
29 Muhammad al-Ghazali, *Kifah Din* (Cairo: Maktabat Wahba, 1991), 228.

Global Supremacy (*Ustadhiyyat al-Alam*). In his infamous speech, Shater firmly reminded his audience that their ultimate objective remains the caliphate, although he intentionally referred to it by the term *ustadhiyya*, which literally translates to "mastery" or "supremacy." The term is relatively new to the Brotherhood's public discourse, and the introduction of this new term coincides with its introduction of different modes of operation and different methodology to implement Islamic expansionism. While they often use the terms *ustadhiyya* and "caliphate" when they communicate with Arabic speakers, they explain it to Westerners as just another international political structure similar to the European Union. During the same speech, Shater said, "Our Prophet established the Islamic state in Medina, then he expanded this state until it covered the Arabian Peninsula, then he started an international Islamic state…until it became the largest on the planet, [it reached] the status of global supremacy."

The propagandistic rhetoric that an international Islamic State would be modeled after the European Union was also suggested by several Brotherhood members, including Brotherhood leader Khalid al-Qazzaz during a Muslim Brotherhood propaganda event at Georgetown University in Washington DC, on April 4, 2012. When the author pressed the speakers about statements supporting a renewed caliphate, Qazzaz called the term a "cliché" and said no one should object to a Muslim superstate that would be like the "European Union."[30]

These are only few examples of how the Muslim Brotherhood uses semantically weaponized terminology. This aspect hasn't just served them when they approached unsuspecting Muslims for recruitment, but it also facilitated their penetration of some of the most sensitive organs of the United States government.

30 "MB Charm Offensive Courts Washington," Investigative Project on Terrorism (Washington, DC), April 9, 2012.

Democracy (*Dimuqratiyya*). Throughout their history, Islamists fought the Western concept of democracy until they reached the conclusion that they can utilize ballot boxes to advance their goals. The Western concept of peaceful transition of power can only exist within the confines of the Western concept of the rule of law. Western democratic tradition began with Magna Carta over eight centuries ago until it reached its modern process. The Muslim Brotherhood considered the concepts of human rights, the rule of law, the will of people, as a form of worshiping *taghut*. Their early honest chants of "Down with the Constitution, Down with Freedom, Down with Democracy, and Down with the Educated" have been recently polished to a form of dissimulation to appease Westerners. It is a fact that every time the Muslim Brotherhood takes control of a nation, they turn ballot boxes into guillotines.

These examples should compel governmental agencies worldwide to recognize that among the various target for infiltrations, are the fields of interpretation, linguistics, and interpretation analysis. Covert Islamists utliize them as part of their counterintelligence operation against the agencies and nations that employ them. The pervious terminology should be incorporated in the testing process of potential employees prior to placing them in sensitive positions.

CIVILIZATION JIHAD OPERATION IN THE UNITED STATES

The Brotherhood's Explanatory Memorandum stated they have a "public Islamic movement," which infers the existence of a secret Islamic one. This was confirmed in the same document when its author wrote about "the urgency" of finding a balance between "special work" and "public work." The term "special work" (*al-amal al-khass*) in the Brotherhood literature is always used in reference to the Special Apparatus.

It is commonly thought that the Brotherhood established the Freedom and Justice Party, as their first official political party, in 2011.

But as is often the case with the group, this is not entirely accurate. A forthcoming example demonstrates the power of the International Apparatus and how its American chapter has influenced the course of the Egyptian organization.

FREEDOM, JUSTICE, AND INFILTRATION

In 2002, the Brotherhood-affiliated Freedom and Justice organization was founded in Texas as a nongovernmental entity called the *Freedom and Justice Foundation*. It was established by Brotherhood sympathizers and potential Brotherhood operatives, Muhammad Elibiary and Sahar Aziz. According to an archived version of their website, Elibiary was the foundation's Executive Officer and Aziz was one of its board members.[31]

Aziz has a habit of removing online evidence of her affiliation with Muslim Brotherhood front groups. For example, she once gave a speech at the Islamic Society of North America (ISNA) titled "Civil Rights Litigation," which she later removed from her website before shutting it down.[32] According to a close friend of Aziz, she is the daughter of a Muslim Brotherhood leader and she seems to adhere to her father's ideas. She was heavily involved with CAIR before her activities were taken off her website. Aziz is known for Islamist agitation against law enforcement, and she focuses much of her work on trying to dismantle counter-terrorism measures by advocating for limits on antiterrorism funding and training, and restricting training manuals to Islamist approved propaganda. Aziz also advocated for blasphemy laws in America to be used against critics of Islam. Aziz

31 Freedom and Justice Foundation archived web page, http://web.Archive.org/web/20101103055218/http://www.freeandjust.org/OurTeam.htm, accessed June 19, 2018; Freedom and Justice Foundation archived web page, http://web.archive.org/web/20100816121231/http://www.freeandjust.org/PublicDiplomacy.htm#WHITEHOUSE, accessed April 20, 2021.

32 Sahar F. Aziz, "Sahar Aziz Presents on Civil Rights Litigation," www.SaharaAzizLaw.com/eventsdetails.php?id=52, accessed November 13, 2012.

articulated her solution to her first amendment problem, stating she knows that State Department lawyers "can come up with a way" to redefine criticism of Islam and Islamists as a form of discrimination.[33]

Aziz's father has used numerous aliases in the United States. This is a standard tactic employed by Islamists to avoid law enforcement detection and surveillance. His real name is Muhammad Samir Muhammad Fo'ad Abdul Aziz.[34]

While Sahar Aziz was involved with the Freedom and Justice Foundation, she was also a senior policy advisor for the Office for Civil Rights and Civil Liberties at the US Department of Homeland Security. Aziz was also a nonresident fellow at Brookings Institution in Doha and is currently a Professor of Law and Chancellor's Social Justice Scholar at Rutgers, the State University of New Jersey.

In 2011, when the Muslim Brotherhood in Egypt founded a political party, they may have looked to their savvy American public relations counterparts in their attempt to portray the Brotherhood as political rather than terroristic. They used the same name as Elibiary's organization when they formed the party. According to the archived pages of the Freedom and Justice Foundation, Elibiary was "a National Security Policy Analyst, has been advising Intelligence and Law Enforcement agencies (ex. FBI, DHS, NCTC, ODNI, etc.) on various Counter-Terrorism (CT) issues (ex. Domestic Intelligence, Strategic Intelligence Analysis, Information Sharing and Radicalization)" while he was working at the institute.[35] Elibiary became more influential under President Barack Obama's administration, and he didn't make an effort to hide his Islamic radicalism nor his ties to the Muslim

---

33 Daily Caller, https://dailycaller.com/2012/09/17/will-obamas-department-of-justice-ever-criminalize-speech-against-any-religion/, October 21, 2011.

34 Muhammad Aziz's real name was acquired from his membership card in the Egyptian Physicians' Union, which he originally posted on his public Facebook page, https://archive.org/details/screen-shot-2017-08-16-at-10.37.03-am, accessed April 19, 2021.

35 Freedom and Justice Foundation archived web page, http://web.Archive.org/web/20101103055218/http://www.freeandjust.org/OurTeam.htm, accessed June 19, 2018.

Brotherhood.[36] In 2013, he became a member of the Homeland Security Advisory Council.

Elibiary described Muhammad Morsi as "Egypt's Mandela." Middle Eastern media often refers to Elibiary as a Brotherhood operative.[37] Moreover, following an Islamic State terrorist attack on Coptic Christians in 2017, when a gunman opened fire on a bus killing twenty-eight people including children, Elibiary celebrated the terrorist attack on his Twitter account, writing, "Reading ISIS's latest mag 'otherizing' Egypt's Copts. Subhanallah what goes around comes around. Coptic [leaders] did same to MB Egyptians." Seemingly gleeful over the massacre, he used the word "*Subhanallah*," which is Arabic for "Glory to Allah." He followed that with the false claim that Coptic Christians in Egypt "did same to MB [Muslim Brotherhood] Egyptians" to justify the killing of Christians, which is a general priority for Islamists around the world. There is no record of Coptic Christians committing acts of violence against any member of the Muslim Brotherhood but much evidence of Coptic Christians being victimized.

Elibiary's radicalism made news prior to this incident. In September 2013, he was widely criticized in the United States and Egypt after he placed the *Rabi'a* symbol—associated with Muslim Brotherhood militants—on his Twitter account's profile picture.[38]

The Muslim Brotherhood's Rabi'a militia's four-finger gang sign is named after the Brotherhood violent occupation of Rabi'a al-Adawiya Square in Cairo, in August 2013.[39] During the Brotherhood's armed siege of the square, they established tents where they abducted, tortured, maimed, and killed their victims.[40] They targeted civil-

36 Meira Svirsky, "Senior DHS Advisor Elibiary: Brotherhood Not a Threat in US," Clarion Project (Washington, DC), October 30, 2013.

37 Al-Youm as-Sabi' (Cairo), May 9, 2017.

38 Sharona Schwartz, "Controversial Homeland Security Adviser Defends Use of Muslim Brotherhood-Associated Icon on His Twitter Profile," The Blaze, September 30, 2013.

39 Al-Youm as-Sabi' (Cairo), August 12, 2016.

40 Al-Masry Al-Youm (Cairo), July 22, 2017.

ians whom the Brotherhood suspected as being police officers or Brotherhood opponents. Among the victims was a carpenter, Amr Magdi, who was abducted, electrocuted, and beaten to death in the presence of Brotherhood members of the Guidance Bureau.[41]

Another victim, Mahmoud Sayyed, was a police officer. Sayyed stated in an interview with the Egyptian newspaper *al-Masry al-Youm* that he was tortured for seventy-one hours.[42] He was also stabbed repeatedly, beaten with chains, shocked, and scalded with boiling water. Incredibly, Sayyed survived his ordeal and was discovered in a cemetery where the Brotherhood had left him to die.

Rabi'a in Arabic means "fourth," hence four fingers. The Muslim Brotherhood claims the signal is a sign of "resistance" and tribute to Muslim Brotherhood operatives killed during clashes with Egyptian security forces. The signal gained widespread use among Islamists and terrorists, such as *Izz ad-Din al-Qassam* Brigades, after Turkish President Recep Erdoğan inspired his followers to use the signal, saying he "wondered if the signal will replace the victory sign to represent triumph in the Islamic world."[43]

After Elibiary posted the terror symbol on Twitter, he remained in his position at DHS. In 2014, Elibiary tweeted that it was "inevitable that 'Caliphate' returns."[44] In the same year, Elibiary was at the center of a controversy involving allegations that former DHS Secretary Janet Napolitano gave him Secret clearance, which allowed to him download classified information. According to Congressman Louie Gohmert (R-TX), Elibiary showed that classified material to a reporter.[45] The former official in President Obama's administration still did not attempt to hide his extremism even after the Muslim

41 Ibid.

42 Ibid.

43 Al-Arabiya (Dubai), September 25, 2013; *CNN Arabia*, September 21, 2013.

44 John Rossomando, "DHS Adviser Says Caliphate's Return Inevitable," Investigative Project on Terrorism (Washington, DC), June 16, 2014.

45 Kerry Picket, "Homeland Security Sec. Johnson Admits Alleged Breach of Classified Docs 'Problematic,'" https://www.breitbart.com/, May 29, 2014.

Brotherhood declared total war in Egypt against all foreign nationals and their embassies, including Americans.[46]

In January 2015, Muslim Brotherhood's *Rabi'a* television station in Turkey, officially declared war against Egypt and announced it would target foreign individuals and "multinational companies in Egypt." The Brotherhood also demanded that diplomats, ambassadors, and embassy employees depart Egypt. They also warned that tourists who plan to visit Egypt should cancel their trips. The announcer said, "We are providing a chance for Western, Arab and African citizens, and all their employees to immediately evacuate the country...or else you will become targets."[47] The announcement provided a deadline of February 28 for the evacuation of foreigners.

This is only one example, in one area of policy and intelligence circles, that demonstrates how coded Islamist terminology, entwined with infiltration, has allowed the world's most violent jihadist group to gain power in America. There are numerous examples of this pattern in education, law enforcement, media, public policy, and other professions where Brotherhood spies are involved.

JIHAD ADVOCACY DAY

Since the spring of 2015, Muslim Brotherhood umbrella organizations, the US Council of Muslim Organizations (USCMO) and CAIR, have been hosting what they call Muslim Advocacy Day to connect national, regional, and state Islamist organizations and community members with their elected representatives in Congress. In 2017, CAIR reported that 400 delegates from thirty states met with some 230 elected officials and congressional staff.[48] Among the dele-

46 Rab'ia Television Network (Istanbul), January 31, 2015; Al-Arabiya (Dubai), January 31, 2015.

47 Ibid.

48 "CAIR: Alabama Muslims Lobby Congress on Record Breaking Muslim Advocacy Day," US Council of Muslim Organizations (USCMO), Washington, DC, May 5, 2017.

gates at the 2017 Muslim Advocacy Day were Muslim Brotherhood leaders directly linked to violent Islamists. USCMO's leadership includes an Islamist once accused by the US government of funding terrorism conducted by al-Qaeda and the Taliban.

USCMO also invited a known terrorist to join the "First International Conference of Muslim Councils," which took place on February 2016 in Washington DC. USCMO's leadership, who annually lobby Congress and are in communication with the US State Department, have strong ties to al-Qaeda.[49]

USCMO's leaders have hosted several Brotherhood operatives convicted of terrorism. Among the most dangerous Islamists frequently invited to attend national events in the United States is Maha Azzam, a designated terrorist in Egypt and the second cousin of Ayman al-Zawahiri. Azzam shares more than just DNA with the leader of al-Qaeda.[50]

A USCMO board member is also associated with al-Qaeda. Mazen Mokhtar is an Egyptian-born Islamist, board member of USCMO, and the executive director of the Muslim American Society (MAS), and he has been accused of fundraising for al-Qaeda and the Taliban.

The Muslim Brotherhood-organized "Muslim Advocacy Day" on Capitol Hill is part of this effort, as Islamists seek to exert influence within the People's House to further their jihadist, totalitarian agenda. They have already had some success. For example, USCMO's leadership claimed responsibility for improving relations between then-Secretary of State Rex Tillerson, Qatar, and the Muslim Brotherhood.[51]

The United States has failed to understand what its allies in the Middle East already know: the Muslim Brotherhood poses a serious

---

49 "USCMO First International Conference of Muslim Councils in the West," United States Coalition of Muslim Organizations (Washington DC), http://uscmo.org, accessed May 21, 2018.

50 Dustur (Cairo), February 23, 2018.

51 Oussama Jammal, "A visit to State Department opens up the topic of the relationship between Rex Tillerson and Qatar," August 17, 2017, Twitter.com/OJammal; *Elaph* (London), August 23, 3027.

threat to national security. USCMO was founded in 2014, by eight American Islamist organizations.[52] One of these groups, CAIR, was labeled by federal prosecutors as an unindicted co-conspirator during the Holy Land Foundation terror finance trial, because of CAIR's pervasive ties to the Muslim Brotherhood's "Palestine Committee," which was established in 1988 to support the terrorist group Hamas.[53]

Another founder of USCMO is the Islamic Circle of North America (ICNA), which has been linked to terrorist organizations in South Asia and to American Muslims for Palestine (AMP), a group widely considered to be part of Hamas's network in the United States.[54]

On May 2, 2017, a Brotherhood-affiliated organization, Egyptian Americans for Freedom and Justice (EAFAJ), was among the groups lobbying Congress during Muslim Advocacy Day.[55] EAFAJ has routinely invited convicted terrorists to its events in the United States, such as Brotherhood Leaders Walid Sharabi and Gamal Heshmat from the leadership of the Egyptian Revolutionary Council (ERC).[56] Both were convicted of terrorism in Egypt and are currently residing in Turkey.[57]

EAFAJ posted a flyer on its Facebook page announcing that its members planned meetings with Congress to deliver a report that would "expose the crimes of Egypt's current military regime against its own Egyptian people." According to Egypt's *al-Youm as-Sabi'*

---

52 US Council of Muslim Organizations website, http://uscmo.org, Washington, DC, accessed December 1, 2017.

53 "Attachment A: List of Unindicted Co-conspirators - In the United States District Court for the Northern District of Texas Dallas Division," The Investigative Project on Terrorism, Washington, DC, accessed November 19, 2017; US Department of Justice, Office of Legislative Affairs letter to Congresswoman Myrick, The Investigative Project on Terrorism, Washington, DC, accessed March 3, 2017.

54 "Pakistani Islamism Flourishes in America," *National Review*, January 24, 2018; "American Muslims for Palestine's Web of Hamas Support," Investigative Project on Terrorism, December 11, 2014.

55 Official Facebook of Egyptian Americans for Freedom and Justice. www.Facebook.com/EAFAJ, accessed May 20, 2018.

56 Farahat, "Islamists with Direct Ties to Terrorists," 10.

57 Ibid.

newspaper, the report referred to members of an Islamic State terrorist cell from the village of Arab Sharkas as "victims of the Egyptian regime."[58] This is typical doublespeak from EAFAJ and the Muslim Brotherhood. Its members make an effort to cite liberal democratic values when they communicate with western politicians, but in private, they express extremist and pro-terrorism rhetoric.

For example, at a November 2016 EAFAJ event, extremist imam Muhammad Elbar declared that Egyptian President Abdel Fattah al-Sisi "ought to be beheaded."[59] On his own Facebook page, Elbar claimed that he is the brother of the Muslim Brotherhood's jihadist Mufti Abdul Rahman Elbar, who is currently in prison in Egypt following a terrorism conviction.[60] The EAFAJ delegation to the 2017 and 2018 Muslim Advocacy Day included activists who identify as members and affiliates of the Muslim Brotherhood.[61] Another EAFAJ Brotherhood operative, activist Yahya Almontaser, was in regular communication with Islamic State.

The audacity of the Muslim Brotherhood's lobby in the United States has gone beyond sending people with ties to terrorism to lobby Congress—they sent an actual convicted terrorist who proudly admitted his involvement in terrorism and who is currently teaching at Union County College in New Jersey.[62]

AYMAN AL-ZAWAHIRI'S COUSIN ON THE HILL

In 2015, during their annual terror-linked lobbying event in Congress,[63] USCMO invited Maha Azzam. She is a designated terror-

58 Al-Youm as-Sabi' (Cairo), May 8, 2017.

59 John Rossomando, "Brooklyn Imam Linked to Qaradawi Group Calls for Sisi's Head," Investigative Project on Terrorism, Washington, DC, November 30, 2016.

60 Al-Ahram (Cairo), May 15, 2014; *Al-Masry al-Youm* (Cairo), January 5, 2017

61 Farahat, "Islamists with Direct Ties to Terrorists," 14-7.

62 Cynthia Farahat, "An Asylum-Seeker Who Needs to be Deported," *American Thinker*, May 7, 2018.

63 Farahat, "Islamists with Direct Ties to Terrorists," 6, 14-7.

ist in Egypt and the second cousin of Ayman al-Zawahiri.[64] She is the granddaughter of Abdul Rahman Azzam (1893–1976), the first secretary-general of the League of Arab States.[65] Abdul Rahman was also the great-uncle of Ayman al-Zawahiri.[66] This is not a simple case of guilt by association. Not only are family dynamics significantly different in the Middle East than in the West, but also Muslim Brotherhood families continue their legacy through their descendants, and Maha Azzam shares similar values with Zawahiri.

Azzam is the president of the Turkey-based Egyptian Revolutionary Council (ERC). It is a radical Brotherhood group that openly advocates for violent jihad, and its leadership is composed of Brotherhood convicted terrorists in Egypt, such as Walid Sharabi, Muhammad Heshmat, and Amr Darrag, a member in the Muslim Brotherhood's Guidance Bureau.[67] In June 2017, Azzam's ERC essentially declared jihad in the Gulf of Aqaba or the Gulf of Eilat, in a statement on its official Facebook page.[68] The Gulf of Aqaba is located at the northern tip of the Red Sea, east of the Sinai Peninsula and west of the Arabian mainland. After a deal between Egypt and Saudi Arabia that handed Saudis control of the Gulf of Aqaba in 2016, ERC called upon Egyptians living in the cities overlooking the Red Sea to "struggle to liberate" the islands and the Gulf of Aqaba and treat them as "occupied territories."

In another veiled call for terrorism, the statement urged citizens to "treat all Saudi companies and institutions as occupying forces." These jihadist undertones suggest that Azzam shares more than just DNA with her terrorist second cousin al-Zawahiri. Azzam is a British citizen

64 Dustur (Cairo), February 23, 2018.

65 Al-Youm as-Sabi' (Cairo), March 24, 2015; "Lamha Tarikhiyya," The League of Arab States, http://www.lasportal.org, accessed May 30, 2018.

66 "Ayman al-Zawahiri Fast Facts," *CNN*, December 14, 2012, https://www.cnn.com.

67 Ahmed Mansour, Interview with Ahmed Abdel Rahman, Head of the Egyptian Muslim Brotherhood International, Billa Houdoud, Al-Jazeera (Qatar), April 22, 2015.

68 Cynthia Farahat, "Gulf of Aqaba Treaty: a Saudi Repudiation of the Camp David Accords," *American Thinker*, June 26, 2017; Egyptian Revolutionary Council Official Facebook Page, www.Facebook.com/ERCEgypt1, accessed May 20, 2018; Ibid.

and an Associate Fellow in London-based Chatham House's Middle East and North Africa Program.[69]

The ties between the Muslim Brotherhood's American front organizations and Azzam should compel American and British intelligence and law enforcement agencies to investigate Azzam. Is she merely a radical relative of Ayman al-Zawahiri, who coincidentally supports jihad and the Muslim Brotherhood—which founded al-Qaeda—or is she potentially acting as a mediator between al-Qaeda, and the Muslim Brotherhood's British and American chapters?[70] Azzam is not the only connection of USCMO to al-Qaeda.

ACCUSED AL-QAEDA WEBMASTER MAZEN MOKHTAR LOBBIES CONGRESS

Mazen Mokhtar is a USCMO board member and the executive director of the Muslim American Society (MAS), a Muslim Brotherhood front organization.[71] Mokhtar is among the organizers of USCMO's annual lobbying event on Capitol Hill. Mokhtar has been accused of fundraising for al-Qaeda and the Taliban.

In August 2004, the US government accused Mokhtar of operating the website www.minna.com, which was a mirror site of www.azzam.com, named after al-Qaeda's Abdullah Azzam.[72] The site solicited funds and recruited Taliban, Chechen, and al-Qaeda terrorists. The website was also affiliated with the Chechen terror group, Islamic

69 "Fact Box: 'Egyptian Revolutionary Council' Visits Washington DC," Atlantic Council, Washington, DC, https://www.atlanticcouncil.org/, February 5, 2015

70 Cynthia Farahat, "The Muslim Brotherhood, Fountain of Islamist Violence," *Middle East Quarterly* 24, no.2 (Spring 2017), March 1, 2017.

71 "Introducing the Muslim American Society," Investigative Project on Terrorism, Washington, DC, September 18, 2007; Patrick Poole, "Muslim Congressman's Ferguson Panel at Chicago Islamic Convention Features Al-Qaeda Webmaster, Taliban Fundraiser," *PJ Media*, December 27, 2014.

72 Dana Priest and Susan Schmidt, "Terror Suspect's Arrest Opens New Inquiries," *Washington Post*, August 8, 2004.

Army of the Caucasus, and its field commander, Shamil Basayev. The Islamic Army of the Caucasus claimed responsibility for the Beslan school massacre in Russia on September 1, 2004. The massacre's victims totaled 334 people, including 186 children.[73]

According to an arrest warrant for terror suspect Babar Ahmad, who operated the Azzam.com website, Ahmad conspired with the US operator of www.minna.com to solicit donations to terror groups and to post instructions on how to donate the funds.[74] Mokhtar was arrested in 2007 and charged with tax fraud, which commentators speculated would be used as an entry point for further terrorism charges.[75] But then-US Attorney Chris Christie dropped the charges in 2008 without explanation, allowing Mokhtar to go free. Today, Mokhtar continues to raise funds for Islamic Relief USA (IRUSA), an organization accused of links to Hamas.[76] In 2014, the United Arab Emirates designated both MAS and IRUSA as terrorist organizations.[77] During Mokhtar's lobbying efforts, New Jersey Senator Cory Booker took a selfie photograph with Mokhtar and posted it on his official Twitter page. He is still resuming his fundraising efforts through the shady Baitulmaal Brotherhood front organization. On his public Facebook page, Mokhtar posted pictures of a Baitulmaal convoy providing aid to Kafr Yahumul camps in Idlib District in Syria

---

73 Cynthia Farahat, "Islamists with Ties to Terror Lobby Congress," *Front Page Magazine*, May 4, 2018; Archived *CNN* article, "New Jersey Man Investigated in Terror Probe," August 4, 2004, http://www.elastic.org/~fche/mirrors/www.cryptome.org/minna/minna.htm.

74 United States District Court of Connecticut, Warrant for Arrest: United States V. Babar Ahmad," Investigative Project on Terrorism, Washington, DC, accessed November 28, 2017.

75 "Middlesex County Man Charged with Tax Evasion, Filing False Tax Returns," United States Department of Justice US Attorney, District of New Jersey, NJ. April 24. 2007; Joe Kaufman, "America's Mainstream Web Terrorist," *Front Page Magazine*, October 8, 2008.

76 Mazen Mokhtar, "Baby Musa, Myanmar Relief Fund," www.GoFundMe.com, accessed November 29, 2017; Gregg Roman, "Islamic Relief: Charitable Support for Political Violence," *Daily Caller*, Washington, DC, September 8, 2017.

77 "List of Groups Designated Terrorist Organizations by UAE," The National, Dubai, November 16, 2014.

in May 2020.[78] Kafr Yahmul is under the control of al-Qaeda's *Hay'at Tahrir ash-Sham* (Organization for the Liberation of the Levant or Levant Liberation Committee) previously known as al-Nusra Front.[79]

Mokhtar and Azzam are not the only alarming examples of Islamists associated with terrorism allowed to roam the hallways of Congress at the USCMO event. Yahya Almontaser is a New-York-City-based activist who was present at their 2017 Congressional delegation and was also in communication with an Islamic State terrorist. Almontaser is a self-proclaimed member of the Muslim Brotherhood.[80] On his Facebook page, Almontaser spent several years regularly corresponding with Muhammad Sayed Taha, a self-described Islamic State terrorist who is currently incarcerated in military prison in Egypt for trying to bomb the Police Academy in Cairo. Taha referred to Almontaser as *ustadhi*, which means my mentor or my teacher. In return, Almontaser praised Taha's jihadist ambitions.[81]

In April 2017, the Egyptian newspaper *Dustur* published case documents relating to Egypt's most famous Islamic State case, known as *qadiat daesh al-kubra*, (ISIL's big case).[82] According to the documents, 170 convicted terrorists were arrested for various Islamic State-related terrorist attacks and activities, including fighting in Syria and Sinai, and attempting to bomb the Egyptian police academy. According to the article, Muhammad Sayed Taha's name appears among those arrested in the "Beni Suef Daesh terrorist cell." The cell is named after the city of Beni Suef, located south of Cairo.

---

78 Mazen Mokhtar Facebook Page, "Zakatul fitr hot meals delivered in Al Zaitoun and Al Rahman camp in Kafr Yahmoul," https://www.facebook.com/mazen.mokhtar.92.

79 Ala al-Basirah (Damascus), September 17, 2018.

80 Farahat, "Islamists with Ties to Terror."

81 Ibid; Yahya Almontaser's Facebook Page, www.Facebook.com/Yahya.Almontaser, accessed September 3, 2018.

82 Dustur (Cairo), April 27, 2017.

THE BASIT CASE: NEW JERSEY'S JIHADIST ACADEMIC

Sahar Aziz is not the only Islamist targeting students in New Jersey. Ahmed Abdel Basit Muhammad, also known as Basit, is a Muslim Brotherhood operative and Egyptian convicted terrorist. He admitted on social media to his involvement in terrorism in Egypt.[83] Hostos Community College and New Jersey Institute of Technology both offered Basit jobs, and he is currently employed as an adjunct professor at Union County College, according to his official Facebook account.[84]

In 2016, an Egyptian court sentenced Basit to death in absentia for his role, along with seven others, in several terrorist attacks.[85] This author has previously reported on Basit's activities and his conviction on *American Thinker*.[86] Basit's conviction was part of a large Brotherhood terrorism trial in Egypt known as "the Case of the Progressive Operations Committee (POC)."

POC was founded by Muhammad Kamal, and Basit was among the Kamal Vanguard cell members involved in the assassination of the country's top prosecutor, Hisham Barakat, according to Egyptian investigators. Prosecutors said Basit played a key role in the POC.[87] According to *Shorouk News* in Cairo, the Egyptian government accused Basit of using Brotherhood funds to purchase arms, ammunition, and bomb-making equipment, as well as to facilitate the travel of members of a POC terrorist cell to Turkey and Syria to receive jihadist training. That training reportedly included firearms lessons and instruction in the manufacture of bombs and improvised

83 Farahat, "An Asylum-Seeker Who Needs to Be Deported."
84 Ahmed Abdel Basit Mohamed. Facebook page, www.Facebook.com/Ahmed.A.Muhammad.102, accessed September 10, 2018; accessed July 13, 2021.
85 Al-Youm as-Sabi' (Cairo), May 29, 2016.
86 Farahat, "An Asylum-Seeker Who Needs to Be Deported."
87 Tahrir News (Cairo), May 10, 2016.

explosive devices, under the supervision of the al-Qaeda offshoot, *Aknaf Bait al-Maqdis*.[88]

The Egyptian government's claims about Basit's terrorist activities are credible. On his Facebook account, Basit has called for a "resounding jihad" against Egyptian government employees, whom he described as "dirty damned infidels."[89] Basit is also connected to terrorism recruiter, self-confessed torturer, and Brotherhood leader Safwat Hegazy.[90] Hegazy bragged on al-Jazeera about his involvement in torture.[91] He is also a leader in al-Gama'a al-Islamiyya.[92]

In a Facebook post on August 16, 2015, Basit admitted to involvement in organizing a violent riot, in 2013, that led to the death of 210 people and the injury of 296 others in downtown Cairo.[93] The riots started at the al-Fateh Mosque. The rioters marched to a bridge in downtown Cairo from which they and reportedly fired automatic rifles at random civilians and police officers. In the same Facebook post, Basit praised a gunman at the riot, writing, "Due to Allah's blessing and generosity, an armed man appeared from the end of the bridge; seeking God, the man started shooting at thugs."[94]

In 2016, Basit filed for asylum in the United States, where he is an immigration activist who frequently posts videos advising Islamists

---

88 Shorouk News (Cairo), June 11, 2015.

89 Ahmed Abdel Basit Mohamed Facebook page, July 28, 2014; Screenshot of Basit Mohamed's Facebook post, Archive.org/details/ScreenShot20171203At8.34.26AM, accessed June 1, 2018.

90 Ahmed Abdel Basit Mohamed Facebook page, May 13, 2012; Screenshot of the post, Archive.org/details/ScreenShot20171203At7.58.42AM, accessed June 1, 2018.

91 Ahmed Mansour, Interview with Safwat Hegazy, "Shid ala il-Asr," Al-Jazeera (Qatar), August 18, 2011.

92 Shorouk News (Cairo), April 7, 2012.

93 Ahmed Abdel Basit Mohamed Facebook page, August 16, 2015; Screenshot of Basit Mohamed's Facebook post, Archive.org/details/ScreenShot20171203At11.57.19AM, accessed June 1, 2018; *Al-Ahram* (Cairo), February 24, 2014.

94 Ahmed Abdel Basit Mohamed Facebook page, August 16, 2015; Screenshot of Basit Mohamed's Facebook post, Archive.org/details/ScreenShot20171203At11.57.19AM, accessed June 1, 2018.

on how to immigrate to the United States.[95] He is an activist in Brotherhood front groups in New York City where is also friends with NYC based terror recruiter Bahgat Saber.[96] Basit is also active in a Washington, DC, Brotherhood front groups such as The Freedom Initiative and its Brotherhood founder Mohamed Soltan.[97] He is also associated with the Alliance of Egyptian Americans.[98] During congressional meetings, the Alliance of Egyptian Americans represented Basit as a victim of political persecution and facilitated his meeting with the late Senator John McCain.[99]

On April 5, 2018, Immigration and Customs Enforcement (ICE) detained Basit for administrative immigration violations.[100] Before learning of the US court's decision about his asylum case, Basit removed numerous radical and jihadist posts and confessions from his public Facebook account. The Huffington Post, al-Jazeera, and several other media outlets framed Basit's arrest as a human rights case, claiming that Basit was "condemned over pro-democracy protests in Egypt."[101] The truth, however, is that Basit was convicted of terrorism in Egypt after organizing a deadly riot. Few people would consider such violence a "pro-democracy protest." While there are many honorable Muslim immigrants who deserve the chance to start a new life in America, a convicted terrorist is certainly not one of them.

The Basit case is a study of the layers of failures by American institutions. Basit traveled to Qatar, where the US Embassy reportedly

---

95 "Asylum and Death Sentence," Save Basit website, https://www.savebasit.com, accessed June 1, 2018; Ahmed Abdel Basit Mohamed Facebook page, February 21, 2018; Al-Jjisr News (Cairo), October 1, 2017.

96 Ahmed Abdel Basit Mohamed official Facebook page, "Ahmed Abdel-Basit Mohamed is with Bahgat Saber," May 1, 2021.

97 Save Basit Campaign, The Freedom Intiative (Washington DC), https://thefreedomi.org/campaigns/savebasit/, accessed February 19, 2022; Ahmed Abdel Basit Mohamed official Facebook page, "Ahmed Abdel-Basit Mohamed is with Mohamed Soltan," August 26, 2018.

98 Farahat, "Islamists with Direct Ties to Terrorists," 21.

99 Ibid

100 Rowaida Abdelaziz, "Exclusive: ICE Detains a New Jersey Teacher Who'd Face A Death Sentence In Egypt," *Huffington Post*, April 13, 2018.

101 Ibid.

issued a visa to the convicted terrorist to enter the United States.[102] Basit then passed through US Customs in the United States. The third problem was his employment at the Muslim Brotherhood-operated school Rising Star Academy, which employed Basit as a physics teacher.[103] The fourth failure was allowing Basit to lobby congressional offices. The only proper government action taken toward Basit was his arrest in 2018. The fifth failure was the numerous media outlets that portrayed him as a victim, despite the overwhelming evidence against him. The sixth failure occurred when an immigration court granted Basit asylum in the United States.[104] The seventh is that he is now teaching American college students.

The Basit case is a classic example of how terrorists are able to create a solid base in the United States. The only positive outcome of the Basit case occurred following his arrest. The Egyptian newspaper *Dustur* reported that according to its source in the Brotherhood's US chapter, their operatives "are terrified" after Basit's arrest and they were even "considering relocating to the United Kingdom."[105]

MEANS TO IDENTIFY COVERT MUSLIM BROTHERHOOD LEADERS AND OPERATIVES

It is hard to counter the Brotherhood's Civilization Jihad Operation when its operatives are covert. Since only a few of the group's leaders publicly acknowledge their membership, the means by which its operatives are identified can be achieved when *all* the following factors are present in the behavior of an individual:

(1) Repetitive engagement in Muslim Brotherhood public events. This entails several involvements in Brotherhood-sponsored political

102 Ibid.

103 Rising Star Academy (Union City, NJ), http://www.rsanj.org/rsa, accessed June 1, 2018.

104 Hannan Adely, "Jersey City Teacher, Facing Death Penalty in Egypt, Has Been Granted Asylum in US," *North Jersey USA Today*, August 21, 2018.

105 Aman-Dustur (Cairo), April 8, 2018.

activities, including Brotherhood affiliate conferences, talks, riots, protests, and/or jihadist activities.

(2) Repetitive public appearances with self-identified national and international leaders and members of the Brotherhood. A Brotherhood member will not only attend events. They also try to gain status within the group through publicly appearing in political and social events with known Brotherhood leaders and members. Furthermore, a Brotherhood operator frequently will associate with their equivalent rank within the group. For example, if an operative repeatedly appears in pictures with Recep Tayyip Erdoğan, this is an indication that they are either the leader of their country's International Apparatus chapter or at least among the leader's deputies.

(3) The subject's adherence to the instructions of the Muslim Brotherhood Guidance Bureau. Brotherhood members are only allowed to publicly express opinions and views and political discourse that conform with the Guidance Bureau's guidelines and positions toward cultural and political issues. For example, after Qaradawi announced that Erdoğan was their new sultan, Brotherhood operatives across the world added the Turkish flag to their pictures on their social media accounts.

(4) Marital relationships. While it can fall under "associations," the marital status of Brotherhood operatives can be an important indicator in revealing the operative's ranking and position in the group, since they are only allowed to wed within the same hierarchical structure in the organization. If the subject under investigation is male, his position in the Brotherhood can be revealed through examining the ranking of the male relatives of his female spouse. If the subject is female, her ranking in the group's hierarchy can be revealed through the position of her father and older male members in her family. When *all* these four indicators are present, it is safe to conclude that the operative is almost certainly a member of the Brotherhood.

An example of this familial dynamic is Dalia Fahmy. She is an Associate Professor of Political Science at Long Island University,

Senior Fellow at the Center for Global Policy in Washington, DC, and a Visiting Scholar at the Center for the Study of Genocide and Human Rights and UNESCO Chair at Rutgers University for 2018. According to Tharwat al-Kherbawy, who has known her family for decades, Fahmy's father is Fikry Fahmy al-Tanbadawi, and his brother is Farid Fahmy al-Tanbadawi. The men married two sisters from another Brotherhood family, and they all immigrated to the US in the 1970s. Kherbawy told the author that the family "significantly contributed to building the International Apparatus in the United States." Kherbawy added that Fahmy's father was "deputy of the Brotherhood chapter in New Jersey for several years. The Muslim Brotherhood assigned her uncle to move to Chicago to become the deputy for their chapter there, where he still maintains the leadership of the group in Chicago."

This set of identifiers suggests that the head of USCMO, Oussama Jammal, could be the leader of the International Apparatus in America. Jammal is also director of the Muslim American Society-Public Affairs and Civic Engagement (MAS-PACE), a division of the Brotherhood front group, the Muslim American Society (MAS). Jammal is also vice president of the Mosque Foundation in Bridgeview, Illinois. In 2003, Jammal raised $50,000 at a Mosque Foundation prayer service for terrorist operative Sami al-Arian, the then-North American representative of Palestinian Islamic Jihad.[106] Under Jamaal's leadership, in 2012, the Mosque Foundation hosted an official delegation of *al-Jama'a al-Islamiyya*, the Lebanese branch of the Muslim Brotherhood, which is associated with al-Qaeda.[107]

Two officials Jamal invited from *al-Jama'a al-Islamiyya* were also in direct communication with Hamas and Iran's Islamic Revolutionary

106 Steve Schmadeke, "Hard-liners Won Battle for Bridgeview Mosque," *Chicago Tribune*, February 8, 2004.

107 Farahat, "Islamists with Direct Ties to Terrorists," 4; Ra'fat Fahd Murra, "El-Harakat wa'l-wa'l-wa'l-Qoua al-Islamiyya fi al-Mujtama' al-Filistini fi Libnan," (Beirut: Markaz al-Zaituna, 2010), 49–51.

Guards Corps (IRGC).[108] Jammal's Mosque Foundation also invited Jordanian Islamist Amjad Qourshah to give sermons at its mosque. Qourshah was imprisoned in Jordan in 2016 for promoting jihadist propaganda.[109] In his lectures, Qourshah has defended Islamic State members and described them as "decent men."[110]

Despite these extremist connections, Jammal and USCMO have long enjoyed access to senior government officials. On June 29, 2021, Jammal held his annual event online in the presence of US Representatives Ilhan Omar (D-MN) and Rashida Tlaib (D-MI).[111] In August 2017, Jammal posted an *Elaph* article on his Twitter account claiming credit for "opening the relationship" between Rex Tillerson's State Department, Qatar, and the Muslim Brotherhood.[112] The article stated that USCMO, CAIR, and American Muslims for Palestine (AMP) had met with high-ranking State Department officials. An unnamed member of the Islamist delegation stated that they are "always in communication [with the State Department] in regard to issues that interest the Muslim community."[113] Jammal appeared in numerous pictures in private and public meetings with Erdoğan. This level of access to the Muslim Brotherhood's sultan and US policymakers may demonstrate Jammal's high-ranking position in the group.

The vast majority of Muslims have rejected al-Qaeda, the Muslim Brotherhood, Islamic State, and their narratives. This is why the Brotherhood is currently more focused on rebranding their agenda under the banners of "ethics" and "morality" as a cover in the Middle East. One example is the Qatari-based Brotherhood-run think tank,

---

108 Farahat, "Islamists with Direct Ties to Terrorists," 3; Helmut Pisecky and Alex Grinberg, "Iran and the Muslim Brotherhood in the Arabic-Speaking World: The Best of Enemies?" Rubin Center Research in International Affairs, Herzliya, Israel, January 14, 2016.

109 Elaph (London), June 14, 2016.

110 "Amjad Qourshah Yoshidu bi Qiadet Daesh," YouTube.com, March 6, 2016.

111 "USCMO Concludes Its National Muslim Advocacy Week With Great Success," US Council of Muslim Organizations (USCMO), June 29, 2021.

112 Elaph (London), August 18, 2017; Oussama Jammal's Twitter account, www.twitter.com/Ojammal.

113 Farahat, "Islamists with Direct Ties to Terrorists," 5.

the Research Center for Islamic Legislation and Ethics (CILE).[114] The center is headed by convicted Egyptian terrorist Emad el-Din Shahin, and it frequently hosts Islamists such as Tariq Ramadan, Qaradawi, and the current head of the Muslim Brotherhood's Propagation of the Message Section, Ahmad al-Raysuni, a designated a terrorist in the United Arab Emirates.[115] CILE is also working with American academics.[116]

The Makassed Foundation still operates in Lebanon under the name al-Makassed Philanthropic Islamic Association of Beirut, where it has twenty Islamic schools. The Makassed branch in the United States was established in 1999, in Washington DC, under the name The Makassed Foundation of America. Makassed also has a branch in the Palestinian territories and runs a hospital in Gaza. The foundation is currently active in American University in Beirut, where it recruits students who continue to operate to advance its Islamists mission.[117] The foundation is a member of a Lebanese-based Muslim Brotherhood-run organization that connects Brotherhood front groups in Lebanon working toward stealthily advancing the cause of reviving the Ottoman Empire under Turkish leadership.

Just as early World War I Islamists exploited terms associated with morality when they established and operated the Islamic Ethics Association, modern pan-Islamist and undercover jihadists are revamping their clandestine proselytism under the same exact banner as well as under the term "ethics."

The Brotherhood's Civilization Jihad Operation has been successful infiltrating Western institutions, which in turn, have systemati-

---

114 "Internal Closed Seminar: Islamic Ethics: State-of-the-Art and Future Directions," The Research Center for Islamic Legislation and Ethics (CILE), Qatar, September 9, 2019; Cynthia Farahat, The Anthropology of Islamic Disinformation," *Middle East Quarterly* (Spring 2020).

115 "CILE 2nd Annual International Conference," CILE, December 11, 2014; "Qur'an and Ethics Conference," CILE, February 8, 2015.

116 Al-Bayan (Dubai), November 5, 2018.

117 The Islamic Makassed Alumni Association in Beirut, http://makassed-alumni.org/, accessed November 5, 2020.

cally worked to legitimize the Muslim Brotherhood by elevating its operatives to powerful positions. This operation is not entirely hidden behind the public banners of benevolent façades. Underneath a thin layer of faux civility, the Brotherhood's true intent emerges once their strategy is uncloaked.

THE MUSLIM BROTHERHOOD AND TERRORISM RECRUITMENT

The Muslim Brotherhood's terrorism recruitment technique and incitement for jihad change depending on several factors, such as their circumstances, their audience, their medium, and the laws and the policies toward Islamists in the counties where the recruiter resides. Modern terrorism recruitment has two forms, overt and covert.

Both techniques follow the same general pattern and the same sequence of indoctrination. First, they begin by narrating inspiring stories of jihadists from Islamic history and discussing their challenges, circumstances, grievances, and guerilla action. Second, they draw parallels between the situations, motivations, and justifications of early jihadists with those in modern times. The third stage always includes incitement, and this is where the type of recruitment becomes either overt or covert.

During overt recruitment, they give direct orders and directions on a specific terroristic action, such as the method, time, and location to execute an attack. Covert terrorism recruitment relies either on coded language and/or terrorism incitement using general terminology, which is difficult for law enforcement to link to specific criminal actions and therefore hard to prosecute. This can include assassination fatwas and calls for ritually sacrificing members of a certain group. Often, those who are actively involved in covert terror recruitment are associated with a wide network of Islamists and jihadists who might be involved in terrorism.

Prior to applying either tactic, there is an important step that precedes recruiting terrorists, and that is normalizing violence. The Muslim Brotherhood has mastered this tactic, and the wider the audience exposed to the process, the higher the percentage of recruits.

NORMALIZING GRAPHIC VIOLENCE

Under President Mubarak's regime, terrorism recruitment was state sponsored and broadcast around the clock on the Egyptian government's Radio and Television Union's communications satellite, Nilesat. For example, on his show on an-Nas television channel, Muslim Brotherhood leader Safwat Hegazy had a daily television show called "*Zaman al-Izza* (the Era of Dignity)." Dignity is also one of the Brotherhood's code words for jihad. On his show, he openly advocated for the genocide and torture of Christians and Jews. He often narrated historic jihadist victories and detailed gruesome means of torture and murder to inspire and instigate viewers with criminal tendencies.

During one of his shows in 2009, Hegazy told his viewers, in graphic detail, that while they should be "neck choppers," real experts murder their opponents by splitting their head in half vertically or horizontally.[118] He quoted a historic Islamic figure saying, "Do not disappoint us, be neck choppers [and] hand cutters." He repeated, "Be neck choppers and hand cutters, and if you fail I don't want to see your faces. If you fail, get defeated, and retreat, I don't want to see your faces."

Hegazy added that under similar historic or political conditions, the reminder of such actions is "required." He continued to say, "Be neck choppers, hack necks, cut necks. When you fight chop necks or mutilate hands."

118 "Zaman al-Izza 4- Uthman ibn Affan Radia Allahu Anhu," YouTube.com, June 13, 2015.

On that same show, he quoted another major historic Islamic figure who taught his son how to fight and protested the manner in which he carried out executions. "You should target the tip of the head, not the stem of the neck. Amr ibn al-As is telling his son Abdullah, I saw you fighting and I didn't like it because you hack the"—Hegazy physically demonstrated the faulty manner by which Abdullah was decapitating infidels and pointed at his bottom vertebrae connecting the neck to the upper back.

Hegazy said that instead of cutting the neck from its "root," Abdullah was "instructed to [target] the tip of the skull, hit the head [in the middle] to split it, or [horizontally] split the head in two." Hegazy added:

> These people taught their children how to fight for Allah, we have people now teaching their children how to pickpocket, or inflict injuries with a knife, [these are] elements of thuggery. Instead our master Amr ibn al-As taught his son [how to hack] the tips of skulls, which was only mastered by strong knights. There were two Muslims known to hack the tips of the skulls, unlike the usual neck chopping. Cut the neck. But [also] split the head in two halves from the middle or cut it horizontally.

Hegazy continued, saying it was done by only two men in jihadist history, "Our master al-Zubayr ibn al-Awwam, may Allah bless him, and our master Amr ibn al-As, those are the two who killed in this fashion." Hegazy said that those two jihadists were so skilled that after they perpetrated a massacre, people could identify how many victims many were "killed by our master al-Zubayr and how many were killed by our master Amr when the skulls were examined." One liked to split skulls horizontally and the other vertically. Hegazy later said that they presented a great example for Muslims, as "Our master Amr told his son, be like your father and inherit his method of killing. Al-Zubayr's son was also like his father, when he fought, he killed like his father."

This level of grotesque and explicit violence was aired on family-friendly television under President Mubarak's regime, where most of the media was under the control of the Muslim Brotherhood, including almost all Islamic television channels and networks. Normalizing violence is in every aspect of the Muslim Brotherhood's message. Even when the discussion involves benevolent topics, they adhere to a strategy of exposing their subjects to extreme levels of graphic violence.

Yusuf al-Qaradawi directs every member of the Brotherhood ideologically, and he is the group's most mainstream and authoritative modern theologian. Qaradawi mastered the tactic of subliminally deadening his subjects' humanity. One of numerous examples is displayed in his book *Fiqh as-Siam* (The Jurisprudence of Fasting). An unsuspecting individual can look at the title of the book and understandably misconstrue the book to be about the physical or spiritual benefits of fasting and rules regarding Islamic fasting. But as with most things involving the Muslim Brotherhood, it is not what it seems.

In his book, Qaradawi covered almost every aspect of person's life, such as regulating the most intimate details during coitus with their spouses.[119] Qaradawi's horror is on full display in the same book, during his fatwa regarding the regulations on using a lavatory. While getting into graphic detail about rules on extraction of biological materials, Qaradawi combined it with horrific sexual torture, saying:

> One should be careful during *instinja'* (rinsing urethra and anus with water); because inserting [your] fingertip in your anus can invalidate fasting, even the smallest tip of the head of the finger; even during defecation if fecal material isn't fully extracted and one has to clench his anus forcing partial fecal material back into

119 Yusuf al-Qaradawi, *Fiqh as-Siam* (Beirut: Al-Risala Publishers, 1993), 105–6.

> the anus, this nullifies fasting…etc., similarly is the woman's vagina, if it was stabbed with a knife and the knife reached deeply into the vagina, it also nullifies [her] fasting.[120]

Another similar example can also be found on Qaradawi's official website. During his fatwa on the legitimacy of brushing one's teeth while fasting during Ramadan and how it should be done, Qaradawi prohibited Muslims from brushing their teeth during the duration of fasting, adding that a fasting Muslim's breath "smells like musk to Allah and it is despised to remove it…the fasting [individual] should accept it. Just like blood, bloody wounds inflicted on a martyr."

Qaradawi merged the innocent question about brushing one's teeth during fasting with gore. Qaradawi continued, saying that "martyrs will be resurrected in their bloodied clothes, the color will be of blood but it will smell like musk…hence, a martyr is to remain in his blood-soaked clothes and it is not to be washed nor have its stains removed."[121] This tactic is almost universally employed by Muslim Brotherhood religious preachers. They intentionally desensitize their operatives to horrific discourse and imagery and frame them in a positive light, while casually bringing up such examples during random conversations.

Qaradawi followed Banna's habit of normalizing cruelty and glorifying murder-suicide. International Apparatus leader Sa'id Hawwa praised Qaradawi's example by recounting one of Qaradawi's speeches in Egypt, "The purest death, the most beloved by Allah is this…" and "He [Qaradawi] raised his hand simulating a throat-slitting gesture for the cause of Allah…while the masses were electrified in front of the seen of [simulated] sacrifice and slaughter."[122]

---

120 Ibid., 86–7.

121 Yusuf al-Qaradawi, "Isti'mal as-Siwak wa-Ma'goun as-Sinan and as-Sa'em", Yusuf al-Qaradawi's official website, www.al-qaradawi.net/node/3738, August 5, 2020.

122 Sa'id Hawwa, *Al-Madkhal ila-Da'wa al-Ikhwan al-Muslimi,* 199–200.

Covert terrorism recruitment is often disguised in religious sermons, whether online or offline. Since the late 1990s, Islamists have been heavily relying on the Paltalk chat program for terrorism recruitment and planning terrorist attacks.

Among the earliest pioneers of cyber jihad is Wael Ghonim.[123] Ghonim is a former senior fellow at Harvard University and former head of Marketing of Google Middle East and North Africa's branch until 2014. He is also a self-confessed member of the Muslim Brotherhood.

In 1997, Ghonim founded the website Islam Way. While the website appears to be benevolent at face value, it also promotes jihad and terrorism through countless Arabic sermons. Numerous lectures on the website incite mass murder and suicide attacks.[124], [125] The website repeatedly incites the persecution and murder of non-Muslims, especially Jews. For example, in 2014, they published an exclusive fatwa titled, "Horror and Terror Defeat Jews." The fatwa was issued by Muslim Brotherhood scholar and member of the Brotherhood's International Union of Muslim Scholars Yusuf al-Astal.[126] Astal said that the best tool Muslims should utilize against Jews is "horror, terror, and fear." He also said that murdering them was "a religious obligation."[127] In 2011, Wael Ghonim received the John F. Kennedy Profile in Courage Award in the name of the People of Egypt. This only added insult to the millions of injuries inflicted by the Brotherhood on the people of Egypt and the rest of the world.

An example of overt online recruitment is delivered by NYC based Brotherhood member and possibly the most famous terror recruiter

---

123 Wael Ghonim, "Kuntu Shaban Adian thuma Indamamt lil Ikhwan wa-Taraktahum," Arabic Post website, ArabicPost.net, September 12, 2019.

124 Islam Way Fatwa, "Kaif Adhak wa-fi A'idi al-Mushrikin min al-Muslimin," Islam Way's Arabic website, https://ar.islamway.net/, December 12, 2013.

125 Hafiz bin Ajab ad-Dusri, "'Amaliyat Istishhadiyya," Islam Way's Arabic website, https://ar.islamway.net/, March 9, 2004.

126 Al-Araby (London), June 24, 2007.

127 Yusuf al-Astal, "Al-Ru'b wa'l-wa'l-wa'l-Irahb lazal Yahzimu al-Yahud," Islam Way's Arabic website, https://ar.islamway.net/, April 2, 2014.

in the world, who operates from his apartment in Manhattan. Almost daily, Bahgat Saber streams live videos on social media that range between two and nine hours in length, during which he incites terrorism, assassinations, and torture against Egyptian government employees and opponents of the Brotherhood's Islamist project.

During the early months of the COVID-19 crisis, Saber urged his listeners to engage in bioterrorism in the Egypt and the US during his Facebook live video on March 1, 2020.[128] Saber said, "If you are a soldier, you can go into the defense ministry and shake hands with all the generals of the military and the police. The same is true with the justice system." Saber added, "If you have contracted coronavirus, you should exact revenge. Avenge yourself, avenge the honor of your women, avenge the people who are in prison, and avenge the oppressed people. Go there. Why die alone? When you die, why die alone?" During the same video, he urged his listeners to spread Covid in Egyptian embassies in the US.

In another one of his terror-recruitment videos, Saber demonstrated how to murder police officers using household appliances.[129] In another Facebook live video, on April 17, 2020, Saber asked for "lone wolf" terrorists to perpetrate terrorist attacks in Egypt, and he identified specific targets and locations for terrorist attacks. Saber and other Brotherhood operatives sometimes refer to terrorist attacks as "revolutionary work." He explained the term saying, "We have a clear mission, and it is revolutionary work, and the definition of revolutionary work is violent work, and the definition of violent work, is work that sheds blood."[130]

The problem of Muslim Brotherhood terrorism recruitment on Facebook is not limited to Saber. Turkey-based Secret Apparatus Youth wing leader Mahmoud Fathy established a Brotherhood terrorist mili-

---

128 Al-Arabiya News (Dubai), March 18, 2020.

129 "Limaza Halet al-La'na bi Misr," YouTube.com, July 17, 2020.

130 Bahgat Saber's April 17, 2020 live Facebook video is currently unavailable online. It is available in the author's personal archive.

tia called *Tayyar al-Ummah* (Movement of the Islamic Nation).[131] His militia has an overt media apparatus where he streams videos with general Islamic and political content, and secret social media channels where he strategizes, recruits, and gives detailed directions on how and when to carry out terrorist attacks in Egypt.

Fathy runs his covert operation by sharing a series of secret documents entitled *Rasai'l al-Istiqlal* (Epistles of Independence). He uploads the documents on his Facebook page for a few days, then deletes them. His manifestos include how to spread political propaganda to augment their jihadist cause; means of recruiting jihadists; regulations on communications between recruits; and details on how and when to carry terrorist attacks.[132]

Fathy also works with US-based Muslim Brotherhood activists such as Texas-based activist Sawsan Gharib and Chicago-based Muhammad Kamal Okda.[133] Facebook's problem goes beyond the Brotherhood's use of the platform for their terroristic endeavors. Facebook legitimized the Muslim Brotherhood political façade on May 6, 2020, when it appointed Yemeni Muslim Sisterhood leader Tawakkol Karman to its oversight board.

United States governmental and nongovernmental institutions actively engage in marginalizing and persecuting Muslims when they empower Brotherhood jihadists who terrorize moderate Muslims whom they consider infidels.

---

131 Mahmoud Fathy's official Facebook Page, www.Facebook.com/MahmoudFathy003, accessed July 12, 2021.

132 The author was able to acquire Mahmoud Fathy's secret documents. Due to their violent nature, the author decided not to republish them online.

133 Mahmoud Fathy's official Facebook page.

CHAPTER THIRTEEN

HE IS NOT YOUR BASTARD

The Failed US Foreign Policy of Dictatorship Maintenance and Jihadist Appeasement

"It is a settled policy of America, that as peace is better than war, war is better than tribute. The United States, while they wish for war with no nation, will buy peace with none."

—James Madison

ONE OF THE MOST DANGEROUS expressions in American foreign policy, which is often utilized by politicians to justify their involvement with war criminals, jihadists, and mass murderers is, "He's a bastard, but he's our bastard." A variation of the statement was attributed to President Franklin Roosevelt in 1939 while referring to Nicaraguan dictator Anastasio Somoza García. It was also attributed to Presidents Harry Truman and Richard Nixon. While the origin of the statement is disputed, it explains FDR's foreign policy of appeasement toward the Soviet Union. This appeasement contributed to the deaths of almost one million victims during the Soviet famine of 1946–1947, after FDR and Winston Churchill capitulated to Stalin at the Yalta Conference in 1945. Churchill took part in this conference as he knew that he couldn't defeat the Nazis without the United States, which had friendly relations with Stalin. In 1941, Churchill warned FDR against his policy toward the Soviets, stating, "Stalin is an unnatural man. There will be grave troubles."[1]

This also ultimately led to the cold war between the USSR and the United States, fought through proxies, resulting in the destruction of millions of lives through mass murder and displacement. During the past few decades, America's "bastards" sponsored worldwide terrorist factions, funded the spread of jihadist propaganda, and normalized radical Islam in the Middle East, resulting in the victimization of millions of people.

A foreign policy of surrender and appeasement has been the general strategy of the United States under both Democratic and Republican administrations for decades. This cynical motto is still widely used in Washington along another equally destructive phrase, "riding the tiger," which is frequently used to justify cooperating with terrorists and mass murderers. German-American duo entertainers Siegfried & Roy demonstrated that one cannot ride the tiger literally, and decades of fatal foreign policy decisions confirm it also cannot be done metaphorically.

Another foreign policy platitude that belongs in garbage heap of history is, "better the devil you know than the devil you don't." Individuals who employ this phrase generally are profoundly ignorant of both devils. Unless these policymakers are themselves worse devils than those they support, they are ill-equipped to understand, predict, or control the actions of the tyrannical entities they are hoping to manipulate.

These so-called devils often operate in a realm of criminality and do not respect contracts and treaties. They are simply better than at being evil than their appeasers. When Western governments think they are manipulating a "devil they know," it often backfires because they are generally incapable of predicting the consequences.

---

1 Susan Butler, ed., *My Dear Mr Stalin: The Complete Correspondence of Franklin D Roosevelt and Joseph V Stalin* (New Haven: Yale University Press, 2005), 154.

For decades, the State Department's strategy by large has been one of dictatorship maintenance. While the US directly supports tyrants across the globe, it also engages in a more destructive type of dictatorship maintenance by aiding and abetting the dictatorial social and religious practices perpetrated by Islamists. The bigotry of low expectations toward foreign populations, combined with moral cowardice and maybe an admiration for perpetrators, are the most probable justifications for these actions.

These damaging aphorisms and their philosophical underpinnings, motivations, and antisocial tendencies should be replaced with the adage, "If they did it with you, they'll do it to you." If dictators, terrorists, and criminals conspired to destroy nations and populations with you, they'll conspire with others to destroy you too.

An important example of the policy of dictatorship maintenance was uttered by President Obama during a speech in September 2014. Obama said he hoped to "shrink" Islamic State's influence "to the point where it is a manageable problem." He didn't say he would eradicate Islamic State, but instead, make them a "manageable problem." To manage something means to control it, not destroy it.

Obama's policies were the culmination of the strategy of "riding the tiger." Obama knew they were "bastards," but he wanted to make them "his bastards." This could explain his consistent empowerment of Islamists and why he infested his administration with Muslim Brotherhood agents. Obama exemplified an end-stage ideological coup against Western civilization. It shouldn't be a surprise that one of his first actions as president was to remove Churchill's bust from the White House. After all, Churchill was the man who said:

> We shall not be content with a defensive war...we shall not flag or fail. We shall go on to the end, we shall fight in France, we shall fight on the seas and oceans, we shall fight with growing confidence and growing strength in the air, we shall defend our Island, what-

> ever the cost may be, we shall fight on the beaches, we shall fight on the landing grounds, we shall fight in the fields and in the streets, we shall fight in the hills; we shall never surrender.[2]

The contrast between Churchill's and Obama's philosophies could not be more stark. For decades, Western leaders aided terrorists and mass murderers by evoking "national security." In public discourse, that phrase is often employed to conceal the lack of ethical and rational justification for specific public policies. This intellectually and morally bankrupt tactic should be challenged. Appeasing aggressors has never won battles, but it has led to massacres, genocides, infiltration, subversion, and destruction of civilizations. Both Western and Arab leaders continue to lose battles because they employ this flawed tactic that gives an inherent advantage to the most violent and most irrational. Appeasement is the surrender of the home field to an opponent and a declaration of submission. It also directly resulted in the loss of hundreds of thousands of lives and the displacement of millions of people in the Middle East.

THE JIHAD INNOCENTS' CLUB

While many appeasers may be well-intentioned and gullible, they often follow a strategy crafted by those who are neither. Islamists, communists, and socialists have successfully employed Soviet and Nazi propaganda tactics toward this end.

One of the most important proponents of the tactic of recruiting naïve activists to carry out destructive conspiracies was Wilhelm "Willi" Münzenberg (1889–1940). Residing in Berlin, Münzenberg was the highest-ranking Bolshevik outside the Soviet Union, with the mission to inflict a communist revolution on the Western world. In

2 Richard Toye, *The Roar of the Lion: The Untold Story of Churchill's World War II Speeches* (Oxford: Oxford University Press, 2013), 70.

his book *The Mighty Wurlitzer: How the CIA Played America*, Hugh Wilford wrote:

> Particularly successful were Münzenberg's various "front" groups, committees superficially devoted to some undeniably benign cause, such as anti-imperialism, peace, or antifascism, whose real purpose was to defend and spread the Bolshevik revolution.[3]

Wilford explained that these front groups "proved irresistible to politically well-meaning progressives, whose participation made them, in effect, 'fellow travelers' of the International communist movement." Currently, it is culturally and politically acceptable and even preferable in Washington circles to be jihad fellow travelers, under the contemporary slogans of inclusivity, intersectionality, and anti-racism. The same strategy is regurgitated with the grievance du jour to be adopted by the "progressives" of today. During the early years of the Bolshevik revolution, these activists and their front groups were called "Innocents' Clubs." Münzenberg said, "These people have the belief that they are actually doing this themselves…This belief must be preserved at any price."[4] Western members of the Jihad Innocents' Clubs, which cater to the ideas and conspiracies of the Brotherhood and their ilk, are themselves tools of the modern Willi Münzenbergs, When speaking in Arabic, Brotherhood leaders often mock these Westerners, just as Bolsheviks mocked their fellow travelers.[5]

An important example of this tactic was exhibited by Sudanese Brotherhood leader Hassan al-Turabi, a friend of Osama bin Laden. Turabi revealed important information about the Brotherhood's Secret Apparatus and showed how Brotherhood figures frequently tell the truth in Arabic. During al-Turabi's interview with al-Jazeera

---

3 Hugh Wilford, *The Mighty Wurlitzer: How the CIA Played America* (Cambridge: Harvard University Press, 2008), 12.

4 Ibid.

5 V.I. Lenin, *Lenin Collected Works* (Moscow: Progress Publishers, 1965), 31: 438–59.

in 2010, which aired after his death in 2016, Turabi mocked intelligence agencies in Arab countries and the West for thinking that they understood security challenges, while they "only scratch the surface." Turabi was correct. Intelligence agencies and academics in the West almost unanimously believe the Brotherhood's misinformation that they dissolved the Secret Apparatus in the 1940s. They accept this contention, despite irrefutable evidence to the contrary.[6]

Turabi highlighted three critical facts. While his discussion centered around the Secret Apparatus operation of the 1980s and the Brotherhood's 1989 coup d'état in Sudan, his admissions revealed tactics currently employed by the Brotherhood worldwide. Turabi provided further definitive evidence to assertions stated in previous chapters.

First, he admitted the Brotherhood still operates both a Secret Apparatus and an International Apparatus. He also stated that an Intelligence Apparatus connects terrorists and Islamists across the globe. He said the Secret Apparatus comprises a secret leadership that operates on behalf of public leaders, in case they are imprisoned or placed under surveillance. According to Turabi, the Secret Apparatus continued to operate even after the Muslim Brotherhood seized power in a country like Sudan. He said the clandestine division of the Brotherhood in Sudan was under the leadership of as-Saffi Nour ad-Din, who is also known as the "secret keeper" of Sudan's Islamist movement. In 2015, Din admitted that he was in frequent communication with then-president of Sudan Omar al-Bashir.[7]

Turabi said that the Secret Apparatuses had "private special intelligence networks," and "international intelligence networks in every country on earth, which links all Islamic movements worldwide...it provided us with information that doesn't get published in newspapers." He added, "we trade all information among each other." Turabi

6 Al-Jazeera (Doha), July 31, 2016.
7 Al-Marsad as-Sudani (Khartoum), February 11, 2015.

confirmed that the Secret Apparatus continues to resume clandestine activities even after they "govern a nation." Turabi also stated that the leader of the Secret Apparatus has a different public title, such as "Secretary of Planning."

The second important admission by Turabi is that the Brotherhood controls the public narrative about their organization and influences intelligence agencies' analysis. He said they infiltrated Sudanese intelligence and the people who report to the Sudanese military and other intelligence agencies of Arab countries. Moreover, Turabi said the Brotherhood infiltrated intelligence groups who communicate with intelligence agencies in the United States.

The al-Jazeera interviewer asked Turabi, "You infiltrated all this?"

Turabi replied, "Of course, all these agencies, through [people] working for them and around them, while they think that they were dependable sources."

He further explained that the Brotherhood's *jihad al-mudafa'a* (defensive jihad) doesn't "just mean that you sit in a cave and fight intruders, but sometimes you should transgress" on the enemy. He said they had successfully infiltrated the Sudanese military, state security apparatus, police, and other state organs that deal with both domestic and foreign policy. "Our plan from the 1970s is to rule Sudan either through a revolution or a coup d'état," he said. These were remarkable admissions about the Brotherhood's penetration of American and Arabic intelligence agencies and their plans for revolutionary jihad against the nations they target.

Third, Turabi said the Secret Apparatus was the governing body of the Muslim Brotherhood. He said that the apparatus had learned from the mistakes of the Brotherhood's Secret Apparatus in the early years. "We learned our lesson from what we have studied about this apparatus…the apparatus ate its own in Egypt, and ultimately became the ruling body in the organization."

Turabi and modern Brotherhood leaders learned that to control the Secret Apparatus, the leadership of the Brotherhood had to operate it themselves. Turabi's damning confessions were aired in Arabic in 2016, the same year Georgetown University professor and Muslim Brotherhood propagandist John Esposito claimed, "Muslim Brotherhood-affiliated movements and parties have been a force for democratization and stability in the Middle East."[8]

Esposito's definition of Brotherhood-affiliated movements, which spread his ideas of "democratization and stability," are genocidal groups such as Islamic State, the Organization of Monotheism and Jihad, Excommunication and Emigration, al-Qaeda, Hamas, Afghan Services Bureau, Taliban, al-Gama'a al-Islamiyya, Egyptian Islamic Jihad, Tanzim Shabab Muhammad, Tanzim 1965, and the Secret Apparatus. The contrast between Turabi's Arabic admissions and Esposito's propaganda to Westerners demonstrates the grave danger of allowing jihad's fellow travelers to spew disinformation that could directly result in death and destruction around the world. They need to be held morally accountable for the devastation they create, whether out of treason, sadism, or ignorance.

Turabi and Esposito are only two of countless examples. Whether or not politicians, academics, and the intelligence community want to admit it, there is a vicious ongoing war of ideas. Denying reality will not evaporate it. The cowardly evasion of the Brotherhood's goals has wasted billions of dollars and thousands of lives fighting wars that could not succeed in stopping Islamism.

Misunderstanding the threat has also resulted in wasteful and ineffective counterintelligence programs. For example, in 2016 the FBI hired New York advertising firms to "fight terrorist propaganda" and "counter extremist ideology."[9] While the FBI is composed of overwhelmingly patriotic and heroic individuals, politicians have distorted the Bureau's mission. How else to explain hiring runway and

8 John L. Esposito, "The Muslim Brotherhood, Terrorism and U.S. Policy," *The Huffington Post* (New York), March 9, 2016.

9 Kaveh Waddell, "How New York's Top Advertisers Are Fighting Terrorist Propaganda," The Atlantic, March 15, 2016.

lingerie advertisers to shape America's narrative around the greatest conflict of our time?

President Biden's and other former presidents' catastrophic foreign-policy failures have threatened the world. Three examples of failed strategy include the United States' policies toward Iran, the Taliban, and the Muslim Brotherhood.

THE IRAN DEAL AND AMERICA'S REPETITION OF HISTORY

Since 1979, the government of the Islamic Republic of Iran has sponsored terrorism and prepared to obtain nuclear weapons. Many American presidents, including Presidents Obama and Biden, succumbed to Iran's agenda as well as the agenda of the Muslim Brotherhood.

On November 4, 1979, a crowd of four hundred men marched toward the US Embassy in Tehran carrying a banner that read in English, "We do not intend to bother you." The US Marine Security Guard was ordered not to shoot the "unarmed students" and a few hours later, more than fifty Americans were taken hostage. This false promise of peace tricked President Jimmy Carter and his advisors into submitting to Iranian dissimulation.[10]

President Obama presided over an incident reminiscent of the Iranian hostage crisis on September 11, 2012, when jihadists attacked US government facilities in Benghazi, Libya. This terrorist attack was perpetrated by Muslim Brotherhood affiliates. Kris Paronto, a CIA contractor who fought off terrorists during the attack, said Americans were ordered to "stand down."[11]

---

10 United States Congress, House Committee on Foreign Affairs, Foreign assistance legislation for fiscal year 1981: hearings before the Committee on Foreign Affairs, 1980, 508–9.

11 "Former Cia Contractor Speaks Out About Benghazi Attack," *ABC News*, May 23, 2016.

In 2015, a false promise of peace was delivered to the American people by President Obama, during his deal with the theocratic eschatological fanatics in Tehran. Obama said his deal "prevents Iran from obtaining a nuclear weapon, without resorting to war."[12] The only thing Obama's deal accomplished was to deliver on the demands Khomeini made in September 1980. Khomeini had conditioned the release of hostages with returning the property of the late Shah, canceling its claims against Iran, releasing frozen Iranian assets, and promising not to intervene politically or militarily in Iran.[13]

The Iran deal is another dictatorship maintenance escapade, which allowed Iranian mullahs to take the world hostage for three reasons. First, the deal was one-sided and not legally binding. Iran did not even sign it.[14] This made it compatible with the radical Shi'it jurisprudence on treaties. The Mullahs believe that "there is no authority which can bind Muslims to non-Muslims under any circumstances."[15] By not signing, the Mullahs affirmed its illegitimacy. Per Articles 77 and 125 of the Iranian constitution, treaties are only considered valid after they are "approved by the Islamic Parliament of Iran" and signed by the "President or his legal representative." Neither of these actions took place, thus providing further evidence that the mullahs don't acknowledge its legitimacy.

Second, since the mullahs did not stage a coup against their own parliament or deactivate their constitution, it's fair to presume that they didn't accept this deal internally. As the Iranian constitution states in Article 153, "Any kind of agreement resulting in foreign con-

12 The White House, Office of the Press Secretary, "Remarks by the President on the Iran Nuclear Deal," August 5, 2015.

13 *The Washington Post*, https://www.washingtonpost.com/archive/politics/1980/09/13/irans-financial-terms-draw-cautious-response-from-us/60245a49-e03a-49d5-8056-32fc99e89796/, September 13, 1980.

14 Joel Gehrke, "State Department: Iran Deal Is Not 'Legally Binding' and Iran Didn't Sign It," *National Review* (New York), November 25, 2015.

15 Kassim Khudair Abbas, www.Haydarya.com, accessed July 5, 2021.

trol of the country's natural resources, economy, army, culture, and other aspects of national life, is forbidden."

Third, the duration of the deal predicts the initiation of aggression by Iran, which would make the arrangement a Shari'a-compliant *hudna* deal. The key constraints on Iran's nuclear program will ease after ten years. The ten-year duration is another major red flag. According to fundamentalist Shi'ite jurisprudence, a truce between Muslim and non-Muslim nations does not allow a suspension of jihad longer than ten years, given that after that period of time, they wage war. While the ruling allows the imam to extend the duration of truce, it still must expire, resulting in imminent aggression.

These factors almost ensure the continuation of Iran's nuclear proliferation. In 2007, former head of the International Atomic Energy Agency (IAEA) Muhammad al-Baradei said Iran was probably three to eight years away from having a nuclear weapon. Of course, this would not have been the case if it weren't for his own pro-Islamist leadership of the IAEA.[16]

In 2016, the full tableau of the 1979 hostage crisis was completed when Obama fulfilled the dreams of Ayatollah Khomeini and funneled $400 million to the Iranian regime, for the release of new American hostages, and $1.3 million in interest on Iranian cash held in the US since the 1970s.[17] Whether for ideological reasons, narcissism, or ignorance, Obama's policies toward the Brotherhood and Iran are similar to FDR's policies toward the Soviet Union. The most critical distinction is that the Soviets were atheists who didn't uphold eschatological fantasies of instigating the "end of times" so they can die while killing their enemies. Unlike the Soviets, Islamists believe they win whether they live or die.

---

16 *The Irish Times*, https://www.irishtimes.com/news/iran-probably-3-8-years-off-nuclear-bomb-iaea-1.807347, May 24, 2007.

17 *Los Angeles Times*, https://www.latimes.com/nation/politics/trailguide/la-na-trailguide-third-presidential-donald-trump-is-right-the-u-s-did-pay-1476931849-htmlstory.html, October 19, 2016.

In 1943, Ambassador William C. Bullitt, an advisor and friend of FDR, wrote a lengthy memorandum warning FDR about Stalin. FDR replied to Bullitt saying, "Bill, I don't dispute your facts; they are accurate. I don't dispute the logic of your reasoning. I just have a hunch that Stalin is not that kind of man. Harry [Hopkins] says he's not and that he doesn't want anything but security for his country, and I think if I give him everything I possibly can and ask for nothing in return, noblesse oblige, he won't try to annex anything and will work with me for a world of democracy and peace."[18]

FDR didn't only ignore Bullitt's warning, he also ignored Churchill's. Francis P. Sempa, editor of the journal *American Diplomacy*, wrote, "As Winston Churchill noted in his brilliant history of the Second World War, the peril of Nazi domination of the world was replaced by the even more formidable peril of Soviet domination of the world."[19]

Obama and Biden's Iran deal and other Middle East policies seek to replace the Soviet domination of the world with an even more formidable Islamist one. The strategies are the same; only the names have changed. Stalin was Hassan Rouhani and is now Ebrahim Raisi. Harry Hopkins was Valerie Jarrett and is now Jake Sullivan. FDR was Obama and is now Biden. Tomorrow the names will change but the misery continues until this vicious circle of dictatorship maintenance is broken. President Donald Trump was the exception to the rule when he voided the Iran deal, but after President Biden assumed office, he led the world back to 1979 and 1943.

---

18 William C. Bullitt, "How We Won the War and Lost the Peace," *Life* magazine, August 30, 1948, 94.

19 Francis P. Sempa, "William C. Bullitt: Diplomat and Prophet," *American Diplomacy* VIII, no. 1, 2003.

THE LARGEST JIHADIST PROPAGANDA CAMPAIGN IN WORLD AND THE PATH TO A SECOND 9/11 THROUGH THE RESURRECTION OF THE TALIBAN

On October 23, 1979, one of the most destructive political meetings in the history of the US took place in Washington, DC. The subject of that meeting was "Covert Action." This meeting needs to be immortalized in history for its devasting implications on the entire world. Zbigniew Brzezinski, then-President Jimmy Carter's National Security Advisor, chaired the meeting. Also present was Ambassador Donald Gregg, National Security Council advisor; Hedley Donovan, special advisor to President Carter; Benjamin Civiletti, Attorney General; John White, deputy director of the Office of Management and Budget; Harold Brown, Secretary of Defense; and David Newsom, Under Secretary of State for Political Affairs. This meeting was also attended by Prince Turki al-Faisal, head of Saudi intelligence, and then-President of Pakistan Muhammad Zia-ul-Haq.[20]

This committee unanimously endorsed a proposal to continue to fund Afghan jihadists, a policy begun on July 3, 1979, after a "Presidential Finding authorized CIA to expend up to $695,000 to support the Afghan insurgents, either unilaterally or through third countries, by providing cash or non-military supplies; and also authorized CIA propaganda operations in support of the insurgency."[21]

The meeting resulted in the largest jihadist propaganda campaign in history, which was perpetrated by the CIA and its allies in Saudi Arabia, Pakistan, Egypt, Jordan, and many other Islamic nations. The joint CIA-Arab jihadist propaganda campaign was arguably more devastating to the world than their arming jihadists in Afghanistan

20 United States Government Publishing Office, Foreign Relations of the United States, 1977–1980, Volume XII, Afghanistan, Document 76.

21 Ibid.

through Brotherhood proxies. The support for Afghan jihadists was done through collaboration with the Muslim Brotherhood, who were responsible for terrorism recruitment through the Afghan Services Bureau—which eventually became al-Qaeda. The jihadist propaganda effort radicalized a substantial number of Muslims worldwide and resulted in millions of deaths in Sudan, Afghanistan, and around the world. The ideas propagated by those jihadists ended up flying into America's tallest buildings on September 11, 2001. Today, President Biden is repeating the travesties of 1979.

TWELVE DEADLY US POLICIES TO RETURN AFGHANISTAN TO AN INTERNATIONAL JIHADIST BASE

Behavioral patterns can show intent; therefore, the evidence of anti-American policy coming from inside the US government suggests that elements within the current and previous administrations have been working to revive al-Qaeda and other terror groups through support of the Taliban. These actions provide a glimpse into the pattern of deadly behaviors that took place over the course of twelve damaging policies, which could have been avoided.

(1) In 2011, the Obama administration formally began negotiations with the Taliban. Then-Secretary of State Hillary Clinton said, "Over the past two years, we have laid out our unambiguous red lines for reconciliation with the insurgents: They must renounce violence; they must abandon their alliance with al-Qaida; and they must abide by the constitution of Afghanistan."[22]

As expected, the Taliban did not comply, and within months they attacked both the US Embassy and NATO's headquarters in Kabul. It

22 US Department of State, *Remarks at the Launch of the Asia Society's Series of Richard C. Holbrooke Memorial Addresses* (New York, NY: 2011), https://2009-2017.state.gov/secretary/20092013clinton/rm/2011/02/156815.htm.

appears the State Department's alleged "red lines" were merely rhetoric aimed for domestic consumption. The Taliban seemed to understand this and used the opportunity to demonstrate to their base their commitment to wage war against the West. Whether out of ignorance, negligence, or treason, the State Department's actions amplified the Taliban and al-Qaeda's power.

(2) In 2012, after the Taliban perpetrated numerous terrorist attacks, they issued a statement and announced their plans to open a "political office" for what they called "The Islamic Emirate of Afghanistan." The Taliban chose the Muslim Brotherhood-affiliated and terror-sponsoring regime in Qatar to host their headquarters. In the same statement, the Taliban requested "the exchange of prisoners from Guantanamo."[23]

Among the terrorists they wanted released were Khairullah Khairkhwa, the former Taliban governor of Herat, and Mullah Muhammad Fazl, a mass murderer and the Taliban Deputy Minister of Defense who was wanted by the UN for possible war crimes including the murder of thousands of Shi'ites. State Department spokeswoman Victoria Nuland commented on the Taliban's request saying, "You don't negotiate with your friends." A more appropriate response, and one consistent with prior US policies, would have been to say the US does not negotiate with terrorists and mass murderers.

Among those involved in the negotiations was Taliban fighter and emissary for Mullah Omar, Tayyab Agha. While he was a close associate of bin Laden, Agha was later described in a report by RAND Corporation as "the most prominent moderate in favor of peace talks."[24]

(3) In July 2013, the Taliban officially opened its political office in Doha, Qatar. The ceremony was hosted by Qatar's Assistant Minister for Foreign Affairs Ali bin Fahad al-Hajri and Jan Mohammad

23 *Kuwait Times*, https://issuu.com/kuwaitnews/docs/04012012, January 4, 2012.
24 Jeffrey Eggers, "Afghanistan, Choose Your Enemies Wisely," RAND Corporation blog, August 24, 2015.

Madani, a UN-sanctioned Taliban terrorist who was under Special Notice of the INTERPOL-United Nations Security Council.

(4) In 2014, President Obama's administration's fulfilled the demands the Taliban had made two years earlier, and he released the "Taliban Five" from Guantanamo Bay, in exchange for US military deserter Bowe Bergdahl.

Consenting to the Taliban's demands will continue to have dire consequences for decades to come. These released Taliban leaders were reinstalled into official positions in the Taliban cabinet in September 2021. Khairullah Khairkhwa, a warlord, was appointed as the Taliban's Minister of Information and Culture. Abdul Haq Wasiq became the Taliban's Director of Intelligence. Norullah Noori, who was sanctioned by the United Nations under Security Council Committee resolution 1267 (concerning Islamic State and al-Qaeda associated individuals and groups), was appointed as Minister of Borders and Tribal Affairs. Muhammad Fazl, the Taliban's former Deputy Defense Minister who worked closely with Osama bin Laden and al-Qaeda in 2001, was reinstated to his position. Muhammad Nabi Omari, either an active member of al-Qaeda or a close associate, was also among the jihadists released. As of 2021, Omari was appointed by the Taliban as governor of Khost. Prior to the agreements between Qatar and US that reinstalled the Taliban to power, the Taliban's office in Doha provided a political front for what was essentially a jihadist coup against the Afghan government.

(5) In 2015, Ayman al-Zawahiri gave his pledge of allegiance to Taliban leader Mullah Akhtar Mohammad Mansour, who was killed by a US drone strike in Southwest Pakistan that year. His assassination seemed counterproductive because of Mansour's willingness to coexist with the Afghan government. It was also unusual because the Taliban was not designated as a terrorist group, and his assassination only served his more radical successor.

(6) In 2016, Zawahiri announced he had renewed his oath of allegiance to the Taliban's chief, Hibatullah Akhundzada. This made

the Taliban leader the acting head of al-Qaeda. After Zawahiri swore allegiance to the Taliban, Obama turned his "red line" into a green light and said, "The only way to end this conflict and to achieve a full drawdown of foreign forces from Afghanistan is through a lasting political settlement between the Afghan government and the Taliban. That's the only way. And that is why the United States will continue to strongly support an Afghan-led reconciliation process[.]"[25]

(7) In 2017, Arabic newspaper *Asharq al-Awsat* reported that Iran had provided the Taliban with military training, arms, and funding. The paper quoted the governor of the Afghan Wardak Province, who said, "The strongest factions within the Taliban are Iran's Taliban," in reference to the Afghan Taliban members who resided in Iran.[26]

(8) In 2018, Pakistan released Taliban cofounder Mullah Abdul Ghani Baradar from prison, based on a request from Qatar and the US. Baradar was a mass murderer.

(9) In May 2019, Iran sent almost three million Afghans back to Afghanistan, citing US sanctions as an excuse. It is more probable that the "strongest" Taliban fighters were sent back to Afghanistan in preparation for their reinstatement in power. A few months later during the summer of 2019, the Taliban became significantly deadlier, perpetrating 3,500 terrorist attacks.[27] It is not a coincidence that the considerable rise in terrorist incidents coincided with Baradar becoming the Taliban's Deputy Commander and the return of Iran's Taliban to Afghanistan.

(10) In February 2020, President Trump resumed President Obama's policies when his administration signed the "Agreement for Bringing Peace to Afghanistan" with the Taliban, who had become the *de facto* leader of al-Qaeda. During the peace conference where

25 The White House, Office of Press Secretary, Statement by the President on Afghanistan (Washington, DC, 2016).

26 Asharq al-Awsat (London), August 6, 2017.

27 Katie Bo Williams, "The Taliban Got Way Deadlier in 2019, Says Pentagon's Afghanistan IG," *Defense One* (Washington, DC), October 31, 2019.

the treaty was signed, Ambassador Zalmay Khalilzad, then-US Special Representative for Afghanistan Reconciliation, shared a panel with Mullah Abdul Ghani Baradar—a mass murderer responsible for the deaths of hundreds of US soldiers. Under Baradar's leadership, the Taliban significantly increased US casualties until his arrest in Pakistan in 2010.

In 2009, *Newsweek* described Baradar as "cunning" and "more dangerous than [Mullah] Omar himself." The same article reported that Baradar said, "Rely on guerrilla tactics whenever possible. Plant 'flowers'—improvised explosive devices—on trails and dirt roads. Concentrate on small-unit ambushes, with automatic weapons and rocket-propelled grenades."[28]

That was the same man Ambassador Khalilzad was pictured shaking hands with in one of the most disgraceful moments in American diplomatic history. Terrorism propagandists circulated that image around the world. Muslim Brotherhood operative and journalist

Abdul Bari Atwan described the deal between the US and the Taliban as an "announcement of defeat" and "surrender" by the US.[29]

(11) In late August 2021, the United States withdrew all troops from Afghanistan, leaving hundreds of American citizens, thousands of American residents, and tens of thousands of Afghan allies to face the Taliban alone. According to *Forbes* magazine, the Biden Administration abandoned an "estimate of $83 billion worth of training and equipment to Afghan security forces since 2001." In 2021 alone, the US military aid to Afghan forces was $3 billion.[30]

(12) On August 16, 2021, Taliban chief Akhundzada ordered the release of al-Qaeda, Islamic State, and most jihadists from Afghan prisons. This action was almost certainly intended to aid the Taliban in spreading terror across Afghanistan. Ten days later, "former" Taliban

28 Ron Moreau, "Meet the Taliban's New Chief," *Newsweek*, July 7, 2009.
29 Rai al-Youm (London), March 1, 2020.
30 Adam Andrzejewski, "Staggering Costs—U.S. Military Equipment Left Behind In *Afghanistan," Forbes*, August 23, 2021.

leaders in charge of ISKP carried out a suicide bombing at Hamid Karzai International Airport in Kabul during the US evacuation from Afghanistan. Thirteen US service members and 170 Afghans were killed, and hundreds more injured. Most media outlets reported that ISKP was battling the Taliban, but if there was even a minor internecine warfare between them, the Taliban would never have released them from prison. In contrast, this attack provided the Taliban with their needed legitimacy as an Islamist government. Western media and politicians who attempt to distance the Taliban from Islamic State are allowing themselves to be pawns of the fake equation of "bad terrorist/worst terrorist."

Al-Jazeera, Doha's state-sponsored media, repeated the narrative that Taliban was battling ISKP and stated that the Taliban had killed ISKP leader Ziya ul-Haq, also known as Abu Omar Khorasani. Al-Jazeera claimed this was evidence to the conflict between these groups.[31] They failed to report that the Taliban killed ul-Haq on August 16, 2021, ten days before the attack on the airport and the same day the Taliban released the rest of the ISKP fighters from prison.

Ziya ul-Haq was replaced by Mawlawi Aslam Farooqi, also known as Mawlawi Abdullah and Aslam Farooqui, in 2019. Farooqi was associated with the Pakistan-based terror groups *Lashkar-e-Jhangvi* (LeJ), *Lashkar-e-Tayyiba* (LeT), and TTP.[32] In 2020 he was incarcerated in Afghanistan, and briefly replaced by Shahab al-Muhajir, until the Taliban released Farooqui from prison in August 2021. He assumed the leadership of ISKP the same day the Taliban killed his predecessor. If the Taliban hadn't killed ul-Haq, he would have been the leader of ISKP instead of Farooqui. Under Farooqui's leadership, ISKP perpetrated the suicide bombing at Kabul's international airport.[33]

---

31 Al-Jazeera (Doha), September 27, 2021.

32 "ISI-linked Pakistani Aslam Farooqui Is the Mastermind Behind Kabul Airport Attack," *The Shillong Times* (New Delhi), August 28, 2021.

33 "Taliban Executes Former IS-K Chief a Year After Afghan Govt Jailed Him: Report," *The Week* magazine (New Delhi), August 19, 2021.

ISKP is TTP, and TTP pledged allegiance to the Taliban. Both al-Qaeda and the Haqqani Network also pledged allegiance to the Taliban. The Taliban is clearly the public leadership and umbrella organization of Sunni jihadist groups. The US government's complicity in the Doha negotiations that led to the return of the Taliban to Afghanistan was done under the guidance and leadership of Qatar's Brotherhood regime. It's possible the Qatari regime is controlling the Taliban in Afghanistan as part of a century-long covert war run by the Muslim Brotherhood's Secret Apparatus. The reprehensible manner by which the evacuation took place will have dire consequences for decades to come. Neither will America's allies ever trust her, nor will her enemies respect her. Now jihadists worldwide have seen the maximum reaction they could instigate from an attack against America, while America has not seen the extent of how far they are willing to go to fulfill their objectives. President Biden's policies toward Afghanistan will almost guarantee jihadists attack on American soil and many more internationally.

THEY ARE NOT YOUR BASTARDS

The Brotherhood is the world's most sophisticated jihadist syndicate. It operates as an *imperium in imperio* with parallel transnational military, intelligence, diplomatic, and educational apparatuses. Western politicians and intelligence agencies who believe they can employ jihadists as allies in their covert missions are delusional. The tactic of allying with jihadist groups is a methodology that inherently gives the advantage to Islamists because of their long-term strategy and their theologically based mission. Jihadists are also better at being bad. They will always win this equation.

While Western communists may believe that they are also capable of executing long-term conspiracies, Islamists also will win this battle, as their covert and overt warfare even exceeds their lifetimes.

Intellectual and militant jihadists view themselves as rings in a long chain that transcend physical limitations, both literally and spiritually. The monastic patience of Islamists allows them to dominate the short-term political cycles and even shorter-term memories in the West.

The solutions to countering Islamism require introspective reevaluation of the failed and destructive policies of Max von Oppenheim, Hitler, Gerhard von Mende, and the US, of utilizing jihadists to fulfill devastating aims. This strategy backfires and allowed the creation and metastasis of the Brotherhood's covert and overt operations. The "good terrorist/bad terrorist" dynamic was mythology created to justify aiding and abetting jihadists. Many of radical Islam's fellow travelers employ this argument to validate their support of the "lesser of two evils" philosophy.

Congressional and political alliances with Muslim Brotherhood front groups such as the Islamist umbrella organization, USCMO, which aid the political mission of groups like the Taliban and al-Qaeda, must be terminated. The US Department of Justice should consider compelling the USCMO and its affiliates to register under the Foreign Agents Registration Act. The Muslim Brotherhood should be designated as a Foreign Terrorist Organization in the US and Europe. Western governments should support the heroic leadership of Middle Eastern and Arab leaders who are fighting this unbridled and unconventional enemy.

Islamists can only be defeated with a strategy consistent with the moral and intellectual standards of America's founders. To rephrase James Madison, as peace is better than war, war is better than appeasement. While America should wish war with no nation, it shouldn't be extorted by Islamists to surrender to none. Either you are with the overwhelming majority of Muslims, and every peaceful individual on earth, or you are with the Muslim Brotherhood.

INDEX

Symbols

A

B

C

D

H

M

T

U

V

W

Y

Z